UNSCRIPTED

Also by Alan Sugar

WHAT YOU SEE IS WHAT YOU GET

THE WAY I SEE IT

ALAN SUGAR

UNSCRIPTED

MY TEN YEARS IN TELLY

MACMILLAN

First published 2015 by Macmillan
an imprint of Pan Macmillan
20 New Wharf Road, London N1 9RR
Associated companies throughout the world
www.panmacmillan.com

ISBN 978-1-5098-0306-4 HB
ISBN 978-1-5098-0304-0 TPB

1 3 5 7 9 8 6 4 2

A CIP catalogue record for this book is available from the British Library.

Typeset by Ellipsis Digital Limited, Glasgow
Printed and bound by CPI Group (UK) Ltd, Croydon, CR0 4YY

Visit **www.panmacmillan.com** to read more about all our books
and to buy them. You will also find features, author interviews and
news of any author events, and you can sign up for e-newsletters
so that you're always first to hear about our new releases.

To John Beattie and Martin Lucas,
two hard-working loyal employees who helped me prosper
in business, making me a successful entrepreneur.

To my uncle John Appel, whose sense of humour I inherited,
according to my wife Ann.

And to Harold Mazin, my brother-in-law, who appreciated
my role on TV and was also a funny man.

CONTENTS

1

THE SO-CALLED TALENT

Landing myself a job on telly

If anyone would have told me ten years ago I would be a TV star and featured on the cover of the *Radio Times*, I'd have said they were nuts. Throughout the course of my life there have been a number of milestone experiences. The first was when I built up my electronics business Amstrad – a rags-to-riches story where a young man from the East End of London became the blue-eyed boy of the stock market, building Europe's largest computer manufacturing company and starting Sky TV with Rupert Murdoch. It brought me to the attention of the financial media, as well as the then Prime Minister Margaret Thatcher. In the 1980s Britain was just coming out of recession and she was delighted to hail me as an example of the ordinary man-in-the-street from Hackney who can do well. This helped break the public perception that only the posh and privileged were able to succeed in business.

When this thirty-four-year-old cockney floated his company on the stock market, the demand for newspaper and radio interviews was tremendous. This was what gave me my first experience in television. The meteoric growth of Amstrad in the eighties attracted so much attention that I was invited on to the famous *Terry Wogan Show* a number of times, and very nervous I was too. When I look back now – knowing what I know about television and TV production – it makes me laugh to think I was at all worried about it.

At the time, Nick Hewer was acting as my PR consultant, and he had organised my appearance on the *Wogan* show just after a stock-market crash which resulted in the market capitalisation (or, in layman's terms, the value) of Amstrad dropping from its dizzy heights of £1.4bn down to something like £600m. This was reflected in my personal wealth as an overnight paper loss of £400m. As you can imagine, this was quite an interesting point of discussion for Terry Wogan and was the reason, as I recall, that I was dragged on to the show that particular week.

Terry asked me how I felt on the morning the stock market crashed and my personal wealth had dropped by £400m. I replied that it didn't make any difference to me. I still got out of the same side of the bed, because what you don't have, you don't miss, and that I viewed it as a paper fortune.

Then I changed the mood by saying, 'But in the meantime, if you could help me out and give me two bob for the coffee machine in the BBC cafeteria I would be very grateful.'

That little bit of wit came about instinctively. I can be a little bit witty at times, and it went down quite well with the audience. Actually, it left poor old Terry rather stuck as to what to say next.

Continuing the journey through my life, people will know that I made what I consider a fatal error: getting involved in a football club – Tottenham Hotspur. They were on the verge of bankruptcy, and as the family and I were lifelong supporters of our local team, I saw it as a community gesture to go in and sort out this great institution. I thought it would be a tremendous challenge but it turned into a nightmare. I don't intend to go through all the mountains and valleys of that experience – which included my bitter court battle with the *Daily Mail* – let's just say it was not a nice time. Having said that, by the time I got out of Spurs I had cleaned up the finances, rescued the club and put it on a firm financial standing. Additionally, as one would expect of me, I made about

£40m for my ten years of grief when I sold my shares to ENIC, the current owners.

One of the side effects of being involved with football was that I was required to do lots of television interviews, most of the time protecting the position of the club and protecting my own position as chairman against criticism from the pundits and fans. My wife, family and friends all say that this era in my life changed me from a reasonably happy, jokey character into a defensive and mildly aggressive person. That came over very clearly in TV interviews during the football days, which is an interesting point, because it was perhaps this aggressiveness, and the fact I was able to answer questions on the fly in live interviews, that brought me to the attention of a certain Mr Peter Moore, the man who recommended me to embark on the next major journey in my life – a television programme called *The Apprentice*.

One day, in March 2004, my secretary Frances informed me there was a young lady on the phone from the BBC who wished to come and speak to me about a possible television programme. I just assumed this was another invitation to participate in *The Money Programme*, then a very popular show on BBC2 covering business matters. They often asked me to comment about the electronics industry or the performance of my company. I'd also been invited on to talk about the football industry, Sky TV and that kind of stuff.

I agreed that this young lady, Sophie Leonard, could come and see me, but it turned out to be nothing to do with *The Money Programme*. She explained to me that the BBC were considering acquiring the rights for a programme called *The Apprentice*. The long and short of it was that *The Apprentice* was a business programme where a group of applicants came along and were divided into two teams to perform certain business tasks; and the CEO –

which might be me – would judge which team was most successful and then fire someone from the losing team. This would go on for a series of weeks until eventually a winner emerged. Sophie asked me whether I would be interested in doing this programme.

My immediate reaction was one of surprise. I said that I would possibly consider it, and she went away saying that she would be talking to a few other top business people. For now, they just wanted to know whether I'd be interested if offered the role. Basically, she was sounding me out.

To be honest, I forgot all about it until approximately two weeks later when I got a message from Sophie, who wanted to set up a meeting with me on behalf of a company called Talkback Thames. Before that, however, she came and talked to me again. This time she explained that the BBC was not actually the *owner* of *The Apprentice* format in the UK; it was owned by an Englishman named Mark Burnett and he had agreed to license the rights of the format for the transmission of this programme in the UK to Fremantle Media, the owner of Talkback Thames. Fremantle Media had bought the rights to produce this programme not only in the UK but also, I believe, in other European countries.

By this time I was totally confused and frankly not interested in all the technicalities. However, it became quite clear after the event that the BBC had in fact been gazumped. I found out afterwards that while they were pontificating about doing a direct deal with Mark Burnett Productions, Fremantle Media had come in and pulled the rug from under their feet. Interestingly, though, another deal must have been done whereby Fremantle Media, although having the exclusive licence for the format, were going to produce the programme for broadcast on the BBC.

As a layman in television, this all meant nothing to me. I asked Sophie who she was representing now. She said she was representing Talkback Thames whose remit was that they were going to actually *make* the programme. More to the point, their search to find the CEO or host of the show had now become very important. And so, once again, she was here to ask me whether I would be interested in doing it.

My interest was raised when I explained to my wife, Ann, what was being proposed. She told me she'd heard from her friends in America that *The Apprentice*, hosted by Donald Trump, was the biggest hit on American television at the time. My ears pricked up at that stage. I called Nick Hewer immediately, saying, 'Nick, this is a must. I have to get this gig. Please get on the case and find out who's really making the decisions.'

My very loyal and good friend Nick, who had worked for many years as my PR consultant, had decided to retire from the general PR practice. He spent a lot of his spare time in a lovely little town in the middle of France, though he did continue to do a bit of PR work for me personally. As ever, Nick beavered away and confirmed that Talkback Thames did indeed have the rights to produce *The Apprentice* and they were going to make the decision as to who the host would be. BBC Entertainment boss Jane Lush was the person who had agreed to commission the programme, and she had her favourites, one of whom was Philip Green and another was possibly Stelios, the owner of EasyJet. I was down the pecking order on her list – something she would totally deny now, preferring to accept the plaudits for her brilliance in spotting Sir Alan Sugar.

To be fair, Jane Lush's idea of Philip Green was a good one because he was a great British businessman, although not perhaps as famous or popular in the eyes of the public as I was. This was partly due to the fact that I was the boss of Amstrad, but mainly due to my years as Tottenham boss. I knew Philip reasonably well and had a gut feeling that he wouldn't really be interested, partly because of the time this thing would take up, but more because he wouldn't have considered himself as proficient in front of the TV cameras as I had become after dealing with the football media for years.

The simplest thing for me to do was to give Philip a call. In some respects Philip is just like me, a very straightforward man. He said he wasn't cut out for the role and, as I suspected, he couldn't afford the time to do it so he'd turned it down. He added that if there was anything he could do to help my cause, he would certainly recommend me as the man for the job.

Philip, being someone who followed football, knew that I was more than capable of holding my own in front of TV cameras. I really appreciated what he said to me at the time and I believe he did indeed put in a good word for me with the powers that be.

Meanwhile, Nick's investigations revealed that one of the decision-makers on the search for the CEO was a fellow by the name of Peter Moore.

Funnily enough, Peter was a Tottenham fan and no doubt knew of my ability to talk on television. He told Nick that he would go in to bat for me, and I sincerely believe he did just that. He fought very hard to bring my name to the attention of Jane Lush and to another gentleman by the name of Roly Keating, who was Controller of BBC2 at the time.

There was a series of frantic phone calls between Nick and me over the course of a couple of weeks.

'How's it going, Nick? Do you reckon we've got the gig or not? What do you think?'

Nick said, 'Look, I have spoken to Peter again. He seems to be really up for it. I'll get you a meeting with him and we'll see how it goes from there.'

When I met Peter for the first time, he was not what I expected to see. Mind you, what was I expecting to see? What did I think a TV production person looked like? Anyway, Peter was a thin chap, about my height, with long scruffy silver-grey hair. He was dressed like a left-wing hippy but had a very eloquent speaking voice, no doubt cultured from his days at Cambridge University. He must have been chosen by Talkback Thames because of his past experience making shows like *Cutting Edge* and *Jamie's Kitchen*. What came over very quickly was his dry wit, so we were going to get on well. There's nothing better than the banter between two people with the same dry sense of humour. What I didn't know was that he also had a fiery temper. You'll read more about that soon.

Back to the meeting, I remember thinking that I really wanted to get this gig because I knew how successful the programme was in the US. On top of that, over the previous years, at the invitation of the then chancellor Gordon Brown, I ran a programme, sponsored by Lloyds Bank, of visiting schools and universities with the aim of teaching young people the value of business, and how to start one's own business – basically demystifying that world. *The Apprentice* would be an opportunity to spread that message on television in a very big way – a way to say, 'You can do it too.'

In the past there had been some business programmes on TV, in particular the one hosted by Sir John Harvey Jones. They were interesting but quite stuffy and not very entertaining – certainly not the type of programme that would attract the young budding entrepreneurial viewer.

By now I had seen some tapes of the American version of *The Apprentice* that someone had sent me, and it was a great format. I knew deep down I could do this with my eyes closed and, more to the point, I knew this show would attract a great following of young people, with its serious business message woven together with the entertainment value of the characters in it.

It finally boiled down to Peter Moore recommending me to his then boss, Daisy Goodwin, the editorial director of Talkback Thames. She came onside and recommended me to Jane Lush and Roly Keating at the BBC. This resulted in a meeting at the Dorchester hotel, which coincidentally I was able to attend because I was there for a charity function that night anyway. I bought them all a drink at the bar and at the end of the meeting Roly Keating said, 'Well, you're fine by me. Peter's the one who's got to make the programme.' Jane Lush knew by now that Philip Green wasn't going to do it, and so it was agreed that night that I'd got the job.

Interestingly, as I was finishing writing this book, Richard Desmond, the so-called media mogul, published his autobiography in which he claimed *he* was first choice to host *The Apprentice* with Philip Green as number two and me as a last-resort third place. Those who were in charge of the programme at the BBC and Talkback at the time have no recollection of this. I know, from talking to Peter Moore and Jane Lush in those early days, who was in the mix and his name was certainly not on *their* list.

I can only think that Mr Desmond's memory failed him when exploring his memoirs. He may for example have confused an approach from his own production company, Portland TV, who might have been looking for a host to fire some of the bimbos used on his soft-porn channels Red Hot TV and Television X. Having said that, I have personally found his autobiography quite useful. I've got an antique table with one leg shorter than the others and his book is a perfect fit.

It is only recently, having spoken to Peter eleven years later (telling him I was about to write this book), that he disclosed to me the document that spelt out, in simple terms, the format of the programme. It reads:

Prospectus for Potential CEOs

1. Talkback has been commissioned to make a 12 x 1-hour series based on the highly successful American format show – *The Apprentice*. The BBC2 adaptation will retain the core attributes of the NBC version, although there will be subtle differences.

2. A knockout competition – with a charismatic business figure (effectively 'the CEO') offering the winner the prize of a significant job – remains unchanged. The contestants will live together during the competition and each week they will divide into teams and compete to make the most profit in a business task. The winning team will share a reward; the losing team will appear in the boardroom to face the music. Judged on their performance, one contestant will be eliminated by 'the CEO'.

3. We will have fewer candidates (14 not 16) and fewer episodes (12 not 14). Having eliminated one candidate each week from 1 to 10 there will be 4 candidates remaining for the final 2 episodes. In week 11, 2 candidates will be eliminated almost at the outset. Then the 2 finalists will be asked to choose from the six runners-up, teams of 3 each, for them to lead into the final competitive tasks. The twelfth and final episode sees the resolution of these tasks and the announcement of the winner.

4. Because there is no one quite like Donald Trump, one characteristic difference with the American version will be the personality of the central business figure (CEO). Trump's name is a brand in America and he is synonymous with fabulous wealth and glamorous living. Our first job is therefore to find someone with charisma, wealth and acknowledged business success who can be the 'star' of our show.

5. The ideal 'CEO' will have to be in a position to offer the winner a year's contract doing a serious job, because that's the prize that motivates the series.

6. This inevitably involves a short but intense time commitment: approximately two months.

7. The CEO's on-screen role is to introduce each episode, set the task for the contestants and preside over the boardroom

dénouement. That person has to eliminate one contestant each week with the immortal words 'You're Fired'. The decision about which contestant is eliminated will be the presenter's alone.

8. In keeping with the Trump version, our ideal 'presenter' CEO will have two close business associates who also appear on-screen to monitor the tasks and advise in the boardroom. The CEO's company will also contribute to the shaping of the weekly tasks for the competition, in collaboration with the production team. And finally the CEO needs to help in the provision of 'treats' for the weekly winners – such as rides in the CEO's personal plane etc.

9. The presenter will have a considerable stake in his or her own portrayal and we acknowledge that.

Peter Moore

Talkback Productions

From that moment on, the whole thing started to escalate. Around May 2004 things started happening very rapidly. The BBC put out the following press release, which was a really big thing for me and my family:

Sir Alan Sugar confirmed for BBC2's *The Apprentice*

The Apprentice, the series that gives a unique insight into the competitive world of business, is coming to BBC TWO with Sir Alan Sugar at its helm. Sir Alan, one of Britain's most successful entrepreneurs, guides 14 candidates as they vie for his approval, and the knowledge that they can make it in the world of business.

Made by Talkback, the series will see the 14 contenders face the longest and most gruelling interview of their lives. They will carry out weekly assignments to test out their business acumen and entrepreneurial skills. Each week, Sir Alan will fire one of them, leaving the rest to go on to another equally challenging task. The one candidate who proves their worth and capability will secure a year-long job with one of his companies and a six-figure salary.

Sir Alan, an 'East End boy made good', has worked hard to get where he is today. Brought up in a council flat in London's East End, Sugar is Chairman of Amstrad plc, the largest individual shareholder in Tottenham Hotspur, owner of Viglen the computer company and owner of one of the largest private property companies in Britain. He has long been a major champion of promoting enterprise in the UK.

Sir Alan says: 'My philosophy has always been to work hard, be honest, be frank, be credible and always learn from your mistakes. My good news/bad news approach to business has earned me a reputation for being blunt but you've got to have what it takes to make it in business.

'I was delighted to be approached for this role. It sits perfectly with my long-held belief in the importance of promoting enterprise. What a great platform.'

Jane Lush, Controller Entertainment Commissioning, added: 'The Apprentice is a breathtaking and original way of using entertainment to bring business to those who might not have thought it was for them.'

Daisy Goodwin, Editorial Director at Talkback Productions, will co-exec produce the series with Peter Moore (*Cutting Edge*,

Jamie's Kitchen), and Tanya Shaw (*Lads' Army*, *I'm A Celebrity . . .*, *Pop Idol*) as series producer. Patrick Uden will be involved as a senior programme consultant.

Daisy Goodwin says: 'I'm very excited to be making *The Apprentice*, the first entertainment show to have a real point – to show what it really takes to get ahead in business.'

Peter Moore says: 'This is a series that tests entrepreneurial skills and rewards the winner with a fantastic job, at the same time acknowledging the British sensibility towards naked ambition and the accumulation of wealth.'

The Apprentice is based on the hit US series of the same name and was created by Mark Burnett and produced for NBC by Mark Burnett Productions. Mark Burnett is British and a former member of the parachute regiment that served in the Falklands. The series was a huge hit for NBC achieving 28 million viewers for the finale in April 2004. The American show will air on BBC2 later this year.

Anyone wishing to take part in the show should go to www.bbc.co.uk/apprentice to apply.

For further info contact:

Communications Manager, Talkback Thames

Publicity Manager, BBC Entertainment

At Talkback's offices in Newman Street, Soho, in the heart of TV production land, I was introduced to what I was told was the production team. This was made up of Peter Moore, the boss of the team, and Tanya Shaw, his series producer (who had been hired due to her experience in the making of *Lads' Army*, *I'm A Celebrity* ... *Get Me Out Of Here* and *Pop Idol*), plus Dan Adamson, Patrick Uden, Beth Dicks and a load of other people whom I have since learned were executive producers, series directors, task teams, house teams ... I had no idea what everyone did.

'This is Dan Adamson, the production team leader,' someone would say, or, 'This is Andy Devonshire, the producer/director.' Now, I can't even remember people's *names* two minutes after I've been told, let alone their *titles*; let alone understand what those titles mean in terms of what they are responsible for! I suggested that a good place for a face-to-face meeting with this whole team would be at my house in Marbella where we could sit down in a relaxed atmosphere and go through all the things that needed to happen before we started the filming process. Sure enough, the invitation was accepted – it could have had something to do with the fact that I sent my private jet to pick them up. Nick came too and we had a nice day or two in Spain.

We spoke about what needed to be done. First of all, we had to determine who my sidekicks were going to be. Peter Moore, who could see the relationship I had with Nick Hewer, said straight away that Nick was the obvious choice.

'Oh, absolutely not, I couldn't do that,' Nick immediately said. 'No, I don't do television, no, no, no, this is not for me; I don't have the capability, etc., etc.'

'Shut up, Nick,' I said. 'It's a very good idea. Please do it.' But I told Nick it would be on one basis which I needed to sort out with Peter.

Up until then we hadn't discussed money. As far as I was concerned I was quite happy, as I told Peter at the time, to do this thing for no fee. But I couldn't ask Nick to work for nothing. (Mind you, if you were to ask Nick at the time he would have jokingly said that he *always* thought he was working for nothing for me – he did moan from time to time that I didn't pay him enough! Sorry about that, Nick.)

This time *I* went in to bat for *Nick* and arranged a very good fee for him to do it. Peter was slightly shocked that I had made such a demand, but afterwards they recognised they would have to pay my sidekicks. And so it was agreed, subject to all the financial terms being ironed out, that Nick would be my left-hand man. This left me with the task of finding my right-hand woman.

Peter had never met Margaret Mountford but Nick had, and as soon as I blurted her name out Nick said, 'Perfect.' He could see immediately how all three of us would work together as indeed we had in our business lives.

Margaret, a senior corporate lawyer at Herbert Smith for many years, had done a lot of business deals for me. At the time, she had left Herbert Smith to do a doctorate in papyrology, studying ancient Egyptian manuscripts. She had also taken on some non-executive director roles in various companies, one of which was Amstrad. My task now was to convince a very prim and proper Margaret to take on this new adventure, which would be totally alien to her.

I agreed to work on that and come back to them, subject of course to Peter Moore and the production team meeting Margaret and approving her themselves.

During that meeting in Marbella we discussed in very broad terms the kind of tasks we would be setting the candidates and how the whole thing would work. Patrick Uden, who attended the meeting, was a very experienced person in television production. He was put in charge of organising the structure of the tasks – making them work as business lessons that could be judged. It was also part of Patrick's job to liaise with the logistics people at Talkback so they could arrange for the tasks to be filmed in certain locations and obtain the necessary agreements. For example, if you are filming in the London Borough of Islington, you can't just bowl up with your camera crew and a bunch of candidates who start running around. You have to get permission from the Borough. And some Boroughs do not give permission.

I think it fair to say that for Nick and me it was a very exciting time. It was a new journey for us; something to re-energise our batteries having been through the rise of Amstrad and its temporary decline, through the football era and court cases, and through other great events like launching satellite TV with Rupert Murdoch. And now here we were about to go on another voyage into uncharted waters, so to speak. Actually, exciting times is an understatement!

I still had to land Margaret though. A few days later at an Amstrad board meeting I took her to one side and said, 'Margaret, here's a videotape which I'd like you to go home and watch,' to which she said, 'I don't have a video and I hardly ever watch television.' Silly me – if you knew Margaret as I do, you'd understand why she didn't have a VCR.

'Right,' I said, refusing to be put off, 'well, we certainly have lots of TVs and VCRs here at Amstrad, so if you like, you can watch it here, then I'll tell you what I want to speak to you about.'

She said, 'Okay, but tell me what you want to talk about first, and we'll work out when I can watch the video.'

'Well, Margaret,' I said, 'I've been asked to do a television programme. It is in fact a replication of a TV programme that's already running very successfully in the US, headed by a gentleman by the name of Donald Trump. And to make a long story short, what happens is: there are fourteen individuals who are trying to win a job with me for a £100,000-a-year salary. They form two separate teams and every week we send the teams out to perform a task. One team will win; the other will lose and in the losing team, one of them gets fired – and I require you and Nick, whom you know very well, to tell me what has gone on while you've been out following these people around in the street monitoring how they execute the task.'

Now Margaret is very bright; one of the brightest people I know. I could see she got it straight away but she didn't want to drop her guard and show her excitement – which would be a Halley's Comet event in itself – so she merely said, 'Yes, I could be interested. Give me the video, a friend of mine has a VCR. I'll watch the tape and I'll let you know tomorrow.'

The rest, of course, is history. And what a great duo I chose there. Nick on one side, the very suave, calm, cool gentleman; Margaret on the other side, the very serious, sharp-thinking, rather posh lady; and me, the geezer in the middle, the rough diamond.

When one looks back, if I say so myself, in TV terms it was a stroke of genius that these three people were so well matched for the job. I will explain later how, to the outside world, those who produce television programmes take the plaudits for this type of masterstroke – but only after it's worked and the programme has become a hit. They conveniently forget that it had anything at all to do with me. In front of their peers it was their 'creative brilliance' and 'wealth of experience' in recognising that this trio would be a hit on television that was applauded. For the avoidance of doubt and to clear up any stories told in the pub by those involved in the early days of the production of *The Apprentice*, it was down to me and no one else. While the three of us did have to be approved by the BBC and the production company, all they did basically was satisfy themselves that we didn't have criminal records or murky pasts, or that we weren't dodgy drunken characters. Nothing to do with spotting a successful trio, I can assure you. But I would've loved to have been a fly on the wall in some of the BBC meetings two to three years later, listening to the BS of those who claimed it was them.

So my team was set up and ready to go. Now we were just waiting for the production people to let us know the starting dates and what we needed to do as far as filming was concerned.

Peter told me there would be quite a significant gap until we got to the next stage of physically doing the work. In the meantime, he and his production team kept me fully informed on the most important thing, which was the development of the tasks. Over the ten years of *The Apprentice* that followed, my input into the tasks would be an essential aspect of the programme.

Shortly after Margaret came on board I was asked to attend a meeting to thrash out the terms of a contract for me. This meeting was attended by Peter Moore, Dan Adamson, myself and a female lawyer from Talkback Thames (this was before the days of Jacqueline Moreton, a very professional senior lawyer at Talkback whom I dealt with in later years, and well before the days of Christine Hall, the current lawyer I deal with at Fremantle).

Usually, a new person being offered a serious role opportunity like this in television would be represented by an agent, but would nevertheless be so desperate to get the gig that they would agree to virtually anything that was in the contract – in other words, a real wannabe. However, this did not apply to me, and my business instincts were such that I said, 'I don't need an agent, but I'm not just going to sign the contract; I would like to read it first if you don't mind.'

'Well, actually, it's pretty standard stuff as far as Talkback's concerned,' said the lawyer. 'It's just a case of getting the formalities dealt with and signed.'

I said, 'Not really, love. I think I'll have a read of it if you don't mind. It won't take me long, so if you go and have a cup of tea, we'll have a little discussion afterwards, shall we?'

'Well, if you insist, but, you know, there should be no problems, we are not tricksters here. We don't try and pull the wool over people's eyes. We don't normally have this problem with the talent.'

'Talent? Sorry, what? You're calling me "the talent"? Okay, that's a new word on me. I'm "the talent", am I?'

'Well, that is the terminology we use – the talent, yes.'

'Oh really?' said I.

'Yes, it normally means that you're a singer, dancer, comedian, ventriloquist, actor—'

'I'm not an actor, love; I'm a businessman. This is a business programme and there will be no acting on this programme. I'm Sir Alan Sugar, but if you wish to call me "the talent", that's fine. In fact, it's rather complimentary I suppose. I am talented, yes, but not perhaps in the manner you've just described. Anyway, may I suggest you go off and have a cup of tea – or as you're a media person, go and sit in Starbucks with your laptop and have a frappy latte shrappy crappolino – and I'll speak to you in an hour or so's time.'

Well, needless to say, inside this contract there were a few things I was not happy with. For example, if I hadn't been careful I would have been effectively signing my life away as being an exclusive talent to Talkback Thames – which many TV production companies want as part of their contracts. I don't blame them, but as one can imagine, the whole kitchen sink was in that contract.

Interestingly enough, *The X Factor* is produced in partnership with Simon Cowell's company and a division of Fremantle Media. I have to wonder what those wannabees sign when they're desperately trying to get in front of Simon. I feel pretty confident that some of the people who turn up for that show – the green-haired blokes with torn jeans and a bone through their nose – do not consult Clifford Chance the City lawyers, and even if they did, I am pretty sure most would agree anything for a chance at fame.

So when the media lawyer came back from Starbucks I said to her, 'You know, I think we need to have a little discussion here. I have red-lined what I'm not going to sign.'

At this point she became a bit flustered. I think this was due to her lack of knowledge of the background events leading up to this meeting. She said, 'Well, if you are not prepared to sign it, the production people may have to go and choose someone else.'

I said, 'No, no, no, dear, we've been down that road already, and I have been selected. I've been signed off by the BBC, by Jane Lush, by Uncle Tom Cobley and all, so that's not going to happen. Now, *there* are the red lines – that's what I will accept. You go take it into consideration and get some instructions – I have plenty of time. And, by the way, you do realise I don't want paying for this thing?'

I didn't want paying as I wanted to get this gig in order to continue my enterprise work promoting business to the young. I was self-confident enough to know I would be a success at it, and having shown what I was capable of after *The Apprentice* became a hit (which I knew it would), I would then have the opportunity to discuss money matters if there were another series.

Interestingly enough, for some reason or other, the BBC (or somebody) insisted that I *had* to be paid, and they threw a figure of £20,000 down on the table.

'I don't really want it,' I told them. 'I'm happy to do this thing for no fee at all. However, if you insist that I have to be paid for some reason, what I'll do is give the money to charity.'

They said, 'We don't care what you do with it, but you have to accept it.'

As is the case in the world of television, the producers are one hundred per cent focused on making the show, so they tend to overlook or not think about the legal technicalities. We were months and months down the line before someone at Talkback Thames or the BBC realised that Sir Alan Sugar hadn't actually signed anything officially! So here they were – Talkback and the BBC – about to sign a deal between themselves for, I guess, a seven-figure sum to produce the programme, when they realised their so-called talent didn't have a contract. So there was a bit of a panic. And that panic was illustrated by how quickly the meeting was called and how quickly they wanted to get the contract signed. Under normal circumstances, someone would present me with a contract and give me at least a week to think about it; then there would be another week of toing and froing with drafts and redrafts going backwards and forwards. But no, they wanted it done *that day* because, I believe, the first tranche of money from the BBC to the production company was due, but they wouldn't pay it until they'd secured me as the talent. I'm liking that word more and more as I go along.

Peter Moore gave me the honest truth about it. He pulled me to one side and said he was in the shit. He explained the cock-up described above, and asked me whether I would kindly be reasonable in my contractual demands to get this thing sorted. His honesty and the fact that he had gone in to bat for me persuaded me to ease up a bit. Not a lot, but a bit. I won't go into any further detail on this, save to say that a lot of my red lines worked and a new contract was mutually agreed that day and signed a few hours after the meeting started, thanks to a bit of quick work on a word processor.

I'm not quite sure what went on with Nick's and Margaret's contracts, but you'd have to be a very brave person to try and pull the wool over Margaret's eyes. I'm sure her contract was precise and watertight. I had arranged a fee for Nick and I insisted that the same fee had to be paid to Margaret. Nick was delighted with the fee. In fact, Nick being Nick, he told me at great length how grateful he was.

I said, 'Nick, it's not me paying it; it's them. It's a done deal. And you don't even know what you're letting yourself in for because, from what I understand, this is going to be bloody hard work.'

'Well, I don't know if I can carry it off, but it's certainly exciting and I am looking forward to it, albeit nervously.'

Daisy Goodwin was Peter Moore's immediate boss at Talkback Thames. *Her* boss was a gentleman by the name of Peter Fincham, whom, I didn't realise, was allegedly in charge of the production of *The Apprentice*. I think he might have been one of the many people who came along to those meetings and introduced themselves. As I said, when I meet a load of people at once, I simply don't take in their names or positions, so Peter Fincham didn't register with me at the time. I hadn't seen Daisy since the Dorchester meeting but she called me one day and said, 'You do *realise* that you have to give the winner of this contest a job for £100,000, don't you?'

'Yes, Daisy, I do realise that.'

'No, no, okay, I just wanted to tell you that this is for real – you've actually got to offer the person a year's contract for £100,000. I just want to be a hundred per cent sure that you fully understand that's what you've agreed to?'

'Yes, Daisy, I fully understand, and I can understand why it's attractive to the applicants.'

'Good,' she said, 'I'm so pleased.'

Clearly that was another panic they hadn't ironed out initially and she needed to get it confirmed. I can imagine she might have lost a couple of nights' sleep over that, thinking that as she hadn't sorted it out, there might be some kind of disaster. As a final note on fees, Talkback Thames and the BBC were very fair and paid all reasonable expenses for people like Nick and me, covering various transport costs, driving us around, hotels and other stuff.

Having seen the Trump television programme, I realised that the thing had to be filmed somewhere in a boardroom. Naively, I offered the boardroom of my company Amstrad at Brentwood House. Tanya from the production company came along to view it, but it turned out to be far too small. She advised me that they would have to set up a new boardroom for me. At the time I didn't understand why our room was too small, but the penny soon dropped when I saw the finished boardroom we filmed in, which was way bigger.

The reason the pictures and the production of the programme

are so brilliant is because, believe it or not, there are up to eight cameras at any one time in the boardroom viewing all the people and the candidates from every conceivable angle, plus all the associated lighting and sound rigs set up in there. What's more, outside the boardroom is the reception area where all the candidates sit waiting to go in. This area has become famous as the place where the young lady says, 'Lord Sugar will see you now.' Off the reception area there are further rooms; some where the production people view what's going on in the boardroom, others where the candidates have to wait, sometimes individually, sometimes in teams.

Seeing this amazing set-up and how the programme is actually made is a fascinating, eye-opening experience, even for someone with a semi-technical mind like mine. When you see it, you realise it has to be done this way.

Behind the scenes there was a lady who got the nickname 'Mummy', who was in charge of the money. Her real name was Sandy Fone and she was constantly having terrible rows with Peter Moore, no doubt over costs going outside the budget. She would allocate the money for paying for the location, paying for the camera crew, paying for the cars to take the candidates around, organising the house for the candidates to live in, and so on. Despite this being a huge logistical task, it is taken care of by just one or two people. The arrangements start several weeks prior to filming and go on even after filming has ended. It's like a mini-company within a company. And Mummy was under strict instructions not to go over budget.

Budget is a word we would hear a lot about over the course of the next ten years, and the person in Mummy's position was key to the production company not going over budget. In simple terms, the BBC pay x amount to the production company to deliver twelve episodes of the series, which includes the fees paid to the talent appearing in it, and that's it. The production company has to make the series within the amount of money allocated by the BBC and hopefully end up making a production fee after paying everybody. There would be fun and games in the future, in this area.

2

I AM NOT AN ACTOR

Getting ready for the first-ever episode

Making the first series was an exciting time not only for myself, Nick and Margaret, but also for Peter Moore and his production team. Peter's team were all TV professionals, so of course they knew the ropes. However, as we were going to make a brand-new programme, none of us really knew what to expect.

One thing they did know was that it had to be different from the US version. I was told that American TV often relies on interviews with people *after the event* talking about how they felt at the time, whereas on British TV we tend to want to follow the action *as it happens*. That's what Peter and his team wanted to achieve in *The Apprentice*. And that's exactly what they accomplished in this first series.

I don't intend to describe, in microscopic detail, everything that happened or every single candidate I've come across over the past ten years. However, for this first series I will go into some detail on the basis that a thorough explanation of the first series provides an excellent template for the series that followed.

Peter explained to me that series director Beth Dicks would be assigned to me. She would be by my side following me around throughout the filming of the whole series. This would start off with something called the 'Titles'. For those who don't know about TV (which included me at the time), the Titles are the build-up to the programme. It would start, 'Who is Sir Alan Sugar? Where did he come from? What did he do? Why is he the boss on this programme? What's so special about him?' etc., etc.

Making the Titles involved me having to spend a couple of days filming around the streets in various locations such as outside the premises where I started my very first business, next to the famous Ridley Road market. They filmed me in front of the flats where I was born in Hackney and walking around in the City of London. All of this made no sense to me at the time, but of course when it was finally edited and put together with music, it was very impressive. They added footage of me riding around in my Rolls-Royce, sitting in the back reading the *Financial Times*, all that type of stuff.

By now I had told the family about the show. They were very supportive and, I guess, also quite excited. They were asking me for a blow-by-blow account. 'What's happening now? When are you filming? Have you seen the candidates? When will it be on TV?'

The first thing I showed them was a small compilation tape containing all the filming Beth had done. It wasn't really impressive at that stage because it was just shots of me walking around, standing in front of places and all that. But one thing did emerge from this Titles business very quickly – I am *not* an actor! I'm fine at speaking off the cuff, but there were occasions where Beth tried to give me a script and I was totally useless – I just could not do a script. I often marvel at how professional actors remember each line they have to say and put it across so brilliantly, because I can't do that at all.

In the end, after many tries and retries at certain points, for example when I was standing by my aeroplane at Stansted airport, I asked Beth, 'Is it absolutely imperative for me to say exactly what you want me to say, word for word? Or can I say it my own way?'

This was, in fact, my first encroachment into the territory of the creative geniuses. One could see that she wanted me to say the *exact* words, so she persevered.

Very quickly the Sugar loss-of-patience and short temper started to kick in and it soon became a case of, 'Beth, I'm not doing this – take it or leave it. I've got the general gist of what you want me to say – now this is what *I'm* going to say, and that's it.'

And, of course, it was perfectly okay. The reason I labour this point will become clear later, but some production people tend to think of the main person (or the talent) – *me* in this case – as the stooge. The talent is told where to go, what to do, where to stand, what to say. So I decided at an early stage, when I got back from this filming session, to politely explain to Peter that this was not going to happen. 'And if for one moment they think they're going to tell me what to say in the boardroom, then I'm telling them right now that all bets are completely and utterly off.'

To be fair, Peter not only agreed but made it clear there was never any plan to script the boardroom scenes. 'Absolutely not,' he said. 'You're completely spot on, Sir Alan. No way are we going to tell you what to say. No way. What comes out of your mouth is what's going to be shown. That's going to be the beauty of this programme. We are not making a scripted programme at all.'

Despite this fact, as the years have gone by, because the programme and some of the sequences have been so brilliant, there have been sceptical people in the media who talk about 'scripted boardrooms'. That is absolute total rubbish and something I'd like to clear up. There is *no* script for the main programme. There cannot be a script. I mean, just think about it: if you've ever been in a meeting somewhere with six or seven people, once the meeting starts you have no idea what they are going to say and how they are going to interact; therefore, you cannot possibly know how you are going to respond. I didn't realise it myself at the time, but it's the same when I get in the boardroom with fourteen candidates – I'm as surprised as anyone else by what comes out of their mouths and therefore can't plan what I'm going to say back to them.

So it was a good thing that Beth walked around with me for a couple of days filming the Titles, because what came out of it was that we cleared the air: there would be no script – they would take what I had to say and use it in their editing.

A couple of weeks went by while the production team beavered away making preparations. We had established that the filming would start at the end of August 2004 and it would run right the way through to late October or early November.

That summer I was on my boat in the South of France and it suddenly occurred to me that if the production company wanted some more great Titles, what better than to show me sailing into Monaco's harbour on a yacht? I called up Peter and said to him, 'Peter, I'm learning the ropes here and I'm starting to understand what you clever people do. If you want some great Titles shots, well, instead of me walking past St Paul's Cathedral or the Gherkin in the City, I've got something much better for you. Get down here and film me on a big white yacht pulling in and out of Monaco harbour.'

His first reaction was, 'It's going to cost us money. We're going to have to fly the people out there,' etc., etc.

'Well, Peter, that's your problem, but I'm just telling you, if you want some great pictures, if you want an image of the high life, you couldn't get anything better than this, and this is a one-time opportunity.'

Of course, they agreed in the end. Beth was delighted that she and the camera crew were going on a two-day jolly down to the South of France, and they did indeed capture some brilliant footage of the boat manoeuvring in Monaco which was used in the Titles. Actually, it might have looked a little misleading, as if I was steering the boat in myself. I wouldn't have a clue how to do it!

When the final programme went to air and I saw the Titles, it was an eye-opener to me to realise that a lot of stuff they film never gets used. A rule of thumb I have picked up over the years is that one hour of filming can sometimes produce as little as ten to fifteen minutes' usable footage. It really is all down to the editors or, dare I use the phrase again, the 'creative geniuses' to decide what will be included. So as a novice, you can imagine that when I saw the first cuts of the things we filmed, I said, 'Why did we waste half a day filming the boat going here or there?' or, 'Why did we waste two hours filming me walking past the Gherkin or up and down the factory floor if you didn't use it?'

They would respond with a blank expression and, 'It just didn't work, Sir Alan.'

This term – *It just didn't work* – would be something I would hear for the next ten years. What it means? I don't know – it's just something in the minds of these creative geniuses.

The next thing I was asked to do was a dummy run. In other words, because the production company and I had never done this before, we did a dry run in the boardroom before we did it for real. The production team recruited about fourteen people from their relatives and friends, and set them a small task: selling something to a hardware store. They explained to me what they had done and asked me to interrogate them when they came back.

This, I think, was the most significant moment in Peter Moore's and Tanya's time on *The Apprentice*. This was going to show whether I had got the plot or not. If this thing went down like a lead balloon they would be scratching their heads saying, 'Bloody hell, we've got a real schtummer here. He doesn't know what to do or how to talk. How are we going to make a bloody programme?'

Bear in mind that I had no clue as to what these people were doing, other than a few pictures and a brief synopsis of where they went and what they were trying to sell; and also bear in mind that I didn't see them or see any film of what they did. At the end of the day they came back into the boardroom, got into their two teams and I started to talk to them.

If I say so myself, I took to it like a duck to water. It went very, very well and it resulted in me firing one of Tanya's relatives. When it was all over I asked, 'Has the filming stopped?'

'Yeah, yeah, very good, very good,' they said.

I turned to the fellow I'd fired and said, 'Sorry, no hard feelings. You looked very upset and disappointed; you looked as if I really *was* giving you a bollocking. I didn't mean it, honestly. You know this is just a dummy run?' The fellow kind of half accepted my apology.

At the end of the day I had made Peter Moore and Tanya Shaw two happy people. When they'd embarked upon this project on behalf of Talkback and the BBC, they took a tremendous risk in assuming I was capable of doing it, but in this case the proof of the pudding was clearly in the eating. We were at the races and off to a very good start.

I was obviously a bit of an unknown to the production people and it's quite clear to me now that there were certain things they kept close to their chests and away from me. It hadn't occurred to me that I should have some input into the selection of the fourteen candidates. It eventually dawned on me one day, when we were getting close to filming, and Tanya said, 'Right, I'd better show you these pictures of the candidates and their brief CVs.' This was about a week before I was due to meet them for the first time.

It didn't strike me as a bit off at the time, but I did begin to think later that I should have had a little bit of involvement in the selection process. However, they felt that they were the organ-grinders here and I was the proverbial talent/monkey. I would be given whoever they chose and they didn't need my input thank you. But more to the point, I think there was a certain distrust of me at the time, being an unknown entity, a fear that I might go blabbing my mouth off, telling the media and other people about who the candidates were and all that kind of stuff. Of course, there has to be a certain amount of confidentiality that goes on in the making of these programmes; however, the team did not share this confidential information with me in the early days.

As you can imagine, being presented with a bunch of papers with pictures of people and their so-called claims to fame didn't really do much for me at all. I just accepted what they gave me. I may have commented, 'How do I know these people are any good?' and they said, 'Leave it to us – we are the experts.'

The reality, as I was soon to find out, is that while they were very good at selecting interesting characters and geeky people, quite frankly, as we will see later, they didn't have a good understanding of business. But then why should they? Let's face it, they are creative people who make TV programmes. They might be experts in choosing good characters for television, but in the end I would be the judge of who had a good business brain. Fortunately, there were *some* credible candidates.

We started to talk about the tasks, and what the first task would be. To be fair to Peter and his team, they *did* discuss this with me and ask for my input. They told me they didn't have much time and so the first task had to be done and dusted in a day. I'm not sure who thought of it, but the first task was a simple one – selling flowers.

Here's where the production people are clever. Selling flowers was very easy for the viewing audience to get their heads round. Secondly, because half the candidates were boys and half were girls, the first task pitted the boys against the girls. Again, this was a deliberate move by the production people to make things easy for the viewer to follow.

We decided that for the setting of the task – the point where I tell the candidates what the task is all about – we had to think of some sort of analogy. Flowers are items that only have a short lifespan; they have to be bought early in the morning and sold very quickly so I came up with the comparison of a newspaper. After all, what is a newspaper good for the next day (apart from wrapping your chips in)? So you get some goods which are saleable for just one day and you have to get rid of them that same day and you can't have any left over. We all loved that idea and the production company arranged for the setting of the task to take place at the printworks of the *Financial Times*.

But before that, it was time to meet the candidates in the board-room for the first time. Up till then I had only seen their pictures and their brief CVs. For this initial meeting, the producers wanted to create an atmosphere of uncertainty and, I guess, fear and ner-vousness. From the boardroom, I picked up the phone and asked the secretary outside to send the candidates in. As they entered, I saw the faces of the candidates for the very first time. I glared at them and moved my head along the line as they filed in and sat down. There was silence for about ten or fifteen seconds as I stared at each of them, peering into their eyes. I can't imagine what was going through their minds, but it looked very good on telly.

And then came my opening speech. I told them first of all that I had in front of me what I believed were Britain's best business prospects and that they were about to embark upon a twelve-week journey of business tasks. They would be arranged in teams, and the team that won would end up getting a treat, while in the losing team at least one person would be fired. After explaining the gen-eral principles to them, I then broke into my famous statement: 'This is not a game. This is a twelve-week job interview. I'm the one who's going to decide who gets fired, so you can forget about flick-ing your hair back and flashing your eyes and having a handsome attack, because it ain't going to make any difference. And here's a bit of a warning – never, ever, ever underestimate me because you will be making a fatal error. I know everything in my business. I can tell you where every screw and every nut and every bolt is in my company. I don't like liars. I don't like cheats. I don't like bullshitters. I don't like schmoozers. I don't like arse-lickers.' This little statement was to be used many times afterwards by the BBC and the production company in what they call 'trails' to promote the programme.

After I finished my tirade, the stunned expression on their faces was a picture to behold – it was a fantastic moment. It did come across to a certain extent on the programme, but it was one of those moments that was much better live.

I told them I'd got them a nice house somewhere in London and that they'd be living there throughout the process. I also told them they would have to come up with a team name which we would refer to during the series. The way the teams went about choosing team names would turn out to be a fiasco, not only in this series but in later ones. However, I have to admit it did make very good telly. The scenes of candidates arguing over team names and the rationales behind their thinking were quite astonishing, not to say entertaining. The boys came up with the name Impact while the girls' team name was First Forte.

It had been explained to the candidates previously that they could be away from home for many weeks and they would not be able to talk to the outside world. This is something that a lot of applicants for *The Apprentice* don't really understand – the candidates genuinely have to stay within the confines of the house we provide and they are allowed maybe one phone call per week to speak to their loved ones. They can, of course, leave the house if they want to give up, but otherwise they are cut off from the rest of the world and they are chaperoned – no mobiles, no money, no internet. Having said that, the production people do have contact numbers from the candidates in case of emergency. The point of all this is they are not allowed to consult externally with anybody once a task has been set. If you think about it, for the competition to be fair they have to be cut off from the rest of the world. Otherwise, for example, they could call up Daddy or their boss for help and gain an unfair advantage on the task. It's amazing how some people who applied for *The Apprentice*, and got through the audition stages, pulled out later in the series when reality set in.

In this first series, after my very sharp and brusque introduction, I told them they would be taken to the house I'd provided for them, and that I would be calling them some time in the near future for a meeting where I would explain what their first business task was about.

Just before the candidates went on their merry way to the house, the BBC and PR people needed a photograph of me with all of the candidates and Nick and Margaret to use for promotional purposes. The reason the photo session was done after the first boardroom is obvious. We wanted to capture the first moment I laid eyes on the candidates in the boardroom and vice versa.

The candidates arrived at the house and settled in, thinking they were just going to relax for the rest of the day. Later that night, they got a phone call telling them to get ready straight away – they were going to be taken to a printworks in Wapping.

I don't know how the production team managed it, but they got the *Financial Times* to agree to allow us into their printworks. Nick, Margaret and I stood beside the printing presses when they started to roll and you could actually see the newspapers being printed. But here was our first taste of how things can go wrong.

The *Financial Times* were excellent in agreeing for us to come into their premises, but they were not going to 'hold the front page' for us while we got everything in place. We were given exact timings for when things had to happen because they had to press the button to start the presses rolling. Unfortunately, the candidates had not turned up by the time the *FT* had to go ahead and run the paper.

Although I say I'm not an actor, we filmed Nick, Margaret and myself standing high on a steel balcony in front of the printing presses and I was talking to an imaginary group of candidates that hadn't even arrived yet! A few of the camera crew stood in their place to give me what they call an eyeline, and I rattled through my introductory speech explaining what the task was about – to no one!

The candidates finally turned up. After they were divided into two teams, one person from each team was invited to put themselves forward as the project manager for this task. Tim Campbell, the eventual winner of the first series, put himself forward as project manager for the boys, while Saira Khan, the eventual runner-up, put herself forward as the girls' project manager.

However, by now the noise inside the printworks was horrendous, and it was impossible to film anything and get clean audio. Nevertheless, they lined up the boys' and girls' teams below the balcony in front of me and ran the cameras, and later they patched it in with my previous speech. It came out brilliantly in the film, and we'd managed to overcome this hiccup that was caused by traffic jams and having to adhere to the *FT*'s print deadline.

Considering the cost of arranging everything for the next day – the camera crews, the sound team, the flowers for the candidates to sell – it would have been impossible to cancel the thing and do it again. However, let me make it clear – anything you see in the boardroom and out on the streets is one hundred per cent as it happened.

The candidates were taken back to the house, and Nick, Margaret and I were left standing like three lemons, thinking, 'What do we do now?' Basically, nothing! Go home. I would reconvene with them all at 6 p.m. the next day in the boardroom where the interrogations would take place over who sold what and which team won.

It was at this point that one could start to appreciate what Nick and Margaret do, apart from sit next to me in the boardroom. The next day Nick followed the girls' team while Margaret followed the boys, literally shadowing them throughout the course of the day. It was about then that Nick and Margaret twigged that Alan had a cushy number – just turning up, setting the task and being there in the boardroom afterwards. Meanwhile, they were going to have to graft; getting up early in the morning to follow the candidates around in the flower market and then onto the streets, all the while making sure they were in the right places to be filmed. I think it was the first time Margaret realised she needed to get herself a pair of trainers because her feet were starting to ache.

I will take this moment to say that my knowledge of what actually goes on during tasks is limited, obviously, by the fact that I'm not there. And so I sincerely say that my eyes and ears are indeed Nick and Margaret (and in later years, of course, Karren Brady). They have to explain to me what is going on, who in their opinion is not doing much, and who in their opinion is the champion on the task. Otherwise, how would it be possible for me to judge things?

So at the end of the task it was absolutely imperative for me to sit down with Nick and Margaret and go through what happened throughout the course of the day. Who said what? Who did what? All that type of stuff. Nick and Margaret were assisted by some of the production people who came into that same meeting because each team of seven boys and seven girls sometimes split into sub-teams and Nick and Margaret couldn't be everywhere at once. So I got my feedback mainly from Nick and Margaret, but also got supplementary information from the production people who followed the sub-teams around. Armed with all this information, I was able to interrogate the candidates.

I always enjoyed seeing the surprise on a candidate's face when he or she started to realise that Sir Alan Sugar was no schmuck. And I didn't shoot my bolt straight away in revealing that I knew what went on. I allowed the candidate to start waffling, and at certain points I might suggest that maybe they'd had a slight memory lapse, referring to the information given to me by Nick or Margaret. The expressions on their faces at those times were priceless.

Sometimes Margaret or Nick would interject. 'I don't think that's exactly what went on,' as Margaret would put it. 'Perhaps you'd like to tell Sir Alan what really happened?' And, of course, as we know, when some of the candidates were talking, Margaret's eyebrows and Nick's expressions were TV gold. They said much more than words.

The boardroom was the first opportunity for me to speak face to face with the candidates at length, and therefore start to know them. A couple of people began to stand out quite quickly. Paul Torrisi, for example – ratchet-jaws or rent-a-mouth as I would call him eventually – would not stop talking. Saira Khan could also bunny off a scratch. Not only could she talk non-stop but she had this amazing way of speaking: very exact but also very fast. One could also start to detect amongst the candidates those who would not allow any person to say anything against them, so arguments arose without me having to stimulate them. During some of those arguments, I would just sit back and let them knock themselves out.

As I mentioned earlier, not everything that's filmed can be included as it's only a one-hour show. It should be noted at this stage that in order to make one episode of *The Apprentice*, believe it or not over one hundred and fifty hours of filming is done in all the various locations, and this has to be condensed into a one-hour programme.

The boardroom session on this first task went on for at least two and a half hours. However, as you may know, the boardroom session of each finished episode takes up approximately twenty-five minutes, so that gives you an example of how much it has to be condensed by editing while ensuring that the important, factual stuff is included. In that first-ever episode, the boys won. Actually, it wasn't until much later that I watched the episode myself, so I'll park that for one moment.

I then had to deal with the losing team. Saira Khan, who was the girls' project manager, was obviously in the firing line. However, thanks to input from Nick, it became quite clear that even though the girls had lost, she was definitely the hero of their team, selling more than anyone else and getting people motivated. In the end, the candidate Adenike Ogundoyin was fired, but not before a tremendous verbal battle between the ladies. Having assessed the situation and consulted with Nick, I concluded that Adenike had to go. She made one serious error that I can recall. I asked her a simple question, 'How many bunches of flowers do you think you sold?' She said, 'Lots.' In other words, she didn't know.

I told her, and this is where the programme is so authentic, 'I have been a salesman all my life, and one thing a salesman always knows is what they've sold, every minute of every day. They know their first sale of the day and they know what they've sold throughout the course of the day. And you're telling me you don't know what you sold. Well, the truth of the matter is, according to Nick and your teammates, you sold nothing.'

The moment of theatre was great. The firing was brilliant. The whole atmosphere was electric. But as she walked out the door, I felt sorry for her. I really did feel sorry for her because no one can understand the pressure that people are under in that boardroom environment; not just with me talking to them and firing questions at them, but the glare of the lights, the physical heat in the room and the fact there are about eight cameramen filming you with profile shots and full-face shots, all at the same time.

If I recall correctly, there was a tear in the eye of Adenike when I eventually fired her in what we call 'Boardroom Three', the final boardroom scene with just the last three candidates. So while I knew it would go on to make brilliant television, I felt a little upset and went out of the boardroom to meet up with Adenike afterwards, just to say words to the effect, 'Look, no hard feelings, someone has to go,' etc., etc. I tried to make her feel a bit better, but to be perfectly honest it was probably to make me feel a little bit better, to show her I'm not the tyrant she might have thought I was across the boardroom table.

When I look back on my ten years in television, I have really enjoyed the whole journey, but let me say that the first series of *The Apprentice* was something special. Even the build-up to making the first episode was truly memorable – like having your first child and, in my case, launching my first Amstrad product. It is something that will always remain very firmly in my mind; and I'm sure I speak for Nick and Margaret when I say that it's something they'll never forget either.

Despite the fact that I went on to do another nine series of the main programme and three series of the junior version – which meant setting a total of 138 tasks to 192 candidates – that first series will always be unique for me. My wife often says it was the best series and very hard to replicate.

That said, in TV terms it clearly wasn't the best series, but it was the ongoing template for a great programme. And I have to take my hat off to Peter Moore and his team who, even though they were experienced in making television programmes, put their trust in me, in uncharted territory, and made a brilliant show.

3

WE'RE OFF AND RUNNING

Series one gets underway

The fourteen candidates taking part in series one of *The Apprentice* had no idea what they were letting themselves in for. As I mentioned previously, I had no idea who *they* were, and they had no idea what to expect when they met me. Over the years, there has been so much media speculation about this that I would like to put the record straight. In every new series of *The Apprentice* I have been involved with, the very first time I meet the candidates – face to face – is when they walk into the boardroom for the first time. This is what we call 'Boardroom Zero'.

For reference, throughout this book: Boardroom Zero is the first time we meet; Boardroom One is when the candidates come back from the task and we go through what happened and reveal which team won; Boardroom Two is when I interrogate the losing team and the project manager chooses which two candidates they're going to bring back in; and Boardroom Three is when those three candidates plead their case as to why they should stay in the process, and one or more of them is fired.

Another thing I would like to reiterate is that I have very little idea – apart from what Nick and Margaret tell me – of what goes on when the candidates are out and about on the tasks or in the house. It is not until several months later that all the footage of them is available for me to view, and of course by then it's a case of 'after the horse has bolted'. It's fair to say that sometimes, had I seen the footage of what actually went on, some of my comments in the boardroom would have been different. All this serves to further endorse the importance of Nick and Margaret, and later, Karren Brady.

While we're on the subject of rumours, there has been a lot of speculation by media snipers about how the boardroom works. Over the years I've heard every sort of nonsense about what goes on. People have said I have an earpiece and get told what to say – that is double-barrelled rubbish. They say my boardroom chair is on an elevated box to make me look taller – also absolute rubbish. I sit on a high-class office chair which can be adjusted up and down to suit, so why would it need to be on a box? I recall the PR people were so pissed off with this rumour that they took a photo of the boardroom set-up from behind to show the media they were talking bollocks.

There are some interesting things that happen before the candidates get to see me. There are some practical aspects to the filming that, if one thinks about it, have to be done to make the series work. These efficient TV practices are very well known and in the public domain, as many members of the public are watching when filming takes place; indeed, these things have been reported many times in the newspapers.

Anyone who watches *The Apprentice* will remember that the first time they see the candidates is when they are walking over the Millennium Bridge in London. This takes place very early in the morning with special permission from the City of London. As one can imagine, the candidates are pretty clueless as far as TV filming is concerned, so there are several attempts at filming this scene until the camera crew get it right. This may involve them having to go back onto the bridge and do it several times over. What the viewer actually sees looks natural and seamless, with changes of shots and close-ups of the candidates. This is because at least four cameras are filming them from all angles walking over the bridge, and that footage is then taken into the editing suite where it is mixed and matched to create those great pictures of the candidates seemingly bouncing over the bridge with a great swagger in their step.

The programme shows the candidates leaving my offices and getting into a taxi after being fired. The way this is done is fascinating, and again, hats off to the experts. Consider, no one knows when each candidate will be fired, but what we do know is that, with the exception of the winner, they *will* all be fired. So at the very start of the series, just after the bridge filming, the candidates are asked to come to my office building with an overcoat and a scarf. Then, one by one, they are filmed leaving my office, getting into a taxi and being driven off. To complicate matters further, we film it once for every candidate during the day and once at night. The reason for this is that sometimes it is clear to the viewer that the boardroom session is taking place at night, so after firing someone you can't have them coming out into broad daylight. So by now, as they say in television, they have pictures 'in the can' of the candidates leaving the office in a taxi by day and by night.

On the day a candidate actually gets fired, we have no idea what they will be wearing in the boardroom – for example, the colour of their shirt and tie. Therefore, every time the candidates come to a boardroom session after completing a task, they must bring with them the same coat and scarf they wore when we filmed them several weeks earlier. The reason for this is continuity, so that when they are filmed *inside* the taxi after they've been fired, they look the same as they did when they walked out of the office and into the taxi (which was filmed some weeks earlier). The coat and scarf neatly cover up what they were wearing in the boardroom when they were fired. Sitting in their coat and scarf in the back of the cab, the loser can waffle and moan as much as they like about their dismissal. Clever stuff by those production people. One of the things that could come back and bite us on the nose was if, for example, one of the ladies decided to have a change of hair colour or style. When they stay in the house they do have a hairdresser come in, but changing their hair colour or style is a no-no.

As I've mentioned, I was consulted on all the tasks; indeed, the second task – to devise some kind of toy targeted at children – was one which I was actually instrumental in devising, along with the production team. Having built my reputation on products and manufacturing, one of the things I wanted to find out was how good the candidates were at coming up with a product. Not only would it show me how creative they were, but also how switched on they were at assessing what the market wanted, and then pitching it back to experts – so it was testing a few different things. The task was supposed to replicate designing a product from scratch and presenting it to me. I had taken advice from a retail expert in this particular field and my remit was that the toy had to be innovative and not seen before.

One of the issues that came up was that we needed prototypes of the designed products to be ready in just a few days so they could be presented to the retail shops' buyers or to me. Fortunately, the production company had found a prototyping house that was used to working very quickly in producing what I call 'mock-up' samples, more or less overnight.

These prototypers would go on to be a very useful contact over the following years as there would be many product design tasks I would set. In the first series, the candidates got off pretty lightly because judging which team's product was best was simply down to my opinion. In later years we asked the candidates to go and pitch their products to experts and buyers in the relevant industries, and the winning product was based on the number of potential orders received.

Over the years I have seen project managers get carried away with their own ideas, refusing to listen to what the market actually wants or the rest of their team says. In the first series, Lindsay Bogaard decided to be project manager for the girls and they went off and brainstormed their ideas. From what I learned in the boardroom afterwards, she became very autocratic and turned down the other ideas her team had come up with. Indeed, they made two products – one was a kind of small robot you could assemble; the other, the idea she finally went with, was a set of semaphore cards for use in the school playground. She claimed in the boardroom that this product would stop kids shouting – instead the children would signal to each other by holding up cards to convey certain messages. What a load of rubbish! I told her, 'If you can stop children shouting, then you don't need to worry about getting a job with me.'

In fact, had they gone with the robot idea, I would have chosen it as the winning product of the day. The boys, under project manager Raj Dhonota, came up with some communication gadget that looked like a walkie-talkie set, but it wasn't very innovative.

Again, the production people showed me they were no fools. Once they found out which products the teams had designed, they went out and looked around the shops to see if they could find any similar products already on sale. When they found these communication devices, they provided me with one of them and said words to the effect, 'Sir Alan, you might want to keep this tucked away under the desk, and when you talk to the boys about their great, innovative product, you can whip it out and say, "This does the same thing, doesn't it?"' When I did this, it was a great boardroom moment. Their faces were a picture to behold.

Lindsay was the first example of a project manager taking no notice whatsoever of her team. She broke all the rules of common sense and insisted upon her idea in the face of objections from everyone else, and that was what cost her. After I fired her, she shot off back to Holland and complained that she was unfairly treated in the edit. In fact, she's one of the only candidates ever to make such a complaint.

In dreaming up the various tasks, we had a look at what the Americans did in the Donald Trump version; however, I don't think there was one task of theirs that met the very high standards set by myself and Peter Moore's team. Generically, of course, there were some similarities – for instance, there's always an advertising task, which is one of my favourites – but in general we had to rely on our own ingenuity. I don't propose to go through every single task in the first series, save to say they were designed to try and test the candidates' abilities and characters. How they dealt with each task's difficulties and pressures helped me decide which of them I should dispose of.

So while Lindsay was fired because she didn't listen to her team, Miranda Rose was fired the following week because she was totally disrespectful to her project manager.

On week four, Adele Lock, who claimed to be a retail manager, just couldn't hack it. On this particular task – to sell items in a concession area within Harrods – which I set up with the famous Mr Al-Fayed, she really fell apart. It resulted in the losing team ganging up on her in the boardroom, saying that she never contributed. Adele tried to swing it round to save face by telling me she had never been so undermined in all her life and that she found the process completely demeaning, and that the people around her were useless. She then started to rant on about this not being a real business situation such as those she was experienced with, and that she had some 'personal and emotional problems' she needed to deal with. Regrettably, this was the first example of someone not taking into account that they would be stuck in the house for many weeks if they were going to succeed in this process. I sensed at the time that she'd sussed she was going and was trying to get in before I fired her.

'I'll make your job easier for you, Sir Alan – I'm leaving today,' she said.

Clearly she thought she was being smart in avoiding being fired. However, I jumped in quickly and said to her, in effect, 'Don't give me all that flannel. Thanks for the speech – you read it right: you knew you were going. I'm sorry about problems you may have in your family, your emotions and stuff. If you can't hack it, that's fair enough, but don't make excuses, because despite what Tim [who was project manager] might be saying about the other members of the team, you *were* going.' In other words, I got in before she did.

Then there was Matthew Palmer – a mature student is how he described himself. He was very confrontational. In fact, his USP was to annoy everybody and disagree with everything that was said. On one occasion he blamed his poor sales on being too tall, to which I replied, 'I've heard some excuses in my time, I've got to tell you, son, but that ranks high on the excuse list. You are doing some of my old football managers out of some of the best excuses I've heard in my life.'

Matthew's most memorable moment was when he tried to open the boardroom door by pulling rather than pushing, and banged his head while doing so. He didn't last too long in the process.

One of the stand-out moments for me was the advertising task. This was something I was very much looking forward to. The task was based around the candidates coming up with an advertising campaign for use on television as well as in the printed media.

Something the BBC was very conscious of was that *The Apprentice* must not be used in any way, shape or form to promote any of my businesses. I signed on and agreed to this immediately. I under-stand, of course, that the BBC is funded by the licence-fee payers and it is obvious that one cannot use the opportunity of a television programme for anyone involved to promote their own products. This I agreed with one hundred per cent.

However, as I was in the electronics business, I said that it would be fair and reasonable for me to build the advertising task around something I would likely be manufacturing. This made per-fect sense and I was certain the viewers would understand because the product would be within my field of expertise. There was a big debate over this and clarification was sought from the BBC. Fortu-nately, there was a product, a CD player, which we were designing for the American market exclusively. As this product would never be available in the UK it was agreed that it could be the subject of the advertising campaign, on the basis that no one would be able to go out to the shops the day after the programme and buy it.

This is just one example of the complexities one must take account of in order to comply with the very stringent but very fair and sensible BBC rules. The task went ahead and it turned out to be brilliant television. One of the candidates, Paul Torrisi, a property developer, had started to rise to the top of the pile as a very fiery, excitable character. After the first task selling flowers, Margaret told me, 'By God, does that boy have the gift of the gab!' He had obviously decided that the way to win was a full-on charm offen-sive and, boy, did he go for it! He was charming kids, grandmothers, builders, you name it.

Paul went quite far in the process; all the way to the interviews episode the week before the final. He actually reminded me of a younger me in a lot of ways, but he had a volatile temper he couldn't seem to keep the lid on, despite me warning him a number of times. At one point he tried to blame his confrontational nature on his Italian blood. Margaret was having none of it. 'That's no excuse,' she told him.

Paul often locked horns with sales manager Saira Khan. It became a real feud. On the advertising task, Paul was leading the filming sub-team and the whole thing was a bit of a mess, with the presentation being a total embarrassment. When they got to the boardroom I asked Paul if the reason he'd brought Saira back in was because of the argy-bargy they'd had the previous week rather than because of her performance on the task. Paul swore blind that they'd made up after the last boardroom, which Saira denied. Paul was desperate to prove to me that he'd behaved well. Having heard Saira deny at least three times that they had made up, Paul said, 'I am a Roman Catholic and as God is my witness I shook her hand,' to which I replied, 'Well, I'm Jewish and I couldn't care less!' That shut him up. After that, I had to split the two of them up and put them on different teams.

Paul acted as director on the filming of the TV advert for the CD player while Saira was sent to deal with the production of the newsprint advertising. The task took about two to three days, after which the teams returned to the boardroom to show me the results of their work. Before we started to discuss the results, I said, 'I've written books on advertising – chequebooks! My hope for you lot is that you run a business one day with a turnover of the amount of money I've pissed up the wall on advertising over the years.'

The difference between the two teams was so obvious that I actually asked Raj, a member of the losing team, to announce who had won. 'Raj,' I said, 'you're an astute man – who has won?'

Raj said, 'I assume—'

'No, I didn't ask you to assume. I asked you who won.'

'They have.'

'Spot on, son.'

Paul Torrisi, one of Raj's teammates, started disputing the decision with me. 'Why did they win?' he said.

I replied, 'Did you ask Raj?'

'Raj isn't going to potentially fire me,' said Paul.

I explained to him, 'An onlooker would not know what the bloody hell your advert was all about! They would have said what my wife says half the bloomin' time when she sees these arty-farty bloody ads on telly: "What was that about?" Where's the product? Not there.'

'It *is* there,' Paul continued to argue.

I said, 'Yeah, if you've got a microscope and you put your head right in front of the TV screen.' That shut him up.

The losing team's television advert was terrible. Actually, bearing in mind they were amateurs, it was so pathetic that it bordered on being funny. But what was really awful was Saira's full-page advertisement for the CD player – it had stupidly formatted text dotted around meaningless pictures of the product. It was so amateurish that it was beyond belief to think that someone could bring such a piece of rubbish like that into the boardroom.

When I set these advertising tasks, I put the professional facilities of recording studios, camera crew and graphic designers at the candidates' disposal. However, bear in mind that the professionals I lay on for them are not allowed to give their advice or input. They are there simply to be told by the candidates what to do. I remember telling Saira in the boardroom that her instructions to the designer driving the Apple Mac were diabolical. She had obviously given him no direction. She came up with some waffle about how she was busy doing other things, whereas in fact she wasn't. I remember saying to her, 'You made a fatal error. You should have stuck to the Mac man like shit to a blanket. You shouldn't have left him until you'd developed a much better proposition.'

Actually, Saira had panicked. Realising that her full-page advert was rubbish, she tore it up before she came into the boardroom, but more to the point, she had seen the reaction of her colleagues and she knew they would blame her for the poor effort. The production people presented me with a pile of torn-up paper. I told them to get some Sellotape and stick it all together. Saira's action in trying to dispose of the advert backfired, and to her surprise I had the advert there on the boardroom table. She tried to defend her dreadful advert, stating, 'I think that what I've produced in terms of layout demonstrates a basic understanding of advertising.'

I told her, 'I think that's a basic layout for the *Dandy* or the *Beano*; not for any newspaper I've read.'

However, the person who got fired for that task was Rachel Groves. In her CV she talked about her experience in producing adverts, so here was the first example of me demonstrating that I would not tolerate people who messed up in their own areas of expertise; in other words, doing what they do in their day jobs.

I was told by Nick of the most embarrassing scene when the team was presenting their proposition to the advertising agency, whom I'd chosen to give me their opinion on who should win the task. At the time I couldn't conceive of what he was trying to tell me, but apparently Rachel went into a room full of executives and put up a 'mood board', which looked like something some four-year-olds had made at playgroup. She then kicked off her shoes, switched on the CD player and started to dance to the music. I said to Nick, 'You've got to be kidding me!'

Nick said, 'You could not make it up, Alan. I wanted the floor to swallow me up. It was one of the most embarrassing moments in my entire professional career.'

Andy Devonshire, who was the director, also told me he couldn't believe what he was seeing but I didn't fully grasp how bad it was until I finally saw the edited version of the episode several months later. You could actually see the industry experts cringing. It was unbelievable, but also wonderful telly. To be fair, the intensity of the process has made candidates do some pretty stupid things down the years. It is so competitive that people will do silly things to get noticed, and Rachel clearly went too far.

*

Another task that stands out for me, and went on to become a favourite of mine in later series, was discount buying. I chose twelve items and told the candidates to go out and buy them for the lowest price possible. The team that came back having spent the least amount of money would win. In the first series, one of the items was a load of jellied eels and another was a bowler hat. At a recent ten-year *Apprentice* party, halfway through Peter Moore's speech he produced the very same bowler hat. He had hung on to it for ten years! On that task, the winning team came out to dinner with me to one of my favourite restaurants, while the losing team was sent back to the house to reflect on the loss – and guess what was for dinner? Jellied eels!

Another of the candidates, Sebastian Schrimpff, was a very nice chap – tall, quite good-looking and very well spoken. He left the process after the task I set at the Hackney Empire, which was an auction of items that the candidates acquired by getting contributions from certain celebrities whom I'd set up to be visited. Mr Griff Rhys Jones, someone I'd had lots of dealings with in the past, in connection with the renovation of the Hackney Empire, kindly agreed to host the auction at the famous old building itself. It was, I guess, a way of me getting the Hackney Empire on telly. Griff had hatched a plan to renovate the Hackney Empire and I paid for much of it to be done. There's a whole story behind that which I won't bore you with, but it was a very long journey and eventually we did it.

Interestingly enough, back when I was trying to land the job on *The Apprentice*, Nick had informed me that Talkback Thames was originally founded by Griff Rhys Jones and Mel Smith. I think they called it Talkback before they sold it on. Because I was involved with Griff and the Hackney Empire, I called him very early on to say that any help he could give me in persuading Talkback to choose me as the host would be greatly appreciated. While Griff was very sympathetic to my request, he made it perfectly clear that he had sold the business a long time ago and didn't know any of the people who were running it. However, he said he'd be more than happy to put in a good word, which I believe he did, though it may have fallen on deaf ears in that Griff was so far divorced from Talkback by then that he wouldn't have had any influence.

The auction at the Hackney Empire went down very well. My family and friends were invited to the venue to watch, and this was the first occasion when they got to see what went on as far as filming *The Apprentice* was concerned. They obviously knew I was involved in this project and were as excited as I was in wanting to see the end result.

The two teams were put in opposite royal boxes while their products were being auctioned by Griff on stage. It was fascinating to see what the candidates had managed to extract from the celebrities I'd laid on. The biggest donation I recall was a high-performance motorbike. Sebastian's team lost, and in the dog-eat-dog world of *The Apprentice*, as nice a fellow as he was, his colleagues ganged up on him, placing the blame in his lap for the lack of contribution. This was endorsed by Margaret who was following the team, and it resulted in Sebastian having to leave.

Ben Leary, who was a headhunter for a living, was an interesting character. He took a rather laid-back position. He wasn't very vocal and to me he seemed quite shrewd in allowing everyone else to fall on their swords. He wouldn't get involved in arguments or point fingers at anybody. I think he had decided that his tactic would be to sit on the fence, keep quiet and hold back. I mention this now because it's a tactic that was adopted again and again in the years that followed. However, it is something I pick up on very quickly after a few weeks and I tend to warn the person that I've got my eye on them. The tactic ultimately backfires because I throw them in at the deep end and appoint them as project manager.

I say that Ben was trying to be a bit shrewd because, despite being quiet, he managed to slip in that he was brought up in

Chigwell, thinking it would impress me as I live there. He said that his mum and dad ran the King's Head pub, and that he was educated in the area. I'm not sure how he thought this would cut any ice with me, but it didn't. He left the process by simply not controlling costs on the task for which he was project manager.

Raj, who claimed to be an internet entrepreneur, also seemed to be trying to assess the process and play it cool. He left because he failed to step up despite several warnings from me to wake up and *do* something and *be* somebody in the process.

Despite the stringent qualification process on *The Apprentice*, there are always candidates who slip through the net. One of those was Miriam Staley, a very nice young lady who was very bright. I recall watching her on the shopping channel task in week ten and commenting from my armchair at home, 'She has not stopped bunnying for twenty-five minutes – she can talk non-stop – she doesn't come up for air. I wonder if she's married. Poor husband, the geezer must be stone deaf!'

It was one of those situations where I had to decide whether she was the right calibre of person to work in one of my organisations, and in Boardroom Three she was unlucky enough to be up against two strong candidates, Paul Torrisi and Tim Campbell. Having listened to Paul plead his case – he said that he didn't think things were fair – I recall telling him, 'We don't do *fair* here, mate; the only bloody fare you'll get is your cab fare home.'

In the end it boiled down to my personal opinion, and I decided that Miriam simply wasn't for me.

Funnily enough, I bumped into her later on, as she got a job in the PR department of Lloyds Bank, who had been my bankers for many years. Long after *The Apprentice* was broadcast, I was at a meeting at Lloyds HQ and they brought her in just to say hello. So at least she had learned something positive from the process as she'd obviously got herself a good job there.

The shopping channel task also rang alarm bells about James Max, the shrewdest person in the first series. A lot of banter went on between him and me. On one occasion he said that he wanted to learn from me, to which I replied, 'I'm not Corpus Christi College – I'm not looking to teach. I don't mind people picking up things but I'm not here to teach. I want someone who's actually going to *do* something.'

One could see from his CV that he was a highly qualified person. He had been involved in real estate and had worked for financial institutions in high-level positions. You could tell throughout the process that he got the plot immediately when others didn't understand what it was all about. At one stage, James was looking like the top contender and the potential winner of *The Apprentice*. However, as time went by, one felt that perhaps James was there for the wrong reasons. He was the classic example of someone who slipped through the net. He wanted television exposure to fuel a media career of his own. And while he performed very well throughout the course of the series, it became apparent to me, and to Peter Moore and his team, that he was never seriously considering coming to work for me if he had won. What he thought he had won was recognition on television.

Saira Khan was another feisty character, and is one of the candidates people remember most from that first series. She was so determined that it bordered on comical at times. I nearly fired Saira on a number of occasions for not being able to get on with her team and having confrontations with people, but in the end she made it to the final and came a very close second to Tim Campbell.

The TV shopping channel task I've already mentioned was designed to test whether the candidates could deal with an extremely high-pressure situation and project their selling abilities on live television. The result would be clear-cut because the shopping channel would be able to tell us at the end how much stuff each team had sold and who the winners were. James and Saira were on the same team, and Saira was directing him through his earpiece as to what to say and do while he was on the air. The product he was demonstrating was a yoghurt-making machine, and some of the stuff that went on in that sequence was fantastic television. Saira was yelling into James's earpiece, telling him to stick his finger in the pot, get a big dollop of yoghurt and shove it in his mouth. Credit to James, he pulled it off brilliantly. She was shouting at him so much, it's a miracle he could get a word out. James was made for this episode – he really excelled. Watching him selling a foam mattress in the broadcast episode, I couldn't help commenting out loud to my TV screen, just like people do on the Channel 4 show *Gogglebox*. He was saying the foam mattress was a technological breakthrough in the way that it sprang back into shape after you laid on it.

'Of course it's going to go back to its original shape,' I exclaimed. 'It's a lump of bloody foam, that's why! What a lot of bollocks. What a pile of tut. A lump of bloody foam for a hundred and fifty-four pounds? Sell any of *them* and you're a bloody good salesman, that's all I can say.'

In the end he sold over two grand's worth, which just goes to show how well he did. I remember at the time saying to Nick, 'We're in the wrong business, mate!'

There was also a sequence where Saira and James had chosen a furry-looking wolf jumper to sell. And it was here that James showed his true colours and why he had entered the process. Because although the item was very naff, and yes, you would have laughed at it, I was told by Nick and to a lesser extent the production people that his reaction to it with Saira when he was trying it on was total theatre. In other words, he was acting, laughing out loud in a false manner. This rang alarm bells with me in that this was not a person's normal reaction during a business transaction trying to assess a product; it was someone playing to the cameras. Armed with that information, as well as my own observations, and not wishing to take a life-changing opportunity away from one of the other genuine candidates, I made the decision to let James go in week eleven. And I was vindicated because, after the series had broadcast, he put himself around to other TV companies for work. Basically, it seemed he would do anything to get on TV. He even appeared in a most ridiculous kids' programme which had nothing at all to do with any skills this guy had; he seemed simply desperate to be on TV.

He ended up getting himself a job working for a radio station and made some appearances on Sky News reviewing the newspapers. I think this work lasted a few years for him. He finally gave most of it up and about a year or so ago he called me to say, 'Lord Sugar, I've decided to get a real job again.' He went back into a business he was expert in, perhaps realising that his media career was not as fulfilling as he had hoped. But he still can't resist doing the odd radio gig.

It is human nature for people to want to be famous and to be recognised on TV, so I don't blame him for that, but what I don't like is when somebody wants to use our *Apprentice* programme as a vehicle for them to become media celebrities. Yes, it's a high-profile series, but it is a very serious process where the prize is massive. I make it very clear that the candidates have to be there for the right reasons. There have been several candidates who tried to launch media careers post-*Apprentice* in subsequent series, but not many have succeeded. More about that later.

I mentioned Paul Torrisi earlier. He was an aggressive young man and, I have to say, one of the star characters of the first series. People asked: did I keep him in the process because he was good TV? Well, I guess as time went by, I was learning the ropes and recognising that one of the things that was going to make this a successful programme was not just the business message, not just watching the task being performed – it was also seeing the antics of some of the characters.

Having said that, the production company knew very well that the decision on who would be fired each week was one hundred per cent mine. It's natural for the production people (and Nick and Margaret) to have their own opinions but I'd signed up only on the basis that they were not going to tell me who they wanted to keep and who should be fired. Despite Paul being great telly, I didn't keep him in for that reason. There are always certain characters, like Paul, who I see a spark in, and I keep them in the process because I want to give them another chance. With Paul I knew he was rough round the edges but he was a super salesperson. It was a no-brainer for me that he had to stay. Of course, the production people loved it when I kept a character like Paul in as they knew he was TV gold, but they also knew that I held the power over who went and who stayed. So while I took note of their hints, I recognised there was a credibility issue as far as I was concerned. I didn't want to be seen by the viewing public as allowing someone to remain in the process who didn't deserve to be there. This would be a topic of debate in the media as the years went by in later series. So I was conscious at that stage that Paul needed to earn his wings to remain in the process. And he did because he was a great salesman, no question about it. Like James Max, he was one of the people who got what the process was all about. As a result, there were some fantastic moments when Paul argued with Saira, which made great telly.

In following the format of *The Apprentice* as defined by the rights owner, Mark Burnett, the penultimate programme is what's known as the interviews episode. This is where the final four candidates are interviewed by a group of external advisors of mine. This was another challenge for me. The production team had told me that I needed to find some trusted people to assist in the interrogation of the final four candidates, and of course, not only should these people have the ability to interrogate well, but they should be interesting too. At the end of this interview process, they were to leave me with just two candidates remaining – the finalists.

4

GRILLING THE CANDIDATES

Picking the finalists, and a logistical problem solved

One of the first names that came to mind as a possible interviewer was Paul Kemsley, a friend of my son Daniel. I'd met Paul, who was a property developer, in Florida and also at Spurs where he was a director. Paul came across as a shrewd, streetwise, fast-talking businessman and it occurred to me that he would make a good interrogator and really push the candidates. I approached him and told him what I had in mind, and asked him to take a look at the Trump US programme to see how the interviews were conducted. He was eager to do it and immediately accepted. My hunch turned out to be correct, he was excellent – and not just at grilling the candidates. He was very entertaining too.

Another gentleman I'd worked with for many years was Claude Littner. He had assisted me with some of the companies I was having problems with in France, Spain, Italy and Denmark, as well as at Spurs where he acted as CEO for a while. Claude was a bit of a troubleshooter and did an excellent job in holding the fort in these companies while they were in dire situations, in need of a leader. I approached Claude about being an interviewer and he, too, was very interested in doing it. Once again, I showed him the tapes of the American *Apprentice* so that he could get a feeling for what he had to do.

The production people had to stick to the format dictated by the rights owner and as such requested at least three advisors. The third one I chose was Bordan Tkachuk, who was managing director of my company Viglen. Bordan was an excellent salesman and certainly had a way with words, and on that basis I chose him. All three interviewers knew me very well and I was confident they would help me choose the right person to get a highly paid job in my company.

This idea of using advisors to assist me on the suitability of potential employees was new to me. I was very interested in seeing what happened when these candidates were being scrutinised by my advisors and, because of this, I decided that the interviews would be conducted at my Amstrad Brentwood headquarters. We were at an important point in the process. We were homing in on the last four candidates and the purpose of this penultimate episode was to end up with two finalists. Therefore, two of the people they were interviewing had to go.

I was pleased at the way Kemsley rattled the candidates' cages and how Claude grilled them. I needed to find out how the candidates would stand up to the interrogations as it would give me a good indication of which of the four were real contenders for the final.

The day after filming the interviews at my Brentwood HQ, we all convened in the boardroom and continued. First, I spoke to my three advisors to get an opinion from them on who they thought were viable propositions for me to employ in the ultimate £100,000 job.

As I predicted, Kemsley was on fire with his comments, and Claude was his usual cutting self. Bordan always tended to side with the conspiracy theories; he would be looking deeply into the agendas of certain individuals. He found himself a bit of a niche, going through the candidates' CVs and picking up a few points here and there that embarrassed them.

Having heard their reports, I thanked the advisors for their help, and they left the boardroom. In came the four candidates, ready for me to decide which two would go through to the final.

After a lot of discussion, debate and argument, Saira Khan and Tim Campbell ended up as the finalists. Ironically, they were the ones who had put themselves forward as project managers for the flower-selling task on the very first week. In later series, rushing in and putting yourself forward as project manager on the first task often turned out to be a poisoned chalice.

The production company laid on a rather lavish final. It was important in such an ambitious series for the final to be a really big event. They always have in mind how the pictures will look on the TV screen. In the first series, the two finalists would each hire a riverboat on the Thames and put on a glitzy themed presentation. I was to arrive on a small speedboat, a bit like James Bond, jump on board each riverboat and see how the task was going.

In reality, it was a bit of a pain in the neck. The Health & Safety people had gone nuts – I had to wear this special life jacket while we were going along the Thames catching up with the riverboats. I took off the life jacket once I got onto the riverboats and it was amusing to see the look of shocked surprise on Saira's and Tim's faces when they saw me come aboard.

To assist the finalists, I had called back some of the previously fired candidates. Tim and Saira each chose three candidates to help them with their final task. This is always an interesting part because the candidates know each other very well from the previous weeks. I suppose it's a bit like being back in the school playground and 'picking up sides' for football. To my surprise, Saira, who had been arguing since day one with Paul Torrisi, chose him to be in her team, as well as James Max.

The day after the riverboat presentations was the final board-room, and Saira and Tim came back with their ex-*Apprentice* assistants. I asked their opinion on how they felt things went and on how Saira and Tim did. After thanking the six of them for their participation, I sent them on their merry way. Then it was time for the final run-in. I had to make the decision on which of them I would choose as the winner.

Before we go on to that, I want to talk about a rather interesting situation that occurred. Before the boardroom session started, Jane Lush and Daisy Goodwin had turned up to see the final being filmed. I'd heard it was pretty typical that the so-called bosses come along right at the end after all the hard work has been done, and true enough I hadn't seen them throughout the previous weeks. But if you've ever heard of the expression 'suddenly the penny dropped', well this penny was more like a lead ball. It had just dawned on everybody that here we were at the end of the filming – in November – with the programme due to start broadcasting in February for twelve weeks, with the final in May. So the big problem was: how were we going to keep the lid on who the winner was for six months?

No one had thought about it, including me! When we discussed it in one of the side rooms, no one had any idea how to resolve the issue.

'If you think you are going to be able to keep this quiet, you can forget it,' I told them. 'The media are very intrusive and once the programme goes to air, especially if it's successful, the nasty media will be only too happy to spoil everyone's enjoyment and break the story on who the winner is. It seems to me there's only one solution, and that is: if the final is going to be transmitted in May, then – even though I have decided – I am not going to announce until May which of these two has won. It will be in my head and I won't be telling anybody, including my colleagues, and more to the point, any of you. Only I will know who the winner is. Therefore, people can speculate all they want, but I won't be revealing it until the morning of the final transmission.'

This created a logistical problem. 'What are you talking about, Sir Alan? We can't just go back to the boardroom again in six months' time with all the costs involved in getting the camera crew and sound team together. And we can't suddenly start editing at the last minute.'

'No, I fully understand that, and I'm a hundred miles ahead of you. Here's what's going to have to happen. We're going into the boardroom today and I'm going to have to do something a bit cruel. Once the cameras are rolling I'm going to interrogate the finalists, drag them through the normal procedure and then say, "I'm ready to make my decision," and then hire one of them. When they jump out of their chair and kiss and hug and laugh or cry, I'm going to have to tell them, "Sorry, I've got something to say: let me explain to you that I can't choose the winner today for confidentiality reasons, because the final isn't going to be broadcast until May, so I'm going to have to take you back a couple of minutes and go through the whole rigmarole again and this time I'm going to hire the other one."'

You can imagine how Jane Lush reacted to that. 'The BBC will never accept that. It's deceptive, it's wrong,' etc.

'Well,' I said, 'you are right, of course, but if you have any other solutions, perhaps you could tell me what they are? You can forget it if you think the media is going to keep this thing quiet or, more to the point, the dozens of production people involved. They are bound to leak it to their mates that they were involved in making *The Apprentice* and that they know who the winner is. Somebody in a pub somewhere is going to blurt out the winner, and if you think that's not going to happen, then you're in cloud cuckoo land. You are going to have to go to the compliance people and the editorial policy people at the BBC and tell them this is the only way we can deal with it. We have no choice – that's what's going to happen today.

'And then we have another problem: what are we going to do with these two people? What are they going to do with their lives? Is Tim Campbell going to go back to work on the London Underground? How can he? He's given up his job! Will Saira be able to go back to the job she gave up? What are we going to do with them for six months?'

'Oh,' said Jane Lush, 'can't we just send them away somewhere, like Hong Kong?'

'Really?' said I. 'Are you going to pay for that?'

'Ooh no.'

'Well, who is going to pay for it then? Mummy's not going to pay for it, that's for sure. It's not in the budget.'

'Well, what do you suggest, Sir Alan?'

'I'm thinking on my feet here,' I said. 'My only other suggestion is that I could take them in to work for me in one of my organisations and give them a special project for six months to keep them occupied. Now that I've seen the last task performed in front of my eyes, I will go into the boardroom session with an open mind regarding my final choice.'

Daisy and Jane were in a complete tailspin having realised that once again something had not been thought through properly. They had steamed in to this very exciting project, but no thought had been applied as to how they were going to keep the lid on it. Eventually, they agreed to my ideas. Peter got the plot quicker than Jane Lush; and because Jane was pontificating and putting obstacles in the way, Peter typically lost his temper and started to walk out of the room. I told him to calm down because we had to solve this problem, and him ranting and raving was not going to help.

Eventually, they had no choice but to go along with the ideas formulated on that day. The proposal was taken back to the BBC and it resulted in the editorial policy people insisting that somewhere on the BBC *Apprentice* website it would clearly state that the hiring would be recorded twice and that the final decision would be withheld until the morning of transmission. And that fact has been set in stone on the BBC site until today. I outlined how this would be achieved: the production company would make two separate tapes – one with Saira as the winner, the other with Tim as the winner – and I would inform the BBC on the morning of transmission which tape to use. Having not been involved in TV before, I thought it was a stroke of genius on my behalf and, more to the point, the only way out.

Even so, this temporary job idea for the finalists was fraught with problems. First of all the media blew it straight away, shortly after the end of filming. Saira and Tim were followed by different journalists who saw them going into my offices in separate locations. One journalist spotted Saira at Viglen while another spotted Tim at Amstrad. Both journalists thought they had struck gold and found the winner. As I recall, we had to put out some kind of press release to say that the media speculation was wrong. Nevertheless, the fact that they were in temporary jobs for six months was out in the public domain thanks to the media. On top of this, there were other problems to do with my existing staff getting the hump, which I'll explain later.

However, it was the best solution, and ever since then, for the past ten years, we have filmed a 'double hiring' so that nobody other than me knows who the winner will be until a couple of days before the final is broadcast. If one thinks about it, as the final is not a live programme, there is no other way – this is the fairest way to deal with it. In fact, this double filming seems to be quite the norm in TV circles. In the award-winning first series of *Broadchurch*, one of its stars stated in an interview that they filmed several endings, and that none of the cast or production people knew what the actual ending would be until it was broadcast.

I spoke earlier about Peter Moore and his fiery temper. Throughout the course of filming, I was told by various people working in production that Peter was known for being a bit of a nutter. He would fly off the handle and lose his temper if things went wrong. To be honest, I hadn't experienced this at all until the day of the final episode. I was in the boardroom waiting to speak to the candidates, but nothing was ready. I was very pissed off at being messed around by the production people, who had got everything totally wrong as far as timing was concerned. The candidates were late and we were sitting around for hours waiting for the production people to organise things. It was a Sunday and it happened to be an occasion when there was a family party going on which I had to miss because of this bloody filming. On top of that, there were some family difficulties we were going through, so I was in a foul mood.

I was in the boardroom talking to Dan Adamson about what he wanted me to do and I was expressing my displeasure in a very despondent way at having to sit around wasting my time. The delay was winding me up and I was not being very nice to Dan. Suddenly Peter Moore, who'd been observing my mood from the gallery and my response to Dan, came flying into the room screaming and shouting that I'd spoilt everything by being uncooperative, despondent and belligerent towards Dan. He screamed that I'd messed everything up. He was ranting and raving like a lunatic, at which point I stood up and said, 'Right, that's it. I've also had enough. You can stick your TV programme where the sun doesn't shine,' and I walked out of the boardroom.

When I reflect on that day, I really don't know what would have happened if I had actually walked out forever, because there they were with eleven episodes in the can (ooh, I sound like a TV luvvy now: 'in the can'), the twelfth and final episode about to be recorded – and the talent having walked off the job! Contractually, I guess they could have come after me, but I would have had a very good defence in saying that I didn't need to be abused by the production people. In truth, I didn't realise at the time what a disaster it would have been for the BBC if I had genuinely got the hump and quit.

Nick Hewer and James, the chief cameraman, followed me out, Nick telling me to calm down, saying he fully understood my frustration and that he felt the same frustration sitting there hanging around.

'This isn't typical of you, Alan,' he said, trying to reason with me. 'You're more professional than this; you've done a good job up till now. You need to calm down a bit and think about this.'

James came up and offered me a cup of tea and told me that it would also be a disaster for him and his team if we had to shut the whole thing down. I can't exactly recall what was running through my mind at the time. I suppose I was envisaging that the candidates (who by now had arrived and were waiting around) would have to be sent home, the whole thing would have to be shut down; there would be a mega row and a tremendous delay. And so, all things considered, it was the right thing for me to concede and go back into the boardroom and finish the job professionally. Also, to be honest, in the back of my mind I was still excited about being on television in this fantastic programme. I asked myself, 'Am I really going to chuck it all away because of my stupid temper?' And I guess on balance that's what sent me back in the boardroom to carry on and finish the thing off. Margaret whispered to me, 'Well done, Alan,' meaning I'd done the sensible thing.

The next morning, I spoke to Peter Moore on the phone and we had a few harsh words. No doubt his interpretation of the conversation was that his words were harsher than mine, so I think at this point it would be better to say that we agreed to disagree. I think Peter was similar to me in that we were two emotional, hot-headed individuals. It's true I sometimes do my nut, but when I calm down I forget about it and in those circumstances I don't hold a grudge. As far as I'm concerned, I just move on. However, sometimes it's quite difficult for the person on the receiving end of my temper to understand how one minute I can be ranting and raving, then a few minutes later I'm back to normal.

*

I'm going to break off from talking about the first series here and talk more generally about some of the logistics of what goes on in producing a television programme like *The Apprentice*.

We have all seen people being interviewed on TV chat shows with a microphone pinned to the lapel of their jacket. Obviously, in *The Apprentice*, in order to make it look as authentic as it does, one can't have microphones stuck on people's clothes. To overcome this, small radio mics are used. Each one has a transmitter that's about half the size of a cigarette packet, and the wire that comes out of the top of it has a miniature mic on the end. In my case I stuck the transmitter in the right-hand pocket of my trousers and the wire ran up the back of my shirt, under my collar, and the mic was tucked into my tie knot. The sound quality was perfect. I say perfect, but I will explain shortly about some of the so-called perfectionists in the sound department who used to drive me bloody nuts.

Now consider that there are fourteen candidates plus Nick, Margaret and me. That's seventeen separate microphones that had to be fitted on people in the boardroom. Each of these microphones sends a signal to a main control unit known as a mixer where the sound levels are adjusted. In the case of the ladies, they had the mics hidden in certain parts of their dresses, but all the men had the mics hidden in their ties like me.

Away from the boardroom, there was the setting of the task to be filmed each time. The candidates would assemble at various locations which were supposed to be synergistic to the task being set. There I would tell them what the task was all about. I would have to arrive very early in the morning, sometimes around seven-thirty, and endure the camera people filming the arrival of my car. The filming, of course, was never right first time, so we would have to drive round the block and come back a second time. Then there would be, 'Awfully sorry, Sir Alan. Apologies, apologies. Someone stepped into the line of the camera. Could you please do it again?'

On one episode we had to go round the block, in a busy part of central London, six or seven times until they got the shot.

In these early days of the first series, being a novice, I just accepted this as part and parcel of being in a television programme. After all, who was I to argue with the production people about this ridiculous situation of not having the thing set up properly and having to retake things so many times? After arriving and stepping out of the car in all kinds of weather, I would have to have this microphone inserted into my tie and then hide somewhere so the candidates wouldn't see me. I'd wait until the production people had the candidates ready and lined up, with Nick and Margaret standing in a certain position, and then I would be called to walk in and rattle off what the task was about.

Sounds simple, doesn't it? Unfortunately, it wasn't. There would be people stopping in the street, trying to get in the picture or disrupting things, or a noisy truck would go by, or an aeroplane would fly overhead. Then it would be, 'Awfully sorry, Sir Alan, could you just step back and come and do that again?'

The setting of the task required me to give the candidates the general gist of what it was all about. Initially, the production people would try to script this opening speech, for example, 'Tomorrow you're going to Harrods and you're going to take over a department there. You're going to have to do this and that [etc.].'

As I'd previously informed the production people, I can *not* do scripts. I'm very good at saying things off the cuff when I have what it's all about in my head, but I'm not going to learn lines. However, some of the production assistants felt they knew more about business than I did, and they would bring out a bunch of statistics like, 'Two hundred and fifty-three thousand people walk through Harrods every day, and seventeen million pounds is spent in Harrods each month,' and so on and so forth. I told them I was not going to remember all that verbal diarrhoea, and anyway, who bloody cares?

They felt they knew better than me, because this was a business programme and the viewer needed to know these things. I told them, 'I cannot remember a string of numbers and statistics, and I'll fluff it every single time. So what we have to do is just leave it to me to put it my way.'

In the end, they were so insistent that I should use these statistics that I said, 'We're going to have to do it in stages then.'

And so I did. I got them to tell me the first part of what they wanted me to say, then I would say it and stop. Then a few more words, and stop. And again, and again. Horrible, totally unprofessional. I discussed this with Peter Moore and told him it was ridiculous, and frankly I wasn't doing it any more.

In the first series the format stated that after setting the task and sending the candidates on their way, I would have to get into my car and talk about what I thought the candidates would have to do in order to win this task. Now this might seem very straightforward to viewers when they watch that sequence. In reality, however, it involves rigging up the inside of my car with lights, a cameraman crouched on the back seat next to me with a special wide-angled lens, and a production person in the front seat next to my driver monitoring the microphone levels. This all took time to set up, and so once again I would have to hang around waiting for it all to happen. What's more, if a task was set in central London, what the production people needed was for the car to be seen to be moving along. Well, have you ever tried to move along in Piccadilly Circus at eight o'clock in the morning? You can't, of course, so it would be stop, start, stop, start. Once again it was a case of, 'Oh, I'm awfully sorry, Sir Alan, we need to go somewhere we can get a good run so we can see the car is moving along; so we can see buses and trees and things like that.'

This would take ages to get right and my patience was wearing thin. But again, as a complete and utter novice, I thought, 'Okay, I'll go along with what you want me to do.' Eventually, the car would be released and I'd be able to go back to the office and get on with some business.

At the end of the boardroom sessions, after I had fired somebody, once again the format called for me to ride in my car and explain why I fired the candidate. This required the car to be rigged up again and microphones to be attached to me. We would drive up and down the road near the boardroom. This was the worst thing I experienced in the whole of the filming process because at the end of the day, having had to absorb all the information from Nick and Margaret about what went on in the task, and then go through the three separate boardrooms, I used to end up mentally exhausted. So it was a real pain in the neck to then be asked to get in the car, go through all the technical palaver and come up with some off-the-cuff opinions on why I fired this person. But, once again, this TV novice just went along with it.

Going back to the microphones in the boardroom, the camera crew and the sound team did not use the same personnel every day. They tended to alternate and occasionally you would get this fellow who considered himself to be a bit of a perfectionist. One day, while I was in full flow in the boardroom talking to one of the candidates, this chap suddenly chimed in, 'Sir Alan, you have to stop.'

'What's wrong?'

'There's something wrong with your microphone.'

'What's wrong with my microphone? I was just talking to Paul Torrisi. Why are you stopping me? I'm losing my train of thought.'

'Well, I'm very sorry, there's some technical problem with your microphone. Someone's coming in to have a look at it.'

And the guy would come in and fiddle with my tie and ask me to count, 'One two three four five six . . .'

'Yes, that's fine, it's okay now. Start again.'

Being a technical person myself, and having been in the audio business for over forty years at the time, I suspected this was a complete and utter load of bullshit and that this particular individual just liked to assert his authority. I say that because these problems never occurred when the other guy, Pete, was on duty; it was always this pain-in-the-arse. There's nothing worse – when you're in full flow; when you've got exactly what you want to say in your head – than being stopped for a technical fault.

On one occasion, the guy came in three times to adjust my tie, at which point I simply got up, walked outside, got hold of Peter and Tanya and said, 'Look, sort this fellow out. I'm sure there's nothing wrong with my bloody tie. It's the same tie I wore two weeks ago. He's telling me that because it's silk it's crackling when I move my neck. Can you hear any crackling on your monitor, Peter?'

'Calm down, calm down. We've got to get it right. Quality is most important.'

The irony was that this so-called microphone expert used to say that certain ties of mine were made of materials that caused problems, and he'd had a lot of experience of this in the past. Really? What he didn't know was that when he wasn't there I used the same ties and the other fellow, Pete, didn't say a dickie bird. I'm sure it was total rubbish.

The feeds from the eight cameras in the boardroom, as well as the audio feeds, all go back to one master control room, known in the TV world as the gallery, where Peter and Tanya would sit together with Andy Devonshire, the series director. In the gallery there were banks of screens, each screen allocated to a camera. Andy would be talking to the individual cameramen to pull in certain shots of people, close-up here, profile there; and he would direct them as to who he wanted the camera on. That said, having explained all this technical set-up, the actual boardroom scene runs as a completely unscripted interaction between me and the candidates.

What used to annoy Nick, Margaret and me were the retakes. We were told that while they were viewing the programme in the gallery they'd heard someone cough, for example, just when Nick or I was saying something and . . . 'We'd like to do a retake, please.'

Of course, by then the candidates had left the boardroom, with one of them fired. Nevertheless, the production people would come in and say, 'Let's do some retakes for Nick, let's do some retakes for Margaret, and let's do some retakes for Sir Alan.'

On most occasions there were genuine reasons to do these retakes because people *would* cough or sneeze, or sometimes two people would talk over each other at the same time and the audio would be garbled. In some cases, after being reminded of what I was supposed to have said, the production people would get my words wrong.

I'd say, 'Hold on a minute, I never said that originally. Why are you asking me to say it now? Sorry, it would be false if I said these words. I don't mind saying something I said before, but let's get it right. I'm not going to say something I never said previously.'

So the fact is, no one told me what to say in the boardroom. In hindsight, onlookers might say it would have been better if I'd said something else. However, I always made it clear – and it was agreed by the production people – that I was never going to add stuff I didn't actually say to candidates, as there would have been a real credibility issue. *The Apprentice* is totally authentic and, as in real life, there have been many times I've been in a meeting or a nego-tiation and after I've left the room thought, 'Oh, bloody hell, I should have said this or I should have said that,' but that's life. At the end of the day, my words to the candidates at the outset also apply to the production people – I don't like liars and I don't like bullshitters. And I have to say, some of the people in the produc-tion team were sailing a bit close to the wind at times, which wound me up no end. And as for inefficiency, well, that wound me up even more.

Some of you reading this might think I was becoming a bit of a diva. That's simply not the case – I just cannot stand inefficiency.

At this juncture, I have to say that, despite my frustration, I know now that what Nick and Margaret, and later Karren Brady, experienced out in the field during the tasks was ten times worse. I take my hat off to them for having the patience to put up with it. On a couple of occasions in later years, Nick and Karren got very, very frustrated and had some face-to-face meetings with the production people, saying that they weren't prepared to do stupid things that were inefficient, time-wasting and very tiring. Of course, I backed them one hundred per cent.

For example, some of the people in the production team were youngsters, twenty-somethings who wanted to climb up the ladder in TV production and film-making. They weren't very experienced but nevertheless they would dish out instructions to people like Nick, saying, 'Could you make sure you're at the house by seven-thirty tomorrow morning as we're going to be filming such and such.'

'Yes, of course. I'll be there,' Nick would say.

Now, imagine getting up at five in the morning, getting into a car and arriving at the house, somewhere in Chiswick, at seven in the morning. And then hanging around waiting for the cameras, lighting and everything else to be set up; only to be told, 'Actually, Nick, we don't need you. We've changed our minds. We *thought* it would be a good idea for you to be here to see something going on, but actually we're running out of time, so sorry.'

From what I gather, that sort of thing went on quite a bit in the early days. Like me, Nick and Margaret put up with it. I guess they, too, thought it was part and parcel of being in a television programme. But as the years went on, they weren't going to take that nonsense any longer. We had to sort the production people out, in particular the young kids running around who thought that Nick, Margaret and indeed I were just stooges they had control over and could instruct to be in certain places at certain times. 'You stand there, my friend, and I'll tell you what to do . . .'

'Er, no. Not really, young chap. It's a waste of time and I'm not going to do it.'

That's not being a diva; that's just gaining experience in recognising that some of these youngsters on the team knew as much about business, or indeed film-making, as I do about knitting. Consider, for example, Nick and Margaret going through this exercise of getting up early, waiting around and being filmed, and then when the episode is aired, that sequence is missing! One can imagine them watching it, remembering the bloody traffic jams they endured as well as the tiring travelling and hanging around – only for the whole lot to be trashed. No wonder they got smart from the next series onwards.

5

'SIR ALAN WILL SEE YOU NOW'

Inside the boardroom over the years

Putting aside the time-wasting and inefficiency, filming in general was exciting. Peter Moore, Tanya and their crew used to observe the boardroom filming from the gallery. As soon as it was all over, we would exit the boardroom and on many occasions would be greeted by Peter, and sometimes Tanya, actually applauding us for what they considered a tremendous session. It was a little uncharacteristic for him to show this excitement. Nick, Margaret and I didn't fully understand why he was applauding – we weren't sure whether he was being serious. But clearly he was impressed, though at the time we had not realised, in TV terms, what a great session we had just filmed. To us, what we had done was no different to what Nick and Margaret or I would do in real life. We were not acting.

It is an opportune moment to talk about the tension that exists in the boardroom, and how that tension comes about. The template for this was laid down by Peter and his team and has existed throughout the whole ten series to date. Firstly, the candidates are told to wait outside the boardroom in the reception area. They must not talk to each other or exchange any comments. In the case of Boardroom Zero it's the first time they have met and so it is critical they don't speak to each other. It is funny to watch them eye each other up and down, a phenomenon that has been seen in every series. This hanging around in reception raises the tension, even more so in Boardroom One when they have no idea if their team has won or lost.

Then comes the phone call: 'Sir Alan [or Lord Sugar] will see you now.'

They will have been briefed on where they should sit when they file into the boardroom, but the tension is so high that on many occasions they've been confused and gone to the wrong places. On these occasions we have to refilm and sometimes they just can't get it right – I think the record to date is four takes. At first, the production people simply tell them to go out and do it again, but as you can imagine, by the third attempt I lose my rag. 'Listen, what is so bloody hard about this? You, Charlie, come and sit there. You, Claire, stand behind Fred. Come on, let's get it right this time.'

If I didn't know better, I might think that the production people do it on purpose to put me in a foul mood. Then occasionally, when the candidates have finally sat down and we've got going, I suddenly look up and realise I can see the microphone sticking out of one of the boy's ties. 'Stop, stop, stop. Get the sound guy in here. Fred's mic is showing.' In comes the sound guy, he faffs around with the mic and we are off again.

As I've said, there is no script, and by this I also mean that the candidates are not allowed to bring in any notebooks or pieces of paper to refer to. They must simply rely on their memory.

Once the candidates are seated in the boardroom, the gallery will ask me to wait a minute while they pan the camera along to film their facial expressions.

Then, if we are filming Boardroom One, this is the moment I walk in. The boardroom has translucent glass panels so that you can see my shadow walking along before I get to the boardroom doors. A production team creative-genius moment and, I have to say, a good one at that.

Once I am in, it's 'Good morning' or 'Good evening' as the case may be, and we are off. It's true to say that the boardroom is a place of terror for the candidates with such a tense atmosphere at times you might think they are fighting for their lives.

I've already talked about meeting the candidates for the first time in the first series. However, being a quick learner, in subsequent series I added some more information for them. The tension would still be the same as I rattled off my introductory speech, but then I would stop and say, 'Okay, stop the cameras. Right, what I am about to say now is not for broadcast, so just relax, chill out a bit and listen. Whenever you're in the boardroom, or indeed when you meet me for setting a task, you may think I am going a bit nuts because I might say something, take a pause and then say it again. Don't worry, I am not nuts. I just want to save time when I realise I've made a mistake, because if I don't do it then, I'll have to do it afterwards. So I would encourage you likewise – if what comes out of your mouth sounds wrong to you, count to three in your head and say it again.

'Secondly, throughout the course of this process you will meet some young people who work as part of the production team. In many cases they are younger than you, but they will be telling you what to do. They have worked in television before and, believe it or not, they know what they are doing.' Just to lighten the moment I might joke and say, 'Well, they think they know what they are doing – ha ha ha.' (There would be lead-balloon expressions on some of the candidates' faces.) I continue, 'So if they tell you to stand here or go there, please don't argue or question why – just do it. It will all fall into place if you are lucky enough to be here for a few weeks.

'Finally, you are here to win this business contest. You are not here to enhance some media career. I will suss that out very quickly and you will be on your bike. So I do hope you are here for the right reasons because, be under no illusions, I can spot it a mile off. And by the way, don't let things go to your head. You are not, repeat not, celebrities – not now and not even if you win. So I am telling you, do not talk down to the camera team or production people as if they are second-class citizens, because if you do, I will hear about it and I will kick your arse out no matter how good you think you are. In other words, there are to be no Jennifer Lopez throwing-a-wobbly moments, complaining that the dressing room does not have white silk walls or white roses and Diet Coke at five degrees centigrade. I think you get my drift, right? Good. So, good luck, and now let's get back on with filming.'

During that speech you would see wry looks and knowing smiles on the faces of the camera crew. They loved it. The camera-men in the boardroom have to show restraint most of the time and of course be silent. It's a sign of their professionalism that they keep quiet when I come out with some of my classic quips to the candidates. I'm told there is a shriek of laughter in the gallery on these occasions, but in the boardroom, the camera crew and Nick and Margaret (or Karren) have to restrain themselves.

Sometimes, boardroom filming takes place when Spurs are playing. I have a secret code with the chief cameraman, James Clarke, a Southampton fan. He lets me know the score as we are going along, not that anyone would detect it, but it might be noticed that I go into a mean streak when I hear Spurs are losing. Or if West Ham are losing I will nudge Karren and whisper, 'Shame, innit? You lot are two nil down.'

In the early days of filming in the boardroom, it was impossible not to notice the number of breaks there would be. I would sit and talk to the production people and ask them what was happening. They told me that the cameramen had to periodically change the tapes in the camera, which was a bit of an annoyance, especially with up to eight cameras on the go.

Back in the days of the first series, even though the cameras were highly advanced for that era, they still used tape, and every so often, while I was in full flow speaking to the candidates, I would be told to stop while the tapes were changed. At this point all eight cameramen diligently changed the tapes and put them in a box. As you can imagine, this was a little frustrating but unavoidable.

There was a very authentic atmosphere in the boardroom, so it would have been wrong of me to turn round after one of these interruptions and say something like, 'Now, where was I? What was I just talking about?' I would have liked to have been able to say that, but I couldn't show my weakness in front of the candidates. So while the tapes were being changed, I was trying to recollect what I'd just been saying and what I was about to say next.

I started wondering what the process was with these tapes. Where did they go? What was done with them? I spoke to some of the production people and camera crew during one of the breaks. They told me that each tape was carefully marked up with the date, time, series, episode and scene – in the boardroom or out on a task. All of these tapes would then be taken to an editing suite and the entire content of the tapes downloaded onto, for want of a better word, a giant hard drive. Once downloaded, the editors would be able to start selecting and editing the clips that they wanted to produce the finished episodes of the programme.

One day when we were filming the second series, I was hanging around in the production office when I noticed a cabinet containing hundreds of tapes. I turned to Dan Adamson and asked him, 'Are those the tapes of all the filming we've done so far?' By then we were on about episode eight of the second series.

'Yes, why do you ask?' he said.

'Bloody hell,' I replied. 'If there were a fire in here, you would lose the whole lot!'

'Yes, I suppose you're right. I hadn't thought about that.'

Considering the amount of money involved in producing the series, not to mention the time and effort, it was horrible to think that all the tapes could be lost. 'What would you do?' I asked him. 'I can understand that no one's going to break into this office and nick tapes, but there could be a fire. Why haven't you got a fire-proof safe?'

Dan shrugged his shoulders and said, 'You're right, but that's how it is in this temporary office.'

It was quite an amazing risk as far as I was concerned, and it wouldn't surprise me at all if there are stories of television producers whose tapes were lost or destroyed.

Years later, different camera technology was employed whereby the cameras used digital disks rather than tapes. As soon as these disks were taken out of the camera, they went into some kind of secure storage unit there which also backed up the disks. So they'd obviously dealt with the issue I raised, maybe because there *had* been one or two disasters. This change took place around the same time as HD-quality recording came in.

When I realised that I'd have to spend quite a lot of time filming, away from my company, I told the production people I needed internet access so that I could bring one of my computers along. This request was granted and I was able to get on with my work there during the long and boring breaks between scenes, or while waiting for candidates to arrive or waiting for them to have their post-mortem at the losers' café, etc.

In fact, there was a lot of wasted time. A boardroom filming day would start around 11 a.m. and you would leave around 8 p.m. At eleven o'clock there would be a briefing for everyone in the production team before the candidates entered the boardroom. After that, I would discuss with Nick and Margaret (and in later series, Karren) what went on in the task.

I'll take a moment to talk about the sometimes conflicting banter between Nick, Margaret, Karren and me over the years in these briefing sessions. This started in series one but continued with a vengeance in following series. I have been employing people for nearly fifty years and one thing I have learned over that time is not to let one person's personal opinion of another cloud my judgement. Not that I have any complaints with Nick, Margaret or Karren but sometimes they would express an opinion on a person's character, perhaps because they were loud-mouthed, flash or big-headed, and I would have to try and see the wood for the trees. While that type of person sounds rather odious in the spirit of this competition, it is not a reason I should fire them. In fact, some of the most successful people in business are like that. Not me, I might add.

The names have been changed to protect the innocent, as they say in the movies, but Margaret might say, 'Alan, you have to get rid of Mary, she is a nightmare. She keeps coming up to me in the strect and calling me Maggie. "Hi, how you doing, Maggie?" What damn impertinence. You wouldn't have someone working for you who called you Al, would you?'

'Fine, Margaret, but with respect that is not a reason to get rid of her today. She hasn't done anything wrong. In fact, you just spent half an hour telling me who the culprits are.'

'Well, I don't like her and I hope you don't choose her. I told her not to talk to me like that.'

Or Nick might say to me, 'Alan, that Fred is a total waste of space. He will drive you nuts if you employ him. I can't see him going too far in this process.'

That's an example of Nick being subtly polite – '*I can't see him going too far in this process.*' Nick had been working for me for a long time and knew my organisation well. He knew the culture of the organisation and most of the senior people within it. As such, he would have a good understanding of who I would get on with or not, and more to the point, who would survive in a Sugar company. However, if Fred was not culpable in the loss of this particular task, I would once again have to see the wood for the trees.

In later series, Karren would get really excited and have strong views. In addition, all these opinions were being expressed in the same room as the lead production team, many of whom had their opinions too, sometimes tainted by the way a particular candidate had been dealing with people in the house, or by some of the slimy things they might have got up to, or intended to divert blame away from another candidate whom they would like to win. This inferno of opinion would fly around the room, doing my head in, so to speak. Eventually, I would have to say, 'Okay, okay. Enough. I've got it, I've got it. I will take it into account.'

Part of the enjoyment for the production team in the board-room was that they could sit and watch what went on – live. They had no clue who I was going to fire so there was a sense of jeopardy. And despite the aforementioned inferno, neither did Nick, Margaret, Karren or the lead producers. I adopted a deadpan expression which gives nothing away. It's famously known as my Bolton face. Once, as chairman of Spurs, I was in the stands at Bolton and we were getting murdered – we were six-one down in the League Cup. The ITV cameras were there and they had the lens right in my face to try and catch me showing emotion. Of course, I knew their tricks and what they were trying to do, so I stared ahead of me with a glazed, deadpan face, bottling in the anger and disappointment at the result.

The Bolton face also came in handy when friends or associates tried to get inside information out of me on the Amstrad share price. 'I hear things are going well with that new computer, Alan. I might buy some more shares, yeah?' Enter the Bolton face. My secret inner thoughts: 'Piss off, I'm not going to jail for you.'

Let's get back to *The Apprentice* boardroom logistics. The first boardroom scene would go on for an hour or so, then we would break while the camera crew went off to film the losing team in the café – the now famous Bridge Cafe in Acton where, I've heard, they have had a large upsurge in business since *The Apprentice* started using it. It was useful to get some clues from the discussion in the café as to who the project manager might be thinking about bringing in. The production people were at liberty to report to me what was being said in the café as well as the general tone of the conversation.

All of this takes time, of course, and that's why I needed my computer so I could get on with my work in the breaks. I also requested that Sky TV be rigged up so I could watch football. Many of the boardroom filming days were at the weekend and sometimes coincided with Spurs playing. On top of that, I was able to keep up with world events via Sky News.

One of the things I've learned about television production is the importance of food. You cannot imagine how much effort goes into feeding the crew, the production people and, in fact, anybody who's involved with the programme. An essential part of the set-up is a kind of restaurant where the food is laid out in abundance. At lunchtime, the crew and production people pour in and line up to be fed. As I say, this is a very serious issue – the crew must be fed!

There was one particular chap in the boardroom by the name of Jack. He was a very nice fellow who assisted the cameramen in putting the finished tapes in boxes and carefully writing them up. I would always see Jack eating, and I think for the next ten years we had this joke about Jack always having a sandwich on the go, or a knife and fork in his hand.

The food was excellent, but there was one downside to it. If you ate too much it would make you feel tired. I used to find it difficult to get the momentum going again after a big lunch, which was between Boardroom One and Boardroom Two, so I used to cut back on the food for that very reason, and I believe Margaret did the same.

In later years the arrangements were changed a little, and in most cases lunch was served before we started filming, so the time between lunch and getting into the boardroom and talking to the candidates was taken up by the briefings from Nick and Karren and the production team. To be honest, during these meetings I would be half asleep if I'd had a lot for lunch.

The candidates, up to sixteen of them, also have to be fed while they're there. By the way, they eat in another part of the building, away from Nick, Margaret (or Karren) and me. Moreover, many of the candidates had their individual dietary requirements, so I guess you can see a picture emerging here – making a TV programme of this size and complexity is no simple thing. There is lots of organisation and logistics to be taken care of, and food plays a big part not just at the boardroom location, but also at the house where the candidates live. In the house there are particular members of the production staff who are there simply to look after all the candidates' requirements, not just for food, but for laundry and hairstyling, and in some cases, a doctor may be needed if one of them gets sick.

Talking of which, one thing that made me laugh was the health and safety angle on illness. Once when I had a headache while we were filming, I asked someone for a couple of Panadol. She said, 'Well, I *do* have Panadol, Sir Alan, but sorry to say that I'm not allowed to give them to you – it's company policy.'

'What? What are you talking about?'

'I've got the Panadol. Look, there they are in my handbag, but I'm not allowed to give them to you.'

'Why not?'

'I don't know. It's some health and safety issue which I'm sure the H&S people at the BBC want us to comply with.'

'So what am I supposed to do then?'

'Unfortunately, you have to go out of the building, pop down to Boots and buy them yourself.'

'Oh, okay then. Can I send a runner to go and buy them for me?'

'Well, not really, because if you sent one of the production people, then it's really the same as me giving it to you.'

'So I've got to send my driver to go and get them; is that what you're saying?'

'Yes, that would be okay. He's not one of our production people. That'd be fine.'

Can you believe this lunacy? I guess somewhere up in the BBC hierarchy there's some manual that lays down regulations like these.

Of course, when it came to something a little more serious, a doctor would be brought in who would be able to prescribe something for me or the candidates, or indeed Nick, who often used to suffer with the sniffles when we were filming in the winter months.

Another eye-opener for me was make-up. Every one of us had to go to the make-up artist to have make-up applied to our faces. Make-up minimises the shine off the camera lens, and they also use it to cover up certain blemishes on one's face, or to get the tones right using different kinds of foundations. For the ladies it was the full monty: make-up, hair, the works. For Nick and I, we would have our faces powdered with the stuff and have this foundation slapped on, which at the end of filming, we cleaned off with some wipes. At the start I was surprised to find the sheer amount of muck they'd plastered on my face. On a number of occasions I rushed out of the boardroom to meet someone off-site afterwards, and forgot to take my make-up off – and I got some very strange looks, particularly from some of my staff. My wife, of course, would notice it if, for example, I was meeting up with her afterwards at a restaurant.

Our first make-up lady, Mandy, remained working for the production company all the way through the course of the series. In fact, I met her a few other times at various TV studios for other television programmes I participated in. I'll talk about those programmes later.

The term 'runners' was new to my vocabulary. These are usually young kids around twenty years old who want to be in TV production. Their job is to run around doing things. 'Go and get a box of tapes for the cameraman. Go and get a coffee for Peter. Get some tea for Tanya.' That's what a runner does. Some of these runners were told to stick close to me and make sure I was happy at all times. Occasionally, it used to get on my wick. An overenthusiastic runner would pounce on me as soon as I walked through the doors into the building. 'Good morning, Sir Alan, is there anything I can get for you? Tea? Coffee? Cold drink? Water?'

'No, no, no. Thank you, I'm fine at the moment. I'll let you know if I want anything.'

'Okay, fine. Thank you so much.'

I'd then go and sit in my room where my computer and work papers are, and I'd try to collect my thoughts for that day's filming. In would burst the runner again. 'Hello, Sir Alan, is everything okay? Tea? Coffee? Water? Fruit? Crisps? Chocolate? A sandwich? Anything I can do for you?'

'No, no. Thank you very much, but I'm all right.'

'Okay, okay. Let me know.'

'Yes, I will let you know.'

Would you believe it? Half an hour later: 'Hello, Sir Alan, just checking in. Anything you'd like? Tea? Coffee? Blah, blah, blah . . .'

'No. Look, let me explain to you. When I want something, like tea or coffee, I'll call you. If I need some tissues to blow my nose, I will definitely call you – you will be the first person I call. So please, don't bother to come back in any more. I *will* call you, do not worry.'

'All right.'

'Okay, fine.'

The irony was, when I did ask for a tea or a coffee, I would then get the next line of questioning. 'Er, how do you take it? White? With sugar? Without sugar . . . ?'

Fair enough, I thought. Everyone likes their tea or coffee their own way, so I said, 'Tell you what, let me come to the cafeteria and I'll make one in front of you, then you'll know how to make it for me in future.'

'Okay, thank you so much.'

The problem with that was, the next day there was a different runner. 'Morning, Sir Alan, anything I can do for you? Tea? Coffee? Water?'

To be fair, Nick, Margaret and I were treated very well. We had little fridges in our rooms stocked up with our favourite cold drinks – in my case Diet Coke, Evian and orange juice – as well as an abundance of chocolate bars and sweets. In fact, the production office looked like a confectioner's shop with the amount of choice that was there for everybody. One would frequently see Nick slipping in and picking up a Kit Kat. 'Energy,' he would say, 'I need it for energy.'

One of the things we didn't do was booze. There was no alcohol there and I think that was wise because we could have easily got into the habit of having a bottle of wine, and the effect of it might have been detrimental to our performance, so it was good not to encourage that type of thing.

Having said this, when there are fifty or so people involved in making a programme, it is inevitably someone's birthday, or someone is getting married, or someone's just had a child, or something else which warrants a bit of a celebration – a cake, a bottle of champagne and all that stuff. So from time to time there would be occasions when everybody got together in the cafeteria and festivities took place.

And one cannot talk about what goes on in TV without mentioning the famous wrap party, when filming is over and everything's 'wrapped up'. Everyone who's involved in the production goes off, at the production company's expense, to some glitzy restaurant or bar, lets their hair down and relives the past weeks, reminiscing on all the funny things that have happened and how wonderful this person was and how marvellous that person was. How brilliantly this person performed and how hard that person worked . . . a real self-congratulatory bash. And good luck to them, because they worked hard and put in long, long hours. The party allowed them to relax and wind down. It was a thank you from the production company to everyone involved in *The Apprentice*.

With filming of the first series over, I was wondering what the next landmark was. When would I be able to see some of this stuff? Peter and Tanya informed me they were now going to spend several weeks at an editing suite in London where all of the footage would be scrutinised and knocked into shape. As I previously said, each episode has around one hundred and fifty hours' filming, and so it started to hit home how important the editors are. These were a separate bunch of highly skilled experts employed by the production company to work on this raw material – what TV people call 'the rushes'. They'd sit with one of the production team for several weeks selecting which clips of film should be used to bring the story of each episode to life.

Nick and I were invited to the editing suite and I will never forget this memorable occasion. Peter and Tanya greeted us there and said, 'Come in and we'll show you some of this stuff. We're editing some of the sequences in episode one, so we'll show you some bits.'

Of course, Nick and I had never been involved in any TV production before, so it was a very exciting moment. They started showing us the scenes of Paul Torrisi running around the streets with bunches of flowers, selling them to some lady, saying to her, 'You buy one, I'll buy one for you also.' Then he was telling some bloke that his grandfather painted Buckingham Palace. He was on fire selling. It wasn't until that moment, when we saw the rushes, that we realised what a fantastic programme this was going to be.

We then watched sequences of the boardroom, partly edited. It was a brilliant eye-opener. It was indescribably exciting at the time, and I'm sure Nick will agree with me that it was a moment neither of us will ever forget.

At that point, the penny dropped with us. We didn't need anybody to tell us – this was going to be a massive, massive hit. We could have both stayed there for hours and hours, but Peter kind of ushered us out and said, 'Okay, chaps, we're very, very busy now. You've seen this little bit. We've got to get on with our work as we're on a tight deadline.'

If I recall correctly, filming of the first series finished around the end of October and the programme was due to go to air sometime in February. I remember Peter and Tanya telling me that this was a massive challenge. Again, not understanding TV production, I couldn't comprehend what was so massive about it. Here we were at the end of October, so we were talking about four months to take all this stuff, edit it and get it ready. *Now*, of course, I realise the amount of effort and hard work that goes into it. People often think of *editing* as manipulating. Just to make things clear, editing is about distilling the story and making the music and everything else work well in the show.

Peter played his cards very close to his chest. At the time, he was still unsure of me from a confidentiality point of view. He obviously spotted my enthusiasm about the stuff I had seen and I was begging him to please give me a copy of the tape so I could show it to my family. 'Anything will do, Peter, even if it's partly edited.'

In his polite manner, he basically said get stuffed. 'I'm not allowed to give it to you. The BBC has forbidden it.'

This falling back on the BBC tactic was something I would often hear. It can be embarrassing to say 'no' on account of your personal thoughts or beliefs – so it's very convenient when you wish to pass the buck to fall back and say, 'Look, I would love to do it, but the BBC says we're not allowed to.'

What I realise now is that the BBC didn't know jack shit about what was going on. All this was Peter's personal opinion because he was, frankly, a little scared that I might give the tape to the media or show it to someone I knew in the media, and that it might leak out. Then he would be in trouble and Talkback would be in trouble – and so on. He relented a few weeks later, after I'd pestered him and said, 'Please, Peter, let me have the latest edit of the first episode – it's to show my wife, Ann,' who at the time was suffering badly with back pains and was flat on her back in bed.

Now, Peter is a very polite chap when it comes to my relatives and friends. Whenever he met them he was very charming, and he did take a liking to Ann, who is a very quiet and polite lady, a non-demanding person. I managed to convince him to let me take this highly valuable videotape. I promised I would not let it out of my sight and I would personally get it sent back to him in the car. I just wanted to show her this episode to cheer her up as she was in very bad pain. He finally agreed to let her see a rough version of the near-finished episode.

I showed the film to Ann and she was very impressed. She, too, had no experience of how TV shows are made, so when we saw the finished product, it was an exciting moment for both of us. I didn't show it to my kids or anyone else because I knew this was going to be a great programme and I wanted them to enjoy watching it for the first time on television. It would have been wrong to spoil that moment for them.

I think I gained Peter's trust by sticking to my promise and returning the tape the following Monday; personally making sure that he had it in his hand. From that moment on, he realised I wasn't going to mess around or break his confidence, and I was able to come in and out of the editing suite quite a few times to see how various episodes were going and, at times, take away tapes of other episodes to watch at my leisure. On one occasion, however, panic set in after somebody in the production team, who was assisting in the edit, showed me an episode.

'Is it possible for me to take that tape?' I asked him.

'Yes, certainly. Take it away.'

I took it home to view it myself, only to get Peter on the phone shouting, 'That guy had no right to give you the tape. I need it back straight away. I need to show it to the BBC . . .'

'Don't worry, Peter,' I said. 'I'll get it sent back to you immediately.'

I hired a motorbike courier and it was back in his hands within hours.

The American version of *The Apprentice* with Donald Trump used Trump's voice as the voiceover to explain what was going on as the programme played out. In hindsight, I'm pleased they didn't ask me to record all that off a script, because that would have required me to attend some studio somewhere to record it. Again, in hindsight, it was right for me not to do it because how could I provide a commentary on what was going on during the course of a task when, in fact, I didn't know?! Remember, I only find out when Nick and Margaret tell me in the boardroom, so that made perfect sense.

At this point, Patrick Uden, who had done a great job arranging all of the logistics for the filming, was tasked with writing the scripts for the excellent commentator Mark Halliley, who did the voiceover on each episode.

Another fascinating part of this whole exercise was the adaptation of the music that accompanied the programme. The musician Dru Masters, Tanya Shaw's boyfriend who later became her husband, wrote much of *The Apprentice*'s incidental music which I believe is still used today. Of course, one of the things that stands out is the classical theme tune to *The Apprentice*, Prokofiev's 'Dance of the Knights', which comes from the *Romeo and Juliet* ballet. One quite amusing story: one of the production people who worked on *The Apprentice* in the later series, Francesca Maudslay, told me that she went with her husband-to-be to the *Romeo and Juliet* ballet, and as this music started to play, she detected the audience nudging each other as if to say, 'Oh, it's *The Apprentice* theme tune,' which I guess goes to show how far-reaching *The Apprentice* is.

Allied to the music, the other fascinating and excellent piece of work was those wonderful aerial pictures of London taken by helicopter; some during the day, some by night. The shots of the River Thames meandering through the centre of London and the high-rise skyscrapers of the commercial district can only be described as fantastic, a piece of artistic genius, and they became a hallmark of *The Apprentice*. Those films were made by Andy Devonshire, the series director, who stayed with *The Apprentice* for many series to follow.

The wonderful aerial photography serves to demonstrate the amount of money invested by the BBC into making this high-profile series the very best it could be. Imagine the cost of hiring helicopters with camera crews, flying around for several hours capturing pictures of the City from various angles as well as the small, subtle things such as plane shadows moving across the skyline. There were shots of iconic buildings such as St Paul's, Tower Bridge and the Houses of Parliament, all put into the can and then brought out brilliantly by the editors.

I have been a manufacturer all my life and I understand how to make stuff. I have run factories and I know the pros and cons of production. It became clear to me that the making of television programmes is very similar to the making of products, as I had done many times at Amstrad over the years. And like anything in life where production is concerned, be it in a factory or a television studio, if you change the personnel, then you will virtually have to start from scratch. So the old saying 'if it ain't broke, don't fix it' kicks in. At the same time, it's a truism that the more you make a product, the better it becomes – that applied to the Amstrad products I used to make where we would continually enhance the product throughout its life. And I will go on later to explain that enhancements are the reason *The Apprentice* continued to be successful and still remains so.

During the build-up to the first transmission dates in February, there were a couple of other events. The big cheeses at Talkback Thames, Peter Fincham and Daisy Goodwin, started to show their interest and were talking of needing to launch the programme at some kind of press conference where they would privately show the film to a bunch of journalists, with me there to do a question-and-answer session afterwards. Of course, I had been to many press conferences and product launches at Amstrad, and Nick would often compliment me on how I was able to handle questions on the fly. He put it down to one thing, quite rightly: I could field any question because I knew my business inside out. Not only was this true at Amstrad's press conferences, but also at those of Tottenham Hotspur. Being such a details person, there was hardly ever a journalist who embarrassed me at a press conference. But a television launch was completely alien to me.

So here I was at a press conference to launch this television programme. Peter Fincham opened the press conference by explaining to the assembled journalists that they were about to be shown the first episode of a new series called *The Apprentice*, which had been running in the United States hosted by Donald Trump, and that for the UK version of the programme, Sir Alan Sugar would be the host. 'So sit back, ladies and gentlemen, and enjoy this programme, after which Sir Alan Sugar will be here, ready to take your questions.'

The episode was shown to the journalists. I don't remember what the immediate reaction was, though I can say that when the programmes were shown to journalists at press conferences for later series, there was always applause at the end of the showing. During those press conferences, senior executives from the BBC and from Talkback would tell me that it was unprecedented for journalists to applaud; however, for this first series the launch was a rather small affair, and from memory there were only around fifteen journalists present. I guess the ones who did turn up came along out of curiosity. Those who didn't come most likely couldn't be bothered. When they saw the invitation they probably thought, 'Oh no, not another new BBC programme.'

The Q&A session started and up sprang, guess who? A negative *Daily Mail* journalist. What was her first question? 'Why are you doing this programme, Sir Alan? I happened to notice that on the boardroom table was one of your phones. Are you trying to promote your products?'

I was ready for that question, to be honest. I knew that the *Daily Mail* was terribly negative towards me. Having kicked their arse a year or so earlier in a long courtroom battle which cost them an arm and a leg, they became, and still are, my major media enemies.

I said to the lady, 'This is a TV programme about my boardroom. Since I make telephones, whose telephone would you expect me to use in my boardroom?'

This brought about a little bit of laughter, and it made her look a bit of a fool. I went on to explain in detail how it had been made very clear to me by the BBC's Jane Lush that this programme must not in any way be seen to assist or promote my business. I, of course, signed on to this and viewers will note that despite the fact my offices were used from time to time, you would never see the Amstrad or Viglen name. Jane Lush must have suspected I was going to try to promote my businesses, perhaps misinterpreting my eagerness to do the show. The media did later make all kinds of suggestions that the production company got things free. I can assure everyone that nothing was free; even when people and companies threw themselves at the production people in later series to use their products or services, they were turned down. There is a strict BBC policy on this and Talkback, despite being on tight budgets, had to pay for everything. That's not to say they didn't drive a hard bargain. I'll tell you a funny story later about me winding up the BBC over product placement. I got very sarcastic with them once because, together with the production people, I played it straight all the way in every series. However, it was frustrating at times that we couldn't use famous brands in the tasks, or if we did, I or the candidates would not be allowed to mention the brand name more than once during the conversation in the boardroom. For instance, if we used Asda in a task, when referring to them in the boardroom, I might have to say to Nick, 'Nick, can you tell me how many the giant supermarket bought?' Or in the case of Harrods, 'Margaret, can you tell me what went on in the famous London department store?'

Back to the press conference, the *Daily Mail* journalist wouldn't give up. Her next stupid question was: 'Of the seven women, did any of them make eyes at you and flirt with you to try to persuade you to treat them differently?'

I replied, 'You've just seen the first episode. Did it look like anybody was flirting?'

The Q&A session continued for another half an hour or so. I explained my reasons for wanting to do the programme, ducked lots of questions about who the winner was going to be, and answered lots of other questions about the prize. I confirmed that the winner would get a genuine job in one of my companies earning £100,000 per year.

All in all the press conference went well, even though it was a low-key affair at a small venue. It was held approximately two weeks before the broadcast date. The reason for this is that tapes of the programme are sent out under embargo to all the TV magazines, such as the *Radio Times* and the *TV Times*. They need this information at least fourteen days in advance not only to publish the TV schedules, but also for the journalists in these magazines to write up their programme summaries and reviews.

The major newspapers were given the tapes about a week before transmission. This really bothered me, bearing in mind I had just come out of the frying pan of dealing with football journalists – where you only had to look at someone the wrong way and it was in the papers the next day – into the fire of TV journalists. Talkback Thames had employed a PR consultant by the name of James Herring whose company were experts in the TV media and I asked him, 'How are we going to keep the lid on new episodes every single time?'

James would go on to be a fundamental part of *The Apprentice* life in years to come but at this point he was still a little nervous of me. He explained very politely, 'We're dealing with a different bunch of journalists here. These are not the same people you encountered in football. These people's jobs rely upon feedback from the likes of me. Their lifeblood of information comes from people like us and the BBC and ITV, and the last people they want to alienate would be us. So if they blow a story early, they may get a bit of glory for five minutes, but they will never get any information again from us or the BBC – and they know it. So you don't have to worry about that – these people, believe it or not, won't spill the beans.'

'You must be kidding,' I said. 'Are you telling me that the *Sun* and the *News of the World* are not going to blow this stuff? I'm telling you, they're the most devious people I've ever come across in my life.'

'Trust me,' said James. 'They will keep it secret, because if they do spoil it for their audience, there's a chance their readers won't buy their newspaper any more.'

I couldn't believe it, but James turned out to be right. And it did play out, over the years, that secrets like who got fired and who won were kept under wraps. It was an interesting learning curve to see how one prepares to launch a television programme.

6

THE BBC HAS A HIT ON ITS HANDS

The first series is aired

Part of my learning curve was watching how the BBC promoted the programme. In the weeks before it was broadcast I started to see clips from the first episode being shown on TV. In TV circles these are known as 'trails' – basically the BBC's own adverts to alert the public that something new is coming. It's difficult for me to convey the excitement felt by me and my family, and I'm sure by Nick and Margaret too, when we started to see ourselves in the trails for the first episode that appeared on the BBC. The trails showed clips of me in the boardroom making the famous statement, 'I don't like liars, I don't like bullshitters . . .' and then some clips of some of the candidates running around in the street during a task.

Not only was this the first glimpse the public had of *The Apprentice*, it was the first time that my friends and colleagues had a clue as to what they were going to see in the programme. A few eyebrows were raised and it created quite an air of anticipation. Obviously my employees at Amstrad and Viglen knew I was involved in making a TV programme, but it's not until you see it on the screen that reality hits home.

Interestingly, these trails had also been picked up by people who didn't know me. I was invited, along with Ann, to 11 Downing Street by Gordon Brown. It was a get-together of a few business-men and women and other well-known people in the UK.

Around the table at dinner was the then Attorney General, Lord Goldsmith, someone I had crossed swords with several years before in the Seagate hard-disk-drive litigation and also in FA litigation. This chap was rather unlucky in the clients he represented, and while he had a reputation as being the best barrister in the UK, on these two particular cases I think it fair to say we kicked his arse. That said, one normally finds that lawyers and people in the legal profession do not hold grudges – unlike me, who always holds a grudge! To them it's just a job. When he saw me at this dinner, the first thing Lord Goldsmith said was, 'I've noticed that you're going to be on TV. It looks very exciting, can you tell me what it's all about?'

This began a conversation around the dinner table amongst all the guests, including Gordon and his wife, Sarah. And what started out as a dinner and discussion on the economy and politics ended up being hogged for at least half an hour by a chat about *The Apprentice*. Frankly, I was quite surprised at the level of interest expressed by the guests. Halfway through the conversation, I started to think about the contract I'd signed with the production company saying that I wouldn't disclose too much information; then the sensible part of me started to become a little guarded about the details.

There were even occasions when I was walking around in public and people would come up to me and say, 'Looking forward to seeing you on that programme, Sir Alan.' Blimey, I thought, if the trails have created that much attention, what's going to be in store when the programme itself starts broadcasting?

The *TV Times* was published and it showed that a new programme, *The Apprentice*, was starting on BBC2 at 9 p.m. on Wednesday 16 February 2005.

Unfortunately, I had a problem with this date. For many years I had talked about going on a skiing holiday, something I hadn't done since I was a young man at school, and I'd promised my two sons I'd take them. Lots of people had told us that February is a good month to go skiing, so Daniel booked a fantastic chalet in Courchevel, a massive, beautiful place. It was decided by the family that skiing was not for the ladies, so it would be a boys-only event – me, my two sons, my son-in-law and three of my grandchildren.

Imagine my horror when I realised that *The Apprentice* would be broadcast for the first time slap bang in the middle of our skiing week – and me and my family wouldn't be able to see it! I asked Daniel to enquire whether the letting agent could fit a satellite dish on the roof. What I had in mind was bringing along one of my Amstrad satellite receivers so that I could pick up BBC2 on Sky. My technical people had checked that the footprint of the satellite would cover that part of France. Luckily enough, the owner of the chalet had a satellite dish, so I brought along my receiver and spent a couple of hours on the first day with the 'technician' trying to get it to work. It was one of those occasions where the so-called technician knew less than me. I won't bore you with the details, but I had to explain to him about the polarisation of the LNB on the dish and how it needed to be tweaked and matched to the receiver I brought. Eventually, we got it working, and as we'd arrived at the chalet on the Sunday prior to the broadcast, we were able to watch all the programmes you could get on Sky, which was a nice bonus.

Then reality hit home, and I should have known this. The thing about satellite dishes is that they conk out in heavy rain and snowstorms. So while watching TV there one day, the picture disappeared. Why? It was snowing very heavily and the sky was full of thick clouds. I was worried that I wouldn't be able to watch the programme on Wednesday night. Fortunately, the weather cleared up by then.

Also holidaying in Courchevel was Paul Kemsley and his family. We invited him, together with some other English cronies, round to the chalet to watch the broadcast. The chef had made an excellent meal that night, and there we were, sitting around the TV at ten o'clock, an hour ahead of Britain, waiting for this programme to start.

About five minutes after the programme began, just after I'd ranted about liars and bullshitters, my mobile phone started to ring. It was Jeremy Beadle. 'Alan, this is going to be a hit. This is fantastic stuff – unbelievable. What's going to happen next?'

'Jeremy mate, can you call afterwards? Keep on watching. It's an hour-long programme . . .'

'All right, no problem. Fantastic, looks good, looks good. I'm telling you, it's a hit.'

Ten minutes later, Bill Kenwright, a friend of mine and owner of Everton Football Club, phoned to say the same thing. 'This is great stuff, Alan. Really great stuff.' Now, Bill is a great impresario, and he knows a thing or two about the theatre and entertainment.

'Thanks very much, Bill. Give me a call at the end of it. There's a lot to happen yet.'

Halfway through the programme, my brother, Derek, rang me from England. 'This is amazing, to see you on television. It's unbelievable, really good, really interesting.'

'Derek, wait a while – you haven't seen anything yet. I'll speak to you at the end of the programme.'

Obviously I had seen the episode that was being broadcast – in fact, I'd seen it two or three times – but it was interesting to watch the reaction of the other guests, including my sons, while it was playing out. All they'd seen up till then was me ranting and raving at the fourteen candidates and then it went straight into the task. No one knew what was going to happen at the end, and they were asking me, 'Where's all this going?' My reply was, 'Wait and see.'

We all watched as the candidates finished the task and started high-fiving and hugging each other because they'd sold the last flower, then the scene changed and the music became tenser. The candidates were now in the reception area, waiting to come into the boardroom. My son Simon said, 'What's happening now?'

'Wait, Simon, you'll see.'

As the boardroom scene unfolded, there was a complete, stunned silence amongst all my guests around the TV. They were riveted. They couldn't believe their eyes when they saw me slating the candidates and their responses to me. What really got them was when the candidates started disagreeing with each other. The viewers were fascinated – no question about it.

Although I had a tape of the first episode, I hadn't played it to any of the family, apart from Ann. I'd told them, 'You really don't want to see it as it will spoil things for you. Just watch the programme like any other viewer. Trust me, you'll be pleased I held it back.'

Meanwhile, back in London, Ann was holding a similar get-together at our house with my daughter and daughter-in-law and a few other friends. As you'll recall, Ann *had* seen the episode when she was laid up in bed with a bad back, but knowing her, she wouldn't spill the beans and spoil it for the others there.

The programme finished and the people with me in the chalet were very complimentary. They all said what a great show it was and that they were looking forward to the next episode. They were asking me questions like, 'Who's fired next? Who's the winner? Come on, you must know who the winner is?'

I replied, 'I'm not going to tell you who the winner is. In fact, I'm telling no one who the winner is going to be. This series has to run for another eleven weeks yet, and during that time I will be keeping my cards very close to my chest.'

With the programme over, the phone was ringing every five minutes, emails were pinging in and text messages were arriving from friends and colleagues. Jeremy Beadle rang again. 'Alan, you have a hit on your hands, I'm telling you. I've been in television all my life, and this is a hit.'

'Great, Jeremy. I'm glad you enjoyed it.'

'Fantastic, well done.'

Bill Kenwright called back. 'You've got a winner there, boy. This is really something new, something fresh. Well done, mate.'

I phoned Ann at home to tell her that my phone hadn't stopped ringing. Well, I say I phoned Ann – I tried to phone her, but it took me at least twenty minutes to get through as the phone was constantly engaged. When I finally reached her she told me that our phone at home also hadn't stopped ringing with calls from friends and family. Apparently, my sister Daphne had called within ten minutes of the programme starting. Ann said to her, 'Yes, Daphne, yes, it is very good, but keep on watching – you haven't seen anything yet.'

There was a clear consensus from all the people who watched the programme with us in France and in England, and from everyone who phoned Ann and me – we had a hit on our hands.

The next day, I was contacted by James Herring as well as David Fraser and Andrew Bloch from my own PR consultants, Frank PR. They told me they had a long line of journalists who wanted to interview me about the programme. Despite listening to James, who was experienced in PR for TV shows, I was still reluctant to talk with journalists because of my horrible experience at Tottenham. To me, it didn't matter how nice and how polite you were to journalists; they would twist your words and come up with headlines that didn't reflect what was discussed in the interview.

David Fraser and Andrew Bloch endorsed James Herring's view that we were dealing with a different breed of journalist here. They said, in effect, 'These people are not like the football scum. They are TV/entertainment journalists from the newspapers and I don't think you need to worry about them. If you can give them a few minutes of your time it will be very good.'

As I was still in Courchevel, I did a number of interviews with the journalists by telephone. Many of them hadn't realised I was abroad; they were expecting to interview me face to face and bring a photographer. In fact, a couple of newspapers were so excited about the programme that the editors wanted to send people out there with cameras. By now, my week's skiing holiday was being disturbed by these constant requests for interviews.

There was good reason for me being reluctant to talk to the newspapers. At the press conference where we launched the show to the media, I gave an interview to a journalist who somehow strayed from the topic of *The Apprentice* and got on to football, asking for my opinion on footballers. I said something like, 'A lot of the guys at Tottenham were great people with their hearts dedicated to the club, but then again there are some who are tantamount to scum.'

Well, no prizes for guessing the resulting headline. 'SIR ALAN SUGAR CALLS ALL FOOTBALLERS SCUM.' These twisted, sensationalist headlines were picked up by all the sports media including Sky Sports, which prompted Gordon Taylor, chairman of the Professional Footballers' Association – the highest-paid union leader in Britain – to come out and say, 'This was a pathetic attempt by Sir Alan Sugar to promote his new TV programme.'

I've always said that some people in football have got no brains and, in my opinion, Taylor comes very close to endorsing that statement.

I should have known better than to speak to that journalist at the press conference. I should have told him, 'I'm not here to talk about football; I'm here to talk about the new programme.'

I slipped up, but from then on, I was very careful to keep what I was saying focused on *The Apprentice* and nothing else. Simple principle – what you don't say, they can't print.

During the various meetings with Peter Moore and those associated with the production of the programme, they would tell me that the success of a programme is judged by the size of the viewing audience. Being a technically minded person, I was intrigued to know how they find out who watches what. Apparently, I was told, there is a sort of antiquated system where in approximately 20,000 homes there is some kind of device that can monitor which channel people are watching at any time. They then extrapolate the data and apply it to the 20 million homes in the UK with TV.

Even as I'm writing this, I can see that this system sounds flawed. For example, when your TV is on, you're not necessarily watching it; you could be in the kitchen having a meal. And if it happens to be tuned to ITV at the time, then the statistics fed back will be that this particular household was watching ITV between nine and ten o'clock, when in fact it wasn't. Having said all that, it was the best technology at the time, and it was the yardstick by which all TV programmes were rated.

I remember Jane Lush saying to me, 'You're absolutely right, Sir Alan. It is totally inaccurate, but think about it – it's inaccurate for everyone, so what you lose on the swings you gain on the roundabouts.'

It was true. Someone could be tuned to ITV and not watching just as they could be tuned to BBC and not watching. From this data, the first episode of *The Apprentice* had 1.9 million viewers. Now to me, this figure meant nothing. Was that good or was that bad? I didn't know at the time. I called Peter Moore and said, 'I've heard the viewing figures were one point nine million.'

He said, 'In TV terms, it's not bad. Actually, it's not bad at all for BBC2, because BBC2 doesn't normally have such great viewing figures.'

I could tell from his tone he wasn't totally happy and said, 'Peter, you seem a little disappointed.'

'Well, you know, after all the work and effort we put into it – and it's a fantastic programme – I just thought we'd have got a bit more than that. So you're right, I'm not exactly jumping up and down.'

This made me feel a little sad, because I also knew how much work and effort had gone into it. I asked him, 'What figures would you have expected?'

'Well, if we'd have got three or four million, that really would be a tremendous hit for BBC2. Bear in mind that programmes like *EastEnders* and *Coronation Street* can get audiences of up to eleven or twelve million – that will give you some kind of comparison.'

So I was learning about the world of television, and feeling a little bit down as a result of this feedback from Peter. You can imagine how further disappointed we were when the second episode went out and it only got 1.7 million viewers. This trend, in TV terms, is normally the kiss of death. It is a way of judging whether you have a good or bad programme on your hands. The controllers of the channel would expect the audience to start growing as the programme rolled out episode by episode. So it was not a good sign.

This was the first occasion on which I'd had to talk to television people when, clearly, things were not going right. I spoke to Jane Lush and Roly Keating, and they were ever the optimists. Television people are *always* very optimistic. 'It's wonderful, darling; it's marvellous, it's super. It's one of the best things we've ever done.'

To be honest, I've never heard these people turn round and say, 'Actually, it's a load of crap.'

I think this enthusiasm was their way of regenerating their self-confidence. They said, 'It's quite normal for a brand-new programme to have to settle in. We're sure the audience will grow. We have seen at least six of the episodes and we know it's a fantastic show. It's just that people don't know about it yet.'

'Well,' I said, 'we've been putting the trails out to advertise it, and people have actually seen the programme now. Surely word of mouth is going to make them want to view it, so why were the second week's figures down?' I felt like I was interrogating them the same way as I did the candidates.

'Yes, Sir Alan, it *was* surprising, but it's not untypical. Please don't panic, let's wait and see what happens.'

They were right and as the programme went out over the course of the twelve-week period, its popularity grew and grew and grew, and the viewing figures rose to a peak in the final episode of close on four million. Yes, BBC2 had a hit on its hands after all.

During the football days, if I was in a public place I would get people coming up to me and verbally abusing me about Tottenham Hotspur, calling me all the names under the sun. On rare occasions a couple of nice fans might come up and thank me for rescuing the club. Sometimes they'd tell me that I didn't deserve all the stick I was getting at the time as they knew I was doing my best. Generally speaking, though, there were a lot of low-life toerags who would shout expletives at me – which I won't repeat here – while I walked along the street or when my car was waiting at the lights. They'd actually come up and shout at the car! Not a nice experience, as you can imagine. When I went to White Hart Lane on a match day, I had to be ushered in quickly to avoid the fans en masse.

However, being on TV in *The Apprentice* was as different as night and day. Walking in public places, people would come up to me and say, 'Love the programme. Can I have a picture? Can I have an autograph?' etc. There was a completely different atmosphere. If I went into a restaurant, eyes would be raised and people would smile at me, some would wave at me. Some even had the courage to come over and speak to me, complimenting me on the programme.

Of course, as you would expect, there was always the idiot, often a little inebriated and trying to impress his girlfriend or his mates, who would walk up to me and shout, 'You're fired!'

Usually, at that point, the only person who was killing themselves laughing was the one who said it. Mostly, I gave them a hollow gaze or said, 'Ha ha, how novel. I've never heard that before.'

The girlfriend of the comedian would often turn round to him and say, 'Shut up, you're embarrassing us. Sorry, Sir Alan, he's a bleedin' idiot,' to which I sometimes replied, 'Well, you said it.'

Apart from those clowns, in general the reaction from the public was fantastic. Of course, anybody who's been on television hosting a programme as important as *The Apprentice* is going to experience this sort of thing. Did I like it? Yes. It is human nature to like being famous, to like being recognised, to like being noticed; of course it is. And anyone who tells you differently is lying. So let me clear that up once and for all – yes, I enjoyed the fame. Margaret, on the other hand, claimed that she did not. She travelled regularly on the London Underground and she didn't like people coming up to her on the Tube and saying hello. Personally, I find that hard to believe, but that's what she told me. She said she thought they were impertinent and invading her privacy.

I remember telling her, 'Well, Margaret, you're going to have to stop using the Underground; you're going to have to get yourself a car and a chauffeur. Or go by taxi.' That comment didn't go down too well with her.

'No, I'm being serious, Alan. I travel across London on the Tube all the time. I don't need people coming up to me in the carriage saying, "Oh it's wonderful, you're very good, it's a great programme," and all that stuff. I really don't like it.'

'Come on, Margaret, what's wrong with it? They're not abusing you, are they?'

'No, no, they're not abusive at all. They're actually quite complimentary, but I just don't like it.' Even as I write this now I can visualise her saying it.

Now Nick, on the other hand, like me, loved it. He tends to hang around central London during the week at his gentlemen's club, and he's out and about most nights dining with friends and associates. He, too, started to be recognised in restaurants and theatres. Nick will tell you that the public at large, who never knew him from Adam before, were very complimentary to him. And as I say, he was loving every minute of it, and good luck to him. Nick went from retirement to a TV star! I will go on to talk about how this has escalated and completely changed his life, for which, I have to say, he is forever grateful. He is always mentioning how he owes his new-found life and prosperity to me!

Before *The Apprentice* aired, I had only met Roly Keating, Jane Lush and the people at the production company. I had not met any of the real top brass at the BBC. Now, however, I started to receive calls and invitations from various senior people, one of whom was Jana Bennett, head of BBC Television. She wanted to meet me.

Once these people smell a hit programme, they feel it's time for them to get involved. Jana was a very nice lady, and I don't wish to undermine the work she did at the BBC, but it is a BBC trait (which I'm sure all BBC people will recognise) that they are happy to enthuse and talk about their wonderful hit programmes and successes, but conveniently go very quiet when there's a schtummer programme.

In my meeting with Jana, she was very gracious and thankful for the work and effort I'd put in. She told me that this was a big hit for BBC2, and said how grateful the BBC was.

The next member of the hierarchy I met was the Director General, Mark Thompson. As I've said before, I am not good with names and titles – somebody once told me it's because I'm not interested, and I think there's an element of truth in that. I have to see someone at least three or four times, or mention their name at least twenty times, before I really know who they are. I met Mark Thompson at a BBC cocktail party attended by a lot of TV celebrities. They invited Ann and me, as well as Nick and Margaret. We four stood in a little huddle, wondering what we were doing there. We figured that even though we weren't directly contracted to the BBC, they were our ultimate bosses as far as the programme was concerned.

Mark Thompson came up to me and introduced himself. Looking back, he must have thought I was very rude because I didn't grovel to him. Anyone else being introduced to the Director General would have suddenly gone into total schmoozer mode. I just thought he was another executive at the BBC rather than the bloke in charge.

He told me how he was really concerned about the financial modelling of the BBC, saying that I, being a businessman, would surely understand the fiscal pressures he was under, to which I just nodded and said, 'Yeah, yeah.' I do recall one bizarre thing from that party. The BBC was having a big relaunch of *Doctor Who* at the time, and standing between Mark Thompson and me was a Dalek!

I spoke earlier about branding and product placement on BBC television shows, and how the BBC insists on no branding and no promotion of the products or businesses of the people who appear in their programmes. I signed up to this, but as is my nature, I wanted to see even-handedness; to ensure that what's good for the goose is good for the gander. I won't say I had the hump with the BBC over this, but as I explained, it verged on stupidity that, for example, one could not mention Harrods more than once. I mean, after all, it's a national icon.

However, on Ricky Gervais's BBC show *Extras*, my hawk-eyes spotted that the brand name MESH had been stuck on the back of a laptop computer that was shown many times in the series, in the scenes in his agent's office. Being in the computer business, I knew that MESH did not have stupid stickers on the rear of their laptops, so it appeared to me that these were stuck on deliberately for some reason. Whatever the reason, of course it had the impact of advertising the brand and made me wonder if the props department of the production company had been given the computers for free.

I called Jane Lush to say that the BBC needed to look into this thing. She gave me the 'it's not my department' answer, to which I said, 'Well, give me the name of the person whose department it is.'

After pestering her a few times she gave me the name of a woman at the BBC to talk to. I lodged my complaint with her, and like a dog with a bone, I wouldn't let go. I wanted to make a point. I must have become a nightmare to her, a real thorn in her side. Finally, she came back and said, 'We have reviewed the issue. You were right and it won't happen again.' She also told me that the *Extras* series was over, so it was academic now, and she added that this production was not made by the BBC but by an outside production house.

Further to that, as an avid *EastEnders* viewer and very conscious of this product-placement thing, I started to scrutinise the Queen Vic bar to see if any famous brands of alcohol were being shown. Indeed they were, but the real scandal involved Nokia mobile phones. Any viewer of *EastEnders* will know that part of the drama is to see, for example, Ian send a text to Alfie. You are shown a screenshot of the text and above the screen is the brand name – Nokia. And it just so happened that everyone in Albert Square had Nokia phones!

'A-ha!' I exclaimed when watching the programme at home. 'I've got them bang to rights.'

'What are you going on about?' asked Ann.

'Ha ha, I've got them now. Let's see them talk themselves out of this.' I told Ann about the BBC policy on non-branding. 'Yeah, they can't show my company name in *The Apprentice* due to BBC policy – okay, fair enough – but look at this tonight! The bloody Nokia name has been in your face all night. Everyone has a Nokia phone in the Square!'

She looked at me as if I was nuts and shrugged her shoulders. 'I was wondering what you were getting so excited about – I thought something had happened to you.'

'No, no, don't worry. I am loving this.'

Why am I telling you this story right now? Well, at this BBC cocktail party, the woman I had hassled over the MESH thing came over to me to say hello and introduce herself. I'm sorry but I can't remember her name, so let's call her Jane – there are lots of Janes at the BBC.

'Hi, Sir Alan, I'm Jane Doe. We spoke on the phone over the MESH computer issue. Nice to see you face to face. I hope you understood what happened and were satisfied with my explanation.'

'Oh, hello. Yes, I did understand what you said about MESH, but I now wish to advise you of the most heinous product-placement crime in the history of BBC TV.'

She was going to be sorry she came over to see me. I gave it to her in full Sugar fashion. 'I'm glad you came over because you need to sort out the props people at *EastEnders*. Please don't go telling me they are an external production company because everyone knows it's a BBC production. Right, here it is: somebody in the props department does not seem to know your compliance rules. I am not going to accuse them of anything, but it *is* strange that every mobile phone shown on *EastEnders* in the last few weeks has been a Nokia, and the name has been right in your face. Every character who is seen texting on his phone in *EastEnders* has a Nokia. That's not right in the real world, is it? So I need you to go off and tell me what you think about *that*, find out who's responsible, and please let me know before I make an official complaint to the BBC Trust. Because let me remind you, we on *The Apprentice* are not even allowed to show my company name, and the blinkin' show is all about me in my boardroom!'

This poor woman. She came over to socialise at a BBC cocktail party and got both barrels from me.

'Well, Sir Alan, I haven't noticed. I don't watch much TV even though I am at the BBC, ha ha ha [pathetic nervous laugh], but I will certainly go and investigate.'

Mark Thompson was standing nearby with his glass of champagne, a bit like Del Boy. I called over to him. 'Er, Mark, can you come over here?'

He looked up and dutifully came over.

'Now, Mark, I've been having an ongoing dialogue with Jane here who, as you will know as the DG, is in charge of making sure that product-placement compliance is strictly adhered to. I won't bore you with all the details, but to cut a long story short I think there is something going on in the props department at *EastEnders*, as all I keep seeing is Nokia phones in the show with their brand name right in your face. Can't be right, can it, Mark?'

'Not at all, Sir Alan. It's the first I've heard of it. Yes, Jane will look into it.'

'Oh, it's the first you've heard of it also? Don't tell me you don't watch telly either?'

More nervous, embarrassed laughter from both Mark and Jane Doe. At that point they left me as if I had the plague. 'Okay, busy night, got to socialise. We will look into this.'

Obviously I touched a nerve. Someone must have got it in the neck at the BBC as a few weeks later all mobile phones in *East-Enders* were blank as far as the brand names were concerned, and to this day I watch diligently to ensure that the policy is adhered to.

Ann has also signed on to this. From time to time she tells me when she thinks she's spotted an infringement of the branding policy on a BBC show.

But it wasn't just Ann on the lookout for this stuff. More seriously, my enemies, the scum at the *Daily Mail*, once thought they'd hit the jackpot. A journalist had cottoned on to the fact that Frank PR, in addition to representing me, also handled the PR for Black-Berry. In one series there was a task where the candidates were asked to create mobile phone apps, and this journalist claimed that BlackBerry phones were blatantly plugged throughout the show, in contravention of BBC guidelines. The journalist, a bloke by the name of Paul Revoir, called up Frank PR, thinking he was about to win the Pulitzer Prize for investigative journalism. He tried to give Andrew Bloch, one of the bosses at Frank PR, a hard time. From what I heard, this journalist thought all his Christmases had come at once and that he'd rumbled some major coup that we were breaking BBC rules. Andrew, who's far too polite to these scumbags (I suppose he has to be in the PR game), pointed out to him that the episode was about designing mobile apps, so naturally you would see shots of mobile phones in the programme. Andrew also told him that if he looked properly he would see that several brands of phones were used in that episode, and the BlackBerry was just one of a handful of models shown. Obviously the candidates needed to test their apps on several handsets, so this was just part of the task. Despite this logical explanation, you have to understand how, in journalistic-scum terms, they cannot let the facts get in the way of a good story, so they published it anyway! They made out that loads of viewers had complained about the BlackBerry product placement. In reality, of course, no one had bothered to complain. Why would they?

It was interesting to note that as the series got underway, people in the upper echelons like Jana were asking to see the next episodes before they went out. As you will appreciate, if you were in charge of BBC Television, it would be physically impossible for you to watch all the programmes that had been commissioned for broadcast. Additionally, you can imagine the number of programme-makers who want to get their work seen by the person in charge at the BBC. It follows, therefore, that these senior BBC executives do not see some of the programmes until they're transmitted – in fact, sometimes they don't see them at all! After all, how can they watch every programme the BBC puts out? My point is, when they are told they have a hit on their hands, they suddenly become very keen and call for the tapes.

Naturally, when a series of *The Apprentice* starts broadcasting, some of the later episodes are still in the process of being edited.

This serves to emphasise how much work and effort has to go into it. I believe that at the time of the first broadcast, only six of the shows had finished editing, with Peter Moore and his team still beavering away to produce the final six.

What I also found out from Peter was that up until then, while the BBC had commissioned the show, they had completely left it to Peter and Tanya to deal with the editing. There are strict BBC guidelines stipulating what can and can't be in a programme, ensuring factual accuracy, but apart from that the programme content and the way it flowed – all the creative work, including the music – was down to them.

However, after the programme was broadcast and started to gain popularity, some new BBC people suddenly wanted to get involved creatively because they saw a hit show and no doubt wished to share in some of the glory, which is normal, I guess. It wasn't a case of them not trusting Peter and Tanya. From what I heard, they started to come along to the editing suite. I would love to have been a fly on the wall when that first happened to Peter and to have heard what he said to them. I'm pretty sure it would have included a few expletives and some very loud refusals.

Why did all this nonsense happen? It's because, when you've got a hit programme on your hands, you, a member of the BBC, would like to tell people that you're involved with it. But as I say, it's funny how people only want to be involved in a programme once it becomes very popular. I'm probably touching a few nerves for anyone at the BBC who's reading this book now; though I'm sure they wouldn't deny that what I'm saying is true. Yeah, I catch on quickly, don't I?

7

BECOMING MR NASTY

The final is shown and fame follows

Let's go back now to the previous autumn and filming the final boardroom of the final episode. The riverboat task had been performed and I had seen with my own eyes both candidates' presentations as well as the work and effort they'd put into all their arrangements for the task. Having been through three boardroom scenes, including listening to the advice of their past housemates and ex-candidates, it was decision time for me. Would Saira or Tim be the winner?

When I came to the end of my final summing up, I told them I'd made my mind up. I turned to Saira, who I knew would give me a very good reaction if she thought she had won. I said to her, 'Saira, you are hired.' She leapt out of the chair with joy. She cried and showed a lot of emotion. Tim's head dropped in disappointment.

Now came the tough bit. When the dust had settled and all the hugging, crying and handshaking had finished, I had to become Mr Nasty. I told them that we were now going to film the scene again, but this time with Tim as the winner. They looked bewildered when I broke it to them that we had to film two winning scenarios. They were confused as hell and I remember saying to them, 'Look, let's get this done, then afterwards, come upstairs to my dressing room and we'll have a chat and I'll explain why we've had to do all this. But for now, let's get it done. Trust me, everything will be explained.'

In my dressing room afterwards, I told them in detail why I had to do it. After my explanation, they fully understood. I also explained they would have to consider what they were going to do from now – the end of filming – until the time the series finished broadcasting in May. I acknowledged that they had given up their jobs and so they were now in a kind of limbo. Therefore, I told them I was prepared to allocate each of them a job in one of my companies during this waiting period.

This meeting with the two finalists after filming the double hiring would go on to become a very important meeting in future series. With the experience of a couple of series under my belt, I would use this occasion to issue a strong warning to the candidates as neither of them would have been exposed to television before. We try to vet the applications so that anyone who's previously been on TV isn't usually allowed into the process (as it may indicate they're trying to enhance a media career rather than being there for the right business reasons). However, we do sometimes discover that they may have taken part in a game show or some other minor TV appearance.

My speech would be something like this: 'As you two have never been on TV before, you don't know what life is going to be like once your face is exposed to the public. Whatever you *think* it's going to be like – it's going to be a hundred times bigger. And here's the bad news: if you have any skeletons in your closet, and not just you but *anyone* you've been associated with – girlfriends, boy-friends, husbands, wives, fathers, brothers, sisters – the media will publish it. Not maybe; *definitely*. I can assure you one hundred per cent that they will find out and publish it. They will search through your life and your family and everything you have ever done. They will write about the party you got drunk at in Cambridge, or the time you got caught smoking a joint somewhere. If you think they won't find out, you are absolutely wrong.

'Now, I don't need you to tell me right now; I want you to go away and think about this, but if there's anything in your life, or your family's, that you feel may create some sensational story, let me know. Please don't be embarrassed, because I'm a big boy – I've been there, seen it and done it and nothing shocks me. Of course, maybe you genuinely have nothing to hide – that's great – but do not think you're going to get away with anything because you won't. So go away and think about it, and if you know of any skeletons, let me know, and together with James Herring, the PR guy, we will handle it. Bear in mind that handling it might mean we will blow a story before the media gets hold of it in order to scupper them and kill off the story that, for example, your father did a stretch in Pentonville. Alternatively, we may take the view that we wait until the media get hold of the story and deal with it then; but if so, at least we are braced with the details. What's worse is that you don't tell me and we're caught off-guard one Friday night at five o'clock when a newspaper tells us they're going to publish an article about you tomorrow, and we've got two minutes to comment before they go to press.'

It should be noted that James Herring's job starts at the beginning of filming and ends once the winner has been selected at the end of the series. From then on, my own PR company, Frank PR, takes over supporting the winner in their new position. Frank PR also, of course, have to be briefed about the aforementioned skeletons. Over the past ten years, Frank PR's David Fraser and Andrew Bloch have given each winner the 'Talk of Doom'. I hear they play a kind of 'good cop/bad cop' routine. The gist of this indoctrination is: 'The real hard work starts now . . . You have to keep your head down . . . You must refer all media enquiries to us . . . Don't worry about the other ex-candidates who seem to be getting loads of publicity putting themselves around, as this will be short-lived . . .'

I feel a bit sorry for the winners. They must wonder why they're not allowed to parade themselves around in *Hello!* and *OK!* magazine when, for example, the runner-up appears in feature articles. They must think, 'What was the purpose of me winning this thing? I'm being told to keep my head down.'

It is a tough time for the winners. I also explain to them that the publicity they are seeing for the runner-up or other ex-candidates is mostly very short-lived – it should be seen as a sort of desperate plea to be famous; to try and move on to another thing – *anything* – in TV. The winner, on the other hand, has a job with me which is a serious professional matter, so I don't want them parading around in stupid photos or, in the case of female winners, in bikinis or less. I tell them that the media are users – they will drop you like a hot potato once they've got what they want from you.

I guess it's very frustrating for the winners and their families to see this lack of publicity. Consider the case of all the candidates, winners and losers. They are from ordinary walks of life and then suddenly they're on telly every week for up to twelve weeks. Of course, they are loving it and their social circles must go nuts. And then, just as suddenly – anticlimax. The show is over and withdrawal symptoms set in. They miss being spotted in the street or in restaurants. They loved the public recognition during the broadcast period and try to recapture that attention by putting themselves around doing all sorts of stupid things. For the winner, this type of sleazy publicity would be detrimental to the job in hand. However, when the time is right and the winner has settled in and reached the stage where whatever they've been working on has come to fruition, then we professionally announce what they are developing or producing with a detailed PR launch. After all, *The Apprentice* is a serious business show and the winner has a big salary and a hard job to go and do. We strive, therefore, to ensure they do not get involved in any cheap publicity other than that which promotes their future mission.

Looking back, the skeletons-in-closets speech I make to the finalists (just after the final is recorded) always shocks them. 'No, Sir Alan/Lord Sugar. I have nothing to hide whatsoever,' they'd say.

'Good,' I would say, 'that's great, but remember what I just said: it's not just you – it might be some girlfriend or boyfriend who thinks they've got something to say about you. Or some ex-colleague, or someone who simply doesn't like you. So as I say, you don't have to disclose anything to me today. Go away and think about it. The programme won't start broadcasting for several months. Write it down on a piece of paper or email it to me – I will treat the matter confidentially.'

Despite these warnings, some candidates still felt they were being clever hiding certain things and, sure enough, the media picked up on them. However, on many occasions I would receive an email or a written letter explaining something that might come up, and this detail was tremendously valuable to James Herring and me. In numerous instances it enabled James and the BBC to deal with the issue in a controlled manner.

Another thing I would say to the finalists in this meeting was along these lines: 'Part and parcel of winning *The Apprentice* is that you do not do any interviews with any newspapers or any media unless it is approved by me or the PR company. The reason for this is that your future discussions with the media must focus on the job in hand. As you have no experience whatsoever, I'm giving you the best advice, and that is when talking to the media you need to have the PR company by your side, advising you on what to say. We certainly *will* be doing interviews with the media, but if you or any of your family are contacted separately, be aware that that contact needs to be controlled, not only for your own sake, but also for the integrity of myself and the BBC who have invested so much time, money and effort into you as the winner of this process.'

*

I was clear at the end of the process that my winner was going to be Tim. My concerns about Saira were that she was a little fiery and a bit uncontrollable. My small misgiving about Tim was that although he was a very nice guy who had really worked hard in the series and had a hunger to succeed, I wondered if he might be lacking some of the business acumen required for the prize job in *The Apprentice*. However, that's what I was there for – to mentor him.

The scenario that played out over the ensuing months would turn out to be an ongoing problem for me in the years that followed. Tim came to work at Amstrad headquarters and, as I had it in mind that he was the winner, it was relatively simple for me to set him the task of reintroducing a beauty product we once made – an electronic face-care unit. Tim used a resource inside the company – the R&D people – to design the tooling for his product, and he also used an external resource – software developers who would devise a program to deal with the way we were going to sell the product. The task was self-contained and little did I know at the time that separating him from the day-to-day business and other people in the company would turn out to be a rather clever move.

The nightmare, however, was Saira. I sent her over to Viglen, my computer company, to help out in sales, which seemed to be her area of expertise. I thought her aggressive and convincing salesmanship would help her sell computers to schools as well as government and council institutions.

What I did not envisage was Viglen boss Bordan Tkachuk saying he was on the verge of a nervous breakdown! While to my face Bordan said, 'Okay, no problem, I will accommodate her. We'll find her something to do. I'm sure she'll be very good,' etc., etc., in reality I found out afterwards from Nick Hewer that he'd had several conversations with Bordan who said that this woman was driving him totally nuts; that he didn't know what to do and it was a complete nightmare.

Bordan was most probably exaggerating. However, it's true that

Saira *was* a bit of a loose cannon. Bordan saw her as an irritant, a thorn in his side, and I believe he set her a task just to keep her occupied. The task was to take some of his redundant models and see whether she could find a place for them. Now, to be fair to Saira, she knew nothing about computers. She was given a bit of training on what they do and what the specifications were and I pointed out to Bordan at the time that to *sell* them you don't need to be a computer expert. In other words, once a salesperson gets to grips with the facts and figures, how the product works is irrelevant. They find a customer who will look at what they're offering them based on the spec.

'Okay,' Bordan had said. 'No problem at all.'

Now here's the problem I had with Bordan. He has never, ever, in all the years I've known him, given any credit to anyone other than himself for doing a good deal. I didn't realise this until *The Apprentice* came along, because at various meetings afterwards at Viglen HQ – to catch up and just see how Saira was doing – I would sit and talk with Saira, Bordan and Mike Ray, the finance director. Every time Saira opened her mouth to speak – 'I've been on to so-and-so and offered them fifty of these or a hundred of those . . .' – Bordan would jump in and say, 'No you didn't, no you didn't. It wasn't you who did that; it was Charlie who pointed it out to you.' Basically, he had a very, very negative attitude towards her. Nick also told me that what was winding Bordan up even more was that Saira was not accepting him as her boss, albeit temporary, and that she was in constant contact with me, bypassing him. This, I'm afraid to say, is a trait Bordan has. He cannot stand it when employees under him contact me directly. I mention this now because I made the fatal error of sending a few more *Apprentice* winners to him in later years, all of whom he treated the same way.

I've often commented, in hindsight, that Bordan's autocratic ways may have held back the advancement of Viglen simply because, although he's a super salesman and very conscious of profits and margins, he tends to try to do *everything* himself.

The nightmare got worse. Saira decided she would appoint her own PR people. I remember calling her one day and asking, 'Where are you?'

'It is now Saira time,' she said. 'I've done enough of this. I've done weeks of filming. I'm sitting here at Viglen having a very difficult time, so now it's Saira time. I'm going to have to work on what's good for me.'

I couldn't quite understand what she meant by that, but it seemed to me that she was already assuming she wouldn't be the winner.

As I mentioned, Tim had been set a special project and was completely isolated from the staff at Amstrad. However, in subsequent years when other winners came through, I would put them within certain departments of Amstrad where they would sit next to colleagues and interact with them. Their new colleagues, of course, would be far more experienced in their field, but get this – they were earning £30–40,000 a year, and in came this person who famously would be earning £100,000. Imagine how you would feel as an employee of my company sitting next to a man or woman who has been plonked in this position by the boss in order to honour his obligation of offering a £100,000-a-year job. And here's you, another of my employees, who has to sit here earning £35,000 a year watching this person who's basically clueless about the area of the business in which they've been placed but is earning more than twice as much as you!

Human nature being what it is, this caused me quite a bit of friction within my companies, and when I look back now I can understand why. To be fair, most of my employees accepted it, but there were a few who really took umbrage.

*

As the series played out over the three-month period, the popular-ity of the programme soared. Other enterprises to do with entrepreneurship or youth employment contacted me and wanted me to attend certain events to encourage young people. In fact, these were similar to the events I mentioned previously which I used to do on behalf of the government at the request of Gordon Brown.

And so the time came when I had to disclose the winner. I asked Saira and Tim to come and meet me for lunch at the Scalini restaurant in London where I would tell them face to face who had actually won.

It was the day before the final was going to be broadcast. I remember being at an Amstrad meeting at British Telecom's headquarters discussing the possibility of a project with them and asking them to excuse me from the meeting as I had to go and make someone a happy person and someone else an unhappy person. I revealed that I was going to meet the two finalists and would be telling them who'd won and who'd lost.

Walking around the BT building that day, heads were turning as I came through due to the popularity of the programme. Every-one knew who I was and I guess those in the boardroom during the meeting were slightly in awe of this 'TV star' visiting their prem-ises. I slipped out of the meeting and met up with Dan Adamson, Saira and Tim at Scalini's restaurant. I told them all that it was best we had lunch before I gave them my decision.

Breaking the bad news was a difficult moment, but in life I have come across many a difficult moment and you simply have to deal with it. Credit to Saira, when I told her she was not the winner, she said, 'Fine, okay. I suspected that, so no problem.' I think she had guessed because in many of the meetings we'd had with Bordan, she would ask me why I hadn't set her a specific task as I had for Tim. By then I had also started to understand what she meant by 'Saira time'. She had been beavering away in the background, signing up with PR companies and doing photo shoots and so forth to prepare herself for a media career.

Consider that the programme had broadcast eleven episodes, and consider how popular she must have become by then in her personal circle of friends and family. Also, think about both her and Tim walking around the streets during that period of time – they were becoming famous personalities. And I guess, although she never confirmed it to me, Saira must have been contacted by some television companies to say that, whatever happened, they would like to talk to her about other projects after *The Apprentice*.

Saira was brought up in Nottingham, the daughter of Pakistani immigrants. She was very feisty on *The Apprentice* and it seems she hasn't mellowed in the ten years since. She was the first member of her family to go to university and she got a degree in town planning of all things, after which she joined the sales team of McVitie's. You can imagine terrified corner-shop owners all over the Midlands cowering behind their counters when she strode into their shop clutching an order book. Saira does not take any prisoners.

After *The Apprentice* she carved out a media career as well as starting up her own children's skincare products company. She still has the same remarkable determination, and this was demonstrated when she took herself off to Pakistan intent on adopting a baby. The story was shown in a moving documentary, *Adoption Abroad: Saira's Story*, where she was introduced to a newborn baby who had been dumped in a skip. From then on, Saira was determined she would take this baby girl home, and after months of red tape and hassle with the authorities, she eventually managed it! Today Saira and her husband, Steven, live in Oxford with their son, Zacariah, and their adopted daughter, Amara.

Saira went on to do a few other TV programmes. She was obviously TV gold as far as her motormouth was concerned and she attracted a lot of attention from television companies who used her in various different shows. Of all the candidates I've had over the years, she is one of only a few who have done quite well in pursuing a TV career as a spin-off from her appearance on *The Apprentice*.

On the same day as our lunch I had to film a supplementary show which would air after the final. The BBC insisted on this due to the popularity of *The Apprentice* and the show became the foundation of the programme now known as *You're Fired*, later hosted by Adrian Chiles and then Dara Ó Briain. Again, not knowing much about TV at the time, I just went along with it. They had created a boardroom scene at the ITV studios on the South Bank. This seemed a bit bizarre to me, but I discovered that these studios, albeit owned by ITV, are rented out to make a host of programmes for different TV channels.

They had selected five candidates from the process, and this programme, which was recorded the day before the final was broadcast, would run immediately after the final. During the programme, each of the candidates was spoken to. I was sitting rather casually at the end of the table answering a few questions from the presenter now and again, and making a few comments. I do remember one hysterical moment when the presenter asked me what I thought of Paul Torrisi. I replied, 'I'll sum it up by saying this: Paul actually thinks he's won!' which had the audience roaring with laughter.

It was just an off-the-cuff remark from me, but I think it described Paul brilliantly in that he could never understand how he could possibly have done anything wrong; he couldn't comprehend how anybody could not consider him to be the best.

Once again, in the time-honoured tradition of TV, when we'd finished recording the supplementary programme there was a little party held in what's known as the green room. Daisy Goodwin came up to me and commented how my performance that night was nicely laid-back; it was just me being myself. She said, 'It is amazing, Sir Alan, how you have not changed. You've been on television and seen the twelve programmes broadcast to the nation. You have become a national treasure, yet you're still the same; it hasn't gone to your head.'

I just shrugged my shoulders. To me, it went without saying that it wouldn't go to my head. However, I guess what Daisy was implying was that she had seen – so many times in her career – the host of a popular programme become a bigshot.

Tim was liked by everybody at Amstrad. I said before that over the years some of my employees took umbrage at working alongside a winner of *The Apprentice*, but Tim soon gained the respect of the staff. He had won the series and the job through his hard graft and had shown himself to have great business potential. He was a really nice guy and today we remain in contact with each other. He worked for me for over two years – his contract was extended and his product was launched into the marketplace. As mentioned earlier, this was an example of allowing the dust to settle in PR terms after winning *The Apprentice* and then, as and when you have something to shout about, arranging for a big PR launch. Tim had designed a new face-care system under the name Integra and Frank PR arranged a massive launch in a place called The Energy Clinic near Old Street in central London. The launch was packed, with every national newspaper and TV company in attendance. Big articles appeared in the media the following day with Tim showing off his products. Indeed, the *Guardian* covered the launch on its front page. It was around this time that I said to Tim, 'I told you that all the plaudits for you winning *The Apprentice* would come through one day, and here we are at a very professional launch.'

Regrettably, the product itself wasn't very successful, possibly because it wasn't a retail item. We didn't sell it into the shops, it was sold direct to the public, and although it might be difficult for people to believe in this day and age, back then the internet was not all singing and dancing. I think if we had time-warped the product to ten years later, it would have been far more successful as we'd have been able to use the internet to promote it.

Tim left the company in 2007 and started up his own organisation. Since then he has set up the Bright Ideas Trust with the purpose of promoting enterprise and start-up businesses for the young and underprivileged, and in 2012 he was awarded an MBE for services to Enterprise Culture. He also went on to do lots of inspirational speaking, from which I believe he initially derived some of his income. He is now a member of Estate Property Consultants, a boutique London property investment company which assists high-net-worth individuals seeking prime real-estate opportunities.

I had the pleasure of being at Tim's wedding and have since invited him to one of my family functions. I also bump into him quite a lot at events organised by my PR company. We always have a good chat when we run into each other.

During the course of the series, I was asked to go on a chat show as part and parcel of the BBC's ongoing promotion of *The Apprentice*. The first time I went on *Friday Night with Jonathan Ross*, I can tell you I was a very nervous guest. Can you imagine being on the famous Jonathan Ross's show? As I mentioned earlier, I had been on the Terry Wogan show many years ago, but Jonathan's show was the bees' knees of chat shows and very popular indeed. Jonathan came to visit me beforehand at my Brentwood HQ, turning up in some flash car which he parked on the forecourt of our offices. The staff at Amstrad were so excited that Jonathan Ross was in the building. He came to see me to discuss what we would talk about if I came on his show, and just to get a general feeling and understanding about me. I've since learned that he doesn't normally do this. I think that *The Apprentice* had made such an impact on British television; it was so refreshingly new, and I was a new character – not an actor; just an ordinary person who'd become a TV personality from out of the blue – so I guess he was a bit intrigued to meet me himself.

We had a little chat and a cup of tea. I remember my secretary Frances being so impressed that Jonathan Ross was actually in my office. We talked through lots of things and we agreed that I would be on the show. He gave me a bit of an outline of what we would discuss. So excited was I that I asked if it were possible for my family to come along and see how *Friday Night with Jonathan Ross* was made, which of course was fine. I'm not sure whether Nick was available, but he certainly would have been invited to attend, especially as he was my ex-PR fellow.

If you recall, on Jonathan Ross's show there were four gay singers in a band called 'Four Poofs and a Piano'. They would have a picture of one of the night's guests on their T-shirts, and, that night, the picture was of me! My son Daniel asked for one of the shirts afterwards.

So there I was at the BBC studios, sitting in Jonathan's green room. Anybody who has seen the show will remember that he talks to the guests sitting in the green room - on the air – and fires questions at them. And while I felt I was quite good at being able to answer questions on the fly, the atmosphere was intimidating even for someone like me.

When I look back now I wonder why I was so nervous, because at the end of the day it wasn't a live show. It was edited and it was going to be cut down, so it wouldn't have mattered if we made a few mistakes. Nevertheless, this show was so legendary, one can understand why I had a few nerves.

I was called onto the stage and, of course, guests can't see the audience because of the bright lights that are on us, but I could hear the audience reaction, normally laughter from some of the banter. It was quite a good interview, though not by a country mile the best I've ever done on a chat show. I remember Jonathan concluded the interview by saying, 'Sir Alan, thank you very much for coming on the show, but I can't resist this: I have to say, "You're fired,"' to which I gave him my trademark blank expression and said, 'Oh, Jonathan, how novel. How funny you are.' He got a little embarrassed, but the audience erupted.

I was being chased by lots of TV channels to appear in various programmes and made one big mistake that would teach me a lesson to be selective in what I agreed to do. Human nature being what it is, I was excited back then and I rose to the bait. When ITV contacted me about making a programme, I asked Nick what he thought this was all about. He told me it was a documentary about the eighties, an era in which my business had seen meteoric success, so it seemed like a good idea, and everything was agreed. I turned up at the place where they were going to film it, somewhere in Docklands, only to find that while it was an ITV production company, the programme was going to air on Sky One. Now with the greatest respect, back then Sky One didn't have many viewers at all. It was then I realised that in the TV world, part of ITV's business model was to make programmes for other channels. I learned that if ITV invited me to do a programme, it didn't follow that the programme was going to be *shown* on ITV. I would no longer be fooled by ITV asking me to do something because they have their own production units and make programmes for other channels.

On realising this, I must admit I had a tantrum at the filming site. I said I'd been tricked into something and was not prepared to do it. The fellow from ITV was very apologetic. He understood my naivety, but in his mind he didn't think he'd done anything wrong. He pleaded and begged. He told me he'd put together a select crew specially to film this thing, blah, blah, blah. To cut a long story short, Nick suggested that I do it on the basis, 'You don't want to make enemies in the TV business.'

It turned out to be the biggest load of rubbish I've ever participated in. I remember my daughter, Louise, saying to me when she saw the programme on Sky, 'Dad, what did you do that for? It was really pants.' Whatever that means.

Another programme I regret doing was the early version of *Room 101*, which was hosted at the time by Paul Merton. The format of it back then was not as it is today where there are three guests. When I did it, I was the only guest. In the same way that Jonathan Ross met me before going on his programme, I met Paul Merton at Scalini's and we ran over what we would be talking about on the programme. As fans of *Room 101* will know, the show is designed for its guests to talk about the things they really dislike and Paul Merton decides whether or not the thing should go into 'room 101' to be trashed.

This was the first example of me being stitched up by a TV production company. One of the things I disliked was call centres; how you would hang on the line waiting to be put through, and how sometimes you would end up talking to some useless person in a foreign country. So we discussed the call centres on the programme, but then imagine how surprised I was when they suddenly played the automated phone message from my company Viglen, where first-time callers are directed to press 1 if they want to talk to technical support; press 2 if they want to talk to sales, etc.

This was deliberately done to make me look an idiot. It wasn't a live programme and I kick myself today for not making a fuss there and then. But again, being new to TV, I just sat there feeling embarrassed about being tricked in this manner.

Another show I accepted the invitation to go on was *This Week*, a political programme hosted by Andrew Neil. I'd met Andrew in the past when he was employed by News International and he asked me on his show to discuss some topical matter at the time. He, too, couldn't resist saying to me, 'You're fired,' and he got my standard response: 'It's been done before, my friend; you're making a fool of yourself. It's not new; in fact it's a bit of a lead balloon.'

The difference this time was that the show *was* being broadcast live. He was immensely embarrassed but he soldiered on, saying, 'Well, maybe it's the first time it's been said on *live* TV,' to which I replied, 'Yep, but you still made a fool of yourself.'

That said, these were all good learning experiences for me, and from then on I refused to participate in any of these peripheral programmes such as *Question Time, Have I Got News for You, Mock the Week, Would I Lie to You, Alan Carr: Chatty Man, Never Mind the Buzzcocks* and others.

You would not believe the number of times I have been asked to go on *Question Time* and *Have I Got News for You*. It must run into dozens. Basically, I weigh up the situation and conclude there is no benefit from being in these programmes, particularly ones where they simply wish to take the piss out of me. As for *Question Time*, it always ends up with members of the public shouting at you. In my case they'd have been shouting at me because I was a Labour peer and former advisor to the government on small business. Why would I want to sit there and have people shout and scream at me, and blame me for things that are nothing to do with me? Of course, *Question Time* is very popular, but it's no more than a mini-*Apprentice*. David Dimbleby sits in the middle and you can see that he gets tremendous enjoyment from the panel getting beaten up, either by each other or by the audience. It's just like *The Apprentice* boardroom in a different format. The participants tend to want to sound off as much as they can, saying things they may not even agree with just to get the applause they crave.

What really made my wife laugh was that some idiot at the BBC called up my PR people and asked if I would go on *Strictly Come Dancing*! I mean, please, where are their brains? Are they nuts or what?

One of the programmes I do like doing is *The Graham Norton*

Show. I believe that Graham is *the* best chat-show host we have in the UK, so I've been on his show a few times and I've enjoyed doing it very much. In fact, the last time I was on there I had a little chat with him beforehand and said I had some rather funny ideas on what to talk about, including me taking over the red-chair session so that I could train him on tactics. It went down very well.

Shortly after the first series of *The Apprentice* was broadcast, I received a phone call from Daisy Goodwin. She was telling me that the series had become so popular it had been nominated for something called a BAFTA award.

BAFTA shmafta, what did I know about these things? I have since learned that it is the most prestigious award one can receive for a television programme. She told me that Talkback Thames and the BBC had a table at the Great Room at the Grosvenor House Hotel where the BAFTA awards would be taking place that year. Daisy said they would very much like Ann and me to attend on this very auspicious occasion. In fact, she was almost insistent – it was something that I *had* to do and the BBC wanted me there because, as *The Apprentice* had been nominated, there would be shots of the stars of the various programmes in the audience, including me; and there was a chance the programme could win.

We turned up at what could only be described as a zoo! There were thousands of people piling into the Grosvenor House. Of course, by the time this event took place, I had become something of a celebrity. And yes, we walked in on the red carpet. Cameras were flashing and people were shaking my hand, stopping me and asking me to give interviews. It was rather overwhelming and unexpected. Once again I got caught a little bit off-guard. My driver had turned up at the back entrance of the Grosvenor House as instructed, but when we got there we saw this complete and utter mass of people. The members of the public were behind barriers, shouting and screaming at the various celebrities as they walked along the red carpet. It was a rather intimidating situation. Finally, having given a few little interviews and had some photographs taken, I ended up in the main waiting area before dinner was served. Hanging around, one saw lots of other TV celebrities passing by. I recall seeing Ricky Gervais, whom I had never met before. He turned to me and waved so I went up to him and said, 'Hello, nice to meet you.'

He said, 'Yeah, nice to meet you too. I waved at you over there but I don't know you. I just thought I'd wave at you because I like your television programme.'

And then there was Harry Hill, a guy who was making a living taking the piss out of me. He came up to me and asked if I'd mind him having a picture taken with me. I said I didn't mind at all, as he obviously appreciated my performance. Various other celebrities came up, complimenting me on this new show, and it was not until that moment that I realised the industry itself had been shaken up by *The Apprentice*. It was the first kind of formatted series that was different. It was a programme hosted by an ordinary person like me and not by a celebrity.

Daisy Goodwin grabbed hold of me and told me we'd been called for dinner. She guided Ann and me through the central aisle of this massive room towards our table. On the way, people were constantly coming up to me. Gordon Ramsay leapt out of his chair, shook my hand and said, 'You're nearly as rude as me.'

'Nah, no chance, mate,' I replied.

Finally we got to our seats. And who sprung up and came over? None other than Bruce Forsyth, a legend as we all know. He shook my hand and complimented me on the programme. Ann and I thought this was amazing. This went on for ages; Jonathan Ross was on another table – he also came over and said hello.

Dinner was served and then the ceremony started. There were

lots of clips of TV programmes being shown in the various categories and awards given out. I was sitting next to Peter Moore and Dan Adamson and a few other people from the BBC, although Tanya couldn't be there.

Then came *The Apprentice*. And we won! It was such a shock – we'd actually won! There was mass applause from the floor and some people actually stood up to clap. We really *did* have a hit on our hands. Peter Moore jumped up with Dan and said, 'Right, come with me, Sir Alan.'

'Come where?'

'Come on, we're going up on the stage!'

'I'm not going to say anything. I don't know what to do . . .'

'Don't worry, I'll do all the talking. You just come up on the stage with me.'

And we walked through this room full of celebrities up onto the stage. Peter made a little speech thanking BAFTA for recognising the show and thanking them for this prestigious award, etc. I stood just behind him quietly, and he ended his speech by turning to me and saying, 'I guess this bloke here must have had something to do with it.' There was more applause and we walked off the stage.

Peter said, 'The press want to talk to you now. Look, you're better at this sort of thing than me – you go and talk to them.'

I thought that was rather strange. Why wouldn't *he* be talking to the press? Anyway, I was ushered to an area where I was photographed by at least fifty cameramen with the BAFTA award in my hand and there was a mini press conference where some journalists asked questions about how I felt winning the award and a few other general questions about *The Apprentice*.

On the way in, I met the famous David Jason, and he said to me, 'I love your programme.'

I remember saying to him, 'You are a legend, sir. When it comes to television, *you* are *my* hero. I loved you as Del Boy and Inspector Frost.'

What a night that was, meeting all these great celebrities. You know, you can tell these people were genuine because they weren't coming up to me for any reason other than to compliment me.

The award, the physical trophy that was handed out, was given to Peter, Tanya and Dan, so in fact there were three BAFTAs. Peter and Dan walked back to the table with the three awards, even though Tanya wasn't there.

When I went to do the photographic session, there were a few spare awards there for me to hold up and be photographed with. Naively, I believed that one of them was mine; that I'd won an award. And as I walked out with the award in my hand, a young lady came running after me and said, 'No, no, that's not yours, Sir Alan. That one is just for photographic purposes.'

I went back to the table and it suddenly dawned upon me that even though I was the host of this show, I wasn't getting one of these things. It had also dawned on Ann, and she said, 'Where's your one?'

I said to her, 'Actually, I don't get one,' to which she said, 'Why not? You're the one who made that programme successful!'

'Yes, yes, I know, Ann, but the point is this: these awards are given out to the producers as the artistic geniuses. They're not given out to the person who appeared in the show. They're for people who *make* television programmes. There are other awards for people who participate in programmes, but this is not one of them.'

'Well, it's not fair,' she said. I must admit, I did feel a little bit peeved at the time.

I talked earlier about a certain distrust of me felt by Peter Moore and Dan Adamson in respect to confidentiality and other things. While Peter had got to know me better by this time, the incident I'm about to disclose proves I still hadn't gained Dan's trust.

The day after the BAFTAs, the BBC called me and said that

tomorrow they would be sending a camera crew to my office to do a piece about the programme, and they needed the BAFTA award in the shot, with me holding it. I told the BBC I didn't have one because I wasn't nominated. They asked me to see if I could borrow one so I got my secretary to call Dan Adamson and tell him I would like to borrow his or Tanya's award for an interview I was doing with the BBC, and could he have the award sent to my office please?

Initially, he refused, maybe thinking I was going to nick the award and not give it back. He smelt at the awards ceremony that both Ann and I were upset about the fact that I should have had one of these awards, and he could have confused my disappointment with an intention to steal his or Tanya's BAFTA.

After Frances told me he had refused, I got in touch with him myself and blasted down the phone, 'I'm not going to pinch your bloody award – which frankly you got because I was so good on the show – I need it because the BBC are doing this piece which involves me holding the award. So I'll have it back to you as soon as we've finished recording.'

He arranged for it to be sent by motorbike and said he'd ask the rider to hang about during the filming so he could immediately take the award back with him. I told him this was insulting; that it was tantamount to being called a thief. I reminded him that I'd promised to send it back to him, which should be good enough, and if he didn't like it, I would be getting on to the BBC and his bosses at Talkback and telling them how bloody stupid he was being. In the end, he sent it.

There's a great story that follows on from that incident, together with an unbelievable revelation, but you'll hear about that later.

8

'AM I SPEAKING ENGLISH?'

**Filming series two with the most emotional bunch
of candidates I've ever seen**

The obvious success of the first series led me to believe that soon someone would be contacting me to discuss a second series. My family and friends as well as Nick and Margaret had been saying to me, 'Surely they must be doing a second series.' It seemed like a no-brainer to me but when I got hold of Jane Lush to talk about it, she was very coy on the subject. Peter Moore was also very non-committal. I wondered whether they were trying to be devilishly shrewd, playing down the success of the first series so that I wouldn't demand large sums of money to sign up again.

I found out later on the TV-mafia grapevine that this delay was because of a certain deliberation (I can only assume by Jane Lush and co.): they knew they were definitely going to make another series because the show was such a hit, but thought perhaps it might be attractive to get some other host instead of me; and, as such, no automatic offer was made to me. I never did discover whether they actually went out and enquired again, but quite clearly the delay in me hearing whether there was to be a second series was at least partly down to whether they were going to offer it to me or not.

There was another reason Jane Lush didn't tell me whether a second series was going to be commissioned. It turned out she was in the process of resigning from the BBC to set up her own production company. The news came to me from the new chief at Talkback Thames, a lady by the name of Lorraine Heggessey.

Everything was changing. Daisy Goodwin had decided to move on to pastures new and also form her own production company, and I heard that Peter Moore was moving along with her. Bearing in mind that I was still a novice in this TV business, it came as quite a surprise to me to see this mass migration of personnel. Even Daisy's boss, Peter Fincham, had moved to take up a job with the BBC.

The fact that all these executives were setting up their own production companies must have come about as a result of policy changes within the BBC, who now wanted to buy in programmes from sub-contractors rather than make them in-house. I guess it was a way of knowing their costs were fixed, as opposed to having a large production team, on salaries, within the BBC where the static costs would be incurred even if nothing new was produced. So I am guessing that a sensible decision was made by the BBC to encourage people to start their own production companies and pitch ideas to them. This way they could cut down on their own static staffing.

I contacted Peter and Tanya to ask whether they'd be involved in the second series and they said regretfully not. Tanya went to take up a post at Channel 4 and Peter confirmed he was joining Daisy in her new venture. He tried to explain to me politely that creative TV production people need a challenge. *The Apprentice* was a great challenge – but now they'd done it, they wanted to move on and do other things.

This culture was rather strange as far as I was concerned, because I thought that one would want to continue to be associated with success – but apparently not! It seems that these people like to take on new challenges.

Lorraine Heggessey had moved to Talkback from the BBC

where she had built up her reputation after joining them in 1978 as a news trainee, moving on to greater things like producing the current-affairs series *Panorama*. Due to her success in this field she moved to ITV and then again to Channel 4 where she worked on the documentary series *Dispatches*. She returned to the BBC and founded the viewer-feedback series *Biteback* as well as making some notable documentaries; in one of them managing to obtain an interview with 'Mad' Frankie Fraser. She was promoted to Director of Programmes and Deputy Chief Executive of the BBC's in-house production arm. She ended up as Controller of BBC1 and one of her last memorable and notable successes was the re-introduction of the new *Doctor Who* series. Shortly after that she took up this position at Talkback Thames, an independent production company. Again, this was a fascinating move, away from a secure position.

I eventually met with Lorraine, a rather short, bubbly and vivacious lady. She came across as someone who knew her stuff and knew the TV industry very well. She told me she was very enthusiastic about the new series and that we would need to get together to negotiate a new contract. She said that she too had moved from the BBC for a new challenge in a commercial organisation where she would be rewarded by results. She also took the time to explain to me how the structure of TV production works. I then understood that most of the people I'd been working with were self-employed contractors. They were not all on Talkback's payroll, so to speak, but were hired for a particular period of time to do the job. I guess they received a lump-sum payment for that period and would have to sort out their own taxation and financial affairs as most of them had their own small company to receive the income.

It was quite intriguing getting to grips with this way of working, and it was becoming clear to me why people tended to move on. It was not so much that they didn't want to do a new series; it was more that their contract had come to an end and they needed to find more work. It is a highly competitive and very mobile industry. The best people want to keep on their toes and move across the industry from series to series.

Lorraine must have thought I was a real nutter because, in the first meaningful conversation I had with her, I was telling her that I had the raving hump over the BAFTA awards thing. It was aggravating me and gnawing away at me.

'Hello, yes, nice to meet you,' I said. 'Bloody hell, things do move about in the TV world, don't they? I hope you've got more clout than the last lot – I'm really pissed off over the BAFTA thing.'

'Yes, nice to meet you too, Sir Alan. Well, as has been explained to you, the award was for the production team for the excellence of the programme they produced.'

'Yeah, I get that, but they wouldn't *have* a bleedin' programme without me! My wife has the hump also, and so does Nick.'

'Well, let me see what I can do. I know people at BAFTA; maybe we can get you one of the awards. Leave it with me, but let me say now that I will make sure your name is put down if the show ever gets nominated again for a BAFTA, so there will be no confusion.'

She did indeed try to get me an award from BAFTA but they told her to clear off. She also kept her promise and listed my name the next time the show was nominated for a BAFTA. And we did get nominated for series two, but we lost out to another new and great series, *The Choir*.

I ended up negotiating a new contract with the same Talkback corporate lawyer as on the first series. Normally, people such as the BBC and Talkback Thames would be dealing with an agent; not directly with the talent. Having come out of the football industry and having met many football agents, lots of whom said they also acted for TV celebrities, you will not be surprised to hear that some of the old contacts I had in football were on to me like a shot, telling me what a great job they could do for me in negotiating my contracts with the BBC. They'd tell me how this sort of thing was a special science which I wouldn't understand, and how well connected they were with the TV producers and TV channels because of their other clients.

I politely declined their offers, saying in effect, 'Can I just remind you that I am a businessman? Why would I need your services? What expertise do you have that I don't? It's a very simple case of going in to bat for an amount of money – just like you used to do with me when you wanted money for your players.'

In truth, I think that in many cases the production company and TV companies welcome the fact that they don't have to get into face-to-face negotiations with the talent. With an agent, there is this buffer in the middle who is able to ward off confrontations and stalemate situations when egos take over.

Nevertheless, I wanted to negotiate the next contract myself. But then came another phenomenon. Because I had the reputation of being a tough businessman, a reputation that was no doubt reinforced by the programme itself, this particular corporate lawyer thought she'd try to flex her muscles and show how she was going to take on the big Sir Alan Sugar and not give in to any of his demands. And so what I felt happened during negotiations was that commercial wisdom and common sense were overridden with this woman trying to take me on. Maybe these were her instructions, but I felt her playing hardball was simply for the challenge.

In the end, I told Lorraine Heggessey that she either had to pull her off the case, because we were getting nowhere, or deal with it herself. By coincidence this particular lawyer left Talkback and Fremantle shortly after my new contract was sorted.

At this point let me make it perfectly clear that both Nick and I were willing to take part in a second series. I was not making any unreasonable demands or pretending I wasn't interested. Margaret, being Margaret, reserved her decision, holding back so she could 'wait and see'. Wait and see what? I don't know!

As you would expect, my business acumen kicked in and I negotiated a new deal where the increased fee I received would be paid into my charitable foundation to pass on to worthy causes. I guess the increase must have been reflected in a reciprocal increase in the contract Talkback had with the BBC. I assume that, being sensible and knowing they had a hit on their hands, they didn't kick up too much of a stink as they probably recognised that Talkback had got away with murder on the fee I was paid for the first series.

But who was going to run the second series? Peter had gone, Tanya had gone; the only person left from the original team was Dan Adamson, who was given Peter's old job. Sanjay Singhal, a really nice polite chap, was seconded from the BBC, and Michael Jochnowitz and Mark Saben also came on board. Mark Saben would go on to remain on the team for quite a few series.

From my point of view, I was pleased that Dan was still there because during the course of the first series I had built a rapport with those involved, so at least Dan was a familiar face.

I got on very well with Sanjay, who had effectively taken over the role Dan had in the first series. A new production office had been rented in St James's and I spent quite a lot of time there in the early preparation stages with Dan and Sanjay, going through the tasks and taking a look at the candidates. For this series I had asked to have a little more input into candidate selection, because on the first series the fourteen people were just given to me as a fait accompli.

While I didn't have that much input in selecting the candidates, I did see the shortlist of around twenty-five people who had got through the auditions and had been narrowed down as the real contenders for the show. I didn't see any video clips of them; just their paperwork: CVs and photos along with comments about them from the production people. But at least there was something for me to look at this time and I felt consulted.

We had thousands of applications for the second series of *The Apprentice*. The BBC quite rightly insisted that people from all over Britain must have an opportunity to participate in the show and, on that basis, the locations for the auditions had to be dotted around the country so as to be fair and reasonable for people to get to. They took place at large hotels in Scotland, Manchester, Birmingham and two locations in London. The prospective candidates turned up in their thousands, and a group of production people put them through a very quick interview process. Of course, when you have so many people arriving for interviews, you cannot afford to have a half-hour discussion with each of them, and I guess it was the first impressions of these people that put them through to the next stage, where they were sent in to see the more senior people such as Dan and Sanjay for a second evaluation. Those who got through that went on to the third stage where they would be asked to say a few words to camera, and it would be these people who would go into the contenders' bowl, so to speak.

At the end of the whole process, after travelling all over the country, there were around two hundred people in the contenders' bowl. The production people would discuss these contenders at length, reviewing their CVs and the video clips that were taken, then finally whittle them down to the twenty-five who were ultimately presented to me on paper. In general, this very fair process has continued throughout the whole ten years of *The Apprentice*, although it has become a bit more sophisticated and I now get to see video clips of the last few selected candidates. More about that later.

The second series, as one would suspect, was a little easier as everyone seemed to know what they were doing and were all a bit more confident. We could afford to relax a bit and respond to things as I wanted to, rather than staying within the very rigid format. And it was this series where *The Apprentice* started to find its feet and hit its stride.

I spoke earlier about the time wasted filming stuff that never makes it into the finished show. One enormous waste of time that Sanjay wanted to add was to show clips of me in other business situations. He arranged for me to fly up to Manchester in my jet and waste a whole day at some boring seminar where I got up on stage and did a Q&A. The crew, as well as Sanjay and my PR guy David Fraser, joined me and had a wonderful time as you can imagine – when else would these guys ever get to go on an executive jet and be fed well? They filmed me getting on and off the bloody thing about six times until they got it right and filmed me inside reading the papers and working on my laptop – all great stuff, of course. In the interest of the show, wanting it to look super cool with great pictures of the plane, I went along with it all. At this point I should mention that the cost of this whole exercise with my plane was down to me! Naturally, the production team lapped it up – the hire of my plane, the crew and the airport fees were definitely not in their budget. However, after offering all that and wasting a whole day, you won't be surprised to hear the whole bloody lot was junked.

In Boardroom Zero of series two, I kicked off the whole thing with another of my welcoming speeches, based on what I'd picked up in the first series. It went something like this: 'You are not here to enhance some form of media career – this is a job working for me – so if you're thinking, gentlemen, of prancing around in your Calvin Kleins showing your three-piece suite bulging, you can forget about it. And similarly, ladies, flashing your hair back is not going to get you anywhere.' You should have seen the faces of the candidates. I heard Margaret grunt as she tried to hold back her laughter when the Calvin Klein bit came out.

A good example of the new flexibility we had for the second series came on the very first task. As before, I split the candidates

up into two teams, boys versus girls, and sent them off to Spital-
fields market to buy fruit and veg. The task was to buy the stuff
wholesale and sell it on to consumers at a profit. The boys went and
negotiated and bought a load of stock, while the girls took the
approach of asking if there was any free stuff – close to going off –
that they could take off the vendors' hands. When we looked at the
costs, the boys had spent over three hundred quid while the girls
had spent around forty. I was a bit uncomfortable when I heard
about this as there was some suggestion the girls had been batting
their eyelashes at the vendors in order to get this stuff for free.

The boys were up in arms as they had been the ones acting professionally while the girls' approach wasn't right and proper. But
irrespective of their complaints, I was informed that during the
task, project manager Ben Stanberry had instructed his whole team
to remain in one place, all standing around the stall, which was a
ridiculous idea for capitalising on the task in hand.

I told him how stupid this was. 'You were at Ridley Road
market amongst stallholders who have done this all their lives –
families who run stalls. Did you see any other stalls with seven
people standing around them, because I never have – they'd be
skint!'

The candidates are told not to mention they are doing *The
Apprentice* when they go out to see vendors or customers, but
simply to say they are recording a show for the BBC. These days, of
course, you'd have to be stupid not to realise what programme they
are filming when you see a load of young men or women running
around with camera crews following them. However, this was only
the second series and not so many people knew what was going on.

Females fluttering their eyelashes and flirting with male vendors has been a tactic used on a few occasions since, but another
phenomenon we've seen is that once traders realise they're going to
be on telly, they go into some strange modes. There is the 'I'm
going to act tough and not accept a deal because I don't want to be

seen to be legged-over' mode. There is the 'I've been in this business forty years, mate – don't tell me about this, that or the other' mode. Then there is the sympathetic mode, particularly to the girls, where they give in easily and show they are Mr or Mrs Nice Guy. We get some great sequences from these people, all of whom have to sign an agreement to be shown on TV as well as allow us to film in their premises. It should be noted, however, that these are *real* transactions. People might act in a more self-conscious manner when the cameras are there, but the deals done are real – it's not just cooked up for TV.

I recall giving the girls a hard time in the boardroom over this first task. 'From what I heard, you waylaid a vendor – more like *railroaded* him, never mind convinced him – massaging his shoulders. This is not business. I can't see any of my employees massaging the buyer of Dixons' shoulders.' (Dixons was one of my biggest customers in those days.)

I was determined to get to the bottom of this flirting lark, so after I'd heard the figures where, naturally, the girls' profit was higher, I did something I'd never done before. I told the girls they had five minutes to come up with a bloody good reason why I should allow them to win the task, then I left the boardroom to give them time to prepare their response. They did come up with a pretty good defence, as it goes, but the deciding factor for me was this: in the end, even if the girls *had* spent the same amount as the boys, they *still* would have won. Therefore, I decided that the fairest thing was to award the girls the win. It was a pretty exciting start to the series.

There were some interesting characters in this new bunch; one in particular, Jo Cameron, I noticed from the start. I clocked her in the boardroom after the first task when she almost burst into tears telling me what had gone on. As the weeks went by it became clearer and clearer that she was a very loud and opinionated sort of person. When I saw the first episode I couldn't believe it – she was jumping around and shouting like a total nutter the entire time. She drove her teammates round the bend. The problem with people like her is that when they actually do something sensible, everyone is so sick and tired of them that they take no bloody notice.

I saw this happen with Jo, for example, when they were set the task of coming up with a calendar for Great Ormond Street Hospital. Her team decided to design one around kittens. Jo was one of the only people to point out that it was a stupid idea that had naff all to do with the charity, but no one listened. She also cried a lot, which didn't endear her too much to the rest of them.

Jo was the first example of a candidate who tried to do my job for me in the boardroom. Once, when she was in the last three in the boardroom, she asked, 'To clarify, are we judging people on their performance in this task or all tasks?'

I get really annoyed at people who try to tell me about other candidates' performances in earlier parts of the process, so I told her in no uncertain terms, 'That is none of your business, quite frankly. *I'm* the one dishing out the job here so don't you start pontificating about other people's performances in other tasks – you're responsible for this task and your job is to tell me who didn't perform on this task. Don't start drifting on to other things because I'm not going to debate that with you.'

In weighing up whether to fire her or not, I recall saying to her, 'You *do* have this determination and this forthrightness; and you *do* have qualities of selling and buying . . . But I don't know if you're just a bloody nutter! That's the problem, because I love people with spirit, but I don't want to be bombarded with a kind of machine-gun rat-a-tat-tat.' This girl did not stop talking.

One of the tasks was to sell second-hand cars from a car lot. Jo claimed that in her day job she was once a director trainer at MG Rover. However, she performed so poorly on this task that she was fired. She begged me three times to reconsider – she would not leave the boardroom! Eventually she left and I recall saying to Margaret and Nick, 'She was at MG Rover training *directors* on how to make a profit? No wonder they went bloody skint!'

It wasn't just Jo who got tearful. I remember thinking when I watched the beginning of series two that I'd never seen such an emotional bunch. Within the first couple of episodes it seemed like half of them had blubbed – men and women – though mostly they held it together in the boardroom. One stand-out moment in the calendar task involved a rather professional and quite posh candidate, Nargis Ara, who was a pharmacist by profession. She was like a fish out of water when she took on the role of pitching her calendar to the buyers and started to drone on. One of the buyers, obviously bored, asked a question, to which Nargis had what was the nearest thing to a Margaret moment. 'Do you mind, I haven't finished yet!' From what I heard from Nick, it was a most embarrassing situation. He said he felt like hiding under the table.

Another stand-out moment was when I set the task to promote a new concierge service to make it easy for customers to hire corporate jets. Once again my naivety in offering up expensive props like two jets as well as arranging for filming to take place where security was high – near the runway at Stansted airport – was accepted with open arms from the production people. They must have thought: 'This Sugar geezer is a right schmuck – let's take it while we can.' It wasn't until I realised the Manchester event had been junked that I got the plot, and it was the last time Sir Alan or Lord Sugar offered any freebies. From then on, when the creative geniuses suggested we do some shots of my plane, or on a yacht, or if they wanted to spend a few days filming my car driving around London, my reply was, 'Sure. If you want the plane to fly to Manchester, that will be around twenty thousand pounds.' And the same when I quoted them the cost of the yacht, car, etc. That shut them up very quickly.

For this particular task, the candidates had to hire actors to make a promotional video. One of the actors was filmed lying back in an executive chair on the plane. He was told to portray a look of satisfaction; of unashamed luxury. As it turned out, the way he was rubbing his hand along his leg at the side of the chair together with his ecstatic facial expression looked more like he was in a dodgy massage parlour! It was so funny and made great telly.

However, the video the losing team made was pathetic; it didn't focus on the concierge side of the task. In the boardroom I was so frustrated they hadn't followed my instructions about what the video needed to concentrate on that I angrily said, 'Do me a favour, folks, watch my mouth – A, B, C, D, E. Am I speaking English? Yes? Good, because for a minute there at Stansted I thought I might have been speaking Russian.'

I turned to the other team. 'As for your video, when Nick gave me a copy of the tape I thought he'd mixed it up with one from his collection – it looked like some 1970s porno, *Debbie Does Dallas*!' A cheeky joke, of course. Nick's tapes are all about the history of farm tractors.

That task really showed up some of the candidates' failings. One of the chaps, Mani Sandher, had failed to communicate the brief properly to the rest of his team. By contrast, a couple of weeks earlier he had received praise from his teammates as being reliable; in fact, they referred to him as 'the anchor'. However, on this task they all turned on him. In the boardroom I commented, 'Two weeks ago people were saying you were the anchor. Funny how things can change in that time – you seem to have gone from anchor to wanker!'

The biggest character in that series was Syed Ahmed. He was the type of person the viewers love to hate, and he really lived up to that image. He was forever at the root of all sorts of arguments. He was also responsible for one of the most unbelievable cock-ups I've ever seen during my ten years on the show. I think it was the first time I just sat there in disbelief when I heard what had happened.

The task was to set up a food stall at the Thames Festival on the South Bank, an event which attracted half a million people. Alexa Tilley led one of the teams and one of her teammates was a fellow called Ansell Henry. When they all got back to the boardroom after the task, I simply couldn't resist saying to him, 'Ansell, tell me about Gretel – was she a good team leader?'

Alexa had decided they were going to make pizzas, not a bad idea for that crowd. But the cock-up came when her teammate Syed had to order the ingredients they needed. The team had already decided they were going to aim to sell five hundred pizzas, which would be cut into five thousand portions. This was the first mistake as it was obviously a ridiculously high number. There was absolutely no way they were ever going to be able to sell that many. In fact, when they got into the boardroom it was pointed out that to achieve this, they would have had to sell one portion every nine seconds! I remember saying to them, 'If you can do that, you don't need a job with me.'

But that wasn't the worst of it. Having decided to try and make five hundred pizzas, Syed put out an order for ingredients. He ordered one hundred whole chickens for the pizza toppings! When these things showed up they were absolutely enormous. Forget having one stall on the South Bank; they could have opened a branch of KFC they had so much stock.

One thing that never fails to amaze me is how, under pressure, these clever people can completely lose their heads and end up making mistakes. It just beggars belief. In the end, they only got round to making ninety pizzas, which effectively meant they had one chicken per pizza! It was totally ridiculous.

That was the first time a team ever came into the boardroom having made a loss from the seed money I had given them to fund the task. I was absolutely furious. Any other week, Syed would have been fired without a doubt. In fact, I told him that I considered him one hundred per cent responsible for this failure. However, he was lucky because the project manager, Alexa, though she was a very nice person, was just beyond useless and couldn't have been less well suited to me for my business, so she had to go. I recall telling her, 'This is not a holiday camp or a college of further education where dummkopfs come to learn to make mistakes – you're supposed to be one of the brightest entrepreneurs in the country!' I think I called her a lightweight before I fired her and it was one of the easiest decisions I'd had to make. Funnily enough, Alexa turned out to be the cousin of Matt Lucas from *Little Britain*. I found this out when I was sitting near him at a later BAFTA awards ceremony. Matt mentioned it to me and he thought it was quite funny.

Syed got a real grilling from me in the boardroom. He still tried to argue his case over the hundred chickens. 'Sir Alan, I am a born fighter,' he said. I responded, 'Well, you're not a born manufacturer.'

I asked him, 'Why shouldn't I fire you?'

'Because I'm a winner, Sir Alan.'

'You're not a bloody winner – you lost!'

Personally, I wanted to fire all three of them, but in the end it had to be Alexa who went. Syed was very relieved when I told him and the other remaining candidate to go back to the house. He remained seated and waffled on about how he was so sorry and it wouldn't happen again, blah, blah, blah. I just raised my head, looked at him and said, 'Bye bye.'

Before he left the boardroom he said, 'Thank you for the opportunity.'

'Cheeky bastard,' I said to Nick and Margaret after he'd gone.

I had cause to pull Syed up again on a task I'd set in selling to the trade in week eight. But in this case my comment to him was a great example of why I do *The Apprentice* and why I see it as a learning tool for some viewers. It all centred around the fact that

This captures the atmosphere after filming the first-ever boardroom. The candidates had no idea what they were letting themselves in for.

Here I'm with Nick and Margaret, modelling the bowler hat from the discount-buying task (one of my favourites) in the first series. Peter Moore kept the hat and produced it at the ten-year anniversary party, which is when this was taken.

RIGHT: All the candidates for the first series of *Junior Apprentice*. The winner Arjun Rajyagor is seated at the front on the right.

BELOW: Behind the scenes of *The Apprentice* is a talented production team.

BELOW: On the famous *EastEnders* set, filming a sketch for *Children In Need*.

ABOVE: After getting a bee in my bonnet and complaining to the BBC about product placement in *EastEnders*, imagine my embarrassment when my autobiography appeared in a scene.

Another present from Mark Saben – a nodding dog to
remind me of Tom the nodding candidate!

Launching the Stylfile with Tom Pellereau,
winner of series seven and my new business partner.

Syed had got back late and had missed the deadline I set. I said, 'I've got a problem with you lot coming back late.'

Syed replied, 'I'd do it again. I went for the sale – there was an accident on the way . . .'

'That's beside the point. You were late – there will have to be a penalty.'

The cheeky sod said, 'That's your opinion.'

'It's not my opinion; it's reality! Let me give you an example of something in the *real* world that happened to me. My company was trying to do a very big deal on a property owned by the government. We were told we had to have the tender in by 5 o'clock, and what happened was that some bloody motorbike rider decided to stop and have a cup of coffee in Starbucks and delivered the envelope at 5.15 – and we didn't get the deal. My people had spent weeks and weeks on due diligence, which all went down the drain. Needless to say we don't use that courier firm any more and the motorbike rider was on his bike.'

In the end I gave his team a penalty of twenty-five per cent.

Meanwhile, Nick and Margaret started to play more of a key role in this series. I suppose they were gaining confidence and began to speak up more when they saw candidates doing stupid things or if they thought certain candidates needed a push in the boardroom. On one particular occasion, instead of actually getting on with the task in hand, one of the teams spent hours discussing how to brainstorm their strategy. You could see Margaret getting more and more exasperated and her face was a total picture. In the end she just couldn't help but interrupt and point out what a ridiculous waste of time it had all been. It was hilarious.

Another of the candidates, Paul Tulip, was quite an arrogant fellow. Some people felt that he'd got through the process on luck, but in hindsight he was actually one of the brightest in this group. He got to the penultimate programme where my advisors interviewed the last four candidates. I think it was Paul Kemsley who turned me off him by telling me, 'Alan, this guy is a two-bob car salesman that you could find if you advertised in the *Evening Standard*.' It was quite a damning assessment. Bordan, who was slightly in awe of Paul Kemsley at the time, added his little bit of VAT, endorsing the verdict on Paul Tulip, whom I let go based on what Kemsley and Bordan had said.

To give you an indication of how confident Paul Tulip was, part of the process the candidates had to adhere to was to bring their packed suitcase to the boardroom every time they reported there after a task; if any of them were fired, they had to be ready to leave there and then with their belongings. Paul was so confident of his progress that he never packed his suitcase for any of the episodes! I guess he was nearly right because he got through to the penultimate stage.

People often ask me whether I think I fired the wrong person. Do I think I made a mistake? Well, on this particular occasion, I do think that Kemsley's and Bordan's comments lost me a reasonable contender.

But rising to the top of the pile as the process neared its end were Ruth Badger and Michelle Dewberry, both of whom made the final. Ruth, now more commonly known as The Badger, was a very shrewd lady. She sailed through most of the tasks, and in many cases her individual prowess was the reason her team won. The nearest she got to being fired was on the cruise task where she was partnered by Syed. Now Syed was a rather good-looking chap; a bit of a charmer and a great talker. When I watched the episodes afterwards, I saw how he could charm the birds off the trees. On many occasions he convinced people outside the process, such as members of the public, or buyers or sellers, to fall for his chirpy-chappy approach. But inside the process, with the other candidates, he was confrontational and argumentative. On a number of occasions there was a hell of a row between him and Michelle Dewberry. I believe that after *The Apprentice* had finished, Michelle and Syed had some kind of romantic relationship, which didn't last long. No surprise there!

After the filming of the final episode, the winner in my head was Michelle. Hers was a rags-to-riches story. She had started off as a checkout girl in a supermarket in Hull and had made her way up the ladder in business working for a telecommunications company. I spoke to her ex-boss, just to find out what he thought of her, and the report was very positive. She seemed a very efficient and bright lady who could be set a task and left to get on with it.

Nick and Margaret had commented to me that Michelle was a bit of a cold fish. I told them that I'm not exactly warm as toast myself.

So I had made my decision but, of course, I couldn't tell the winner the good news yet. Ruth went to Viglen for the six-month waiting period. I have to say that of all the people sent to Viglen under the watchful eye of the very nervous and demanding Bordan, she got the best report. He told me she was doing quite well; that she was a nice, hard-working girl.

Michelle came to Amstrad headquarters at Brentwood and shared an office with the previous year's winner, Tim Campbell. She was set a task by me to look into the then fashionable recycling business. Health and safety and EU regulations had demanded that it was now the manufacturers' responsibility to ensure that old equipment such as computers, monitors and TVs were disposed of in an environmentally friendly fashion. Since those times, a big industry has sprung up and there are companies who specialise in dealing with these issues, but these were early days in industrial recycling, and it transpired that the physical work that had to be done in order to strip down a piece of equipment was an enormous, capital-intensive task. Nevertheless, Michelle beavered away, working on the project. Ultimately, her six months' work would enable me to decide whether to get into this business or not.

Because Michelle and Ruth both had self-contained tasks, there was nothing to alienate any of the other Amstrad or Viglen employees. The staff at both companies obviously knew who they were, but like everyone else they had no idea who the winner was nor which of the girls was going to encroach upon their territory. Hence, the 'I've got the hump over the hundred thousand pounds' syndrome hadn't kicked in. Yet.

I visited Viglen's headquarters every so often in my general day-to-day business and, on one occasion, Ruth called me aside. She asked me whether, if she *were* to win, there was any way I could accommodate her working in Manchester where she and her partner lived. She told me she didn't fancy a job in London. This came as a bit of a shock to me because part of the application for *The Apprentice* spells out that the candidate who is successful in getting a job with Sir Alan Sugar has to be prepared to move to work in one of my companies, which, as everyone knew, were in London. I reminded her of this and pointed out to her that neither Viglen nor Amstrad have offices in Manchester. I was taken aback to find that I had someone who'd gone all the way through this gruelling process only to tell me, a couple of weeks away from the final, that she didn't really want to work in London. However, surprising as this was, it was all academic because, in my head, Michelle was the winner.

Another aggravation was that the nasty media had got busy tracking down Michelle's family and there were some horrible articles about her father and sister. In fact, it was because of these negative articles that in future years I decided that the talk I have with the finalists – where I warn them about hidden skeletons – was to be an imperative part of the procedure for me. These spiteful articles convinced me that if I'd have had that conversation with

Michelle, she could have told me beforehand what was likely to come out, and no doubt we could have fended it off.

Once again it came to that dreaded time when I had to reveal to the finalists who the winner was going to be. I met for lunch with Ruth and Michelle as well as Dan Adamson and told them my decision. Obviously Ruth was disappointed at not being the winner.

The second series was the first time that the programme *You're Fired* was commissioned. *You're Fired* was a thirty-minute show on BBC3 that aired straight after every episode of *The Apprentice*. Each week, the person who was fired came on to this show for an after-math discussion, hosted by the brilliant Adrian Chiles, accompanied by a varying panel of so-called experts who talked about the demise of the fired candidate.

It was an excellent programme and one which I was very proud of. It had the balance of a common-sense business message and some very dry Adrian Chiles humour, complemented by contributions from the occasional comedian they had on the panel.

This programme, which was masterminded by Sally Dixon, was in some ways a more difficult show to produce than the main pro-gramme. This is because *The Apprentice* itself has about a hundred and fifty hours of film per episode which takes several months in the editing suite to trim down to a one-hour programme; however, Sally and her team had to trawl through that same footage to show some of the things that had not previously been seen. Then it had to be arranged that the *You're Fired* candidate, who was actually fired many weeks before, was there at the recording. The recording normally took place in front of a live audience on the Sunday or Monday prior to the Wednesday broadcast of *The Apprentice*. So Sally and her team had to look at the hundred and fifty hours of rushes, pick some incidents that she wanted to show in this pro-gramme, compile some of the highlights (or lowlights) of the candidate in question, show some examples of how the candidate got things wrong or some of their confrontations with other candidates, as well as give Adrian a kind of script to work to, in order to produce an exciting thirty-minute aftershow.

Obviously the recording of *You're Fired* takes much longer than thirty minutes. In fact, I believe it takes about two and a half hours from when the audience arrives to the end. First, they watch that week's episode and see who gets fired; then the fired candidate comes on to the stage and is interviewed by Adrian and the panel.

Now consider this: when all that has been filmed, it has to be rushed off to a special editing suite where they *don't* have the luxury of months to polish it – they have to get it ready for broadcast on Wednesday at ten o'clock. A completely different beast, and a completely different method of producing a TV programme.

From what I understood, the BBC were delighted with both the second series of *The Apprentice* and the new programme, *You're Fired* – an hour and a half's worth of entertainment on BBC2 and BBC3 which, with respect, doesn't normally attract much of an audience. But we had record-breaking figures for BBC2 with something like three or four million viewers watching the main programme, followed by unprecedented viewing figures for BBC3.

An interesting element of *You're Fired*, which I believe was Sally's idea, was to give the audience some cards: green for hired, red for fired. Towards the end of the show, Adrian would invite the audience to give their opinion on whether or not they felt Sir Alan had made the right decision by holding up their cards. On most occasions in the second series I think the audience was with me. It was a clever move and you would normally see a sea of red cards and a few green cards. As you'd imagine, the green cards tended to be those of the friends and family of the fired candidate.

There were some occasions in that second series where the audience didn't agree with me, and neither did the three panellists assisting Adrian. But then again, some of the panellists were comedians rather than business people. They tended to make an emotional decision and say that Sir Alan was wrong because they *liked* the person, while ignoring the actual reason I fired them.

I signed up, as part of my contract, to contribute to this after-show, which meant some additional work for me. I would have to do some extra filming at the end of every boardroom, summarising why I got rid of that particular candidate. Doing this work, as well as having to do virtually the same interview in the car afterwards (for the main show), was very, very tiring. It was mentally exhausting having to collate in my head all the facts about what this candidate had done wrong and that candidate had done right in order for me to make the decision.

Imagine, when everyone has gone from the boardroom, they reset the cameras again and we film this bit, which was specifically for use in *You're Fired*. And then I had to leave, have the car rigged up, get in and do exactly the same thing all over again for use in *The Apprentice*. Extremely tiring mentally, but one could understand that the production people were trying to save costs as all the camera crew were still there and they didn't want to arrange to record me at a later time.

Regrettably, things didn't work out too well with Michelle Dewberry. She was a very enthusiastic employee and was stationed at Viglen – as Viglen was the company which had the more urgent requirement on recycling issues. She worked very efficiently and very fast, and was forever saying, 'Right, I've done that; what do you want me to do next?'

Eventually, it became clear that the project she was working on would have required us to invest in a massive factory with a lot of expensive capital equipment. We concluded that it was not viable and that we should use the resources of an external company to deal with our recycling.

Hence, we needed to redefine a role for Michelle. Bordan came up with a few other ideas, but I think Michelle hoped that winning *The Apprentice* would bring her greater personal rewards than just a job. I remember James Herring telling me that Michelle had phoned him lots of times asking when she was going to be invited to parties or presentations or television events. James tactfully explained to her, 'Well, no one is actually asking for you.' I think Michelle felt that she was going to be far more sought after by the media than she was at the time.

She came to see me a few months after taking up the job and tendered her resignation. Obviously this was a brave thing to do because she was earning £100,000 a year! One would have thought she'd be better off sticking with the job and leaving at the end. However, she left midstream and went on to pursue a project with a business partner of hers.

Today we see her from time to time commenting on the newspapers and on Sky TV. She's also written quite a few articles on enterprise and encouraging the young, using herself as a glowing example of how you can start off as a checkout girl from Hull, and go on to succeed in life.

Interestingly enough, on the odd occasion when someone has a gripe at me about *The Apprentice* and the media are looking to get hold of a story about somebody aggrieved by Sir Alan or Lord Sugar, Michelle often seems to be their first port of call. They think she will spill the beans and slag me off. I will go on to write about one winner, Stella English, and the bitter employment tribunal case, and once again the media drove Michelle mad to get some dirt on me and *The Apprentice* process. However, Michelle is very professional and honourable to me and won't have anything to do with the gutter press. She has always had the courtesy to call me and tell me they are driving her nuts and that she's told them to clear off.

*

The second series was even more of a success than the first. In BBC2 terms its ratings were astronomical, culminating in a record 5.7 million viewers tuning in to see the final. Like the first series, the second series was also nominated for a BAFTA. As I said earlier, this BAFTA thing was still niggling me from last year, the reason being: the TV world had gone nuts about *The Apprentice* and, not wishing to sound like a big-head, while the format and the idea of the elimination process is great, the reality was that *I* was the character who created the drama and the conflicts in the boardroom, which in turn got the candidates going, and this made the whole thing interesting and great television. So it *did* niggle.

9

'WHAT IS IT WITH THESE PEOPLE?'

Working with celebrities on *Comic Relief*
and *Sport Relief*

With *The Apprentice* now on everyone's radar at the BBC, I was contacted by Jana Bennett, Head of Television, who asked if I would be interested in doing a mini-*Apprentice* where the candidates would be her and her contemporaries at ITV, Channel 4, Channel 5, etc., for some kind of industry bash that takes place every year in Edinburgh. It would be a bit of a wind-up programme made on the cheap, just for showing at this industry bash, because *The Apprentice* was The Hot Item. I would set the five Heads of Television a mini-task, they would go and perform it, then they'd come back and I would interrogate them in the boardroom, and in the end I would fire one of them.

It sounded a bit of fun to me, so I agreed. Patrick Uden organised the filming and editing, though it wasn't made in the same painstaking manner as the original programme because it was just a spoof. Nevertheless, it goes to show how *The Apprentice* had become so popular that it was now going to be a feature of this industry bash spanning many TV networks. For the record, the bloke from Channel 4 was fired.

For some reason or other, the wannabe tough-guy lawyer also got herself involved. As I say, people like to be associated with success stories in the world of television. Suddenly they were all crawling out from under the rocks wanting to be part of this great phenomenon.

More significantly, the success of *The Apprentice* led to us being asked to take part in *Comic Relief* and *Sport Relief* – very worthy charities. These events normally play out on a Friday evening in March for seven or eight hours and raise millions of pounds for very good causes.

In autumn 2006 Lorraine Heggessey informed me that the *Comic Relief* team (headed up by Emma Freud and her partner, Richard Curtis) had asked if they could do a version of *The Apprentice* where the candidates would be well-known celebrities and I would put them through their paces on a business task. In the same way as the 'civilian' version, one of them would be fired. This sounded like a lot of fun, so Nick, Margaret and I agreed to do it. It would be recorded in the boardroom shortly after the third series of *The Apprentice* was finished. Again, Lorraine asked Patrick Uden to be the lead on this production.

News had got round that *Comic Relief Does The Apprentice* was about to be recorded and there was a rush of celebrities who wanted to get on to this excellent new show. I say a rush of celebrities, because while they were all prepared to give up their time for the charity, some of them really wanted to relaunch their careers and would do just about anything to get back on television. I won't say that all of them in this first *Comic Relief* show were in that category, but there were one or two.

When the first series of *The Apprentice* was being aired, Piers Morgan called me one day from his car while his sons were listening in on the speakerphone. They were in awe of *The Apprentice* and Piers had told them that he actually knew Sir Alan Sugar. So while he was driving along, he asked me to say hello to his sons, which of course I did. When the news got out that there was going to be a *Comic Relief Does The Apprentice* with celebrities, Piers rang me and asked whether I could do him a favour and make sure he was one of the celebrities in it.

I had known Piers for quite a few years in his capacity as editor of the *Daily Mirror*, but he had recently been fired for the famous front-page story he did with the picture of the soldier urinating on an Iraqi. The picture turned out to be fake and in the end Piers got the sack. To be frank, he called me up and asked me if it would be possible for him to be in this programme in order to help relaunch his career.

To its credit, I have to say that the *Daily Mirror* was the newspaper that gave me the greatest support during the football nightmare period. This had a lot to do with a journalist by the name of Harry Harris, but more, I guess, to do with the editor who, as an Arsenal supporter, was loving every moment of the football scandals at Spurs and my attempts to sort out the mess there. As an example of his support, during my bitter court case with the *Daily Mail*, I remembered various nasty articles they had previously written about me, which I wanted to show the court. This was long before the days of the internet and Google, so I needed to dive into the press-cutting archives to find these articles. I would call Piers, on some occasions waking him up at six in the morning. He probably thought someone was phoning him up with a scoop, but instead he got me asking him to do me a favour. The *Mirror* were able to find archive material from all newspapers, and within minutes he'd be on the fax machine sending me through exactly what I was looking for. So I was happy to put him forward as one of the candidates on this celebrity *Apprentice*. It's true, he was a mate of mine, but he also had a reasonable sense of humour and a thick skin, so I imagined he'd be able to get on quite well in my boardroom.

Another friend I put forward was Maureen Lipman, the famous actress. When I first told her I was going to appear in a television programme, she gave me lots of advice. We went out to dinner one night with some mutual friends and she said that I should 'be very careful of these TV people'. I remember her mentioning something called the rushes. 'What you need to do, Alan, is to insist upon seeing the rushes.'

I didn't know what she was talking about at the time. Now that I know what the rushes are, I can see the point she was making – the programme would be heavily edited and I should have some control over the edit. How true were those words?

I asked Maureen whether she would like to join in with this *Comic Relief Does The Apprentice* and she, too, accepted. Like Piers Morgan, I think she also felt it would be a little bit of a boost for her TV career.

In addition to Piers, we also got Danny Baker, Alastair Campbell, Ross Kemp and Rupert Everett to form a boys' team. And joining Maureen Lipman on the girls' team were Jo Brand, Cheryl Cole, Trinny Woodall (of Trinny and Susannah fame) and a bright young businesswoman by the name of Karren Brady. When I invited her to join the girls' team she told me she was very excited and thought it would be fun and a good way of raising money for charity.

As usual on *The Apprentice*, the celebrities convened in the reception outside the boardroom. Nick and Margaret were in position in the boardroom and the celebrities were called in and sat down. I made my usual grand entrance then sat down and looked along the line of faces, peering into their eyes the way I normally do to get a bit of tension going. Some of them were smiling at me. I didn't return their smiles. In that twenty seconds of glaring, Morgan piped up, 'Come on, let's get on with this. We've got no time to waste here.'

I turned to him and said, 'Shut it, Morgan. Be quiet.'

I made my speech to them, telling them what the task was about. It was a brilliant task thought up by Patrick Uden where the candidates would run a funfair which would raise money for the charity. More about that later, but what I'm going to admit to now is the worst boardroom speech I've ever made in all my years on television. I made the fatal error of trying to be a comedian in front of all these pros. I was cracking jokes that went down like the biggest lead balloons you have ever seen. It was cringingly embarrassing and you could see the awkward looks on their faces and hear the polite chuckles at some of my terrible lines.

One of my big clangers was trying to make a joke to Rupert Everett, purposely confusing him with Hugh Grant. I came out with things like, 'Ah yes, I know you . . . you're that fellow from *Four Weddings and a Funeral*, right? How's Liz Hurley then?' Even as I recount this now I want the ground to swallow me up – again!

I made Ross Kemp furious by suggesting that the tough-guy show he was doing at the time was a bit fake because off camera he had about ten security guards around him. He, too, was not a happy camper and did not appreciate my humour.

As these jokes bombed, I could see Maureen cringing and shaking her head. The only saving grace was that it was a recorded session. When I realised very quickly that I was making a double-barrelled idiot of myself – a bit like a Piers Morgan clone – I kind of pulled myself together, got into businesslike mode and carried on explaining the task. To be honest, I couldn't get them out the door quick enough.

The funfair was set up on the parade ground of the Old Royal Army Medical Corps headquarters next to the Tate Gallery on the Embankment. There were merry-go-rounds, coconut shies and all that sort of thing. The first job for the girls' and boys' teams was to invite as many of their celebrity friends as they could get to come along and to get some donations out of them. (Looking back, I'm trying to remember the logic of what blagging donations out of rich and influential friends has to do with a funfair, and I have to admit I still have no idea!) Nevertheless, the gist was: they invited these celebrities along who participated in the events and donated certain items. For instance, Karren Brady got Sir Philip Green to donate something substantial and Trinny managed to get a large donation from a client of hers. Piers Morgan had the audacity to get on to David Dein, the then Chief Executive of Arsenal, and ask *him* to donate something to this charitable event – an event being run by the ex-boss of Dein's arch-enemy, Spurs! Having said that, it was all done in good spirit and David, whom I knew quite well at the time, contributed handsomely. The event attracted a lot of celebrities. Mick Hucknall of Simply Red manned the coconut shy, McFly turned up en masse, Gary Barlow was there, as was Clement Freud!

Now Patrick Uden is a very nice fellow and a very experienced chap in the TV industry. However, he had his own views on the way that this programme should roll out. To put it bluntly, he didn't want me to feature in it much at all – I would just be seen as some person asking a couple of questions in the boardroom, with the real entertainment coming from the candidates themselves.

At first I didn't know about Patrick's Big Idea, but my suspicions were aroused when I said I would like to come along on the evening of this event, just to watch it in real time. Patrick said, 'No, I don't think we need you there.'

I said, 'Well, I'm sorry, it is my event and I'm coming.'

'No, really, Sir Alan, it might spoil the thing. Seeing you might mess up how the candidates act . . . There's supposed to be an element of surprise in the boardroom . . .'

'Patrick, cut the crap. I'm coming, okay? I'm not asking you to film me doing anything; I just want to observe it myself, first hand.'

Apart from doing this for charity, it was quite an exciting thing to be involved in, and I just wanted to watch the thing unfold on the night. I don't think there was anything wrong with that. Patrick reluctantly agreed and I went along.

After he edited the show and I saw the proposed broadcast he had prepared, we started to have some major disagreements. He had cut out quite a lot of my dialogue. I complained to him, at first in a reasonable fashion, saying that the programme didn't make sense in the way it was edited – it was, after all, a business programme. However, he was digging his heels in and he had this view that the less Sugar in this programme, the better – 'It's all about the celebrities.'

'Who told you that, Patrick?' I asked. 'Who told you that? You're making this up yourself; that isn't what you've been told to do. This is my programme and I've been asked to kindly do this on behalf of the charity, which I've agreed to do, and you're trying to tell me that it's nothing to do with me; it's all to do with the celebrities? Well, sorry, Patrick, I don't agree with you, and I'm going to talk to Lorraine Heggessey about this and have it out with her.'

I had some very serious discussions with Lorraine about it which kind of put her on the spot a little – in a rather awkward position between me and Patrick, who was effectively her employee. She'd given him the job to do and he, being a member of the creative-genius society, was beyond reproach, as one must never dare encroach upon their creativity – that would be worse than not paying their salary into the bank. The talent, in fact, is supposed to be the stooge and should most certainly not have any input at all. This was like a red rag to a bull. Loads of excuses were being thrown in my face, like, 'Actually, the edit is under the control of Emma Freud and Richard Curtis – it's really not our programme; it's their programme. They're the ones who have control of the edit.' (In fact, the truth was: the BBC controlled the edit.)

'Okay, if that's the case, let me speak to them because this is not right. Nick, Margaret and I didn't put our time and effort into this just to be seen sitting there like three tailors' dummies doing nothing, so let me talk to them.'

Well, all those excuses and explanations from Patrick and Lorraine turned out to be a bit of BS, because when I finally managed to get hold of Emma she was very apologetic indeed. She said she was very upset that I was upset and wanted to stress that she was so thankful that Nick, Margaret and I had contributed our valuable time to this wonderful cause.

'Don't worry,' she said, 'it's going to be great. Leave it with me, it will be sorted out. You can be sure that whatever you need to put back in will be put back in.'

These were typical luvvies' words because it was not as simple as that; the BBC and Talkback still had control. There was lots of toing and froing over the edit, and eventually we came up with a reasonable compromise. However, Patrick was not at all happy because someone had stepped on his territory. It was not a case of Nick, Margaret and I wanting to seek more glory in a charity show; it was simply that in my opinion Patrick got it wrong in wanting to focus solely on the celebrities. He forgot the principle that it was *Comic Relief Does The Apprentice* and, like it or not, *The Apprentice* has the dynamic trio in it. In his first cut he may as well have had cartoon replicas of us in the film.

I have to say that it's not in my nature to make threats. I see it as tantamount to blackmail to say 'If you don't do this, then I won't be doing it any more.' I never resorted to that kind of stuff, but believe me it was getting close to that because this was absolutely outrageous. We had just worked for many weeks on the original series, then we were asked to hold on and give another week of our valuable time for this. Nick, Margaret and I were very tired from the gruelling process of recording series three, and while we were happy to do this extra bit for a great charity, one must understand that when you put in all this hard work, then you watch it and see hardly anything from us three, it's really demoralising. But, in the end, we got there. The thing went out and it was a great success.

On the show, Piers – being Piers – was being objectionable to everyone. He was in charge of the stall where somebody that people dislike goes into the stocks and everyone throws wet sponges at them. I imagine he made a fortune when it was his turn to be the victim! He, of course, immediately clocked me and asked whether I'd take a turn in the stocks. I told him to get lost. Some of the other celebrities running other stalls saw me there and also asked me whether I would like to participate, which I graciously declined.

Cheryl Cole had pulled in a few celebrities. Apart from inviting her then husband Ashley Cole, who came with Chelsea captain John Terry, she also invited a gentleman by the name of Mr Simon Cowell. He saw me and obviously knew who I was, because by then you'd have had to be living in Siberia or on the moon not to know *The Apprentice*. Yet I felt that he deliberately avoided me; almost as if he didn't want to acknowledge my importance there at the time. He may have said a quick hello, but he was pretty cold towards me. We all know now, of course, that Simon believes he is God Almighty and it has to be All About Simon, so I'm guessing that the leopard's spots were already forming back then.

The following day, the candidates reconvened in the board-room. This time I realised that I shouldn't try to be smart with any more of my lead-balloon jokes – I would just be myself, which is what I should have done in the beginning. I remember walking in and saying to them, 'I have heard that collectively we have raised a hell of a lot of money for charity, so well done. I will go through the details in a moment, but I can tell you right now that it's several hundred thousand pounds. It's not very often you see this smile on my face – it pretty much coincides with Halley's Comet.' That broke the ice at the start of the boardroom scene, but soon after I continued, Jo Brand interrupted and said, 'Sir Alan, I've brought some gifts along for you. Here's a Kit Kat bar for Mr Hewer, here's a cigar for you, and here's something for Margaret.'

It kind of threw me a little. I guess it was meant to be funny but it didn't actually go down too well at the time. I tried to make it amusing by saying that while it was a very nice gesture, until I found out who the winner of the task was, it could be tantamount to bribery, which would not be correct in the eyes of the BBC. Obviously a joke, or another lead balloon, whichever way you want to look at it.

Karren Brady was the project manager for the girls' team, and being a businesswoman, she came in as the winner. In fact, when all the celebs were first assembled in the boardroom to receive my opening speech and the briefing for the task, I pointed out to them that Karren was the only businessperson in the group and that she had the most to lose. At that point, she told me, she thought, 'What the bloody hell have I done?' Luckily, she won by a huge margin so, as I pointed out to her, her reputation was intact. To this day she always says that she's the only person in the history of *The Apprentice* who has sat on both sides of the table.

The boys' team suffered a mini-disaster when Rupert Everett pulled out. I don't know whether it was because I insulted him by 'confusing' him with Hugh Grant, though I heard it was nothing to do with that. In fact, I was told that he just doesn't do this type of thing – he's a serious actor and he couldn't adapt to the ad-lib way in which the boardroom and indeed the whole process played out. He was used to dealing with a script; learning his lines and doing retakes on camera and all that stuff. On top of that, he couldn't pull in any celebrities to get money from, so he decided to quit.

Piers kicked up a stink about being a man down, so partway through the process we had to find a replacement. It was a bit late to try and find a professional who would drop everything and give up their valuable time for free, but then Margaret came up with the inspired idea of getting hold of Tim Campbell, the winner of the first *Apprentice*, and bringing him in. Tim readily agreed to do it to help me out and became, as one would expect, one of the better candidates on the boys' team, albeit they lost in the end.

After I grilled the losing team, it was inevitable that Piers would be fired, not only for the mistakes he made in the task and the manner in which he led his team, but also for his disruptive behaviour. He was having constant blow-ups with Cheryl Cole in the boardroom. Cheryl was married to Ashley Cole, who had left Piers's beloved Arsenal to join Chelsea, and Piers continually harassed her on this subject. At one point, she screamed across the room, 'Will you shut up about my husband, Piers!'

On top of this, he had a flaming row with Trinny, who had caught him trying to pinch some of her documentation at the hotel where they ran their team offices organising the task. He also kidnapped the girls' team's chef and had a fight with Trinny when she came to reclaim the chef from the boys' suite. The fight ended when she stabbed Piers in the hand with a biro. Piers was a complete and utter brat, no question about it, and he had to go. To be fair, he played along brilliantly and it made a great show.

I remind him to this day that I launched his television career, something he finds very, very difficult to admit. Similarly, I guess that *Comic Relief Does The Apprentice* also launched Cheryl Cole in a TV role other than as a member of a pop group. And as we know, she went on to be part of the judging panel on Simon Cowell's *X Factor*. On *The Graham Norton Show* she admitted that being in the celebrity *Apprentice* was how she met Simon Cowell, which led to her success in show business. She explained how at the funfair she got his number and called him, telling him he needed to get to the event and donate some money and, by the way, he should also be aware that their phone conversation was being filmed and likely to be shown in the programme when it broadcast. It was quite a clever ploy and I think he donated £25,000. To be fair, he's a good sport when it comes to things like that.

Piers also befriended Mr Cowell and got himself a gig as a panellist on a new programme that Simon was producing called *Britain's Got Talent*. He became a panellist in the US version of the programme, too, *America's Got Talent*. This programme, which was his American TV debut, together with his appearance on the

Comic Relief version of *The Apprentice*, brought him to the attention of Donald Trump, who was going to make the first *Celebrity
Apprentice* programme in America. It's interesting to note that
while America was first to show the original *Apprentice* programme, Britain was first to make a celebrity version.

Piers managed to finagle his way in as one of the contestants on
the US *Celebrity Apprentice*. 'Good luck to him,' I thought. He was
obviously trying to boost his recognition in the United States. I
didn't think much more about it until around April 2008 when I
was in America and saw the programme. They were broadcasting
the pre-recorded episodes and I'd noticed that Piers had got all the
way through to the penultimate stage, so I was interested to see
how far he'd progress. I didn't have to wait long to see him get into
the final, which was going to take place in New York – live!

He called me on my mobile, telling me he'd got himself into the
final. I couldn't hear him very well as the line was breaking up, so I
said I'd ring him back on the landline in my Florida home. We had
a long conversation, a conversation he always finds difficult to
admit to. Basically, he was looking to me to give him some hints
and tips on what he should do or say to help him win.

'Piers, tell me one thing,' I said. 'Is this final really live or will it
be recorded?'

'What do you mean?' he asked.

'Simple. Look, is it going to be broadcast live or is it going to be
recorded and edited?'

'No, no, no. It's definitely going to be live.'

I said to him, 'Okay, Piers, you've won!'

'What are you talking about, you idiot – *I've won*? I haven't
even gone there yet to take part.'

'Trust me, Piers, if you say exactly what I'm about to tell you
now, you will definitely win.'

'What are you going to say?'

'Well, it's all about Mr Trump's ego. You've got to understand that he puts himself across as one of America's best business-men, so if you play upon that, you will be able to box him into a corner whereby he has no other choice than to make you the winner.'

'Go on.'

'Okay, let's look at your opponent. He's a well-known country-and-western singer and, on the face of it, if Mr Trump had to make a decision based on who's more famous and popular in America, then it's a no-brainer – it'd be this guy. But here's what you've got to say: "Mr Trump, the whole process of this series has been you sending us out as teams to bring in the most amount of money for a charity. Every single time I made more money than anyone else. This fellow here, lovely though he is, has been kept in the process because all his project managers liked him as he's a nice chap, so they never brought him into the boardroom which means you never had the opportunity of firing him – that's why he's sitting here. But, Mr Trump, you are a businessman and you set us a task to come in with the highest amount of money. Now, Mr Trump, you cannot go back on everything you've preached about all your life as far as business and commerce is concerned – it's a no-brainer decision, Mr Trump: I must be the winner because I am the one that followed your instructions to the letter, and any decision other than a win for me will make a farce of this process, because you are the one who laid down the rules."'

'I can't say all that,' said Piers. 'He'd whack me one.'

'Come on, Piers, I know you've got some guts, so here's the point. You're in the middle of a whacking great big studio, all the lights are on, there are a thousand people in the audience. He's not going to get up and do anything to you. Just bite your lip and blurt it out. What's the worst he can do? He can't shoot you. Look, it's live on television and that's the thing that's going for you here. You're live and they can't cut it and they can't stop it.'

I'm not saying that Piers gave my suggested speech verbatim, but it was more or less ninety per cent of what I said. And I was absolutely right – Piers was pronounced the winner.

Oh dear, there wasn't a door in America large enough for him to walk through after that. His head got bigger and bigger. And did I get a thank you the next day from him? No. Did I *ever* get a thank you from him? No. If I ever bring it up in front of him, he waffles and has difficulty remembering the phone call. The only good news is that my dear lady wife, Ann, was there at the time, listening in to what I was saying, so she knows it's absolutely true, and that *does* embarrass the old chap when we meet and she is present. I don't hesitate to throw it in his face every time. He won't admit it but he knows it's true.

The *Comic Relief* episode came across very well and the shots of the funfair were brilliant. The whole thing created a very good impression and was, in fact, the star attraction of that year's *Comic Relief* event. Rather cleverly, they showed it in two parts. After the celebrities had carried out the task, the programme broke away to show some other *Comic Relief* specials and do some more fund-raising on screen, then around half an hour later they came back and showed the final boardroom scene. This was a good idea and it kept the audience guessing as to who was going to be fired.

Comic Relief happens every two years. On the years in between there is a similar event called *Sport Relief* and, sure enough, the following year the BBC asked me if we were prepared to do exactly the same thing after filming the fourth series of *The Apprentice*. The celebrities this time were Hardeep Singh Kohli, Phil Tufnell, Nick Hancock, Lembit Öpik and Kelvin MacKenzie for the boys; Lisa Snowdon, Jacqueline Gold, Louise Redknapp, Clare Balding and Kirstie Allsopp for the girls.

They put out the usual publicity to say we were going to do *Sport Relief Does The Apprentice*, but on this occasion the production company had a problem finding celebrities who could afford to donate their time – which might be as much as four or five days out of their busy schedules. Obviously, if they were currently employed on other business or appearing in some show, then it would be very difficult. On that basis they needed to go to various agents throughout the country to look into the availability of people. Unusually, I received a call from Paul Kemsley, who told me that his wife's very good friend Louise Redknapp, who was married to footballer Jamie Redknapp, would very much like to be involved. Paul said I would be doing him a great favour if I would select Louise as one of the candidates. I thought Louise was perfect for the show and told the producers it would be a great idea to get her.

I knew Jacqueline Gold through her father, David Gold, who was then chairman of Birmingham City Football Club. We had met on a few occasions in the boardroom at Tottenham. Jacqueline was a very successful businesswoman who also, I guess, wanted to promote herself and her company on television.

We also had Phil Tufnell, the England cricketer, who was a fiery and funny character, as well as Nick Hancock, who used to host the TV sports quiz programme *They Think It's All Over*.

The format was the same as the previous year, starting with the initial boardroom meeting where I set the task. Learning from my lead-balloon experience of the year before, I tried to be slightly humorous but professional in introducing the task, which was that both parties were going to try to raise lots of money with what's known as a pop-up shop event in the heart of London. Once again, we wanted them to drag in as many celebrities as they could to donate various things to sell.

At this first meeting I decided I would have a quick chat with the candidates on camera to say hello. Regrettably, Hardeep Kohli took something I said the wrong way and threw a complete and utter wobbly. I happened to say that in my early days of business when I used to ride around in my van, I'd often visit a family called Kohli in their shop in Manchester, so I wondered whether Hardeep Kohli was a relative of theirs as they were a very nice, warm family. I can still remember the mother standing behind the shop counter while her two sons ran the business. She would always be urging me to try out her chapatis. And so, as Hardeep Kohli had recently been on a celebrity cooking programme, I wondered whether he was any good at making chapatis. Quite an innocent bit of banter, I thought. I really did like the Kohlis and I did a lot of business with them as a young man, and the mother was a wonderful character.

When we finished the filming of the task being set, I was told by the producer that Kohli was going to walk off; that my remarks were tantamount to racism. I could not believe what I was hearing. I rushed round to see him and asked what the hell was he talking about? From my point of view it was a light-hearted discussion about a family called Kohli whom I really liked and how the mother, being a typical mother, wanted to feed this young lad, and so she offered me food whenever I went there. And because Hardeep Kohli had been on *Celebrity MasterChef* I thought I'd ask him the question. I couldn't see how, in any way, shape or form, this could be construed as racist.

'And by the way, my friend,' I added, 'in case you didn't know, I'm Jewish, so I'm the last person to make any racial comments. Now if you like, what I *can* do is make sure the production people do not include that bit in the edit, but I'm not having you telling me that was any kind of racist remark. Ridiculous – you're being oversensitive.'

He accepted my explanation and continued to take part in the programme.

Jacqueline Gold did not turn out to be a popular person amongst the celebrities, who thought she was a very bossy project manager. Of course, she was a businesswoman and used to bossing people around, but I believe there was an altercation between her and Kirstie Allsopp. I was getting all this feedback from the production people and starting to wonder, 'What the hell am I getting involved in here? What *is* it with these people and their big personalities?'

I turned up at the event, which took place in a very large shop in Bloomsbury, and saw the various celebrities who had been roped in to attending. To their credit, the teams did manage to drag quite a few in. David Walliams and David Baddiel were there. Simon Cowell *had* been there beforehand. I knew that because there was an artist doing caricatures of people and he had done one of Simon Cowell. On the picture, Simon had written, 'I have given £50,000 for this caricature – come on, Sir Alan, you do the same.' This was rather cheeky, but fun. Obviously I asked the artist to do a caricature of me and agreed to match the £50,000 for charity.

Jamie Redknapp was there, supporting his wife, of course, together with his cousin Frank Lampard. These two lads knew me quite well from the football days and we had a bit of a chat about what was going on in the Premier League and football in general. It was a very nice event, very well organised.

In the boardroom the day afterwards, you could feel the hostility in the girls' team towards Jacqueline and I learned a lot more about what had gone on. Things had started amicably at first, but soon started to deteriorate, ending up with Kirstie flouncing out of the planning meeting because Jacqueline chose not to make the most of Kirstie's list of contacts.

But if the mood in the girls' team was hostile, that was nothing compared to the boys' team where the mood was downright violent! Kohli had volunteered to be project manager, but after a short while his teammates began to complain about his dictatorial leadership style; so much so that Kelvin MacKenzie said to him, 'You're not flaming Hitler, you know.' Kohli was outraged, demanding that filming be stopped, and once again threatened to walk off the show. As before, he was being oversensitive, though I do think Kelvin was a little out of order there. After a bit of calming down, Kohli agreed to continue but did not want to carry on as project manager, so Lembit Öpik took over.

At the end of the first day, the girls had already passed £100,000 in pledges to their team while the boys had no pledges at all! It was looking like a humiliating defeat for them. In the end, the girls did win, but the boys put in a late rally when one of Kelvin's contacts, Tamara Ecclestone, persuaded her father to join in the event. Bernie Ecclestone made the biggest single donation of all, helping the boys' team raise £316,000, though the girls' team topped it with £412,000.

The boardroom after the task was entertaining and explosive. Each and every time the girls' team discussed the business they did and who arranged what, one of them would try to jump in and take the credit for it while playing down Jacqueline's managerial contribution. But the most aggressive rows erupted on the boys' team between Kelvin MacKenzie and Kohli – outrageous stuff following on from the Hitler remark. Sometimes they dragged this Lembit fellow into the arguments. I couldn't resist it – I kept calling him Lemsip, one of my jokes that actually went down quite well as it happens.

The three boys in the final boardroom were MacKenzie, Lemsip and Kohli, and in the end Kohli got fired. Afterwards some of the other candidates came up to me and, bearing in mind his earlier accusations of racism, said, 'That was a brave decision you made there,' to which I replied, 'One thing has got nothing to do with the other.' To me, the decision was all about who deserved to be fired, and from what I heard, he was the one who had to go.

10

STARTING AFRESH ON BBC1

**Selling cheese to the French and other disasters
in series three**

Returning to the main *Apprentice*, after the second series was finished, Lorraine told me that all the production people, including Dan Adamson, had moved on to greener pastures and that we needed to get a whole new team together. I really couldn't believe this business of starting from scratch every series. I had been building a relationship with Dan Adamson whereby we both had a kind of general understanding of each other, only to find that he was now off the case and I was going to be introduced to another bunch of new people.

Lorraine told me she had found two ladies who currently worked for the BBC, Michele Kurland and Kelly Webb-Lamb, and that she was in the process of persuading them to join Talkback Thames and run *The Apprentice*.

She added that, due to the success of the programme, the BBC had decided they were going to move it from BBC2 to BBC1. When Lorraine told me this, she expected me to jump for joy. I just said, 'Really? What difference does that make?'

I was about to learn that, for some strange reason, the same programme on BBC1 would attract lots more viewers than it would on BBC2. Being a relatively technical person, I thought about it with a scientific mindset and said to her, 'I don't get it. I don't understand why that should be the case because, for example, if I wanted to watch the FA Cup Final, and say it was being shown on Channel 4, I'd pick up the remote and press 4. So if viewers want to find *The Apprentice*, surely they'll go and find it whatever channel it's on? Why does it make any difference whether it's on BBC2 or BBC1? And in any case,' I continued, 'BBC2's Roly Keating gave *The Apprentice* his backing, and now it seems you're taking away one of his best shows – not that it's any of my business.'

Lorraine told me it was a known fact that BBC1 has a massive audience. I kind of shrugged my shoulders and said, 'Fine. You know best.' Indeed, they *did* know best, and when the new series started to broadcast on BBC1, the viewing figures outstripped anything we achieved on BBC2.

Before making series three, Lorraine arranged for me to meet Michele and Kelly at the offices of Fremantle Media, the ultimate owner of Talkback Thames. She wanted me to be comfortable with these ladies. I don't quite know what she meant by 'comfortable' considering these were two people I'd never met before in my life. All I could think was, 'Here we go again with another bunch of people who have most probably got their own ideas and want to reinvent the wheel. How can I be comfortable with that?'

The meeting went quite smoothly. Michele, a bubbly lady, told me she was from Ireland and came over to work in England and ended up at the BBC working on various projects including a business programme called *I'll Show Them Who's Boss*. She said that whenever they were filming the programme on Wednesday nights, everything would stop when *The Apprentice* came on and all the crew would watch it together. She was a petite, fast-talking lady and one could immediately see that she was a shrewd, clever individual. Kelly, her right-hand woman, had worked with Michele for quite a while at the BBC and there was good chemistry between the two.

Lorraine told me she was ninety per cent sure she would be able to drag these two out of the BBC to take on the job, but it had to be kept confidential. Well, *I* certainly wasn't going to tell anyone.

It's never been clear as far as I'm concerned what the deliberation was about, but looking back, I think perhaps they weren't sure whether or not to leave the BBC until they'd met me and seen my body language and gauged whether we'd be able to work with each other. In the end they did leave. This probably wasn't a big issue for the BBC because, at the end of the day, they were leaving to come and produce what was to become one of BBC1's flagship programmes.

So Michele and Kelly took over for series three. Michele was given the title executive producer and Kelly was series editor. And, typically, it is the two people in these roles who I work with the closest. They are my point of contact for everything to do with what actually goes on in the series and the finished programmes.

One really good change that Michele made to the format for series three was to show the surviving candidates, after the firing, returning to the house at the end of the episode. In the first two series this scene had been shown at the start of the following episode. It made much more sense the new way that Michele arranged it.

Another thing we changed for this series was that we started off with sixteen candidates rather than fourteen. There were times in the previous series when it would have been useful for me to have had the flexibility to get rid of more than one candidate at a time. However, that wasn't the reason for increasing the number of candidates to sixteen. Michele was concerned that we had been lucky up until now that no one had pulled out for medical or compassionate reasons, and she felt there needed to be backup. On top of that, *The Apprentice* is an amazing opportunity and now we could let two more people into the process.

As it turned out, Michele was right to get backup, as you'll read later on. That said, the additional candidates did come in handy for double firings at times, though I want to go on record now and make it perfectly clear that these double firings are not a gimmick. Naturally, I was always conscious of the fact that if I fired more than one person it could throw out the whole process of balancing the teams in future weeks, or even leave us short of candidates for the interviews episode; however, I never allowed this to stand in the way of firing any candidate who really had to go.

I have to say that Michele and Kelly really worked hard. The number of hours they put in was unbelievable. Although they were part of a massive team, those two roles are ultimately responsible for everything about the series. They were responsible for holding the auditions, selecting the candidates, working with me to design the tasks, managing the teams who set up the tasks, managing the camera crews who run around filming the candidates, overseeing the house team, liaising with the BBC, dealing with press enquiries, dealing with the candidates, consulting with the legal people as well as overseeing the editing of the programmes and ultimately deciding what content makes it into each programme. For the people in these two roles, making *The Apprentice* is an all-year-round job. I was delighted that Michele remained in her position for a number of years, which I believe is the reason why *The Apprentice* went on to be so successful. We did make a very good team and I didn't have to go through the learning curve over and over again with new people.

The BBC had obviously invested quite a bit of money in this series because it was going onto BBC1 and at this point Michele introduced me to a lady called Ruby Evans. Ruby would also go on to be part of *The Apprentice* team for many series; in fact, I think she remained with the programme from the third series to the tenth. Ruby took over Sandy Fone's position and became the new Mummy. However, the job was now a much bigger one as the scope of the tasks became more complicated and the pressure to increase the on-screen value became more important for a programme that was going to be on BBC1. *The Apprentice* is an enormous operation, and managing the organisation of it is like mobilising a small army every year. That's where people like Ruby come in. Ruby, whose title was line producer, was very experienced and her team of production managers, production coordinators and production secretaries went on to make sure that everything ran like clockwork, that everyone knew where they needed to be and that things were set up when they got there.

For each episode of *The Apprentice*, every single person who is participating in the production of the programme receives what's known in the TV industry as a call-sheet. This is a very detailed document that tells you what's going to happen in the programme, right down to the last detail. For example: *Sir Alan Sugar will be needed on Monday 14th at 07:00 at St Paul's Cathedral.* It will explain what time the camera crew will be there, what cameras and lighting will be set up, when we have to vacate the area and all that stuff.

Whenever I read this documentation I'm reminded what a massive organisational undertaking this is. Say we were filming me setting the task at the British Museum. First we'd have to get permission to film there. In the case of the British Museum, this was no problem, they were delighted to promote the place by having it appear on such a prestigious programme as *The Apprentice*. But then consider: the camera crew had to get there at six o'clock in the morning and set up their cameras and lighting; then Nick, Margaret and I came along and we did the filming, all against a time constraint. Bearing in mind that the museum opens at nine o'clock, the whole thing had to be done and dusted in a short window of time, including setting up, filming, shutting down and moving out. And all this, as anyone who watches *The Apprentice* will know, is for a sequence that takes up no more than two or three minutes of the one-hour programme. This gives you an indication of the amount of detail and cost that goes into producing just one small sequence like this, yet its inclusion is important so as to lend an air of grandeur to the programme.

Ruby and her team would organise all this stuff. Knowing that I'm a stickler for efficiency, the filming schedule was normally produced a few weeks ahead. This would allow me to decide how I could weave in my other business activities or commitments. Ruby was also appointed by the team as the 'person to talk to Sir Alan' if there was a problem or some bad news that they knew would wind me up. On occasions when things didn't go according to plan, she was the one who had to call me and say, 'I'm sorry, Sir Alan, we're going to have to shift filming on this day, or the boardroom session on that day. Is that okay? Can you fit that in with your schedule?'

To be fair, I was very cooperative in most cases as I understood the enormity of the logistics, but on some occasions it was really difficult because I'd made appointments on certain dates to do certain things, so it needed a bit of shuffling. But we got through and we had a good working relationship on this.

When I signed up for the new series, I happened to mention worst-case scenarios like all of the tapes going missing and what a disaster that would be. I found out that all of this kind of stuff is covered by insurance; in fact, the whole of the production cost had to be insured in case of mishap. One disaster would be, for example, if I were medically unable to continue midstream. Because of this, the insurance company said they required me to have a medical examination and wanted me to go to see some boffin in Harley Street. I told Ruby I was not doing this. I asked her to go and negotiate with the insurance company, explaining that I'm a healthy chap and that once a year I have to have a Civil Aviation Authority medical exam to maintain my pilot's licence. Having successfully passed that, the medical certificate from the CAA ought to be good enough for the insurance company. After a bit of argy-bargy and negotiation they agreed, and ever since then I have sent them my annual CAA medical certificate – which is probably better than the

Harley Street doc would have provided as it includes some pretty stringent tests such as an ECG.

Dealing with Michele, Kelly and Ruby was very refreshing. They realised I was a hands-on person who liked to get involved in the detail, completely different to the people they'd worked with in the past who were just happy to turn up and do what they were told. I considered *The Apprentice* production as my baby and still do today. It's no different to anything else I've produced as a man-ufacturer. Therefore, when I put my name to it, I need to know what is going on. I think that Michele and the BBC grew to under-stand how passionate I am about the programme, down to every single detail, and how from time to time I would get a little hot under the collar if things started to go wrong from an efficiency point of view – not so much at Talkback but at the BBC. There was no question about my devotion to the programme, and if you speak to anyone at the BBC, Talkback or Fremantle Media, I'm sure they'd say I'm unusual in that sense.

The audition process was the same as for the previous series, with venues up and down the country. Michele and Kelly went to great lengths to whittle it down to about seventy-odd candidates, and then made video clips of them. They were a little concerned that I wouldn't have the time to view these video clips but nevertheless made them available to me together with the candidates' CVs. I was really appreciative of this gesture. In the past, the producers felt they needed to take it upon themselves to home in on the final twenty or so for selection.

On one occasion Michele suggested that I come along to a London hotel to get a feeling for what it was like to see thousands of people turning up for interviews. I went along and she showed me how they sift through them. As one can imagine, people recog-nised me and I almost needed a couple of minders to keep them from coming up and trying to talk to me. Obviously when the applicants came along, they didn't know what they were letting themselves in for, and they may have thought I'd be part of the interview process. It was an interesting eye-opener.

There were a couple of other changes for the third series. The selected candidates would have to agree to the production company running a CRB check on them to see if they had a criminal record or history. Additionally, and more surprisingly, they also had to be vetted by a psychologist! I guess someone at the BBC felt that the grillings I put the candidates through might be considered traumatic, so they insisted all the candidates chosen for the process would have to be checked out by a shrink. They realised more and more that it could be quite a stressful process and needed to know that the people were robust enough to take part. Not that *The Apprentice* sets out to upset candidates – it has a very serious prize and a serious business message – but still they had to provide this 'duty of care' to ensure nothing was done that might damage the health of the applicants. To be fair to the BBC, I think this procedure was quite novel as not many formats that use members of the public go to such lengths to protect the contributors.

Michele and Kelly would get really excited by a potential candidate who seemed full of promise, but then the psychologist would dig deeper and show that being in such a demanding process as *The Apprentice* maybe wasn't in their best interests. In such cases there was no argument or negotiation with the psychologist – if they said no, that was that. The BBC had brought the psychologist in to do a job and you couldn't override them. We did lose a few interesting people at that stage, but I think overall it was a good idea because the candidates can be cooped up in the house together for many weeks. The psychologist, therefore, has to assess whether they are able to be away from their families, whether they're able to hack it in this kind of environment, and whether they will be able to stand up to interrogation by me in the boardroom.

For series three, Michele and Kelly had done a tremendous job and we mutually agreed on the final sixteen candidates. At this point I'm always tempted to meet these people beforehand, and maybe have a chat with them, but the integrity of the programme has to remain intact and I'm in complete agreement that the first time the candidates see me should be when I walk into the board-room.

As well as giving me a bit of an overview of the candidates, another thing Michele and Kelly were keen for me to see was the house they had selected for the candidates to stay in. Viewing the property was another great eye-opener for me. Being in the real-estate business, I was interested to know how one could suddenly acquire a mansion for sixteen excitable candidates to run around in for up to twelve weeks. Who in their right mind would allow you to rent a house to a mob like this? This was another of Ruby's tasks. She had to find a willing landlord who would allow their house to be rented to a TV crew, no easy feat. Ruby told me that as soon as they heard the words BBC and *The Apprentice*, it was 'ker-ching, ker-ching' for the letting agents. The pound signs lit up in their eyes and some of the prices were outrageous. On occasion it was touch and go whether we would even *have* a house for the candidates, because everything was ridiculously out of budget. For this particular series, however, they had located a nice place in Notting Hill.

Then the house has to be kitted out for use during the twelve-week process. As well as providing food for up to sixteen people, there have to be enough places for them to sleep. It goes without saying that it's not a sixteen-bedroom house, so in the early weeks of the series the boys would sleep four in a room, as would the girls, so things could be a bit crowded; not to mention the bathrooms, showers and toilet facilities. On top of that, the house has to be supplied with furniture, TVs and all the food and drink that the young entrepreneurs would be ligging. This is where the services of a very talented chap called Derek came in. He would go on to kit out the houses over the course of the years – quite an amazing feat. Suddenly a truck would arrive with furniture, beds, ornaments, flowers, paintings, lamps, desks, computers, etc., and a team of people would install the whole lot in a day, ready for the candidates. A huge logistical task, and very well executed by Derek, I have to say. But also hats off to Ruby for keeping the price at a reasonable level. And the expenditure doesn't end there – a clean-up team is required afterwards, bearing in mind the house has to be vacated in the same condition as it was at the start.

I did question at one stage whether it would have been a good idea for the BBC to buy a house somewhere. In hindsight, I'm sure all the money that was spent over the years renting these places must have added up to a huge amount.

One thing Michele said that I found difficult to understand was about my opening speech to the candidates in the boardroom for series three. I wanted to say, in effect, 'Now, you know what this process is all about. You must have seen this before in the previous two series. You know what you're here for,' etc.

'No,' she said, 'please don't say that. You've got to start from scratch as if this programme has never been broadcast before.'

'What do you mean, Michele? That's ridiculous; it's nonsense.'

'No, no, this is BBC1; it's a completely different audience. We have to start afresh. Please, can I just ask you not to make any reference to previous series or anything like that? We've got to imply that we're kicking off from scratch here.'

I could never understand that logic, but on this particular occasion, because we were going over to BBC1, I'd learned not to argue as these people knew what they were doing. And so in my opening speech, though it was difficult, I went through my usual thing about how tough it was going to be, how they'd be set tasks every week, how one of them would be fired, how Nick and Margaret were my eyes and ears, and all that. It seemed a bit silly to me, but there you are, that's what we did.

Some of the candidates were nodding as I spoke, as if to say, 'Yeah, we know all this, Sir Alan, we know.'

Nevertheless, I continued with the usual stuff. 'You will be going off to a house that I've laid on for you. I want you to get together and come up with team names and I will be contacting you to let you know what your first task will be.'

The boys' team came up with the name Eclipse, and the girls' team came up with Stealth. We'd decided that year to mix up the girls versus boys approach we had adopted on the first two series. I *had* originally split the candidates into boys' and girls' teams, but then, as a surprise in week one, I made the project managers swap. So, in this case, Jadine Johnson, who thought she was going to lead the girls' team, led the boys, while Andy Jackson led the girls.

At this point it's worth mentioning that the project manager on the first task always tends to get stitched up by the others, and we filmed some great sequences where you could see how the other boys tried to back off from taking the job yet remain semi-macho. One or two of them suggested Andy as the man to be project manager, then the others would start agreeing, 'Yeah, he sounds like the right guy to run the team.' If ever there was a classic example of a stitch-up, this was it. It was brilliant television watching them get poor old Andy to take the helm.

This first task was running a mobile coffee stall. Unfortunately, Andy and the girls' team lost. As an example of the pressure these people are under, I recall that when the task was over, before they knew the result, Andy called all the girls together, thanked them for their support and then got very emotional and started to cry. Some of the girls were patting him on the back and saying, 'Come on, you did okay. Let's get back to the boardroom and see how we fared.' As it turned out, even though Andy was a nice chap, his team lost and he wasn't a very good leader, so he had to go.

*

We only had to wait until the second week of the series to see that Michele's decision to have sixteen candidates was a wise move. That week's task was for the teams to come up with an item to do with pets and outdoor wear. The project manager for Eclipse was a fellow by the name of Rory Laing, a self-confessed bankrupt entrepreneur who had failed in several ventures. I've often said that you only learn by your mistakes, and he was allowed into the process because he had at least *attempted* to start various businesses, albeit they had failed. Rory was a rather posh-talking chap. He reminded me of an army officer and I remember him dictating to his team that he would run things like a military operation. He opened with, 'Discipline, guys, is something I go fucking crazy for. You will take your jackets off while we're brainstorming; only I can leave my jacket on. If you are over-talking, I *will* send you out; I won't have it, okay? And can we please try and stop swearing?' He was a bit of a nutter.

At one point during the day, there was a heated exchange between Rory and Tre, who was a feisty character. Rory said, 'I just want you to do as you're told . . . I am your boss.' Tre came back at him, 'You are not my boss – you're nothing to me.'

Rory proved to be great television but I'm sorry to say he was completely and utterly useless. He came up with some ridiculous utility belt for dog owners, with lots of useless pockets and hooks to clip dog leads on to. I remember he asked one of his teammates, Lohit Kalburgi, to actually wear the belt and demonstrate it in the boardroom. It was pathetic, though hilarious, and of course the task was lost.

However, before I decided which team had won, I talked to all the candidates about how they felt the task had gone. When I got to one individual, Ifti Chaudhri, I could see I was getting no response to my questions. 'Ifti, have you got a problem? You don't seem to be tuned in to what's going on here.'

'No, Sir Alan, you're absolutely right,' he said. 'My head has gone. I have to say that I'm missing my son; I'm missing my family. I don't believe this thing is for me. I'm awfully sorry, but if it's okay with you, I have to leave.'

It was clear this man was quite emotional and desperate to be cut loose. There was no way I was going to try and encourage him to stay on, nor did I think it appropriate for me to criticise him in any way, so I just let him go.

At this particular stage, Rory and the rest of the candidates must have thought their boat had come in. They must have figured that Ifti's departure was good news for them because I had said at the beginning that *one* candidate would be fired each week. So now that Ifti was gone, they reckoned everyone else must be safe. However, due to the fact that Michele had recruited sixteen candidates, this situation fell right into my lap. I said to the remaining candidates, 'Well, that's an unfortunate turn of events, but it's an indication of the pressure that you'll *all* be experiencing in this process. As you know, the stakes are high – a six-figure salary working for me. Nothing in life is easy, so we have to move on.'

It was quite interesting to see their faces as the penny dropped that it was still game on. I told them, 'I suppose you think you've got off lightly there – that because Ifti's gone, you can get back to the house. Well, as I've said once before, never underestimate me, and don't try and second-guess what's going on because I'm telling you, as unusual as it is, one of you is *still* going to get fired.' I turned to Rory. 'Rory, you're a disaster – I'm sorry, an absolute, total disaster. I've given you the chance to explain yourself and you haven't. I was told you were bankrupt – there's no shame in that. In fact, I hear you've been bankrupt twice. Well, here's the hat-trick. Rory, you're fired.'

As I've mentioned before, people at times have accused me of keeping candidates in the process because they're a bit nutty and make good telly. This is not the case; they stay in for the right reasons. I mention this again now because if ever there was a case of keeping someone in for the purposes of good telly, Rory would have been it! But he had to go – it is a business programme after all.

One of the tasks I was involved in developing saw us sending the candidates out to make money by offering different services in the Richmond area of south-west London. I thought it would be really interesting to see what they came up with and whether they could capitalise on what made most money. It is really important that as well as sticking with tried-and-trusted tasks, we come back each year with new business models to challenge the candidates. We try to do this as often as possible, otherwise the tasks in *The Apprentice* could become predictable and stale.

For this task, some of the decisions the candidates made were dreadful. The girls, for example, decided to do a sort of kissogram service, selling kisses to drunken blokes in pubs. It was all very embarrassing and I remember telling them in the boardroom that what they were doing reminded me of another old profession I could mention. It was tawdry and disappointing and I told them so. If I recall correctly, the other team performed gardening services, which was really the sort of thing I had intended when I designed the task.

The stand-out task that year was when I sent the candidates to France to try and sell typical British produce in a French farmers' market. The project manager for one of the teams was Paul Callaghan, an ex-army lieutenant. Paul for some reason got it into his head that it would be a good idea to go to a massive cash-and-carry warehouse, Makro, and buy a load of cheap Cheddar cheese to flog to the discerning French customer. I could not believe my ears when Nick told me about it. Nick, who has a house in France and knows the country very well, thought it was the most preposterous thing he had ever heard. He called it a triumph of hope over optimism. I called it plain bloody stupid. As Nick pointed out, the

French have hundreds of varieties of exotic cheeses – why in the world would they buy this whacking great lump of Cheddar that Paul had bought from Makro? I gave Paul hell in the boardroom.

'I sent you out on a mission to France to sell quality British products. I gave you a list of organic farmers, of people who use tender loving care to create something special that they take a pride in – and what do *you* do? You go to Makro and buy a breeze block of bloody Cheddar!'

Another idea of Paul's was to buy some traditional English sausages and offer them to the French public. Now that wasn't such a bad idea because, as we all know, our British bangers are great, and the aroma of sausages sizzling away might well have attracted some passers-by. The problem was, however, that Paul's policy was to try and keep costs down, so instead of buying a little primus stove to cook the sausages on, he did something a bunch of boy scouts might do if they were stranded out on the moors. He got an empty baked-bean tin, banged some holes in the side, tried to light some firelighter gel inside the can and then placed his frying pan on top. When he eventually got the thing going, it was just about hot enough to melt a pat of butter! He thought he was being clever and resourceful, but it was completely pathetic. One of the more practical candidates, Kristina Grimes, took control of the sausages. She managed to convince a French restaurateur to lend her his kitchen for a while, cooked all the sausages and cut them up so the rest of the team could sell them.

The teams returned from France by ferry. The giant slab of Cheddar did not sell and it had to be disposed of at the dockside back in England. I saw pictures of Paul throwing this giant chunk of cheese into the garbage dumpster.

While dissecting the task in the boardroom, somebody blurted out that Paul had been having 'an inappropriate relationship' with another ex-military person, Katie Hopkins. Katie was one of the more prominent candidates that year, always ready with some nasty jibe about her teammates, a trait she's miraculously managed to turn into some kind of career since leaving the series! Her teammates were up in arms about the romance – they felt it affected decisions that were being made, and I have to say I don't blame them. The allegation, I think, came from Kristina who in reality was trying to protect her position as she was in the losing team. She said that Katie was protecting Paul because of this relationship that was going on.

As it happened, I took no notice of Katie's input and concluded by saying, 'Paul, I sent you to sell the best of British to France. You spent half the bloody day frying sausages on some stupid contraption that boy scouts could have made and, worse than that, you went out and lost me money! You're a total shambles. You're fired.'

The TV shopping channel task was used in this series and once again I viewed it live as it went out on the air. I find this a very useful task because the bottom line is – it's *live*. The candidates realise that as they're talking, the broadcast is being seen by hundreds of thousands of people, so it puts them under a lot of pressure. This time the pressure was getting to Kristina. She was demonstrating a floor-cleaning device and accidently swore when the thing started to go wrong. She also had this trait of saying 'okay' every few seconds while she was supposed to be explaining the cleaner in her sales pitch. While I was watching, I commented, 'If she says "okay" one more time, I'm going to hit something.'

And just as I spoke, Kristina said, 'Okay, now here we have . . .' It was so pathetic that I just laughed and shook my head in sheer amazement.

Series three also featured what must still be the narrowest margin of defeat in the history of the show – 97p! It was a discount buying task where the teams run around trying to buy all the items on a list at the lowest price. In the end, the team that won did so by less than a quid.

I don't much like it when the result is that close, because often what happens is that the candidates on the losing team tend to have the attitude, 'Well, it was only by a pound, so we didn't really do anything wrong.' This is fundamentally not the right attitude, but one has to sympathise with them because if they had bought one of the items for a pound or two less, they would have been the winners. As you can imagine, it's difficult for me to criticise the losing team too much when the loss is just 97p; it's more justified when the loss is £50 or £200. Nevertheless, the project manager of the losing team was fired for his poor management.

Getting back to Katie Hopkins, she made it as far as the interview stage that year, but by then I was starting to have real doubts about her commitment to the process; I wasn't sure if she really had a genuine desire to work for me or just wanted her five minutes of fame. That was the feeling coming through to me.

I remember telling her on one occasion that she was a loser because she had been in the losing team five times, as well as being in the final three in the boardroom three times. When I accused her of being a loser, her face went bright red and she said, 'I am not a loser, Sir Alan, I am not a loser. It is not right to call me a loser.'

I said to her, 'Katie, it's very, very simple. It's a bit like the football results. Your team has lost.' I continued with the analogy. 'Katie, every Saturday night at five o'clock on the radio, somebody reads out the results: "Tottenham Hotspur 3, West Ham United 1. Hamilton Academicals 2, Partick Thistle 3." The results speak for themselves. In your particular case the announcer would read, "Simon Ambrose 1 defeat, Katie Hopkins 5 defeats." You're a loser, dear, do you understand? You're a loser.'

'Well, when you put it that way, Sir Alan, I understand what you're saying.'

'Good.'

Katie was a tyrant in the boardroom and I remember in the discount buying task how she gave Adam Hosker hell, accusing him of being best friends with Mr Pinot and Mr Grigio, suggesting he was a boozer. Katie was annoyed by being brought into the boardroom, so she ranted, 'Your reasons for bringing me in here just do not stack up. But if you want to go personal, I'll go personal. At a business level, you have one speed setting, and that setting is slow, slow, slow! Someone put the wrong speed dial in when they created you, sweetie, so you know what? You're just barking up the wrong tree!'

After her rant was over, I said to Adam, 'I wouldn't expect a Christmas card from her this year, son.'

She was a formidable candidate and the audience thought she made entertaining TV, but in the penultimate episode, when she was asked how she proposed to arrange her future life if she got the job working for me – considering that she lived in Exeter with her children – she decided that, yes, it might indeed be a bit difficult, and at that point suggested to me it might not be appropriate for her to continue.

Simon Ambrose was a credible candidate. He was a Cambridge graduate, an internet entrepreneur, and was clearly very shrewd. I found out later that he was a member of Mensa, having recorded an IQ score of 174 at thirteen years old. When I was in the boardroom discussing what went wrong on tasks, you could see this fellow was on the ball; he'd got the plot. He could understand things well ahead of his colleagues. Having said that, when it came to jokes, his were nearly as bad as my lead balloons. On his application form where it asked him to state any allergies, he wrote, 'Cocaine.' Hmm, made me worry a bit. It *was* a joke.

Even though Simon Ambrose was obviously no fool, he had one or two not-so-clever moments during the series. One memorable moment springs to mind, which is hauled out on TV every single time they show funny clips of *The Apprentice*. It was the occasion when he was demonstrating a mini-trampoline during the selling-on-TV task. In the demonstration, he stood the trampoline on its side and leant it against himself in such a way that when he was screwing the detachable legs onto the trampoline it looked as though he was in a rather compromising position! I'm sure that clip must haunt him to this day.

So after the interviews we were left with Simon, Kristina, Katie and Tre. Before Katie's departure, I decided to let Tre go. He was too fiery a character and I couldn't honestly see how he'd settle down and work harmoniously within my organisation.

Katie then gave me her 'I don't think I can take the job' speech, at which point I let her go. The doubts I'd had previously were vindicated – I could see she had been in this process for what I consider to be the wrong reasons. A clever woman, though, and one who would have been a contender.

And then there were two. Katie's exit left Kristina and Simon to go head to head in the final. The final task, to design a building for a site I owned on London's South Bank, endorsed my feelings that Simon was a worthy winner.

As I mentioned earlier, Katie Hopkins went on to pursue a media career of her own. The first thing we saw of her in the newspapers after *The Apprentice* was that she'd had an affair with a married man and decided to consummate this relationship in a field, completely naked. It could be that there just happened to be a member of the paparazzi enjoying a countryside stroll who stumbled across this scene, or the pictures could have been staged. I have no idea but I know the woman just wanted publicity and she continues to this day to be very controversial. I recall at the wrap party after the *You're Hired* recording, she was the only candidate standing on her own. No one was socialising with her, so she obviously hadn't made any friends in the house. I remember going up to her and having a little chat because I felt a bit sorry for her. Perhaps in hindsight I shouldn't have bothered.

11

'I WON'T BE YOUR ROBOT'

Refusing to be seen as a fist-banging, shouting tyrant

When my friend Maureen Lipman advised me to have a say in the edit and demand to see what she called the rushes I didn't see the necessity for it. But now, with two series under my belt and the third ready for editing, I could start to see what Maureen was getting at. I was giving my all to *The Apprentice*, lecturing the candidates in the boardroom and trying to educate them as to where they had gone wrong on a task or in their business philosophy. Unfortunately, those types of lectures are not possible to condense into a string of four or five words; they tend to last as long as a minute. In telly terms, that was too much, and a lot of my words of wisdom were cut from the boardroom scenes. This resulted in me being like one of those toy dolls that spoke when you pulled the string on its back. They were reducing my dialogue with the candidates to little soundbites like, 'Who was the project manager?' or 'Who decided to go to Streatham?' or 'Why couldn't you find the jellied eels?'

I complained to Michele about this in one of the later series. I said, 'You're treating me like a robot. In fact, you don't need me in the boardroom any more – you could just get one of those robots and program it with stupid four-word questions: "Who did the pitch? Why didn't she speak? Who sold the most?"'

I went along to the editing sessions for series three with Michele and Kelly. When they showed me some of the episodes they were about to send to the BBC for final approval, I started to kick up a bit of a fuss as I noticed that a lot of my work and effort had been thrown out. To be fair to Michele, in later series she started to realise that I know more about this programme than anybody else. I was a fast learner, and the new wave of people coming in to assist Michele were novices to *The Apprentice*. It took Michele a while to sign on to the fact that I'm not just the dumb talent; I'm somebody who understands that of course the programme has to be entertaining, but it also needs credibility. I wasn't very happy with some of the cuts that had been made, but it was a bit late to make any changes as they'd edited the first few episodes ready for BBC approval, so there wasn't much scope for my input.

This was a very sensitive issue. From the BBC's point of view, *they* held the editorial control, but I felt I had to ensure the business message came through and I wanted the opportunity to point out to the production people – who were not business experts – what *I* thought were the important elements.

Contractually I had no rights to assert what I wanted included or excluded from the programme, so it was really a case of me putting up a fair and logical argument along the lines of, 'This is supposed to be a business programme and at the moment I'm starting to worry that, if we're not careful, what you'll be creating here is a kind of *Big Brother* on wheels, and I don't like it.'

I was also shown some of the cuts of the later episodes, this time at an earlier stage, before they actually went off to the BBC. I would pop into the editing suite just to have a catch-up on what was going on and would be issued with a 'raw' DVD, which might be something like an hour and a quarter long. It was a very rough cut without the finishing touches like the opening titles, the 'Previously on *The Apprentice*' section, the closing titles, etc. I got this DVD in order to get a flavour of how the edit was going.

Deep down I wasn't happy, but I had no authority to change

things. I certainly felt that if I was going to do any more series of
The Apprentice, then the next time I signed up there would need
to be something in the contract that gave me some say on the content – at least on the words *I* said. By this I didn't mean editorial
control – just some input into the use of the stuff I'd said in the
boardroom. And not just business messages – also some of the stuff
that made me look a little more light-hearted.

I remember a hilarious moment in the boardroom after a funny
quip I had made that referred to Dot Cotton from *EastEnders*.
When I got to see the episode, the joke was missing! It was such a
great moment, that's why I remembered it so well. I asked Michele
and Kelly what had happened to it. Kelly made the fatal error of
bullshitting me with, 'Yes, it was wonderful, Sir Alan, but unfortunately when we watched the tape, someone had coughed or sneezed
just at that point, so we couldn't use it.' This, I'm afraid to say,
wasn't true, and from that moment on I lost a little respect for
Kelly because, as my very first opening speech stated in series one,
'I don't like liars, I don't like bullshitters,' and I'm afraid to say this
was double-barrelled BS. There was no coughing, there was no
sneezing – I knew because I'd seen the rushes, which caused her a
great deal of embarrassment. In the end it boiled down to the fact
that the tape had already been compiled and it was too late to add
anything, so my little gem got missed. Kelly should have just been
upfront and told me that.

This incident endorsed my thoughts that in future I needed to
have some say. I knew, however, that this was going to be very difficult for them to agree to because, as I've said, the creative people
who make TV programmes see this as their territory and they don't
like anybody encroaching upon it. Funnily enough, in some
respects they would listen to a twenty-year-old junior director
sooner than listen to me, even though, having done three series, I
knew more than they did in many cases.

*

The third series was broadcast on BBC1 for the first time on 28 March 2007 and ran until 13 June. The *You're Fired* programme had also been promoted from BBC3 to BBC2.

Regrettably, there was a nasty situation on the day of the filming of *You're Hired*. It was that time where I had to speak to the finalists and let them know who'd won. Of course, it was very easy for me to tell Simon that he'd won, and obviously he was delighted. However, when I informed Kristina that she'd lost, she got very upset. Michele and Kelly had been chaperoning the finalists, but when Kristina heard the bad news, she ran out of the Talkback building and disappeared. This was a terrible shock to the production people because in a couple of hours' time we all needed to be at the *You're Hired* recording, and Kristina had gone on the missing list!

Fortunately, Michele tracked her down and found her in a church, praying. She was very emotional but Michele did a good job of calming her down and explaining to her that she had to act professionally now. She reminded Kristina that nothing that had happened that day was different to anything she'd been warned about at the outset – the simple reality was: Sir Alan had chosen Simon as the winner. Nevertheless, you had to feel sorry for her.

At the *You're Hired* show after the final, I met Simon Ambrose's mother and father after it had been announced that he was the winner. His parents came up to me and thanked me. His mother also told me that Simon was a highly intelligent young man who had passed all his exams at Cambridge with flying colours, but had a bit of a grasshopper brain and liked to play a lot. Basically, she was asking me to keep him under control and make something out of him, which I thought was rather strange, but then again a mother knows her son.

I guess, looking back, one can see that he *was* a bit of a joker. I recall from one of the episodes that he was quite good at rapping and dancing, and I believe he did like to frequent certain West End nightclubs. With his intelligence I felt he needed to join my real-estate division and with that in mind I insisted he went on weekly day-release to college to become a qualified chartered surveyor. The fact he was a Cambridge graduate was helpful, but his degree was no use in real estate. He was responsible for designing the Amsprop property website, one of the first websites that allowed interested parties (such as the lawyers of potential buyers) to delve right into the deepest level of documentation related to each of our properties, with access via special passwords. This doesn't sound like rocket science today, but back then it was very innovative.

Simon did a good job in conjunction with my IT manager, Danny. He finished his two-year chartered surveyor course and worked in my property company for nearly two and a half years. At the end of that period I could see he was a bit restless. He hadn't found the real-estate business stimulating enough and he didn't really have a passion for it. Nevertheless, he picked up some tricks of the trade working for us. His father, I understand, gave him an inheritance of some kind and Simon became a property landlord in his own right. He left the company, saying he was going to manage the property, as well as open his own nightclub.

I talked earlier about the difficulty of a new member of staff coming to work for me on a published salary of £100,000. Simon was a classic example of how this caused problems. Obviously he had very little knowledge of the real-estate market and there he was plonked smack bang in the middle of our real-estate department. Some of the staff there got the right hump. It was difficult for me to explain to these people that the guy came through a twelve-week process and deservedly won the prize, which is a £100,000-per-year contract with my company. His salary in the second and third years of his employment would be based upon how well he did in the first year, so it didn't necessarily mean he would continue to get that rate of salary unless he deserved it or had brought in so much business that it would be a no-brainer for us to want to keep him.

Despite explaining this to a couple of employees, you could see their despondency, which I guess was understandable. So it was a bit of a difficult time for Simon because there was resentment and, even though he was a very personable, easy-going fellow, some people didn't treat him very well and were a bit negative towards him. I had cause to speak to those people on occasion and say, 'Look, get over it. This is what's happening – deal with it.'

Well, Lorraine Heggessey was right. The change of channel to BBC1 was deemed to be a blinding success; the programme peaked at 6.8 million viewers on the week of the final, and the BBC wanted to commission another series.

I went to visit Jana Bennett, Head of BBC Television, to discuss a new deal. What they wanted to make me do was sign up for more than one series. In the meeting, Jana thanked me for my performance and for helping to create a great programme for the channel. I explained to her that I had agreed to do these three series for a very moderate fee because it was an exciting new venture for me; it was never done for any personal financial gain. Nevertheless, as everybody else in the TV world seemed to be getting paid a lot more than me, my business instinct kicked in. I said that despite the fact I would be giving my earnings to charity, there was no reason for me to be working for a pittance compared to some of the other figures who were famously being paid enormous amounts as the BBC's 'top celebrities'. I recall her giving me some kind of wishy-washy excuse that I couldn't be compared to some of these people – whose names I won't mention right now – because they were deemed to be professional TV celebrities, in other words, 'proper' TV stars.

'I don't quite understand what you mean by that,' I said. 'They may have been in television for a long time; they may have made their way up the showbiz ladder by being famous singers, comedians, presenters or whatever. However, just because I'm a businessman who happens to have a hit programme on my hands, that doesn't mean I should be paid any less, so I don't follow your logic.'

And at this point I politely pointed out to Jana that I was no longer going to be available on the cheap and that Talkback would have to pay the going rate they'd normally pay somebody on one of their top TV shows. I reminded her that the good news was the money would be paid into my charitable foundation and there would be some very grateful charities benefiting from it.

Things started to get complicated from then on because while in the past Talkback had negotiated an all-in fixed fee with the BBC to produce the programme, now that I'd demanded to be paid the going rate, there was an extra element of cost that had to be taken into consideration when Talkback quoted the BBC for the upcoming series.

I was a willing participant for the fourth and fifth series. I knew they wanted to commission another two and so at the end of our meeting I told Jana it would be best if I picked up this matter with Lorraine and let *her* come back to the BBC and tell them how much the whole deal was going to cost them.

There were other issues to discuss with Talkback; not just the money. I needed to put a clause in the contract that gave me the right to have a little say in the edit, at least on the things said by me in the boardroom. Fortunately, Talkback had hired a new lawyer, Jacqueline Moreton, who knew her stuff very well and I found her a lot more straightforward for me to deal with; not because she would give in to things more easily – on the contrary, she was a tough negotiator – but because our discussions would always be about the commercial issues in hand, as opposed to her predecessor who I felt was trying to flex her muscles just for the sake of belligerently taking on the big Sir Alan Sugar. Jacquie and I worked through matters in a businesslike and logical manner, not always agreeing but both being very professional. One had to respect her for that, and I got on very well with Jacquie over the years. She dealt with quite a few series of *The Apprentice* on behalf of Talkback.

The financial side of things ended up in horse-trading about the money that would be paid to my charitable foundation. Off the record I had spoken to a few celebrities' agents and asked them what *they* thought I was worth. They gave me an indication, without prejudice, of course. Frankly, I'm not sure why they did it because normally they would ask for their ten per cent!

In the end, the financial side of things was agreed. What took a bit of doing was finding the words to specify how I would have some input into the final edit. My main argument was that I wanted the programme to have a business message, and as I was the boss of the process, I needed to be able to advise on what I said in the boardroom. I didn't come into *The Apprentice* to be a referee in a slanging match between candidates. It was supposed to be a business programme; a programme where the business message *had* to come through, albeit in an entertaining way as well. I had fully signed on to the need for the programme to be entertaining, but I was no longer going to do it if it just became a brawling contest. What's more, I wanted my words of wisdom to be heard in the appropriate places when a task had gone wrong or a task had gone right, so that I could explain the business angle of it.

Something else was niggling me. After the third series was broadcast, my wife and some of my family were starting to get a little concerned that I was coming across as a really nasty piece of work, always banging my fist on the table and shouting at people, which wasn't a true portrayal of me in real life. I mean, I *am* a fiery character for sure, but you don't have employees working for you for twenty, thirty and even forty years by being a horrible individual. Ann was really concerned about this; in fact, it was the first time she'd ever poked her nose into my business.

'It's not nice what they're doing to you,' she said. 'You shouldn't do any more of these programmes unless they lighten them up a little bit and show you in a better light, even slightly better. There's no problem with you being a bit tough, but this is getting ridiculous now.'

The thing is, the atmosphere *is* quite light-hearted in the boardroom on a lot of occasions. There is some laughter and joking around, and there is some quick-witted banter. Of course, it's mixed in with my sharp tongue and my anger when people get things wrong. The trouble is, I believe the direction for the programme – and who it came from, I don't know – was that Sir Alan Sugar always has to be seen bollocking people and giving them hell, a bit like the way Gordon Ramsay is depicted shouting and swearing at people. (Incidentally, one of the things I decided at the outset of *The Apprentice* was that you would never get me swearing on the programme – at least not using what I would class as the really bad expletives. That is a standard I've maintained throughout the ten series.)

The editing negotiation was quite a tough one, and it ended up with Jacquie and me at stalemate. She could not agree to include words that gave me any rights, because that wasn't in her remit. She referred me back to Lorraine Heggessey to see if we could sort something out. In my discussion with Lorraine, who was also a very straightforward and honest lady, she said, 'Alan, you should know by now, having met these very talented people, that the edit is sacred territory. On top of that, I cannot cede control over the editing of the show as this would be against the BBC producers' guidelines. These people do these jobs so they can say that *everything* that was broadcast was their artistic creation. They would not work for me if I had to tell them that the final say on the edit was taken away from them. They'd see it as an insult; they'd see it as an encroachment on their professional integrity. So we have a real problem here, Alan.'

Her explanation was fair and very logical, but it didn't solve *my* problem. I needed a say in the edit of *my* words, the words *I* spoke. I made it very clear that I wouldn't poke my nose into the editing of anything else: the candidates out on the tasks or in the board-room, anything that Nick or Margaret said or any of the storylines in the programme. However, for what came out of my mouth, I insisted on having the right to say that any particular sequence be included.

'Can you elaborate on that a little bit more, Alan?' Lorraine said.

'Look, Lorraine, after doing three series of *The Apprentice* I know by now what goes on. I appreciate that sometimes a particu-lar storyline doesn't get used, so if what I say refers to something in that particular storyline, I fully understand that it can't be used. For example, if we were doing a fruit and veg task and most of the story centred on the apples and there wasn't room to include the story on the oranges, I can see that anything I wanted to include to do with oranges couldn't go in – I get that. I'm talking about when a storyline *has* been chosen, anything I've said businesswise that's relevant to that story needs to be included.'

I restated that I was willing to participate in the next two series, but I felt very strongly about this and I wasn't prepared to agree anything until the matter was resolved. I politely told Lorraine that at this moment in time – and it had nothing to do with money – we would just have to agree to disagree on this edit issue. I suggested she go away and think about it, talk to Michele and come up with some solution, because there was no way I was going to be treated like a robot any more, where my words of wisdom end up on the cutting-room floor.

It's difficult to explain how I felt at the time, and I don't want to come across as some demanding prima donna, but when you've seriously put your heart and soul into the programme and seen some of the stuff you've worked on just thrown away, it's very demoralising. And I'm not talking about some of my jokes or throwaway remarks; I'm talking about stuff I spent lots of time researching in order to come up with sensible comments and advice for the candidates.

The point that I kept making to Lorraine was, 'I care about the programme; I care about its integrity. In fact, you should be *grateful* that I'm worrying to this extent. I'm committed to *The Apprentice* – it takes up nearly a year of my time. I know the filming doesn't take a year but I'm constantly having to deal with things during the build-up, then post-transmission I'm having to provide a serious job for the winning candidate. This is a full-time job that I have to do amid my other day jobs. Anyone else would just turn up, do his couple of hours' worth, get in the car and piss off. I'm not that type of person. This is a product I'm proud of and it's got my name on it.'

The deadline was getting very close for Talkback to seal a deal with the BBC and the message had got back to the BBC that I was not ready to sign. People from the BBC were calling me up, asking whether they could help, and I told them the issue was nothing to do with money but with logistics. I didn't want to go into detail with them. Instead I referred them to Talkback and said they needed to sort it out with them.

Eventually, Lorraine called me and said, 'The issue is becoming quite critical at the BBC. They want to know why you will not sign up and I'm finding it embarrassingly difficult to explain to them. It's going to come to a stage where, regrettably, they might turn round and say that if Alan Sugar doesn't want to do it, we will have to go looking for someone else.'

Now the way Lorraine put that across to me, to be very fair to her, was in an unthreatening manner. It was in a tone where she was kind of saying, 'God forbid we have to do that – we don't want to do that.' But despite Lorraine trying to say this in a polite way, the hairs on the back of my neck stood up. However, I thought to myself, 'Bite your tongue, Alan, and shut up. Do not lose your temper. Do not start shouting down the phone to Lorraine – she is trying to be diplomatic. Just bite your tongue.'

I remember saying to her, 'Look, ever since I've been doing this programme, all I've ever seen in the papers is people saying, "I was asked to do *The Apprentice* but I turned it down." I've had friends of mine come to me saying, "One of my mates in north-west London was asked to do that programme; they turned it down because they were too busy." This one claimed he turned it down; that one claimed he turned it down. Duncan Bannatyne [who was becoming popular in *Dragon's Den* at the time] said, "I could do it much better than Alan Sugar." So there you are, Lorraine, you've got plenty of choice. You won't have a problem replacing me because there will be people queuing up wanting to do it. However, if I say so myself, and you might call me a bloody big-head, none of them are in my class, darling. None of them at all. You know it, I know it, and the BBC knows it. Let's face it, the issue we have here, Lorraine, is that you've already appointed Michele as the boss of the programme. If we were having this debate prior to you appointing a *new* Michele, this problem wouldn't arise because you could tell the *new* Michele that she can only do this job on the basis that Sir Alan wants to have a little input into the edit. Unfortunately, you cannot now go back to Michele and tell her you wish to take away her licence to control the content of the programme. I fully understand that and so I think it best that you and Michele get together and hammer this out, because I'm telling you right now – I'm still not signing, love.'

Then Lorraine threw something new into the pot: 'Well, we simply can't put these kinds of words into the contract. The BBC won't accept it.'

'Oh no, Lorraine, come off it. Don't go there. You're talking to Alan Sugar here now; you're not talking to some bloody wannabe who's applied to Channel 4's *Big Brother* programme. Please don't go down in my estimation, Lorraine. Right now I rate you as a good person to do business with, so please don't resort to falling back on the BBC and all that sort of stuff, because I don't believe it for one moment.'

In the end we reached a compromise. Michele, Lorraine and I had a nice meeting and we found some words for the contract that suited all of us. Words, of course, as you know, don't mean anything unless you're going to take someone to court. Really, what's more important was that I had an eye-to-eye agreement and shook hands with Michele and Lorraine on an understanding of what my rights were. Part of the agreement was that they would have a DVD recorder in the gallery and burn me a DVD of each boardroom scene so I could see and hear everything that went on. After filming, I would go away, watch the DVD and write up some notes for the benefit of Michele, saying in effect, 'Only if you're going to run this particular storyline, I think we need this little sequence included.' That was the deal that was done, and that is the deal that still exists today.

Credit to Michele, she stuck with the deal. However, I will go on to explain how some of the other people she hired for later series didn't feel they needed to sign up to this agreement. Nevertheless, in essence we agreed we would have more of a business message coming out of my mouth in the boardroom, as well as a bit of light-hearted banter in order to portray a slightly different side of me from the shouting, fist-banging tyrant they'd previously shown. And that's what I believe we achieved from the fourth series onwards.

12

CHILI AND THE LORD

**Still waiting to be big in America, and shaking
things up in series four**

Chili Scot Cru was the representative of Mark Burnett Productions, the owner of *The Apprentice* format. Just as in Britain where people like to be associated with a hit, the growing success for the third series of *The Apprentice* had raised eyebrows in the US, and Chili started coming over to be at the final. Now, Chili is the epitome of the smooth-talking television executive. If you listen to him, your head will get so big that it'll be impossible for you to walk out of the door – that is, if you take him too seriously. He is so complimentary, it's unbelievable.

We have this ongoing banter about all the things he's going to do for me vis-à-vis popularising me in the United States. Chili is very enthusiastic, with lots of ideas for some programme or other I can be involved in, and this repertoire plays out at every *Apprentice* final. I said to him after series ten, 'Why don't you just bring a little DVD along with you and play it to me every year to save your breath? I'm still waiting for this Great Breakthrough in America you keep promising me.'

Banter aside, he has been instrumental over the years in acting as a kind of arbitrator between me and the production company when it came to the renewal of my contract for further series. As I understand it, for every series that is broadcast, Mark

Burnett Productions receives a royalty payable to them by the BBC or Fremantle Media, hence Chili's involvement.

On one occasion during the negotiation of a new contract, I was informed that Fremantle had been approached by an Australian TV company who wanted to buy the UK version of *The Apprentice* to run on Channel 7 Television in Australia. This sounded very exciting to me, to be seen not only in Britain but also in Australia. Naturally, my commercial acumen kicked in and I asked, 'How much will we be paid for this?'

And here is another story that any young businessperson should take heed of. I have often said that you learn by your mistakes, and once bitten twice shy is the appropriate lesson here, as I will explain. We were negotiating over the various elements of my fee, one of which was that I would get a share of the revenues, owing to Talkback, of the UK programmes that were shown abroad. Also getting a share of the revenues would be the BBC and, in some markets, Mark Burnett Productions. This all seemed fair enough. The thing was slightly complicated by the fact that Mark Burnett Productions were going to get a share of the revenues of the programming shown in the rest of the world with the exception of the US, where they themselves would take the English programme and arrange for it to be broadcast in the US, but again, fair enough.

Where it all went wrong for me was that I got done up like a kipper, as we East End boys say. What happened was, and I cannot remember the actual figures, but let's talk about an index scale of 100. Let us say the product was being sold to Australia for 100 and my deal said I was going to get 50 per cent of revenues, which sounds great. No such luck, and here's why. Fremantle Media, the ones who put the deal together to sell the programme to Australian TV, took 20 per cent. The BBC took, from memory, let's say 20 per cent. Mark Burnett took, again from memory, let's say 20 per cent. Then there was the fact that the licence to use the music in the UK version was covered by an overall agreement that the BBC has with the copyright owners and would not apply when the programme was transmitted in other countries.

As a side issue to this story, in the thousands upon thousands of television programmes that are broadcast by the BBC where directors and creative people use popular music to enhance the programmes, the rights owners of that music are entitled to be paid each and every time the programme is played out. Obviously this must have been a monumental task to try to resolve over the years, and I believe there is an authority somewhere that collects all these royalties en masse for all the rights owners and I understand that the BBC at some stage did a deal with that authority to pay what must have been a flat fee such that they can go and use anything and not have to report song by song on the music they use in their programmes.

With that understood, you can see the deal did not apply to the music being used in Australia. Therefore, one of two things had to happen: either we paid extra to the rights owner of the music, or we cut the music out by re-editing the programme especially for Australia, and in this case the latter occurred. And guess what? There was a whacking great fee for doing this – a Talkback Thames edit fee. So a picture is emerging here of how the 100 of total revenue has now been reduced to around 12, in terms of the revenue that Talkback would get. 'And yes, Sir Alan, you're entitled to half – that is, 6.'

So you can imagine my disappointment when reality hit home. Now I can picture people reading this and thinking, 'You're supposed to be quite shrewd – how did you let that happen?'

It was, I suppose, a case of failing to delve into the small print and detail. More to the point, it was my lack of experience in how things were done in this industry. In fact, when I complained bitterly to Lorraine Heggessey, she kind of brushed it off in a matter-of-fact manner as if to say, 'I don't know what you're going on about, Alan, this is all normal.' She went on to explain to me that *of course* when Fremantle sell a programme they must get a commission, and *of course* the BBC was entitled to this and *of course* Mark Burnett was entitled to that. And *of course* the music has to be paid for and re-edited . . . 'I don't quite understand what your issue is here, Alan. This is normal; it goes on all the time.'

'Er, not really, love, no, no. It doesn't go on all the time in *my* world because when someone says to me, "I'll flog something for a hundred and you're entitled to fifty per cent," then I'm expecting to get fifty, but in this scenario, I've ended up with six. Now come on, this is a bloody joke, a total, absolute joke. I feel like I've been legged-over.'

I think Lorraine got it in the end as I put it to her very simply: 'Are you telling me that after all the extra promotional work I did for the Australian television company, and all the fuss and noise and press releases that we put out, all you're going to pay me is this pittance that comes back to me? You must understand, Lorraine, this is a total and absolute joke.' I had virtually done the whole PR thing – talking to loads of people from the Australian media (just as we'd done for the UK version) – all over again. Maybe I should have insisted on a fee for all that, just as Talkback had insisted on a fee for the music edit.

So there you are, another lesson learned on the way the TV business works. And as you can imagine, next time round I made it perfectly clear that revenues for overseas sales of the UK programme to foreign broadcasters was an issue they would have to sort out themselves as far as the commissions they paid to Uncle Tom Cobley and all were concerned; I just wanted an absolute cast-in-concrete percentage of the gross amount being paid by the broadcaster. In the end we achieved that because the programme became quite popular in Australia as well as in a few other countries like South Africa and Scandinavia where English is the first or second language.

Back with Chili, he was very excited about getting Sir Alan

Sugar on American TV. To be fair to him, he did a really good job in getting the British *Apprentice* broadcast on CNBC, which was primarily a business channel broadcast on cable networks in America. Unfortunately, however, Chili's great efforts backfired. CNBC aired the programme around the same time as the Lehman Brothers banking disaster occurred in the United States. It was the worst time you could pick to try and take up valuable space on what was effectively a business and financial channel. The programme ran for two or three episodes and was then, to be frank, simply trashed. It was thrown away because the financial business disasters took over the majority of the stories. That was a disappointment, but credit to Chili, he didn't give up. He did a deal with the BBC in the US to relaunch the programme on the BBC America channel, which again is broadcast on the cable network, though it isn't as popular as CNBC. However, at least he put in the effort to try and get it broadcast in America, which was quite exciting. I recall being in my house in Florida when a gentleman from BBC America asked to come and visit me to do some promotional interviews to put on the channel prior to it broadcasting. This very nice chap came along and we spent about half a day filming a few bits and pieces for the titles and trails for the programme.

Now this you're not going to believe. When they broadcast the programme on BBC America, on some occasions when I was speaking they put up subtitles! This was because, they claimed, the Americans couldn't understand what I was saying! Actually, when I'm in America a lot of the Americans say to me, 'Are you from Australia? It's a funny accent you've got.' I have to admit, if I talk very quickly, they do tend to ask, 'Sorry, what did you say?' But I never thought it was as bad as needing subtitles on the programme.

Unfortunately, the programme wasn't a great hit on BBC America. It wasn't a heavily viewed channel and it certainly wouldn't be a programme that Americans on the whole would want to tune in to, especially bearing in mind the hundreds of TV channels available to them. But Chili did his best and, to this day, he is still beavering away trying to find an opportunity for me on American television because he's a great fan of mine, and I guess I'm a great fan of his because he's quite a funny chap in his mannerisms and his schmoozy ways. He's just a likeable fellow all round.

About a year or so later, he called me again while I was in Florida, telling me that Mark Burnett Productions had acquired the rights to produce *Dragons' Den*; from a Japanese company, I understand. They wouldn't be calling it *Dragons' Den* – instead they would call it *Shark Tank*. Chili enquired of me whether I would be interested in participating in *Shark Tank*.

When he asked me that question, I had visions of the British version of the programme and pictured it being hosted not by one person but most probably by about five. I told Chili that if I were to do something in America, I would prefer to be the main host of the programme and not, for example, one of five co-hosts. So that idea went away as I'd rejected it. Call me big-headed maybe, or maybe not, but what I had in my mind was doing a programme similar to *The Apprentice* in America that focused on me giving out business advice. It also occurred to me that, being British, if I did participate in *Shark Tank*, how could I invest in an American company when I spend most of my time in England? In *Dragons' Den* the panel invest in companies and then get involved after the event. In a US version, it would be logistically difficult. This was a point I raised with Chili in later years but, still resilient to my negativity, he said there could be a role for me in *Shark Tank* like a cameo appearance as a non-permanent member of the panel; perhaps on occasions when they had people pitching products that had an international twist to them. This did make a bit of sense to me but I am still waiting, years later, for Chili to phone me up and tell me to get my arse over to Los Angeles for some filming.

While on the international front, it was quite strange being in America where nobody knew who I was. This was in stark contrast to the UK where, by the end of series three, the programme had become so popular that if I was walking in the street somewhere I was always recognised by the British public. In America they are very much focused on their own marketplace. I've often said that many Americans don't even know there are countries outside America. Lots of Americans have never been abroad and don't own a passport; indeed some of them have never even left their own *state*, let alone travelled overseas. So in America I can walk around freely. I can, for example, go shopping occasionally with my wife in a supermarket, something I haven't done in England for forty-five years. Not that I like shopping in supermarkets, but I do like to keep up with how things are marketed. So in America I can walk up and down the aisles freely. It's a similar experience in France and Italy, but to a lesser extent in the south of Spain where a lot of British people hang out. I'm not complaining about being recognised in the UK; I'm simply raising the point that if I want to go somewhere and not be recognised, America is the place to be.

Having said that, the last time I met Chili was at the very fashionable Soho Beach House Hotel on Miami Beach where he was attending some annual TV convention. I agreed to meet him there, together with some other people from Mark Burnett Productions. On coming out of the hotel I was approached by two or three ladies who wanted to have a picture taken with me. They were obviously British and they were there for the convention. It was funny observing the car jockeys and other Americans outside the hotel watching these ladies make a little bit of a fuss and having a picture taken with me – meanwhile these onlookers had a face on them as if to say, 'Who the bloody hell is he? What are they getting excited about?'

That reminds me, a friend of mine sometimes invites me to his country club close to the Florida Atlantic University. The club's catering department frequently employs a lot of British students who are studying at the university, so whenever I'm invited there for lunch I'm often asked to have photos taken with these students who obviously know who I am. When this happens, I see the same phenomenon with the American citizens looking on bemused, wondering what all the fuss is about. On one occasion, and this really made Ann and me laugh, after having watched all these kids getting their pictures taken with me, an American woman who didn't even know who I was jumped up and said, 'Can I also have my picture taken with you?'!

After the increased exposure that moving the third series to BBC1 had brought, we received twenty thousand applications for the fourth series, more than we'd ever had before. From that we went about our usual whittling down, ending up once more with the customary sixteen candidates.

Going into the fourth series I was glad that Andy Devonshire was still there as series director and the young Mark Saben was still with the production team, having previously assisted on series two and three. Mark would go on to take senior roles in the production of later series, and is a classic example of somebody who rose through the ranks as he learned his trade.

Another gentleman who plied his trade in series three was Tom McDonald, a very talented chap who became senior producer. Tom was very creative with some of his ideas, and he would go on to produce the *Junior Apprentice* programme, which I'll talk about later. Additionally, enter a lady by the name of Cate Hall, who went on to become the production boss in later series. I was pleased to see a bit of consistency developing in the team rather than everyone running off afterwards to pastures new. At least we now had what looked like the skeleton of a good team as we started the fourth series.

As usual I needed to consider what I would say to the candidates in Boardroom Zero. At the end of the day I couldn't just repeat what I'd said in the past and needed to refresh the message. I started by saying, 'Nervous? Good, you should be.' And I continued with my explanation of what the process was all about, including snippets like, 'Don't start telling me you're just like me because you're *not* like me – I am unique.'

There were some amazing characters in this fourth series. One of them was Nicholas de Lacy-Brown, a trainee barrister, artist and property developer – a very posh, well-spoken chap. In the first episode he got himself into a lot of hot water implying that some of the other people in the boardroom with him, like Alex Wotherspoon, were perhaps not as academically blessed as he was because they preferred football to academia. This caused the first row of the series in the boardroom. Alex went ballistic.

'What are you talking about? I *am* educated. The fact that I like football has got nothing to do with it. It's outrageous! You're the one who made the mistakes on this task; you spent too much on the fish. It's not my problem.'

It was a great start to the series, right from the first boardroom in episode one.

In fact, Nicholas was a fish out of water in this process and he had to go in week one. I told him, 'Having read your CV, it says you were devastated at school when you got a B in your GCSE French. Well, you're going to be even more devastated now because you've got a big F – for fired.'

One of the other stand-out candidates in the fourth series was Raef Bjayou, an extremely plummy young entrepreneur. I remember he caught my attention in the very first week when he said in the boardroom that he got on with princes or paupers. I asked him whether he thought he was a prince in his own eyes, which he quickly shied away from answering. At the time I remember thinking to myself, '*Who* talks like that?'

Raef made a name for himself as a particularly dapper sort of chap, even if a lot of the time he sounded like he'd swallowed a bloody thesaurus. Often, when the teams returned to the house after a boardroom firing and changed into more comfortable jeans and T-shirts, Raef would enter the room with immaculately pomaded hair and be sleekly dressed, *à la* Noel Coward, in a silk dressing gown. He lasted until week nine when he made the ultimate mistake on the advertising task. The thrust of the task was to create a TV advert to promote a new brand of tissues as well as design the packaging and come up with the brand name. Raef joined up with Michael Sophocles and the pair of them spent the entire task waffling about how they were going to shoot the advert, thinking they were Martin Scorsese and Steven Spielberg. Raef in particular got really carried away. He had told me in the boardroom previously that he had acted in a lot of Shakespeare plays, which included playing Malvolio in *Twelfth Night*. He got a bit of a surprise from me when I started to question him about his role as Malvolio, especially when I threw him a few lines of the play. He looked a little shocked and taken aback. The reason I was able to do this is because when I was sixteen my school put on *Twelfth Night* and I had a part in it, which has stuck in my mind ever since. So here I was in the boardroom with Raef – him telling me he'd been involved in *Twelfth Night* and me rattling off the part that I played – and his face was a picture to behold. Margaret also gave me a very strange look. She, too, never thought I'd be cultured enough to recite Shakespeare. She was mumbling to me, 'No, no, no, that line's wrong . . .'

'No it's not, Margaret. It's right, I'm telling you, it's actually correct.'

Anyway, that's a side issue. The point I'm trying to make here is that Raef got so involved with the TV advert, thinking he was filming the remake of *Ben Hur*, that he completely lost the plot about showcasing the design of the tissues and focusing on the brand name and the logo so they were recognisable on the screen as well as in the shops where the product would be sold. The reason he made such a mess of things was because he spent so much time being arty-farty, he forgot to get a close-up of the bloody product, making the entire advert completely pointless.

Raef was a very nice chap and a charming fellow, and to this day has been very supportive of *The Apprentice*; indeed, from time to time he's called upon by the media to comment on certain things about the programme. But on this occasion, unfortunately, there was no coming back from this complete cock-up, and he was fired.

Raef wasn't the only candidate who stood out that year, because they were a right bunch – some for good reasons, others not so good. I remember a fellow called Simon Smith, who showed me in the early tasks that he was a real grafter. He was actually a satellite engineer and he knew about my involvement with BSkyB at the time, producing dishes for them at Amstrad. In the boardroom he couldn't resist telling me how he installed loads of these dishes and, of course, the Amstrad ones were much better than anyone else's, grovel, grovel. Simon was the type of chap you'd put in charge of production, and in the first task of the series, which was to sell fish, he was a trooper. I recall amazing pictures of him hacking the head off some giant eel on a market stall to accommodate the require-ments of a customer who wanted the eel's head to make some soup. Another task he excelled at was the industrial laundry where in fact he carried his team through the task – he was seriously impressive. However, when it came to tasks that were less to do with manual labour and more to do with strategy, he really struggled. To be per-fectly honest with him, I told him in the boardroom that if I needed him to build a wall or dig a ditch, he'd be the perfect man, but as a key employee in one of my businesses, I just couldn't see it, and I had to let him go.

The laundry task was absolutely brilliant. It is still a firm favourite of mine as well as a lot of other people's in the production team. In my view it really tested the candidates from a business perspective. They had to negotiate contracts with people to take away their laundry, cost up the whole operation and then perform the service – in other words, collect the stuff, clean it, bring it back and charge for it. This could be going to hotels and restaurants and asking to take their linen, or it could be just knocking on people's doors and taking six shirts, dresses or whatever. Obviously the business acumen needed to kick in here. I've often said: why waste your time talking to somebody where the deal is only worth £25 when you can use the same energy talking to somebody where the deal is worth £2,500? It was amazing how some of the candidates on this task wasted their time and energy seeking out an individual who gave them, for example, just four shirts to clean. In fact, at one point the customer complained that one of the four shirts given to the team got lost. This sparked a big argument within the team as to who was responsible for losing it. I have to admit, it ended up being pretty brilliant television.

I couldn't believe some of the things they got up to on this task. One of the candidates, Lindi Mngaza, tried to charge £5,000 for a contract which should have cost no more than a couple of hundred quid. When the people she was negotiating with pulled her up on this, she tried to justify the cost by offering a free 24-hour laundry hotline in order to make the quote more appealing. When I got her in the boardroom I questioned her about this hotline.

'What sort of business wants to ring someone up at three o'clock in the morning to find out how their sheets are drying? Was this a joke or what?' In fact, I mimicked picking up the phone and said, 'Hello, girls, how's me pants doing? I'm just calling the 24-hour hotline to find out the progress of my Calvin Kleins.'

It was a hilarious moment and one which I'm pleased to say was included in the broadcast.

It was a great series, and another outstanding task was when we went to Marrakesh, to the souk. What fantastic pictures James Clarke and his camera team created there. Absolutely brilliant television. I can still see it today with the candidates running around in

Marrakesh. This particular task was the one where I asked them to go and find ten items and the team that came in having spent the least would be the winners.

Now as any fan of *The Apprentice* will know, from time to time the teams fall down on this task by not correctly interpreting the actual product I want, so apart from getting it at the wrong price, they sometimes get the wrong product. In that instance the product is disallowed and a fine is imposed on the team, which can cause them to lose the task. Even though this particular task was performed years ago, when you ask members of the public to name their favourite *Apprentice* moments, Marrakesh will often be on the list.

One of the items I asked them to find was a kosher chicken. In fact, Mark Saben, who knew I was Jewish, thought this up. He thought it would be rather funny to send them to look for a kosher butcher in an Arab country, and it did turn out to be hilarious. Lee McQueen, the guy who ended up winning the series, *did* manage to find one. Obviously we couldn't set an *impossible* task – in fact, Mark Saben had previously gone out to research Marrakesh and had made sure that a kosher butcher did exist there. However, the other team made a real pig's ear of getting this kosher chicken. First of all, they had no clue what they were looking for and they ended up asking a stallholder selling halal chickens if he had any idea where they could find a kosher chicken. With the cameras around, the stallholder, a mischievous fellow, told them, 'Yes, no problem, my friend, I can give you a kosher chicken.'

One of the candidates, Jenny Celerier, said, 'I understand that a kosher chicken has to be killed in a certain way and has to be blessed?'

'Yes,' said the fellow on the stall. 'I'll get somebody from the mosque to bless the chicken for you.'

What a total mess.

When they got back into the boardroom, I watched Jenny

trying to distance herself from this fiasco, which made me absolutely livid. She was trying to push the whole thing on to Michael Sophocles because he was Jewish. I said to Jenny, 'Are you kidding me? Have you never heard the word "kosher" in all your working life? Surely you must have heard that word?'

'No, Sir Alan, I really do not understand what it means.'

I was stunned.

I turned to Michael. 'Now, Michael, in your application for this process, you said you were a nice Jewish boy, is that right?'

'Er, well, erm . . .'

'Come on, Michael, either you are or you aren't a nice Jewish boy.'

'Er, well, er . . . well, yeah, okay, I am a nice Jewish boy.'

'Because if you're not sure, we can pull your trousers down and have a look!'

I continued, 'Michael, are you telling me you do not know what a kosher chicken is? You've gone to a halal butcher, a Muslim, and asked him to sell you a kosher chicken and say a prayer over it – are you having a laugh? I don't know why you didn't go the whole hog and find a Roman Catholic priest to take the butcher to confession!'

I think the reason Michael hesitated about his religion was that his mother is Jewish and his father is not. In fact, as his *mother* is Jewish, in the eyes of Jewish Law that actually makes *him* Jewish; but more to the point, he stuck it in his CV. I assume this was to impress me, whereas of course it makes no difference to me what race or religion a candidate is. Having said all that, Michael *did* seem a bit mixed up because sometimes, before going into the boardroom to be grilled by me, he was filmed crossing himself!

I recall Nick trying to support Michael in the boardroom by saying, 'He can't be a complete fool, Alan; he's a pretty educated bloke. He read classics at Edinburgh.'

Before I could respond, Margaret said, 'Well, clearly Edinburgh isn't what it was.'

When that remark was broadcast there was an amazing uproar from Edinburgh University. They put out a statement saying their classics department was top-notch, that they had many eminent professors, etc., etc. We had no idea one little quip would cause such a big academic hullabaloo.

In week six I set a task to produce a greeting card. Michael was in the winning team and when the result was announced he punched the boardroom table in excitement and roared, 'Come on! Come on!' and Lee McQueen shouted, 'Yeah, that's what I'm talking about!'

Well, you should have seen Margaret's face. She was disgusted and shocked at such behaviour. I told them, 'This is not a football match. This outburst of yours is not something I would condone in this boardroom.'

Michael responded, 'I apologise, Sir Alan, but I think I've shown glimmers of brilliance here.'

I shut him down. 'Don't get carried away with yourself – you're no Bill Gates.'

Another interesting character was Lucinda Ledgerwood, a zany sort of girl but quite intelligent. She stood out to me because of the strange, brightly coloured clothes and berets she wore. She spoke in a quiet, posh voice, making her points very logically. I think she felt a bit intimidated and ostracised by the others. I heard from the production people that when the candidates got back to the house in the evening after a task or a boardroom session, Lucinda didn't join in with the general discussion, preferring instead to take herself off to bed. I recall in one boardroom when she was in the last three she came out with a classic. I said to her, 'Lucinda, you are a risk manager – what is the risk of you being fired today?'

'Well, the probability is one in three,' she said.

What a brainstorm that was.

*

One of the things we decided to do in series four was to shake things up a bit. Instead of having two candidates in the final, as we'd had in the previous three years, we decided to have four, with two teams of two paired up as joint project managers. For the final I asked them to come up with a new fragrance for the male market.

Alex Wotherspoon was still in the process, and he teamed up with Helene Speight, a clever young lady whose day job was a Global Pricing Leader – whatever that means. The other team comprised Claire Young and Lee McQueen. Claire, who was a buyer for one of the pharmaceutical retailers, had risen through the process. She was one of those who *did* get the plot on the buying and selling and business tasks, but then you'd expect that from a professional buyer. She came close to being fired a couple of times and I have to admit I gave her such a rough time that on occasions I nearly brought her to tears, but she was pretty shrewd and clearly a tough girl.

Lee McQueen, on the other hand, came across as a hard-working grafter who was prepared to learn. He'd managed to get through to the penultimate episode, the interview process, where my advisor Bordan Tkachuk did some investigations on some of the claims Lee had made in his CV. Lee claimed he had a degree, and this turned out to be total nonsense. Bordan had called the university in question and guess what? They'd never heard of Lee McQueen. Now some have said to me that this should have been a fireable offence, and I guess, in a way, they're right. However, I suppose I had a little sympathy for Lee. He explained quite eloquently after the interviews why he had embellished his CV, and I kind of forgave him and let him move on to the final, mainly because I'd had my eye on him as the ultimate winner due to the sensible way he went about executing the tasks throughout the course of the whole process. When you gave him a task, you got a feeling this fellow knew what he was doing. Of course, the media latched on to this CV-embellishment thing and had a field day with it. To this day it is still referred to when they discuss people fibbing on their CVs.

During the interviews episode, Paul Kemsley discovered another claim to fame that Lee had put in his CV – apparently he could do a great impersonation of a pterodactyl. This was too much for Kemsley to let go, so he insisted that Lee show him this impersonation. And Lee did it! It was a really cringey moment, and when I saw it broadcast I thought, 'Why did you do that?' But then this was Kemsley talking him into doing it, and the TV production company loved it of course.

It was a difficult decision to make between Claire and Lee. While I had my eye on Lee as the winner, there were a couple of negative issues, such as the CV thing, that could have changed my mind because Claire was definitely a great contender. But, on balance, I chose Lee in the end.

I still speak to Claire quite a lot. She decided not to go back to working as a buyer but instead started up her own business which involved inspirational speaking to young people. She has been very successful in it, and good luck to her. In fact, I attended one of her seminars in the East End of London and I took part in a Q&A session. She is very supportive of *The Apprentice* and me. I think that she, along with many of the people who have participated in the programme, realise that the opportunity of even *being* in the process is something they'll never forget for the rest of their lives. Moreover, these people have the utmost respect for me despite the way I may have been portrayed on TV as giving them a tough time in the boardroom. And I have to say that, with the exception of a few people, who I will discuss later, the respect shown to me post-series has been unbelievable, so I must have got something right!

After the third series I was acutely aware of the problems of having ex-winners planted in my company, so I decided to think up something for Lee that was completely new – something that my other employees were not involved with. It was fortunate that my son Simon had just set up Amscreen, a new division of my group, whose remit was to place screens in various locations like petrol stations and send adverts to those screens. We had acquired a company in Bolton who had the proprietary software which, to explain in layman's terms, incorporated a mobile phone that sat in the back of a screen, and by using mobile network technology, chunks of data could be sent via the mobile network to this device, which converted the data into an advert that appeared on the screen. This company was in its infancy and it was an ideal opportunity for Lee to join a new venture that would not encroach upon any of my other employees' jobs. In other words, the rest of the staff wouldn't need to have anything to do with him. It was simply him and Simon together.

After Lee had won *The Apprentice*, it was agreed that he would take a few weeks off to rest and settle down. We fixed the exact date that he would start at Amscreen, but when it came to that date, he couldn't make it! Whether it was a massive attack of nerves, neither Lee nor I know, but he called on the morning he was supposed to turn up at the office saying he was sick. He actually had a sick note on his first day! He said it was some violent stomach problem, which I still think was nerves. Quite funny when we look back, though not funny for him at the time. The media, of course, lapped it up. In fact, the reason they found out he hadn't turned up for work was because they were waiting to doorstep him on his first day. So once again they went to town speculating on this explanation and that, and once again generated another few pages of chip wrappers.

As it turned out, Simon and Lee got on with each other very well. They formed the foundation of Amscreen there and then. Lee really got in on the ground floor. Initially, Simon asked him to specialise in the medical market, putting screens in doctors' surgeries

and clinics (as we had also acquired another company that specialised in this niche market). Lee's first task was to start enhancing
this division in the medical market, and I was quite impressed with
the way he took to it. The thing about new people you employ is:
you need to watch them and observe them to see how long it takes
them to get the plot. In this particular venture there were a lot of
new things we all had to learn. For instance, you can't just bomb
down to the doctor's surgery and put a screen up on the wall. There
are procedures within the NHS organisation, permissions to be
granted and all that sort of stuff, so it's not as simple and straightforward as it might sound. And I have to say, as various obstacles
were put in our paths, Lee took to overcoming them like a duck to
water. He was very good at getting the medical side of things
underway.

Lee was a passionate Tottenham Hotspur fan and would chat
with me from time to time about the misfortunes of the club.
Nothing positive, naturally – he was a typical Spurs fan after all –
more along the lines of, 'What are we going to do to try and sort it
out?' By then, of course, I was no longer the chairman of Tottenham so I was able to be a little critical myself. Unfortunately, the
media being the media somehow got hold of a video clip of Lee
being a bit overenthusiastic, looking a bit yobbish, at a Spurs
match. One of his mates had taken a video of him in the stands and
had flogged it to a newspaper which tried to portray Lee as, to put
it mildly, an overexcited football thug.

Lee stayed with Amscreen for two years, during which time he
started to see it grow. Eventually, he asked me if he could leave to
start a business of his own. I would never stand in the way of
anyone who wants to start their own business; I always encourage
it. I listened to his plan and told him that if I *were* to stand in his
way – if I asked him to hang on and wait for the Amscreen business to really start motoring; telling him he'd be a very big cog in a
very large wheel – it would constantly play on his mind that he

never took the chance to go it alone. And I know how that might feel – he would always be looking back, thinking, 'I *wanted* to do it but I didn't.'

So I made that point to Lee and encouraged him to take his opportunity. He had picked up some valuable lessons in the two years he had worked for us, including a lot of business acumen and the fact that one needed to control one's costs all the time; useful stuff if he was going to start his own business.

During his period of employment he witnessed a tribunal claim against Amscreen from one of its employees. In fact, it was from the person from whom Simon had bought the medical screen business. I won't go into the detail of that derisory claim save to say it gave us all a headache, including Lee, who was cited unreasonably. This particular claimant turned out to be a really nasty piece of work and basically cost us a lot of money in defending the action before she withdrew her claim. This was because the tribunal system at the time allowed people to bring claims and not have any liability for paying the legal costs of their opponent if they failed. In this particular case, Amscreen was the opponent and we had to spend a lot of money with lawyers defending the issue. She, on the other hand, found an ambulance chaser who thought his boat had come in as he was attacking a company owned by Sir Alan Sugar. The ambulance chaser was working on the basis that we would simply cave in and pay their client a lot of money. They soon learned this would not be the case, and Lee, regrettably, was dragged into the mess, though I suppose he can look upon it as one of life's lessons, and I guess it must have helped him to know in his future dealings just what can happen.

The soaring popularity of *The Apprentice*, reflected in the record number of candidates applying for it, coincided with a new trend in the TV world. It's funny how each of the broadcasters likes to follow the other. Channel 4 had started to spend a lot of money on street posters and billboards advertising forthcoming or existing programmes. ITV followed suit by also buying up advertising space on the streets. And so the BBC did the same. Jana Bennett authorised a massive advertising campaign for *The Apprentice*. It was phenomenal – every single bus stop in London had a picture of me advertising *The Apprentice* on BBC1. Everywhere you looked there were street hoardings with my face looking at you as you were driving along in your car. I don't know how much money was spent on it, but you have to take your hat off to them as they really did get behind the programme, promoting it before the broadcast started. I make this point because at the time it was a fashionable thing for the TV broadcasters to do, but now has almost completely stopped as they see it as a waste of valuable cash – I imagine to the great disappointment of companies like JCDecaux. That said, I do occasionally see the odd street hoarding advertising something on Channel 4 and Sky. I remember my friends and family saying to me at the time, 'Wow, everywhere we go there's a picture of you looking at me – it's unbelievable!'

If being on street hoardings wasn't amazing enough, imagine how I felt when I was slapped on the front of the *Radio Times*. I'm told in TV circles this is a great honour. Being a TV personality is one thing, but in my wildest dreams I never would have thought I'd be featured on the *Radio Times* cover. And it wasn't just once either. Over the years I've appeared there five or six times.

I have to say that I could only see this as very complimentary by the BBC. Of course, I had no objection to it whatsoever – why would I? As I've already said, the fame side of things was something I quite enjoyed.

13

OFTEN COPIED, NEVER EQUALLED

The popularity of *The Apprentice* – spoofs and spin-offs

I really do *not* like going to awards ceremonies. I had been to a few since that first BAFTA ceremony in 2006, and in truth I found them quite boring. In fact in March 2007 I was kind of forced to go to the Royal Television Society awards where *The Apprentice* actually won. Our nomination was for the second series, for which Dan Adamson had been in charge of production. I went up to accept the award with Dan and whispered into his ear, 'By the way, you can keep your dirty mitts off this thing because you're not having it, mate – I'm keeping it this time. Never mind all your creative arty-farty stuff – this is mine. I'll do my best to get you a replica from the people giving out the awards, but you ain't having it – sorry, son!' which he accepted graciously because he knew how pissed off I was about the BAFTA fiasco. As it happened, the people dishing out these particular awards were quite generous. They did indeed supply a couple more afterwards to some of the other people who were involved in the production.

It's nice to win but these awards ceremonies seem to be occasions when anybody who's involved in television, be it production or on screen, likes to turn up in their dinner suits and evening gowns and have a good old booze-up. It's all about being seen walking down the red carpet and having one's picture taken and mingling with other guests and all that stuff.

I know I'm starting to sound like a miserable old sod here, but I have to say that this just isn't my scene. Now my good friend Nick Hewer, on the other hand, loves it. He laps it all up. He'll go to these events and he'll stand there yakking to anyone who wants to come up and talk to him.

The success of *The Apprentice* resulted in us being invited to a whole host of awards ceremonies and it's quite amazing to see the number of awards the programme has received. At the last count I believe there have been twenty-four, including a BAFTA, a National Reality TV award, a Royal Television Society award for Features and Factual Entertainment, a *Guardian* Edinburgh International TV Festival award, a Television Bulldog award, a *TV Quick* magazine award, a *TV Choice* magazine award . . . the list goes on and on and on.

On one particular occasion I got a call from Jo Wallace, the BBC's commissioning editor for *The Apprentice* as well as *Strictly* and *The Voice*, and a tremendous supporter of the show. She has been the main point of contact for Talkback Thames and Fremantle Media, and is the person who signs off the shows from an editorial and compliance point of view. She was asking me whether I was going to attend the National Reality Television Awards which were being held in some posh hotel in London.

'Sorry,' I said, 'if you don't mind, I really don't want to go.'

It's bad enough sitting through an awards ceremony, but doing so and not winning anything is worse still. Take for example the National Television Awards (NTAs) which are ITV's annual awards. ITV are always very proud of saying that the winners are voted for by the public. I remember being called by the ITV people to come along and be there because *The Apprentice* had been nominated. Effectively, what they needed were high-profile celebrities, so to speak, to be seen sitting in the audience so they could pan their cameras over them in order to enhance the credibility of the awards show. Not knowing too much about telly, I did think it was a little bit strange that an ITV-sponsored awards ceremony would be dishing out awards to BBC programmes. Maybe I was being a bit cynical, but then they did say it was the public's vote that counts. Well, I have to say that in all the years *The Apprentice* has been nominated for an award at this ITV bash, it has never ever won!

So I guess you can understand why I was sceptical when Jo asked me to go to yet another awards ceremony. I was adamant that I was not going to go. I'd already put up with too many of these things, turning up at this bum rush of people prancing down the red carpet, driving me nuts by coming up to me and nattering away about a load of boring rubbish. I was no longer going to sit in the audience as a stooge so the camera could zoom in to me – when it was time for our category to be read out – and try to capture any possible signs of disappointment when we didn't win. On the first two occasions where I naively wasted my time at the ITV NTAs I simply adopted the Bolton face.

But when I told Jo that I did not want to go to this other awards ceremony, she wouldn't take no for an answer.

'Why don't you want to go?'

'Well, Jo, it's a waste of time really. We sit around and we never win anything. And *they're* not going to tell you if we've won or not. Look, let me be blunt – if you *know* we've won, I'll go.'

'Oh no no no, the organisers won't tell us whether we've won, but we really would *love* you to be on our table. It is a prestigious event.'

'Well, not really, Jo. I really don't fancy it. Next time maybe.'

But she persisted and persisted and on this occasion she wore me down. Eventually I agreed to come along to this thing. Joining us on our table was Theo Paphitis from *Dragons' Den*, James May from *Top Gear* and a few other guests. The evening was kind of enjoyable as I was talking to James about flying (he's also a pilot).

Finally it came to the time for the award nominations in our category. It turned out that Jo's persistence was based upon her *maybe* having a little bit of inside information – because on this occasion, we won! For the best business show.

The timing of the National Reality Television Awards night coincided with me being right in the middle of negotiations on a new contract for the next series of *The Apprentice*. At that point we were at a stalemate because I was holding out for a more substantial fee. As we were there at the table, Jo asked me whether we could try and sort this out once and for all. Of course it wasn't really the BBC's problem because fee negotiations were always conducted with Talkback – the BBC just paid a lump sum for the programme. However, the reality was that my fee would have an impact on the final fee the BBC paid Talkback. More to the point, they simply wanted me to sign up so Jo called Jana Bennett over to the table and between the pair of them they tried to beat me up so that I'd curb my demands. It was hilarious.

Even though the financial numbers had nothing to do with the BBC, I took one of the menus from the table and started to write some figures on it which might be acceptable to me. The menu was being passed back and forth between Jo, Jana and me in a sort of horse-trading fashion. Quite honestly I think Jana and Jo were enjoying it because it was a way of negotiating they were not used to. Of course, we did not conclude negotiations that night, but the good news was that a day or so later it was sorted out with the Talkback people. It was quite a funny situation and Jo and I still talk about it occasionally.

As Jo oversaw the compliance and editorial side of things, her name was taken in vain on a few occasions by some of the people in the production team. I spoke earlier about my disappointment over the way that some of the editing had been done and how some of my words of wisdom had not been included, well there was a time when a couple of people at Talkback, who will remain nameless, failed to take heed of my opening message in series one:

'I don't like liars, I don't like bullshitters.' They used poor Jo as the excuse for why certain parts of what I'd said were omitted. I knew that Jo was a very busy person, so I very much doubted she was involved in the deep-dive, nitty-gritty detail of things. Certainly she had to watch the programme to make sure it was in line with all the compliance rules and also to make sure that editorially it was keeping up to what was promised; however, I knew she would not be getting involved in the nuts and bolts of every single word I said. In most cases she was presented with what I'd say was a ninety-percent-finished film. So to be fair to her, she would have no clue as to what else was in the rushes of the two or three hours that were filmed in the boardroom. In other words, it was all a bit of BS.

I overcame this very quickly by calling their bluff. I said, 'Okay, I'll have a word with Jo and tell her why I think this should be kept in,' to which I usually got the response, 'No, no, Sir Alan, no need to go to that trouble. Don't worry about it, we'll go off and have another look at it.'

Of course it wasn't Jo who didn't want something included; it was somebody there telling me a little porky.

Going back to the night of the awards ceremony and the menu negotiations, Theo Paphitis had clapped eyes on what was going on and I remember him shouting across the table, 'I don't bloody believe it. He's only bleedin' negotiating his fee here and now with Jana Bennett and Jo Wallace!' which he really thought was funny.

Someone who didn't think things were funny that night was that weird-looking bloke who introduces *Dragons' Den*, Evan Davis. He was really upset that once again *The Apprentice* had beaten *Dragons' Den* to an award. He was not a happy bunny and he came up to me, half joking of course, saying, 'Bloody hell, you've bloody done it again. Honestly!'

Now and again I've met the cast of *Dragons' Den*, usually at one of these bashes. The photographers seem to love to get me photographed with them. None of us minds doing it, and I get on quite well with all of them, Duncan, Theo, Deborah and particularly Peter Jones. We always have a bit of banter when we meet up at these events.

One of the effects of a successful TV show such as *The Apprentice* can be summed up by the expression 'often copied, never equalled', and that was certainly true of a number of copycat programmes that started to surface. For example, ITV decided to commission a programme called *Tycoon*, to be hosted by Peter Jones. It was a competition featuring entrepreneurs and their ideas, the winner being chosen by the public. The problem that most of these copycat programmes come up against is Mark Burnett Productions' ownership of the format. It's a sort of copyright protection so that people cannot replicate the way *The Apprentice* is conducted.

Tycoon, which aired in summer 2007, was one of many pathetic attempts to try and work around the copyright and end up with an elimination process. In the end it proved two things: firstly, the Mark Burnett format is brilliantly thought out and impossible to replicate by work-arounds; and secondly – dare I say it myself – I'm a much better host than my mate Peter Jones. Now we do get on quite well and I'm sure he won't take umbrage at that comment; in fact, I'm pretty sure he would agree that I'm much better in *The Apprentice* than he was in *Tycoon*. Sadly, in TV terms it failed miserably. It was originally given a prime-time slot on ITV on a Tuesday and it achieved fewer than 2 million viewers, which is 2.5 million below ITV's average for that time slot. The programme was eventually dumped by moving it to a different time. The final episode attracted about 1.3 million viewers and, needless to say, it wasn't recommissioned.

The media cast their verdicts on *Tycoon*. *The Times* described it as a shameless rip-off of *The Apprentice*. The *Scotsman* declared it 'ITV's shameless rip-off of both *The Apprentice* and *Dragons'*

Den'. Thomas Sutcliffe of the *Independent* was more positive, suggesting that it *might* succeed, but berated Peter Jones for trying to take off Sir Alan Sugar. And, finally, the *Sun*'s Ally Ross dubbed the show 'The Crapprentice' and commented that while *The Apprentice* has brilliant tasks and epic firing scenes, *Tycoon* has, well, nothing really.

Away from the media, Mark Thompson, the BBC Director General at the time, accused ITV of copycatting, also claiming that *Tycoon* was very much like *The Apprentice* with a bit of *Dragons' Den* thrown in.

Another show, *Natural Born Sellers*, which was produced by Dan Adamson and Daisy Goodwin after they left *The Apprentice*, used the services of John Caudwell. Again, it was a rather pathetic attempt to rip off *The Apprentice* and it, too, struggled with the same problem of having to work around the Mark Burnett format. Rumour has it that Mr Caudwell, who spent a lot of time recording the programme, was allegedly cut severely in the edit, basically because the production people didn't feel the show was very interesting as shot. Again, this is a story I've been told; I don't know whether it's true or not. However, I do remember watching the programme and thinking to myself, 'Hold on a minute, where is this Caudwell chappy? He's hardly in the thing.' He seemed to be in it for a few minutes at the beginning, a few minutes at the end, and a couple of seconds in the middle, and one couldn't work out what the programme was really about. Like *Tycoon*, it only ran for one series.

Believe it or not, even ex-candidate Saira Khan presented a children's programme with a format closely resembling *The Apprentice*, though it wasn't an exact copy. I believe it was commissioned by CBBC. To nutshell it, she was setting young kids tasks to do things and then had to decide which team was the winner. I remember watching this programme and seeing her trying to weigh things up, deliberating over her final decision. I have to say, with all due respect to Saira, her acting abilities were nil. She was trying to create suspense over who'd won, who'd lost and who her choice was going to be. I'm afraid to say it was a lead-balloon moment. The programme carried on for a few series, but not all with Saira.

If the failure of these *Apprentice* rip-off programmes wasn't enough of a lesson, more recently another ex-*Dragon*, Hilary Devey, was seconded by Channel 4 to come up with yet another kind of *Apprentice* programme for young people called *The Intern*. This, funnily enough, was produced by Talkback who by then had changed their name to Boundless. Sometimes you have to ask yourself: why would Boundless take on a project that was effectively an attempted replication of another series they were making successfully? However, from what I gathered, they didn't see it as a conflict because different departments work autonomously and they get deals to make programmes across all the TV channels. One of their divisions had taken a liking to Hilary Devey – who, let's face it, was a very interesting character on *Dragons' Den* – so they thought, 'She's going to be TV gold.' Regrettably, that programme didn't do very well either.

Aside from the copycat shows, impressionists and comedians also jumped on the bandwagon to try and exploit the success of *The Apprentice*. Rory Bremner did an impression of me on *Bremner, Bird and Fortune*. He kind of faked up a boardroom where I was grilling the candidates for the London mayoral election: Boris Johnson, Ken Livingstone and Brian Paddick. After each of them failed to get a single vote, I hired myself for the job and stated that I would actually make a profit on City Hall.

In *Dead Ringers*, they impersonated me having magic powers, castigating a contestant on *The Sorcerer's Apprentice*. Another TV show that lampooned *The Apprentice* was *Kombat Opera Presents: The Applicants*. Paul Merton and Ian Hislop, famous for *Have I Got News for You*, also parodied the show during a promotional advert for their series, and the children's show *Horrible Histories* features 'Historical Apprentice' as a recurring sketch. This directly referenced *The Apprentice* and me, featuring two teams from different historical periods. There was also a scene in the hit show *Outnumbered* where the little girl, Karen, acted out a boardroom scene with her teddies.

On the internet *The Apprentice* was lampooned on the Boleg Brothers website where it is animated in Lego, then there was that Cassetteboy thing on YouTube which has had over six million hits. Unbelievably funny.

Off the screen, a number of university student groups created local competitions by sticking to the format and coming up with tasks in what is known as 'Student Apprentice' competitions. They've been hosted across the country at a number of universities, particularly in London. The events became very popular and I got bombarded with requests to come along and be a judge. I also believe that *The Apprentice* format has become part of the curriculum at school, albeit unofficially, where pupils have to perform a business task and try to follow the programme format.

From that point of view I find it very heart-warming and positive to see this stuff going on because, as I've always stated, a very large part of the audience are young people who love the programme not only for its entertainment value but also for its underlying business message.

There have been a number of different TV shows that have done tributes to *The Apprentice*, for example *Ant & Dec's Saturday Night Takeaway*. A couple of kids competed to be the new Little Ant and the new Little Dec, and they used *The Apprentice* format to make the decision.

Jon Culshaw on *Dead Ringers* and *The Impression Show* would often do an impersonation of me; one of the best I would say. In fact, out of all the impersonators, if I had to give an award to the person who gets the nearest to me, it would have to go to Jon

Culshaw. I bumped into him at one of these TV awards ceremonies, and what's quite funny is that these impersonators get a little bit embarrassed when they meet up with the people they're taking off. They're almost frightened to face them in case the person is angry. I remember Nick ushering Jon over to me, saying, 'Come on, Jon, come and meet Alan. He doesn't care, he's not offended . . .' We shook hands and had a good laugh, and I said to him, 'Jon, out of all the tossers trying to impersonate me, you definitely get the tosser of the year award.' I obviously said it in a very light-hearted manner, and told him genuinely that he is the one who does my voice the best.

The really annoying sod was Harry Hill. He would exploit something that had gone on in the previous week's *Apprentice* after getting permission from Talkback or Fremantle to include the relevant clips in his Saturday-night show. Initially, they granted permission without referring to me, but I got a little bit pissed off with him in the end because he was taking things too far. Eventually, my PR company would call me up asking whether I would give permission for certain *Apprentice* clips to be used on Harry Hill's show. I refused on several occasions and I believe that on one of his shows he actually mentioned it.

Now I've got a very broad sense of humour and quite a thick skin, but I'm afraid I didn't share Harry Hill's style of comedy – I think he went just a little too far in taking the piss. When I met up with Harry Hill recently on *The One Show*, he reminded me of how I used to refuse to let him use some of the *Apprentice* clips. I told him it was because his show was getting boring and repetitive, and it felt like I was being used as cannon fodder for him, providing a lot of his content each week. I also said that I noticed, after I'd cut off the supply, his show seemed to go downhill and wondered whether this had had anything to do with his show being dumped. He didn't know whether or not I was joking when I said this. Even if I was, many a true word is spoken in jest.

Harry came back with, 'Of course that's not the reason why it was dumped. I decided that I didn't want to do any more.'

'Yeah, right, Harry. Okay, I got it – you wanted to go on to better things like *I Can't Sing! The X Factor Musical* at the theatre. Yeah, that was a great success, wasn't it? Hmmm, never mind.'

You may remember from an earlier chapter that I had this bee in my bonnet about product placement in *EastEnders*, which I kept pestering the BBC about. You can imagine my embarrassment when in one episode of the soap a young fellow playing the part of Darren Miller, a budding entrepreneur, received a present from his girlfriend and it was the Alan Sugar autobiography. And there it was, in full view, as she handed it over to him on the screen. She gave it to him because many a time in the script they would jokingly call him the Lord Sugar of Walford. But how embarrassing for me over the product placement! The person I was giving hell to over the Nokia phones business could easily have got back to me and said, 'Aha! What do you think about that, Lord Sugar, eh? What's good for the goose is good for the gander?' Fortunately, they never picked it up.

EastEnders, one of my favourite soaps, often refers to me when they're talking about some business deal or shrewd operator. Now and again someone will come out with, 'Who do you think you are – Lord Sugar?' The same thing happens in *Coronation Street* – when one of the characters is showing a bit of business acumen someone will say to them, 'Hey, you're the next Alan Sugar.' I have to say I feel proud to be used as an example in such iconic British institutions as *EastEnders* and *Coronation Street*. In addition to those two great soaps, there have been a number of other TV shows where my name has been quoted as synonymous with a tough businessman who doesn't mind giving people a bit of stick.

Another thing I did on TV was a cameo appearance for

Children In Need. I was asked to turn up at the *Dragons' Den* studio and pitch a Pudsey Bear telephone to the dragons. This was a hilarious day and we thoroughly enjoyed it. It was interesting to see the *Dragons' Den* set and how it operated. The sketch worked out very well. Having said that, on the day for some reason (which I think was my fault) the dragons had not arrived when I got there. I must have frightened the production people by telling them I didn't have all day to mess about and that I would give them a maximum of two hours and then I was off. Quite honestly, if you don't lay down terms of agreement on these things, you can be hanging around for ages. Once bitten, twice shy, is what I say. I remember once when I was doing some promotion or other, I was at the bloody studio for five hours – and all I had to do was say a one-line sentence!

Anyway, the production people didn't dare ask me to wait, and for this *Dragons' Den* sketch, despite me saying I am not an actor, that's exactly what I had to do! I had to say my bit while talking to five empty chairs. The production people simply put a large card with the name on the seat and asked me to imagine the eyeline as if, for example, I were talking to Duncan. If I say so myself, I performed it quite well, and it was all done in about ten minutes. The bloke on the BBC production team told me they had allocated an hour to get it right, and couldn't believe how quickly I did it. But then came the 'D'you know what, Lord Sugar? Could we take it one more time? Just in case.'

'In case of what?' I asked.

'Well, you know what it's like, maybe the second one will be a bit better, and then we'll have a choice.'

'Oh, all right, let's do it again.'

I had read the script they'd written for me and told them there was no way I could do it parrot fashion as I was not an actor. The best they would get was for me to understand what they wanted and then they'd have to let me do it my way, to which they agreed. And although I agreed to do what the telly people call a retake, when I do something my way – off the cuff, in my own words – I feel it's never as good when I have to do it a second or third time.

They recorded what I did and played it on a big screen placed in front of the dragons who were now sitting in their five chairs. The dragons then responded to the video with what they had to say, which was duly recorded and edited into a great sketch. I was still there when this was going on and decided to stand behind the video screen to give the dragons an exact eyeline. I recall saying to Theo that he was being too polite to me in one sequence. I told him to do it again and give me a bollocking, and not to hold back.

Following on from that, I was asked to take part in an *East-Enders* sketch for *Children In Need*. I rolled up in my car at the Queen Vic and stood in the Walford street market giving stick to some of the regulars in the cast. It was a great eye-opener for me to actually be on the famous *EastEnders* set. There was so much to take in, seeing the familiar places shown in the programme. Hats off to the BBC production people – it is a fascinating place to walk around.

Most of these sketches have to be filmed when the set for a particular show is already built, so in the case of *Dragons' Den* it was obviously done while a series was filming; but, of course, the *East-Enders* set is always there.

I also remember that it was bloody freezing that day and I had to be filmed in just my suit getting out of the car and walking up and down the market. Like all filming, there were stops and starts and resetting cameras, so in between I stood inside the shop used as the Minute Mart, with my coat on, in front of an electric bar heater. One of my grandsons, Alex, who's a great fan of *EastEnders* and fascinated by theatre and TV production, came along with me. I'll tell you a bit more about him later. There was a great script which was hard for me to pick up because, as I've said, I don't like doing scripts, but I was able to ad lib a little and it came out very funny. I think it went down well in its *Children in Need* slot.

In fact, I thought up a sketch myself that I put forward to the *Children In Need* and *Comic Relief* people, this time based on *The Voice*. I would walk on stage with my iPod playing a Frank Sinatra song into the microphone while the four judges are waiting in their chairs with their backs to me. They're thinking this bloke on the stage is fantastic and you can imagine how funny it would be when the chairs turned round; not to mention the banter I could have with Sir Tom and the rest of them. Unfortunately, they haven't taken that idea up yet – maybe they didn't think it was that funny – but I'll carry on trying to pursue it.

Over the years, *The Apprentice* boardroom with Nick, Karren and me in it has been used many times in some form of promotion for other programmes. One example was when I made a cameo appearance in a *Doctor Who* sequence which was filmed in the boardroom. We were also filmed giving *X Factor* host Dermot O'Leary some stick as he supposedly came to get advice from me on how to host a show. This was used as part of the promotion for an awards ceremony he was going to host.

All of these spin-offs have been very interesting and I've been pleased to participate in them, and they've all come about because of the popularity of *The Apprentice* and me as a character.

Now, most of us have watched *The X Factor*. As we know, it starts off with an auditioning process before they go into the live shows. In that auditioning process it normally ends up with the judges, say Sharon Osborne, Louis Walsh, Gary Barlow or Cheryl Cole (now Cheryl Fernandez-Versini), hosting a shortlist of people at some exotic place where they decide who is actually going through. I refer to this because at least three of the judges I've mentioned seem to try to replicate the jeopardy that occurs in *The Apprentice* boardroom when it's decision time on who's staying and who's going. By this I mean making statements that for one moment sound like they're going to reject someone and the next moment sound like they're going to accept them. They'll say, 'I think you've really let me down,' or 'I've heard you sing that song much better before,' and it's all doom and gloom, then suddenly they'll do a complete about-turn and say, 'I'm sorry . . . but . . . I'm going to have to take you through to the live shows!'

My wife, Ann, who used to be a fan of *The X Factor* but no longer watches it, said to me, unprompted, 'They're trying to copy you, Alan! Look at them; they're useless, completely useless. They're actually trying to copy you to create some sort of jeopardy so you don't know which one they're going to choose, but they're pathetic.'

'Well,' I said, 'there you are, Ann. You don't realise what a gem you live with.'

'Hmmm.'

As I said before, 'often copied, never equalled'. And I think it's true to say, as far as *The Apprentice* format is concerned, that is exactly the case.

14

'A VILLAGE SOMEWHERE HAS LOST ITS IDIOT'

Filming series five with Pants Man and
***Junior Apprentice* is born**

Series five got off on the wrong foot when one of the sixteen candidates, a bloke who lived in Chigwell, funnily enough, decided he couldn't go through with it and pulled out at the last minute. It was too late to contact one of the reserve candidates because it was literally the night before we were going to start filming Boardroom Zero. We decided to proceed with fifteen candidates instead. I understand from the production people that the chap said he had realised at the last minute he just couldn't bear to be away from his wife and children for that long. As I've explained before, the production people warn the potential candidates again and again about the lack of contact with the outside world, and how long they might be away for, but even though they remind them until they're blue in the face, there are still some who seem to be taken unawares and bottle out when it's time to start the process. Having said that, this was the first and only time so far that someone has pulled out at such short notice.

When we filmed Boardroom Zero the next day, the first thing I told the fifteen candidates was that one of their number had already bottled it. After that, we got on with the series as normal, albeit the boys' team was one light. I couldn't resist mentioning that this process was the job interview from hell.

'First prize, you get to work for me. Second prize doesn't exist. Think you can play me and second-guess me? Well, let me tell you – I am as hard to play as a Stradivarius. And you lot, I can tell you, are as easy to play as bongo drums.'

As it happens, Mark Saben bought me a set of bongo drums at the end of the series as a memento gift.

Of the fifteen candidates who made it to Boardroom Zero, there were some really interesting characters as well as the usual quota of loudmouths. One I recall was a young man by the name of Rocky Andrews whose claim to fame was that he ran a chain of sandwich shops in the north of England. Michele Kurland was very enthusiastic about him because he was the epitome of what the programme is supposed to be about – young people and enterprise. However, I felt a little sceptical about this chap. It seemed too good to be true that a fellow of his age was running an organisation, which he claimed to be his, on his own. I mean, it wasn't just one sandwich shop; it was a giant organisation. I suspect to this day that his father was also heavily involved in the business. No doubt Rocky worked with him, but I think he might not have realised that he didn't own it. The reason I bring this up is because the second task in the series was all about catering for corporate customers in the City, and part and parcel of doing this was preparing the food which included – guess what? – sandwiches, albeit a bit more sophisticated than the norm. Obviously Rocky was placed in charge, but regrettably he failed miserably; not on the commercial side of things but on the practical production side, which you'd have thought he'd be able to do with his eyes closed.

I often say in *The Apprentice* that the project manager appointed should always be somebody who has experience, or as near as possible, of the task in hand, and this task was tailor-made for him. I do recall Michele's disappointment when my suspicions were confirmed that Rocky, bless him, was perhaps overstating his position. I had no choice but to fire Rocky.

Another who stood out was Ben Clarke, a trainee stockbroker who fancied himself as a bit of a military man. In week three, when James McQuillan was project manager, Ben said that James's leadership wasn't exactly Winston Churchill.

I replied, 'You mean it was more like Churchill the nodding dog?'

From the first day I clapped eyes on him, Ben would not stop going on about the fact that he'd been offered a scholarship at Sandhurst. It seemed like every time I asked him a question or every time he piped up in the boardroom, he would mention this bloody Sandhurst scholarship, even when it had nothing to do with the matter in hand. In the end I'd had enough of him and the last time he brought it up, I snapped.

'Will you stop going on about Sandhurst?' I said. 'I was in the Jewish Lads' Brigade – trainee bugler – but it didn't help me sell computers when I got older.'

That shut him up, and I heard afterwards that the production people in the gallery thought that moment was brilliant television. Cate Hall, who worked on the series, still says it was one of her favourite *Apprentice* moments of all time. The fellow had thick skin. I fired him in week nine.

Another funny moment was when one of the candidates, Noorul Choudhury, was finally let go by me after failing miserably in one of the tasks. Regrettably, he was not the right calibre of person for the process and after firing him I remember chatting with Nick and Margaret and coming out with one of my famous one-liners: 'I hope whoever employs him keeps the receipt.' Apparently someone snorted coffee all over the equipment in the gallery when they heard that one.

One candidate who let his mouth run away with him was Philip Taylor, who famously came up with 'Pants Man' as a mascot for a breakfast cereal. I had set the teams an advertising task and he had some bizarre idea about teaching kids not to put their pants on outside their clothes. He actually thought this was complete genius. I thought it was idiotic. I don't know why I didn't fire him there and then to be honest. I don't care if you've got two minutes or two years to come up with an idea, anyone who thinks that Pants Man is the best way to advertise breakfast cereal is probably not the right person for me.

I'd told the candidates to come up with a jingle for their advert and off they went to a recording studio. Philip sang the Pants Man jingle and was strutting around like a peacock saying how brilliant he was. 'One take,' he kept saying, meaning he didn't have to rehearse it; he just did it right first time. The producers had asked Dru Masters, *The Apprentice* composer, to help mix these jingles overnight. After watching Philip walk about as if he was the greatest thing since sliced bread, Dru commented, 'I think he thinks he's Bono!' It was a killer line at the time and made us all laugh.

One good thing that Philip did – and perhaps it went a little bit to his head – was to come up with the Body Rocka. This was a task I set to produce a piece of equipment to sell to the sports industry. The other team devised some monstrosity that was basically a wooden box with springs and bits of string hanging out of it – which was a complete and utter joke – but Philip to his credit came up with a plastic moulded item which you laid on and it allowed you to exercise. It was accepted very well and got great praise from the retailers they offered it to, and his team came in with a handsome victory. After he left *The Apprentice* process, he wanted to see whether he could further it commercially. I'm not completely sure what happened because I do believe that Talkback Thames owns the copyright of anything that is invented by the candidates during *Apprentice* tasks, so he would have needed to have those discussions with them to see whether they would be prepared to release it for him to exploit commercially. It is important to note that any profits or profit-share from products invented in the various series that are received by Talkback or Boundless are given to charity. From what I saw in a newspaper from 2010, Philip seemed to have done a deal with them and was able to sell it by promising that a chunk of money would be donated to charity. It went on sale for £34.99. I don't know how well it did, save to say that on Amazon today it's selling for £12.95.

Philip was a controversial character and had been fighting with one of the other candidates, Lorraine Tighe, for weeks. Philip was actually fired in week seven, after I'd sent them off to secure items to sell on behalf of a designer. He failed to shift a single unit, but when he got in the boardroom for that task, Lorraine grassed him up about the flirtatious relationship he was having with another of the candidates, Kate Walsh. I understand they became a couple after the series and I hear they're still together – she's certainly managed to put up with him for longer than I could!

I happened to visit the *You're Fired* studio when they were recording the programme on which Philip was fired. Philip went through the normal *You're Fired* process and then he got out a guitar which he'd brought along and asked whether he could possibly sing, thinking perhaps it would be shown on TV and he'd get his big break. It was bizarre and totally out of context with the reason he was there. I believe the production company indulged him and let him play and sing to the audience, but I'm sure that never for one minute did they intend to allow it to be broadcast, and of course it wasn't.

On the subject of Philip and Kate, there were some pathetic attempts from them to play on their romance. They were both filmed – and I do believe it was set up – walking around Hatton Garden, the diamond centre of London, holding a jeweller's-shop bag to imply they'd just bought an engagement ring. It was a kind of PR stunt; a stunt which perhaps Kate was surprised to learn I'd heard about even before it hit the press. Little did Kate know that she and Philip had visited the shop of my good friend Clive in Hatton Garden. He was quick to tell me that he'd had visitors that day who asked, funnily enough, for a small, empty carrier bag which they used as a prop in their arranged photoshoot.

One of the things everyone remembers most from series five is not a quote from a candidate, but from Nick. Nick seems to have this knack for being right in the thick of it just when the candidates realise they've made a right pig's ear of something. I had sent the candidates off to make some bath and beauty products. The candidates on Noorul's team were extremely pleased with themselves, having had a relatively smooth day producing their product. The other team, led by Paula Jones, were making a right hash of things and were just totting up their costs when Nick wandered in and mentioned that not only had they confused one of the ingredients in the formula, they'd also miscalculated the amount and therefore the cost of that ingredient. They'd mixed up Cedarwood, a relatively cheap ingredient, with Sandalwood, one of the most expensive; and worse still, they'd plonked half a kilogram of it into their formulation! When Nick pointed this out, it was like he'd just thrown a hand grenade into the room. Their stunned faces were a picture. And with perfect timing, Nick cheerfully said, 'Anyway, I'll leave it with you.'

A lot of people still say that was their most memorable Nick Hewer moment. Incidentally, if the team had not made that mistake, they'd have won the task, so it's little wonder they were horrified. I think the maths was: they'd purchased 450 grams of Sandalwood when they thought they were going to use 5 grams of Cedarwood. So they got the ingredient, the price and the maths wrong, and they ended up spending over seven hundred pounds on fragrance oil instead of about a fiver. No wonder they lost the task – their costings were miles out. I said to Paula, whose day job was working in HR, 'Paula, you know how to work out redundancy on a calculator, don't you? So why didn't you get the numbers right here?' She simply didn't get it and as project manager she was fired.

Another interesting candidate in the series was James McQuillan. I recall questioning him about his CV. 'James, you say here that when you wake up in the morning you can "taste success in your spit". Is that right? What did you have, a curry last night?'

James was a bit of a joker. I don't know why, but his voice and some of his mannerisms reminded me of that famous comedian Tommy Cooper. I recall on one occasion Ben Clarke was trying to imply that the reason they had failed on a task was due to James's incompetence. He was banging on and on, running James down and trying to palm the blame off on him. Getting a bit fed up with this tirade, I stopped Ben and said to him, 'What are you trying to say? That a village somewhere has lost an idiot?' That little comment shut Ben down quickly.

James was a nice fellow and he got on very well with the other candidates. They really warmed to him as he never laid the blame on any of the others. Unfortunately, I didn't think he was the right calibre for my organisation, but on the day he was fired some of the girls in the boardroom shed a tear or two as they were sad to see him go.

Another of the candidates, Debra Barr, started off as a really aggressive person in the opening weeks of the series. I was constantly pulling her up for being confrontational and nearly fired her for it on more than one occasion. One of her outbursts we found slightly shocking. I'd set the candidates a task that we called 'Everything must go', the premise of which was basically the reverse of the discount buying task (where I give them a list of items to buy at the cheapest possible price). This task was the opposite – I gave them a load of stuff and told them to flog it for as much money as possible. As it happened, both teams made a complete mess of it; in fact, I think this was the first time that *both* teams ended up making a loss. The team Debra was on made the bigger loss and, when they got into the boardroom, Nick *dared* to make some comment on Debra's sales. Debra forgot who she was talking to, disagreeing with Nick and saying that he was completely wrong. Moreover, the manner in which she spoke to him was totally disrespectful. I told her, 'If you ever open your mouth like that again, don't even bother to come back into this boardroom.' I was not having it.

Funnily enough, Nick and Debra stayed in touch after the series. I think he's rather fond of her now. She got to the penultimate stage because she was a classic example of a candidate who learned as she went along in the process and got better and better. Her aggression was terrible at the beginning but, as the series progressed, not only did she show some good business acumen but she also managed to learn to curb her aggression and conduct herself properly. She went on afterwards to start her own business, which revolved around selling discontinued product lines from manufacturers. I believe she now has a lucrative business dealing with close-outs of products that manufacturers have discontinued, which have to be sold into a special marketplace so as not to disturb the main market. It was a bit of a shame, actually, because despite Debra making a big effort to learn and change, I did fire her in the end. It came down to a toss-up between her and Kate Walsh to go into the final with Yasmina Siadatan. I'm not sure what it was at the time that tipped the scales as to why I let her go instead of Kate. Perhaps it was still playing on my mind that her volatile nature might yet resurface and I couldn't risk her coming into one of my companies and upsetting people as she had done several weeks earlier.

I'm a little sorry I fired Debra because, to be frank, I feel let down by the fact that Kate Walsh, who did come close to being the winner, actually had it in her mind to pursue a media career. She got herself a job with Channel 5 as a presenter on *Live from Studio Five* alongside celebrities such as Ian Wright and Melinda Messenger. It was supposed to be Channel 5's version of BBC1's

The One Show. I'm afraid to say that it failed miserably and the owner of Channel 5 ended up dispensing with her services.

I hear that despite trying to get more work in media circles, she's now had to go and get 'a proper job' which, to be fair, she's very capable of succeeding in. I don't know why she had this desire to follow a media career. I guess the fame bug – being on television – gripped her. As I said earlier, after being recognised on the streets for up to twelve weeks while the programme is on, candidates often get withdrawal symptoms after an *Apprentice* series is finished.

The much-deserved winner of series five was Yasmina. She joined Amscreen and worked hand in hand with Lee McQueen, the previous year's winner. Like Lee before her, Yasmina was given the job of concentrating solely on the medical side of things, putting screens into doctors' surgeries, clinics and hospitals. Yasmina worked for the company for over a year but left when she became pregnant and decided not to return to the company after having her child. I believe she has since had a second child and, the last I heard, is working for James Caan, who was once one of the dragons on *Dragons' Den*.

Yasmina was one of those candidates who was already running her own business before she came into *The Apprentice*. She had a small restaurant and I recall talking to her just before I chose her as the winner, asking her what she was going to do with the business if she won. She said she would allow another member of her family to run it while she was employed by me. I'm not sure whether that restaurant still exists today, but apparently it was a nice little bistro.

At the end of filming series five, the BBC requested that we do another celebrity *Apprentice* sketch for *Comic Relief*. By this time *The Apprentice* was really hot property, which was endorsed by the fact that the fame-factor of the candidates who wanted to partici-pate had really gone up. The boys' team comprised Jonathan Ross,

Alan Carr, Jack Dee, Gok Wan and Gerald Ratner, while the girls'
team consisted of Michelle Mone, Patsy Palmer, Fiona Phillips,
Carol Vorderman and Ruby Wax.

The filming of the *Comic Relief* sketch coincided with the time
when Jonathan Ross was having problems with the BBC over a
prank that he and Russell Brand had played on Andrew Sachs,
which resulted in Jonathan being suspended for a while. I thought
Jonathan would be a great asset to the sketch because he's such a
funny fellow and I had some very lengthy conversations with the
BBC saying that because the programme wouldn't be *broadcast*
until much later, surely they could give him dispensation to do it.
They finally agreed. However, to my surprise, I then had another
obstacle to overcome – Margaret Mountford! When she heard that
Jonathan Ross was going to be in the programme, she told me she
didn't want to participate in it. She felt that the well-publicised
prank he and Russell Brand had played was morally incorrect and
therefore she didn't want to be seen to be involved with him. I
recall telling her she was overreacting and being overcautious, and
that it wouldn't rub off on her own integrity – one thing had nothing at all to do with the other. So I asked her to kindly reconsider,
as it was far too late to pull out. To refuse would leave us in an
untenable situation as I couldn't suddenly bring in a reserve for
her – the whole structure of *The Apprentice* at the time was Nick,
Margaret and me. She finally agreed to do it.

The task I set the celebrities on this occasion was to come up
with a toy or game which could be sold to the toy-shop market. The
boys' team came up with some kind of miniature models which
were supposed to become an 'epidemic' product where kids would
keep buying more and more of them to form a family of these little
items. The girls came up with a sort of jumpsuit that was made of
Velcro – the idea being that kids would put these jumpsuits on and
get stuck to each other when they were fighting. We held a launch
at a hotel on the South Bank where the two teams had to pitch their

products in front of a whole host of guests and celebrities. Somehow the media had learned about Jonathan's participation in the programme despite his being banned from broadcasting on the BBC for a while. There were photographers outside trying to take pictures of him through the hotel window while he was on stage helping his team present their product. A bit of panic set in and we had to stop the proceedings. In the end we stuck a temporary curtain up to deter the photographers.

I have to say that, on this occasion, the *Comic Relief* celebrity *Apprentice* was not enjoyable. Regrettably, the celebrities were not getting on with each other, particularly the girls, and there were endless arguments between Patsy Palmer and Michelle Mone. I don't know what the arguments were about, but Margaret was telling me that it was all a bit of a nightmare. I remember her whispering in my ear in the boardroom, 'For God's sake, Alan, don't let the girls lose, because if they do, it'll be carnage. They'll scream and scratch each other's eyes out.'

The decision I made on this occasion as to the winning product was based upon my technical background and my experience in manufacturing. The product the boys had come up with would have needed a hell of a lot of investment in tooling and advertising, and for that reason alone I felt it was unviable. Therefore, I chose the girls' product which was an easy item to make – effectively a piece of clothing with Velcro attached to it – and I awarded them the win. This created a terrible atmosphere behind the scenes in the boardroom. The boys were outraged that they'd lost. They felt their product was superior to this stupid Velcro jumpsuit and that what they had devised was a far better business model. I guess if you looked at it from one angle, for example if they were a giant toy manufacturer, then you could say they were right, assuming they had the investment. But the task stated that the thing had to be able to be made easily and go on sale in the next few months. Gerald Ratner, the ex-jewellery retailer who famously made the biggest lead-balloon statement in the history of business – a statement that led to his company going down the pan – had been chosen as the boys' project manager. He argued with me vehemently. Basically, he was fuelled by testosterone, flexing his muscles as he was the only businessman in the team. When I was giving critical informa- tion about why their business model didn't stack up, he was actually arguing with me. By then I could see I was just wasting my time. It wouldn't have mattered if I'd said to him this piece of paper was white, he'd say it was black just for the sake of it.

More to the point, the general light-heartedness of this celebrity version of *The Apprentice* was rapidly being lost. This was com- pounded further by the fact that when I sent the boys' team out after Boardroom One to have the customary chat amongst them- selves as to what went wrong, Emma Freud, the boss of *Comic Relief*, sided with them and told them the decision made by Sir Alan was outrageous: 'It was terrible, it was unfair. Your product was far better.' Then she said, 'Don't worry, boys, we've got lots of connections in the industry and we're going to make that product and sell it. *Comic Relief* owns that product and we will sell it to someone else.' As it happened, it went nowhere afterwards; no one bought it and no one was interested in licensing it. Michele Kur- land told me about this conversation between the boys and Emma Freud, and they confirmed it when they came back into the board- room to discuss their team's loss. They were very, very belligerent and were being quite rude to me, saying I'd got it wrong and that the producers, namely Emma Freud (who in fact wasn't the pro- ducer), had agreed with them. I was furious because here I was, doing all this work, right the way through a senior series and then on into November filming virtually non-stop – having agreed to do this show for a great charitable cause – only to have everyone inter- fering and disputing my decisions.

Afterwards, when the whole thing was over, I got hold of Emma Freud and her husband, Richard Curtis, and told them I felt it was outrageous what they did, and that I would find it very difficult to ever again participate in *Comic Relief*. Her comments had put me on the spot and wound up the boys' team. She should have known better than anyone that it was all supposed to be a bit of fun. The idea was that the likes of Alan Carr or Jack Dee or Jonathan Ross, no matter whether they won or lost, would take it all in good humour, with me giving them a bit of stick and firing them, but in reality the whole thing turned rather sour.

Fortunately, the editors managed to pull it around and it looked a little more light-hearted than it actually was. Gerald Ratner had let Jonathan Ross and Jack Dee off, so the final three were him, Alan Carr and Gok Wan. And for no apparent reason I decided that Alan Carr was the one to be fired. The way I put it to him was that it wasn't because it was his fault; it was because I felt I had to get him away from the two horrible people sitting with him in the boardroom. I guess a kind of fifty-per-cent lead-balloon comment.

Halfway through the broadcasting of series five, which went out between March and June 2009, it was announced on *You're Fired* that we wished to recruit some young people for a new spin-off programme, *Junior Apprentice*. It was always customary for the production company to negotiate with me for the next series before the current one had finished, so I would know where I stood. I'd been feeling for a while that I wanted to send out a bigger message to the young community. I was also getting slightly disturbed that the senior programme was going a little off course by being so entertaining that it was losing the focus of the business message, and I think it fair to say that I wasn't as enthusiastic as I usually am when it came to discussing a sixth series. So I approached Talkback and asked them to consider the idea of us making a junior version because this would give me a shot of adrenaline to recharge my batteries, as I was very enthusiastic about promoting enterprise to the young. After quite a bit of discussion with Talkback, they told me they'd got the BBC to agree to commission a junior version, albeit with fewer candidates and only six episodes long.

Another step along the learning curve for me was to understand the problems attached to filming young people. And here you have to take your hat off to the BBC in recognising their commitment to complying with the rules and regulations in this area. Initially, I'd thought we'd have people as young as fourteen or fifteen as candidates in *Junior Apprentice*; however, I was told this was impracticable because children of that age would not be able to live away from home and, in fact, would still be under the control of their Local Education Authorities who would have to grant permission to film them; this despite the fact that the filming would be taking place in their private time during the school holidays. I know it sounds bizarre but it's true. It turned out the law stated that even under strict guidelines we were only permitted to film people from the age of sixteen to eighteen if we wanted them to be able to stay in a house for up to seven or eight weeks, away from their parents. Also we had to adhere to very, very strict guidelines on the amount of time they could be out working or filming. And this was all down to the rules and regulations within the BBC guidelines. I say hats off to the BBC because I recall that Channel 4 got a lot of criticism for what I can only describe as a terrible programme, *Boys and Girls Alone*, which filmed how a group of young children fared living in a house without their parents. The programme didn't last very long as it wasn't that popular, and Channel 4 got a lot of stick for the manner in which they allegedly exploited the young.

So for *Junior Apprentice* we had our hands full with rules and regulations. Once it was commissioned, we realised it could only be filmed during the summer break, after finishing their GCSEs or A levels, because the candidates needed to be free for up to eight weeks for filming.

The audition process was exactly the same as for the senior version in as much as youngsters up and down the country were interviewed to give people from all regions the opportunity of entering. The prize on this occasion was not a job with me but a special £25,000 trust fund which I explained to the candidates would be controlled by me and only released as and when I decided that the use of the money was for proper purposes; either to further their education or to be the seed fund for the start of their own business.

Before I go on to talk about the first series of *Junior Apprentice*, a couple of other things happened in series five; the most important being that at the end of the series, Margaret told me she'd basically had enough of doing *The Apprentice* and wanted to go on and complete her other interests in academia. She said the programme was really hard work and that she had decided to give it up.

I thought long and hard about who to replace Margaret with and decided on Karren Brady. I had previously asked Karren to be one of the interviewers in the penultimate episode, a role she'd also taken on the year before. She had done a great job in that role; in fact, that episode in series four got over 9.75 million viewers, an enormous figure for any show. I'd also known Karren for quite a long time from the football industry and respected her businesslike qualities. And, of course, she'd been project leader in *Comic Relief*'s first celebrity *Apprentice*. Incidentally, she tells me she much prefers the side of the table she's on these days.

In another farewell, series five turned out to be the last time Adrian Chiles would present the *You're Fired* programme. He decided to quit the BBC and go and work for ITV.

We were all extremely excited about *Junior Apprentice* being commissioned, especially me because it had been my idea. It had taken a long time to get to this point, but finally we were ready to go. The BBC had agreed to commission a six-part series and we had auditioned and chosen the ten young candidates from the thousands who had applied. They were all between the ages of sixteen and seventeen and, although most of them were still studying, many had shown entrepreneurial flair.

The series editor for this programme was a chap by the name of Tom McDonald. I'd previously worked with him on the main series and he was excited about forging something new with *Junior Apprentice*. Tom later went on to be executive producer of hugely successful shows like *24 Hours in A&E* before joining the BBC as a commissioning editor.

The production team for *Junior Apprentice* was the same as for the senior series: Andy Devonshire, Tom McDonald, Michael Jochnowitz, Michele Kurland, of course, and another lady by the name of Sue Davidson. Ruby Evans was there too, looking after the dosh.

As Karren had agreed to take over from Margaret, *Junior Apprentice* would be the first time she would be in position as my right-hand lady. It must have been a bit of a culture shock, but she took to it very quickly. It was good that she didn't try to imitate Margaret at all and instead approached it in her own way. That said, she did tell me later that she'd chatted with Margaret from time to time during her first couple of series, just to get a few hints and tips.

One of the things that came out of this *Junior Apprentice* was a near falling-out with my dear lady wife, Ann. I had been so caught up in the enthusiasm of doing the show – an enthusiasm Ann shared – that it only later dawned on me that the filming period would be July and August, during the school holidays. What I'd also overlooked was that the sixth series, which I was already contracted to do, was going to roll straight on from September all the way through to November. Lady Sugar was not a happy bunny that her husband was going to be missing for the whole of the summer holidays. I think she forgave me because of my passion for *Junior Apprentice*, but it was a rather gruelling work schedule for myself, Nick and Karren because we would effectively be shooting two series back to back. The same applied to the crew and the handful of production people who were working across both shows. Filming a series of *The Apprentice* is utterly exhausting and once we get to the end of a series we're all totally done in. Nick, Karren and I would feel completely wrung out and the production people would be total wrecks.

In the past, of course, everyone got to recover a bit, whereas this time we had to go straight into the whole thing all over again. It was pretty relentless, and for the three years we were making both series in tandem, it was tough to keep our stamina up, I can assure you.

I remember the relief I felt on the first day of filming *Junior Apprentice* to finally be up and running with this thing. Then when the ten juniors, as we called them, first walked into Boardroom Zero the atmosphere was electric. Some of them, such as Rhys Rosser, looked so young it was like they were kids wearing their dad's suits. Others, like Tim Ankers and Zoe Plummer, looked more grown up, even beyond their years.

It was obvious to all of us, me especially, that we needed to tone down *Junior Apprentice* to be a bit softer than the main series. These were brave young people and being young meant they were inexperienced. I wasn't about to crush all the spirit out of them and knock their confidence just because they hadn't done well in a task. At the same time, we still wanted to keep the process authentic as a business test, so mostly it was down to me to make sure, when we got to the boardroom at the end of each task, that I managed to balance the tone correctly. Everybody agreed that it worked extremely well. Normally I'm very good with young people and while I was still tough, I found the balance of making them feel comfortable and not blaming them too heavily, but at the same time asserting a kind of headmasterly tone.

I needed to be particularly sensitive in the third week when one of the candidates, Adam Eliaz, fell ill. I had set the teams the task of selling cupcakes and by the time they got to the boardroom, the poor young lad looked like death warmed up. I suggested he should go home and focus on getting better and that he had nothing to be ashamed of for leaving the process.

One nice touch for the juniors was that instead of getting into the usual black cab after they were fired, they were filmed being driven away in my car AMS1. I thought this was a great idea as it served to demonstrate that every single one of the ten who took part in the first series were all winners in a way, even though only one of them could actually win the ultimate prize.

What became instantly obvious on the programme was that these kids were really sharp and a seriously capable bunch. Some of them would give the senior candidates a right run for their money. One week I set them the task of sourcing products from a designer in Amsterdam and then pitching them to retailers here in the UK. One of the teams made almost £40,000. It has since been bettered by the adults but at the time it was the most *any* team had won by, and the fact that it had been done by the juniors just went to show how right I was to pursue the idea of *Junior Apprentice*.

There were some great characters in this first series. Jordan De Courcy, a young Irish chap who unfortunately got fired on the first task, remains in contact with me and is successfully running his own juice-bar business, a really nice fellow. When he took on the role of project manager in the first task, he started to realise during the day just how tough it was. Nick and Karren took him aside and calmed him down a little because he was getting a bit stressed, as anyone would, no matter whether they're sixteen, twenty-six or thirty-six. But he took it very well and, as I say, we've remained in contact ever since.

Adam Eliaz, the chap who had to go home sick, also started his own business. He, too, contacts me from time to time. In fact, I called all the juniors back to have a celebratory lunch about a year after we filmed the first series, and Rhys Rosser, who was so short when he first came into *Junior Apprentice*, had shot up by what looked like two feet!

Zoe Plummer, although only sixteen, spoke and acted like she was twenty-six – a very, very smart girl. I remember telling her at one stage that she needed to slow down a little bit and not carry on as if she really *were* twenty-six. I told her there was a lot of learning she still had to go through. She was a little disappointed when I let her go but she now runs a vintage-clothes market stall and, from what I've heard, is very successful.

There were four candidates in the final task in this series, which was to come up with a new brand of bottled water. Arjun Rajyagor and Tim Ankers were in one team; Zoe and Kirsty Cleaver were in the other. At their launch presentations we invited professionals from that industry and their applause at the end of the presentations was genuine – they could not believe their eyes, that these sixteen- and seventeen-year-olds had come up with such great ideas. It just so happened that Arjun and Tim's team won with their simple branding, and it was left for me to decide which of the two was mainly responsible for the win. It was a very tough decision, but in the end I had to go for Arjun ahead of former farm worker Tim.

Arjun was a very worthy winner and has continued with his education at university. He has only pulled down small amounts of the prize money to buy equipment for his sideline business of computer repair work, which he does to supplement his income. At the time of writing this book the lion's share of his prize money, several years on, is sitting there quite sensibly, not because I've refused anything, but simply because he hasn't called for it yet. He, too, of course, remains in contact with me. Needless to say, the same goes for many of the seniors with whom I've kept in touch. As I say, there are not many people in *The Apprentice* who have a bad word to say about the life-changing experience they went through participating in this great process.

Anyway, with *Junior Apprentice* in the can by the end of August 2009, it was straight on to the filming of series six. But before I get to that I need to take you back a few months to a phone call that changed my life and saw all hell break loose, with certain politicians saying that the BBC should no longer allow me to host *The Apprentice*.

15

'LORD SUGAR WILL SEE YOU NOW'

Becoming a member of the House of Lords,
and series six opens with a banger

Around May 2009, while cycling up a mountain in Spain, I received a telephone call from 10 Downing Street. The operator told me they had the Prime Minister, Gordon Brown, on the line and that he wished to speak to me. There I was in my cycling gear, about fifteen hundred feet up in a place called Istán near Marbella, looking out over the sea and talking to the British Prime Minister!

Gordon came to the phone and after the usual pleasantries he told me that as a key member of his Business Council, he'd like me to come in and see him to discuss an ambassadorial position with regard to business. Gordon Brown's Business Council was a group of businessmen who would meet every month in the Cabinet office in Downing Street to discuss the general economic climate in the UK. Other members included Sir Richard Branson, Sir Terry Leahy of Tesco and Stuart Rose of Marks & Spencer. Gordon asked if I could pop in later today or tomorrow to meet him and Baroness Shriti Vadera. I explained to him that I was in Spain right now and I wouldn't be back in England until next week, so we arranged an appointment for when I got back.

The meeting at Downing Street was quite interesting. I was called the day before and asked if it would be possible *not* to arrive in my Rolls-Royce as it would attract a lot of attention. I thought this was rather surprising as I'd always turned up in the Rolls at Downing Street for the Business Council meetings. Why on this occasion did they want me to arrive incognito? And, what's more, why did they ask me to come in through the back entrance?

What I didn't know at the time was that Gordon was having a government reshuffle and had in mind for me to become a minister and appoint me to the House of Lords. The public was already aware there was going to be a reshuffle that day, and obviously the sight of me arriving in a Rolls-Royce would have got tongues wagging that I was about to be appointed in some sort of government role.

In the meeting with Gordon and Shriti, he said to me that he would like me to become a member of the House of Lords and take up a ministerial role on enterprise, concentrating in particular on the banking sector, working to encourage banks to start supporting small businesses again. After the banking crises of 2007 and 2008, there was a need to rebuild the confidence within the banks so they would lend to small businesses.

My overriding feeling was that I was very honoured. The first thought that flashed through my mind was of my mother and father, who had passed away several years earlier, and what they'd have felt about their youngest son, born in a council flat in Hackney, being a member of the House of Lords. Immediately I recalled the last time I ever spoke to my mother. She was lying on her deathbed and was unresponsive to me when I arrived there. I said, 'Mum, it's me. Do you know who I am? It's Alan.'

She answered, 'Course I know who you are. Who do *you* think you are? Lord Beaverbrook?' Even with her dying words she still had that sarcastic wit.

So when Gordon asked me, I said, 'Of course. I'm honoured to accept an appointment to the House of Lords,' but I told him I didn't understand what the ministerial position meant. Gordon explained the role briefly and told me I would have backup at the

Department for Business, Innovation and Skills (formerly known as the Department of Trade) in Victoria Street, where staff would be allocated to me to give me all the support I required in the House of Lords.

Then it suddenly occurred to me: how could I do all that and take a full-time position in the House of Lords without there being a conflict of interests with all the businesses I owned, on top of the fact I was a BBC presenter? I raised these issues there and then with Gordon, half thinking to myself, 'Bloody hell, here I am being offered membership of the House of Lords, and I'm effectively turning it down because of a conflict of interests.'

Gordon and Shriti asked me to think about it. I went back to Downing Street for another meeting on 4 June, at which point they said, 'Well, if you cannot agree to become a minister, then you could be an Enterprise Champion and effectively carry out duties of overseeing and surveying the activities of the government with respect to small business and banking support.'

At the end of that meeting it was kind of agreed that I would become a member of the House of Lords with the title of Enterprise Champion. I'm going to make this story a bit shorter. A lot of paperwork flew around and I had to fill out lots of forms, make lots of declarations and disclosures in order for me to be eligible for the House of Lords. Despite pulling up at the rear of Number 10, by the time I'd left the building the paparazzi had assembled and started to take pictures of me. When the press release was put out the next day all hell broke loose. At the same time, the phone at the office of Frank PR started to ring off the hook.

The timing of this media onslaught couldn't have been worse. It was 5 June 2009, the day I was to unveil Yasmina as the winner of series five of *The Apprentice* at the *You're Hired* filming, which took place two days prior to the broadcast of the final on TV. On top of that, I was meeting Simon Cowell for lunch. Amidst all the hoo-hah going on over my appointment to the Lords – with the whole world and his brother going nuts about it – I found it quite strange that Simon didn't say a word on the subject. I'm not kidding you; you'd have had to be locked up in a dungeon all day to have missed it. But Simon did not say anything or congratulate me. As he didn't mention it, neither did I – I just thought he was a very strange man. After lunch we left the restaurant and as we walked out my driver and his were comparing the identical cars we had. This is the bit I love: Simon's driver saw me and said, 'Congratulations, Sir Alan, on your appointment.'

I looked at Simon while I said thanks to his driver. Simon was kind of embarrassed and said, 'Oh yes, congratulations, Alan.'

Apart from that light-hearted moment, the rest of the day was a bloody nightmare. It was a day that neither I nor Andrew Bloch and David Fraser of Frank PR will ever forget. There we were, trying to deal with the usual things we deal with during *The Apprentice* final – speaking to the winner and the runner-up, preparing for the recording – while at the same time we were juggling minute-by-minute enquiries from the media, including whether I'd be giving up my role on *The Apprentice*, and fending off ridiculous accusations as well as speaking to the BBC's PR department, which was also being bombarded with enquiries. It was an absolute, total nightmare.

I was doing my best to try to keep a cool head while all this was going on. Meanwhile I had the production team in my ear saying 'Sir Alan, we're ready for you to come on now and start talking about why you decided to hire Yasmina and all the other chit-chat about why the runner-up Kate wasn't going to be hired,' etc., etc. As you can imagine, my head was about to explode. Even while I was on stage, David and Andrew were being inundated with more enquiries.

When the filming was over that night and the wrap party started, I recall that David Fraser, Andrew Bloch, Nick Hewer and I were huddled around a table drafting press statements. Everyone else was eating and drinking and enjoying themselves, but we were locked down there until late into the night.

This story was cannon fodder for the media, particularly the *Daily Mail* – they must have thought it was Christmas. They came out with lots of nasty articles that ran, believe it or not, for a whole week – one per day from different journalists, slagging off this appointment and me personally. Again, I won't bother to articulate all this stuff, but what else would one expect from the *Daily Mail*? However, the biggest problem came from the then Shadow Culture Secretary Jeremy Hunt, who complained to the BBC Trust that I could not take this role of Enterprise Champion and also be a BBC presenter.

The logic was ridiculous; it made no sense whatsoever. But in political fighting, nothing makes any sense – it was just a spoiling tactic. After all, why would the Conservative Party, the opposition at the time, worry about me? However, the BBC took the complaint very seriously and, because of their procedures, had to go through a whole exercise in order to officially answer the complaint raised by Jeremy Hunt. This resulted in lots of meetings between me, the BBC and my lawyers in consultation with Shriti at Number 10. Finally, myself and the BBC agreed the exact guidelines of what I could do and couldn't do as far as being a government advisor was concerned. Basically, what I couldn't do was be seen to have a political opinion during the run-up to the forthcoming general election in 2010 – meaning that I must not be seen to be election-eering on party political broadcasts for the Labour Party, as that would be a breach of the BBC's codes. However, I was allowed to take up the role of being a government advisor for the purpose of assisting people in enterprise.

It was a real mess. The BBC agreed with me that it was a ridic-ulous scenario but they asked me to bear with them as they *had* to go through their procedures. They bent over backwards and did their best to come up with a solution that accommodated my becoming a member of the House of Lords as a life peer while maintaining my position as presenter of one of their biggest programmes.

But it didn't stop there. Despite the agreement being made and a clear understanding established between the BBC and me, this Jeremy Hunt fellow kept gnawing away.

The result of all this was that the BBC Director General, Mark Thompson, was under extreme pressure from the BBC Trust to do something about it because the general election was coming up, and already in the can was a full series of *Junior Apprentice* and of course the forthcoming series six of *The Apprentice*. The latter would normally have been broadcast around the March-to-June period of 2010, but because the general election was going to take place in May, Mark Thompson decided that, in view of my position as a government advisor, the programmes could not be broadcast during the election period.

This created a terrible problem as far as I was concerned. When I made *Junior Apprentice*, I wanted above all to ensure that it would be broadcast during term time when young people were still at school. I knew it would generate a great deal of discussion and therefore become an epidemic programme that *had* to be watched every week. Imagine my dismay when the BBC1 Controller at the time, Jay Hunt, explained to me that due to the political pressure brought about by the general election, *Junior Apprentice* was now scheduled to be shown in July and August, outside the election period. I explained to Jay that this was ridiculous; that the whole point of the show was that it needed to be broadcast when the kids were at school so that it would create some excitement. If they weren't able to talk about it in the classroom or the playground, it would definitely damage the programme. After a lot of debate, we both agreed that it had to be scheduled in term time, and it eventually broadcast on 12 May 2010, approximately one week after the election. One has to appreciate the cooperation of the BBC in successfully juggling the balls, so to speak, to keep everyone happy.

But the bigger problem was with series six. It had been recorded in autumn 2009 and was due to be transmitted at the traditional time, starting in March and finishing around June. This was now delayed until October which created a massive problem, a problem we have effectively never got out of, and I will explain why.

Once series six had been moved to October, it was difficult to record the next series and then bring it back to its traditional slot. The then Controller of BBC1, taking over from Jay Hunt, was Danny Cohen. The first time I met Danny he was Controller of BBC3, after which he was promoted to the position of BBC1 Controller, and then promoted again to become Head of BBC Television. We have had many conversations in the past, particularly about supporting *The Apprentice* and marketing it prior to the transmission of each series. Anyway, Danny felt it was unacceptable to have one series of *The Apprentice* broadcast in October and finishing in December and another one starting just three months later in March, so series seven moved to May. And that's how the timing of *The Apprentice* got changed from its original slot in early spring.

Another problem with the delay was that the two finalists of series six, Stella English and Chris Bates, were expecting to have the normal six months' waiting period before they knew whether they were the winner or not. That waiting period had now doubled, which, as you can imagine, created a tremendous disruption to their lives. Eventually, series six started broadcasting on 6 October 2010 and finished on 19 December, so it wasn't until 17 December that the final episode and the hiring took place, which turned out to be *over a year* after the filming of the series had ended.

Aside from the timing, series six as a whole turned out to be an excellent series which generated some very high ratings. Series five had an average rating of around 8.37 million viewers and series six ended up at around 7.9 million. The drop was put down to the fact that changing the traditional timing of its broadcast had thrown the viewing public, as that time of year – October to December – was traditionally a busy time in the run-up to Christmas, with all the TV stations, including ITV, giving *The Apprentice* strong competition.

My opening speech on series six included another of my gems. 'I've read all your CVs – on paper you all look very good, but then again so does fish and chips.' I went on to warn the candidates, 'I'm not looking for any Steady Eddies or Cautious Carols – I'm looking for someone exceptional.'

We had decided that the series should mirror the economic mood of the nation at the time. People were losing their jobs and companies were struggling, so we thought it only right that this be reflected in the candidates we selected. Some of them, like Alex Epstein, had been made redundant; others, like Raleigh Addington, were graduates fresh from university and struggling to find work.

Sadly, Raleigh's time in the process was cut short. He had to leave in the second week when the terrible news came through that his brother, who was serving in the forces in Afghanistan, was seriously injured. We all felt terribly sorry for him and obviously wished him and his family well and immediately sent him back home to his loved ones.

The series started with a bang, or more accurately, bangers. That year we decided to film Boardroom Zero at midnight. Afterwards, instead of sending the candidates back to the house, as we normally did, and starting the first task the next day, I told them they were about to work through the night producing sausages to sell tomorrow. 'This is a tough task,' I said, 'and it's going to push you to your limits. It's sink or swim, and as you've most probably worked out, I don't do life jackets.'

The first episode of that series was absolutely brilliant and sausages turned out to be a really interesting task. In the end, the boys lost and I fired the project manager, a chap called Dan Harris. His teammates and Karren told me he had been extremely rude and dictatorial throughout the task, an attitude which was perfectly apparent to me in the boardroom when he was leaning back inso-lently in his chair with his legs crossed like he was on the sofa at home. There was no way this bloke was going to be right for me and my organisation, and I remember saying to him, 'You're sitting there as if you're having a chat with me in the golf club. Do you mind sitting up straight like everybody else? Who and where do you think you are?'

But if the boys' performance was poor in week one, they got their act together in week two at exactly the time the girls' team fell apart. It was the product design task and I'd set the challenge of designing a new beach accessory. The boys came up with a product they named Cüüli, which was a beach towel that kept things cool. They explained that you could also put things in it like your keys, wallet and credit cards. I named it the 'Swiss Army towel'. For some reason they had used German umlauts in their logo for the Cüüli. I asked them, 'What are the two umlauts doing there? Is it because of connotations that the Germans always grab the towels in the mornings?'

The girls came up with the Book-eeze. It was a thing you put together with plastic rods for holding your book upright when you're on the beach. I thought it was total garbage, and it turned out the experts they were pitching it to agreed with me. When Karren read out the results in the boardroom, she told us that the product did not get one single order – yes, zero units – the first time this had ever happened on a design task in the main series. In the boardroom after that dismal performance, the girls' bickering was getting worse and worse until they were all shouting at each other. At that moment Karren stepped in and made her famous speech. She gave them a right earful about representing businesswomen and how badly they were behaving. I agreed with everything she said. Here we were, supposedly representing business and providing opportunities for women to show they can be successful and professional in business, and the scene we witnessed in the boardroom was absolutely disgraceful. It was like a bunch of old washerwomen squabbling with each other and Karren quite rightly shut them down.

There were some impressive achievements in this series. One week I set them the task of selecting items to sell to massive retailers. One of the teams very sensibly chose a Babygro which changed colour according to temperature and managed to get one single order worth £99,000. In the end the team made over £120,000 in total, a record-breaking win. The person responsible for doing that pitch was investment banker Liz Locke. She did a very good job selling that amount of Babygros to the retailers.

Not every week was so successful. For the advertising task that year I asked them to design a campaign for a new cleaning product. One team came up with Octi-Kleen, the idea being that this cleaning product made you feel as if you had eight arms, like an octopus, so you could get the cleaning done faster. The others came up with a product called Germinator which had, get this, a picture of a child on the front of it. Who in their right minds would use a child as the face of a toxic cleaning product? Ridiculous. I told the team that the advert depicted the most horrible thing I'd seen in the bathroom since *Psycho*.

The Octi-Kleen TV advert was pretty naff. It starred one of the candidates, Christopher Farrell, and an actress they had chosen for the ad. Christopher was playing a husband who wanted his wife to hurry up and get the cleaning done so they could get an early night. It was like something out of the 1950s. I told the team, 'What you did was focus on the advert – which you wanted to make people laugh and be memorable – but you forgot the product! *Titanic* won eleven Oscars but it wasn't a good advert for cruise ships, was it?'

I remember Karren complaining that the advert was ridiculous; that it made the wife look like a real skivvy while the husband was sitting in his armchair shouting, 'Come on, get on with it!' Also, when the wife finally came in, we joked amongst ourselves that it looked like the start of a porno movie. I remember commenting in the boardroom that Nick would know about this due to his modest collection of adult films at home. As I've mentioned before, this of course is not true – it's a total joke we ran with for many series.

Nick came out with one of his famous lines during this task. He was commenting in the boardroom about one candidate's over-enthusiasm and said to him, 'You were all over it like a tramp on chips.' It was hard to keep a straight face in front of the candidates because one doesn't want to drop one's guard and be seen to be making light of the matter, particularly when the subject we were discussing was a serious error. It *was* difficult sometimes to bite your tongue and not burst out laughing when Nick came out with these lines.

There were some candidates in that series who stood out, not always for the right reasons. One of them, Paloma Vivanco, clearly thought she was being shrewd by pointing out all the flaws in her teammates. On occasions it was perfectly obvious that instead of focusing her attention positively on winning, she was going out of her way to set up other people on her team for a fall, so that if they lost and she ended up in the boardroom she could point out each and every one of those flaws. What she didn't count on was that when she did that, she was making herself less appealing to me as an employee.

The night she was fired, she was the losing project manager but wasn't in the least responsible for the loss of the task. In fact, I was about to clear her of any blame and decide on which of the other two candidates I would fire, when she piped up, 'Lord Sugar, can I just say one last thing?'

I allowed her to speak, then she blew it by comparing herself favourably to the two candidates alongside her, rubbishing their business skills and putting herself up there as some sort of superior being.

I was shocked at such arrogance and said, 'Paloma, I don't like your last outburst, and going by my forty years in business and my gut feeling, I don't like what I've seen across the table here today. You've talked yourself out of this – if you'd have shut up a while back, it may be someone else going, but Paloma, you're fired.' And with a look of horrified amazement, she left the room.

I really cannot stand people being underhand. On top of that, Paloma was one of the only candidates who broke the rules about leaving the house. For this particular series, the candidates stayed in a very nice, recently refurbished house in Bedford Square, right near the British Museum – the perfect central-London location. Ruby Evans had done a great job in getting the landlord to let it to us for the duration. I believe he felt that letting it to us would reap dividends as his property would be exposed on national TV. The poor sod – little did he know (due to the rescheduling delays) that he would have to wait a whole year to see his house on TV!

One problem we had with the house was that the property next door was undergoing major renovation works. Every time the crew showed up to start filming something, such as the candidates leaving the house and getting into the Chryslers, someone would start drilling or angle-grinding and making a very loud noise. They had to keep stopping and starting the filming, which drove them nuts.

Back to Paloma. One day she just decided to leave the house and go out to meet her boyfriend somewhere on Tottenham Court Road. On another occasion she went out to find a hairdresser to get her hair done; all this in total disregard for the rules we had laid down for *The Apprentice*. I remember Michele Kurland going mad at her and telling her that she'd be reporting the matter to Lord Sugar who, as a consequence, might send her home there and then.

When the candidates try and get slippery with me, I give them short shrift. One thing that candidates have tried on occasion is to force my hand on who to fire by deliberately bringing people back into the boardroom who are not responsible for the failure of the task, but whom they perceive are in a perilous position in the process. This always backfires and usually results in the person who thought they were being clever getting fired themselves, as happened in Paloma's case.

Probably the most noticeable candidate that year was Stuart Baggs. In fact he was one of the most memorable candidates I've come across in all my time doing *The Apprentice*. Regrettably, at the time of writing this book, I got the very sad news that he had suddenly died at his home on the Isle of Man. This came as a big shock to me as he was such an energetic character and he was so young. I have so many memories of him in the series, as I'm sure his friends and family do too. I felt very sad for them when I heard this bad news. Here are a few of his stand-out moments.

In the first episode of the series, Stuart took the mickey out of project manager Dan Harris in the boardroom by tapping numbers into an imaginary calculator, saying, 'Dan, how many sausages did you make? [tap tap tap] Zero.' Right from the start he made an impact with crazy boasts like, 'Everything I touch turns to sold,' and he carried on like that the whole way through the series. He once pleaded with me not to be fired. I asked, 'Why shouldn't I fire you, Stuart?'

He replied, 'If you give me a hundred grand a year, I will deliver you ten times that. And if I don't, have it back – a money-back guarantee.'

I told him, 'I had an offer like that from Nigeria once, but funnily enough it didn't stack up.'

There were times when he drove the other candidates completely spare. I remember there was one incident which was so famous within the production team that they called it the Battle of Trafalgar Square. I'd sent them out to put on an open-top bus tour for tourists, and Stuart, who was project manager, and Chris Bates, from the opposing team, were having some sort of tiff about who was allowed to sell tickets in a particular spot. In the end, it all got very heated.

Stuart was enthusiastic, I'll give him that. But as I pointed out to him, 'A fly's got enthusiasm – it doesn't stop headbutting the window.' His team lost that week and they ended up in the board-room. He made the most impassioned plea you've ever heard. He claimed that he wasn't a one-trick pony or even a ten-trick pony, but that he had a field of ponies. I recall commenting to him that he was waffling again.

'Stuart, in the past few weeks, some of the stuff that's come out of your mouth is a lot of hot air, so in the interests of climate change and thinking about the glaciers, just make sure you *think* before you talk. You certainly believe in yourself but it wasn't that long ago you believed in the tooth fairy also.'

At one point, when he was under extreme pressure in the boardroom, he suddenly came out with, 'Lord Sugar, I don't feel well – I'm about to faint,' which took us all by surprise. Obviously we immediately stopped filming, offered him a glass of water and any assistance we could give him, only to find that about ten sec-onds later he'd pulled himself round and was firing on all cylinders again. He was so desperate to win, he said, 'My workday won't be nine to five, I'll be working twenty-four-seven,' to which I replied, 'I don't need a night watchman.'

He called himself 'Stuart Baggs – The Brand' and I remember him getting his comeuppance from Claude Littner in the interviews episode. Claude started reading out loud from Stuart's CV: '"I'm Stuart Baggs – The Brand". What on *earth* are you talking about? You're a twenty-one-year-old kid. You're not a brand.'

Stuart started to explain, 'I think that when you look at what a brand means . . .'

You could see the steam rising from Claude. 'No, no, don't tell me what a brand is. You are not a brand. You're not a brand.'

Stuart also claimed he was a big fish in a small pond, and Claude famously said to him, 'You're not a big fish. You're not even a fish.'

As Stuart made it right the way through to the interviews, Bordan Tkachuk, one of the other interviewers, did some digging and discovered that some of Stuart's claims were, to put it mildly, somewhat exaggerated. This made me angry at the time, because Liz Locke, who was quite a credible candidate, had been let go in a prior episode and I had kept Stuart on because I thought he was an enterprising young man in the telecoms industry.

Margaret, who was one of my interviewers in this series, added her tuppence-ha'penny worth by saying she'd found out that Stuart was unable to handwrite his application form and that he had asked his girlfriend to write it for him because he couldn't write by hand. The only way he could communicate in writing was by computer. I asked Margaret whether she was sure she'd got that right, and she swore on a stack of Bibles that that was what he had told her. He started off on the wrong foot with Margaret when he walked into the interview room and blurted out, 'Margaret! Pleased to meet you.'

He really picked the wrong person to be arrogant towards. Margaret swatted away his impertinence by asking, 'Would you normally address an interviewer by their first name?' It was a great moment and Stuart was lost for words for once. I have to say, after hearing Margaret's, Claude's and Bordan's feedback on Stuart, I decided to let him go.

I've always had the utmost respect for the hundreds of candidates who have been through *The Apprentice* process over the ten years. This fellow was actually very smart and I hoped that he would now concentrate on business, as he did have a seed of a good idea in his telecoms enterprise. However, he could not resist being a bit of a joker and, as such, couldn't stop himself from thinking he would be able to maintain a media career afterwards by doing many, what I would consider, silly things, like appearing in panel shows where it was clear they were just taking the mickey out of him and using him to clown around. Needless to say, his media career was very short-lived. He did appear in a few things but, as usual, the media used him and then dropped him.

I think he got a bit more sensible as he got older, and did indeed start to concentrate on his telecoms business, and from what I heard, in the week that he died, he announced a new service he was about to offer. Anyway, it was a very sad ending to the life of a real character. I am sure he will never be forgotten by all those involved in *The Apprentice* series six.

There were a few other candidates in series six who stood out. Shibby Robati, who was a qualified surgeon, messed up a baking task with his autocratic manner as project manager. The task was to produce bread rolls for selling to hotels and restaurants. His team had been very successful in getting a massive order from a hotel group while the sub-team in the kitchen set to work busily making the rolls – all well and good. Then Shibby announced that he'd got another order, this time for a hundred croissants. The sub-team told him they didn't have the ingredients for croissants as it was never planned to make them. The whole thing turned out to be a total disaster. He was due to turn up at the hotel and deliver the rolls and croissants at six o'clock the following morning so the chef could prepare breakfast for the guests. Out of a thousand rolls, Shibby had to explain to the chef that he only had sixteen. It was a most embarrassing moment. He had to pay the hotel compensation with some of the seed money I had given them to carry out this task – a complete and utter shambles.

This task was a total disaster for Shibby. Back in the boardroom

I asked his teammates, 'Was he Doctor Dolittle or do-a-lot?' There was a long silence.

As this task was to do with baking, I couldn't resist saying to the losing team, 'I've heard of the expression breadwinners, I'm looking at seven bread-losers here today.'

In the same way that Shibby dithered on the task, he was indecisive on who to bring back with him into the boardroom. Due to my frustration, I said, 'Shibby, I tell you what my doctor says to me when I've got a headache: "Take two of these and it might go away." So please, which two people are you bringing back into the boardroom?'

He brought back Sandeesh Samra, who had made some wild claims on her CV; one of which made me comment, 'Sandeesh, according to your résumé you're going to propel me into world domination! That's going a bit far – there was a bloke in Germany who had a bit of a problem with that!'

But playing on Shibby's medical background one last time, I could not resist saying, 'Shibby, after a thorough examination, I have got some bad news for you – you're fired.'

One very confrontational character was Melissa Cohen. She claimed to be a food business manager but she messed up on a task that was synergistic to her field of expertise. She also used to make up words that didn't exist in any dictionary! I remember telling her, 'You remind me of these knock-off DVDs – at first glance you're quite convincing but after a while you're impossible to follow.'

She was the only candidate I can recall who, as she walked out of the boardroom after being fired, had a go at her teammates. Instead of thanking me for the opportunity as most candidates do, she stormed out of the boardroom, saying to the two remaining candidates, 'Well done, ganging up on me – horrible people.'

Joanna Riley was a great story. She got herself right the way through to the penultimate episode and all my advisors liked her a lot because she had a young family but also fended for herself by doing cleaning. In fact, she started her own cleaning service when she was only twenty-two and was a real grafter. It was a sad moment letting her go and my best advice to her, which was endorsed by Claude, was that instead of trying to become something else, she should try to enhance her cleaning business and concentrate on that, which I believe she went on to do.

I spoke earlier about the stringent application process that we apply in trying to make sure the candidates have no skeletons in their cupboards. Regrettably, in series six, the skeletons came out of the cupboard for Christopher Farrell. Once his face appeared on screen, it was disclosed that he was involved in some kind of illegal mortgage brokering. This resulted in him having to go to court to face charges. Melissa Cohen, too, was accused of some alleged financial impropriety in her past, the exact details of which I can't recall, but I remember all of this causing James Herring, the PR consultant for the show, a bit of a headache at the time.

The two finalists were Chris Bates and Stella English. Chris and Stella had both worked their way through the process efficiently. Chris was an investment banker and quite a shrewd lad. Stella, meanwhile, came across as a very capable person who claimed to be the head of business management for a bank.

The final task was for them to come up with a new alcoholic cocktail, and as usual we called back some of the old candidates to assist in the task. One funny moment in the boardroom came when Shibby, trying to critique Chris Bates's drink – which was pink in colour – said, 'The first taste of a drink is with the *eye*.'

'Really?' I said to Shibby. 'I know you're a doctor but I'm *not* sure about that. Next time, I'll have a cup of tea through my eye then. By the way, what is your area of medical expertise, just out of interest?'

'Bones,' he replied.

'Right, I'll make sure I don't break my leg near you then.'

*

A few days after the customary skeletons-in-cupboards talk I give the two finalists, Stella informed me about some things that might come out about her private life, which she agreed I could share with James Herring. I was grateful for this information and sympathetic to its content at the time. And so we were very prepared to brace ourselves for quite a lot of adverse media attention. She told us it might be reported that her partner had some connection with people who were involved in the Stephen Lawrence murder. In fact, it turned out that he had nothing to do with them at all, but the media, of course, put two and two together and started to create an unjustifiable fuss. There were also disclosures by Stella about some matters relating to her mother and brother that I don't feel are appropriate to discuss here, but there was a possibility these might also be picked up by the press, so we were well braced. Conversely, in the case of Chris Bates there was nothing whatsoever.

Stella went to work for a while at Viglen while waiting for the show to broadcast, and I had chosen her, in my head, as the winner. During the course of the twelve months' waiting time – brought about by the election delay – there were lots of nudges from her and Chris to try and get me to indicate to them whether they'd won or not, which of course I would never do.

On one occasion, Stella showed what was to become an all-too-familiar trait – her suspiciousness.

'I know I'm not the winner,' she told me, 'because I haven't been filmed in the final Rolls-Royce shots where the winner is revealed.'

'Stop being so paranoid,' I replied. 'The Rolls-Royce shots have not been taken because we are nowhere near the final yet. They will be taken after the BBC has decided on the broadcast date. And by the way, the Rolls-Royce shots are taken with you as the winner *and* with Chris as the winner so we have both recordings available when I reveal my decision.'

This suspicious attitude of hers would come back and smack me in the face later.

Stella was eventually announced as the winner, and Chris of course was disappointed. Interestingly enough, he went off and was hired by James Caan, the ex-judge on *Dragons' Den*. I don't know what it is about this James Caan fellow but he must track the programme, because Chris was the second ex-candidate, after Yasmina, he decided to take on. He obviously feels they have potential having seen them in *The Apprentice*.

Stella was set an administrative job at Viglen working with Bordan. I knew she was an efficient person from how she'd conducted herself in *The Apprentice*. I also knew Bordan wasn't very happy with employing *Apprentice* winners, but I told him she was of a very high calibre and that he needed to invest some time in giving her a good managerial position. I'm not exactly sure which department she was placed in, and of course she was not an expert in computers, but to her credit she tried to pick up some of the technical side of the business, albeit she would be working more on the administrative, support and sales side.

Unfortunately, the chemistry was not right between Bordan and Stella. On numerous occasions when I went to meet Stella at the Viglen offices, you could see there was a conflict when we were discussing her progress during meetings. Bordan would jump in and, in his usual way, try to play down things that Stella claimed she had done; maybe because he felt she hadn't done them, or that she shouldn't take the credit for things she wasn't responsible for. Having said all that, Bordan will be Bordan.

All of this culminated in a situation where, just a few months into her contract, she simply got up and left the company! I contacted her and asked what she was playing at. I told her it was very unprofessional simply to walk out. I remember saying to her at the time that she was doing herself a disservice.

Because of the negative publicity she'd received from the *Daily*

Mail and other national newspapers, she had this thing in her head that it would be a disaster if the *Daily Mail* got to hear about her leaving. I couldn't quite understand what she meant by 'if the *Daily Mail* got to hear about it'.

I recall telling her, 'I don't give a damn about what the *Daily Mail* thinks. If you want to go, you go. But you have a £100,000 contract which I'm quite happy to honour, so I can't understand why you have simply walked out without any notice.'

She explained to me that she just could not get on with Bordan, and felt the job she had there was not challenging enough for her. She also explained that she didn't know where she would go now, and that having wasted over a year waiting for the programme to be broadcast, and now, having worked for just a few months at Viglen after winning, it was going to be difficult for her to pick up a new career somewhere else. I understood and recognised this, and told her that perhaps I could find her a position with a company I'd recently become chairman of – YouView. She agreed with this proposition and so Amshold, my company, continued to pay her contract while her services to YouView were given free of charge by me.

Unfortunately, however, that didn't turn out too well either. She spent a couple of months at YouView on a project to do with finding contractors to deal with the security of the YouView system then being developed – a highly important job – but once again, she simply tendered her resignation and walked out without giving any notice.

At this stage I kind of gave up on her. Regrettably, there had also been a lot of media stories about her, including matters to do with her partner, which were untrue, but other things were also popping up such as her allegedly not paying for the house she had rented and allegedly not paying for a wedding dress she had hired. Lots of strange things were occurring which in themselves were none of my business. In fact, I heard she was in trouble again recently. After her courtesy car had been caught speeding by cameras, she claimed her au pair was driving but did not say who the au pair was, and was convicted of failing to identify the driver.

But imagine my surprise when at my headquarters one day we received a writ (for want of a better word) in the post! Stella had decided to try and make a claim for unfair dismissal; a claim that was to be heard by an employment tribunal. The allegations made in this claim were totally outrageous and ridiculous. And here's an amazing mystery – within seconds of this writ arriving on my desk, somehow or other the *Daily Mail* had got hold of the story! For a newspaper that slagged her off so much when she won, and then slagged her off again in respect of her family and partner, it seemed that suddenly the *Daily Mail* had become her new best friend. One can only assume she had informed them of this action she was taking, and the headlines told the tale: STELLA ENGLISH, WINNER OF THE APPRENTICE, TAKES LORD SUGAR TO EMPLOYMENT TRIBUNAL.

In my opinion the tribunal system can be abused. It is very easy to make a claim at a tribunal whereby the claimant has no exposure to legal costs. However, the person or company they are claiming against has to employ legal advisors to defend the case. On a previous occasion in relation to another employee, we had spent a fortune with lawyers defending a case which we won, but at the end of the day we had no chance of recovering our costs from the claimant. You can end up with a bill from top-quality lawyers for as much as £250,000 defending a derisory claim. Meanwhile, this type of claimant finds what we call 'an ambulance-chaser lawyer' who knows only too well that the company will most probably take a view that they don't want to spend huge sums defending a claim because even if they win they will have no chance of recovering their money. So you'd have thought that a sensible businessman like me would recognise this, cut my losses and pay her off.

With me, however, the ambulance chaser and Stella English

had rolled the dice and lost, because having bent over backwards to try and accommodate her in two jobs, and constantly tried to calm down situations between her and her fellow employees at Viglen and YouView, not to mention keep the press off her back with regard to her personal affairs, this was a real smack in the face for me. I decided I didn't care how much money it cost, I would not take this lying down. Unless I was directed to do so by the tribunal, I would not be giving her one penny in compensation.

I explained the situation to my lawyers. They said, 'That's fine – if you want to spend money then it's up to you, but you have to realise, Lord Sugar, that if this thing goes to the tribunal, you will have to turn up, you will have to be there and you will have to give evidence.'

'So *what* if I have to?' I said. 'I'm doing it. I'm going to take a stance because I'm sick and tired of these derisory claims, not just from Stella English, but when I read through the national newspapers and see these stereotypical people who claim they have been "treated badly" and get large awards from companies who cave in and can't be bothered to turn up at tribunals, this really, really annoys me.'

I do believe the tribunal system is completely and utterly flawed. I know that nowadays they've toughened it up a little bit by making claimants deposit a certain amount of money, albeit a very small sum, before they bring a claim.

The toing and froing between my lawyer and the ambulance chaser that Stella had employed went on for about a year. There were pathetic attempts to try to get us to make an offer. Her lawyer was told in no uncertain terms that she was getting nothing at all because she had no claim. The ambulance chaser was not in court when the tribunal came about and Stella English had found some female barrister who, I have to say, did not pull up any trees.

Stella English thought she'd become some kind of martyr, taking on the mighty Lord Sugar and proving how brave she was going to be, as if she were some sort of people's champion. I think she came out with some statement – again to her new ally, the *Daily Mail* – along the lines of, 'Never underestimate someone who's got nothing to lose.'

The *Daily Mail* of course was lapping it up and loving every moment of this. As I turned up at the tribunal, the cameras were flashing like mad and the journalists were trying to get comments from me as I walked in. My PR consultant David Fraser was by my side the whole time and was ushering me into the building along with my legal team. Some of the employees at the tribunal building were being typical civil servants, telling me, 'I don't care who you are – you might think you're a high-profile person, but we have no special rooms for you to sit in. You have to sit in the waiting room with everyone else.' After a while, a more accommodating young lady – who could see the embarrassing scene with people coming up to me and journalists surrounding me asking questions – found us a small meeting room we could sit in for a while. A few minutes later, one of the niggling civil servants came into the room saying, 'What are you doing here?'

'We were told to sit here,' I said.

'Well, I may need this room soon, so be warned.' Awful, petty people, just trying to assert their authority.

The tribunal hearing was an uncomfortable situation but I was going to go through with it. There was no way I was going to succumb to what I thought was commercial blackmail by Stella English (by which I mean she thought I would pay up rather than go through the embarrassment and effort of attending the tribunal to be cross-examined). In the tribunal room, the whole of the press area was packed. Stella gave evidence first, and of course the journalists were beavering away, writing down every single word she said. Her case was terribly weak. You can imagine what rubbish she came out with and, of course, that same rubbish was reported in the papers the next day.

My wife, Ann, and a lot of my friends were saying to me, 'What the hell did you get mixed up with this woman for? She is horrible, she is nasty. She's not telling the truth – why are you getting yourself so involved?'

I told them, 'This is a matter of principle; it's not a matter of money. I have faith in the legal system in the UK which has always been very good to me. Besides, I've been in uncomfortable positions in court cases before, and this is just another one. So don't worry, I'm okay, I will have my minute in court.'

And my minute I had.

Outside the tribunal room there was a BBC camera team with a BBC journalist who was reporting what was going on. Stella English would walk past the cameras every day smiling as if she were on the red carpet at the Oscars. Meanwhile, I would be pictured walking in and out of the tribunal looking glum.

In my head I knew what I was going to say when questioned by Stella English's barrister and by mine, and I was hoping that the BBC reporter would be there to hear me. When it was my turn to respond to a question from her barrister, I said, '*This* is an abuse of the tribunal system. The tribunal system was designed to look at genuine complaints from employees who have been treated badly by employers. I am here today to explain to the tribunal what an absolute outrage and disgrace this case is. The tribunal has already heard detailed evidence on which they must be forming an opinion, essentially that the matter should never have come here. This is simply the case of an ambulance-chasing lawyer and an opportunistic woman who thought that I was going to cave in. As soon as the lawyer heard my name, he thought, "Ker-ching, ker-ching, we're in the money." Well, members of the tribunal, as you will notice, that lawyer is not here today because he realised there is no money in this, and that unless you, gentlemen [they were all men on the tribunal], inform me that I am in the wrong, I am not going to pay this woman one penny whatsoever because this is commercial blackmail. Not only am I standing up for myself, I am also standing up for many other employers who've suffered as a result of the abuse of this system. What's more, because I'm a relatively high-profile person, you will see in the back row over there all these journalists who are lapping up every single word of this. I was humiliated by the stuff they produced yesterday, which the tribunal may or may not have read. If they *have*, then the tribunal will have seen that it doesn't bear any resemblance to what was actually spoken – but, of course, never let that get in the way of a good story. And here I am, standing here today because the ambulance chaser and Miss English never thought I was going to turn up.'

Well, I got that off my chest. My lawyers' faces were beetroot red because they had told me I shouldn't get excited or get angry, but I couldn't resist it. To me, that was worth every minute of what I'd been put through.

Then it was time for Stella English to be interrogated again by my barrister. Unbeknown to her, I had learned that she had sold stories to the newspapers in the past through a famous PR consultant she had hired – Max Clifford. I had dealt with Max when I was chairman of Tottenham Hotspur. I believe he was hired back then by Terry Venables to try and assist him but, for some reason unbeknown to me, Max fell out with Mr Venables. Max was no friend of mine but I had come across him a few times and, as such, I was able to pick up the phone and talk to him frankly, and he always spoke to me frankly too. I asked him point blank, 'How much did Stella get paid by the newspapers?' He told me she'd received approximately £12,000 from two different newspapers to sell her story about her awful experience on *The Apprentice*.

In her witness statement, Stella had said she'd received £6,000. At one stage, when she was in full flow telling her sob story, my barrister interjected and asked her, 'Why did you use the services of Max Clifford?'

Stella was stuck. She began to stumble over her words and started waffling, 'Well, erm, well, er, well . . .'

'Miss English, please tell me. You're somebody who tells us you have no money – well, surely Mr Clifford must have charged you a lot of money?'

'Well, erm, well . . .'

She was really shocked that we'd learned about Max Clifford as it hadn't been disclosed in any of our witness statements. My barrister then went on to question her about the fact she had claimed in her witness statement that she'd received only £6,000 from the media, and he asked her politely whether she felt that was correct. She started to waffle again, 'Well, erm, I can't remember exactly.'

'I'm sorry, it's not a case of remembering,' he said. 'When you wrote that witness statement down you must have known – surely you have bank statements and all that type of stuff, don't you?'

In the end, her barrister jumped up and said, 'Perhaps we can reconvene tomorrow and look into this a little bit more.'

This was a total shock for Stella English and her barrister. They had underestimated the amount of information we had, and of course the next day she had to declare that what she had said in her witness statement was wrong – in fact, she'd received £12,000.

It was absolutely clear to me and everyone else in that room that she was not going to win her claim. The tribunal sent us away and it was rather disappointing to hear them say that because this was a high-profile case attracting a lot of media attention, they wanted some time to deliberate on it. Indeed, it took them over a month before they made the expected announcement – clearly we had no case to answer. Stella English had lost her claim completely. The tribunal went so far as to say this was a claim that should never have been brought.

The following press release was sent out on the day the verdict was announced:

EMPLOYMENT TRIBUNAL DISMISSES CLAIM IN *APPRENTICE* CASE

Lord Sugar brands case 'a sham and a total abuse of the tribunal system'.

The employment tribunal proceedings brought against Lord Sugar by former *Apprentice* winner Stella English have today been dismissed and labelled as 'a claim which should never have been brought'.

Following the hearing, which took place in East London last month, employment judge John Warren today issued his judgement, in which he rejected Stella English's claim that she was constructively dismissed from her roles with Lord Sugar. In his judgement, Judge Warren ruled the following:

On the claim:

'There was no dismissal of the claimant – the claimant resigned. Therefore the complaint . . . fails and is dismissed.

'We have found that the conduct complained of . . . did not occur. We do not find that any of the conduct . . . was conduct which destroyed or seriously damaged trust and confidence entitling the claimant to terminate employment.'

On the job:

'What was clear and what did happen was that the claimant . . . was given a "real job." It was a real job with scope for advancement and learning for the claimant.

'The tribunal rejects the claimant's argument that she was given demeaning work.'

RIGHT: I was so impressed with Susan Ma, in series seven, that I went into business with her too! We launched Tropic Skincare in 2011.

BELOW: Zara Brownless, who won the second series of *Junior Apprentice*, was outstanding throughout.

BELOW RIGHT: Ashleigh Porter-Exley, who had a mature head on her young shoulders, was the winner of the third and final series of *Young Apprentice*.

LEFT: With Andy Devonshire and Mary Berry at the BAFTAs.

RIGHT: Since I wasn't given an award for the BAFTA-winning second series of *Junior Apprentice*, I made my own – with one for Nick and Karren too. My grandson Alex recorded my acceptance speech!

LEFT: I'm thinking of setting up a new company, Amsaward. BAFTA, if you need any more of these made, I can knock them out cheaper than your current supplier.

Pitching a Pudsey Bear phone on *Dragons' Den* for a *Children In Need* sketch. The dragons weren't actually there when I did it so I think I acted quite well!

The winner Ricky Martin, who was brash to start with but really grew throughout the eighth series. Our joint business, HRS, is going great guns.

ABOVE: Series ten had some ambitious tasks, including an advertising one in New York. This billboard of Nick, Karren and me is a nice keepsake.

LEFT: The view from the window of the Leadenhall Building, where the interviews episode was filmed.

With series ten winner Mark Wright at the launch of Climb Online.

I've worked with Claude Littner for many years and he's popular with viewers of *The Apprentice* for his Rottweiler treatment of candidates.

In 2014 Karren became a member of the House of Lords.
It was cheeky, as we were in different political parties, but I brought
her into the House for the introduction ceremony.

At the end of series ten, when this photo was taken, we said
goodbye to Nick. Working on *The Apprentice* has been an interesting
and wonderful journey – and for me, it's not over yet.

On comments made by Lord Sugar:

'Lord Sugar should have let the claimant walk away – Lord Sugar did all he could to support the claimant . . .'

(In response to allegations that Lord Sugar said, 'he did not give a sh*t'): 'Lord Sugar was certainly not using those words referring to the claimant.'

'[Lord Sugar] had gone out of his way to ensure the claimant was placed in a role . . . from which she could learn new skills, a job which she agreed to and which she enjoyed doing.'

Lord Sugar said in a statement:

'I am pleased that the tribunal has returned this verdict and feel vindicated in the judgement that I, my companies, the BBC, the TV production company and my staff acted properly throughout Ms English's employment. There was never a case for us to answer but her need for money and fame meant that the whole system was subjected to this charade.

'I have been cleared of a derisory attempt to smear my name and extract money from me. The allegations were without substance, and I believe this case was brought with one intention in mind – the presumption that I would not attend the tribunal, that I would not testify and that I would settle out of court, sending Ms English on her way with a tidy settlement.

'I'm afraid she underestimated me and her reputation is now in tatters. I have principles and I am not going to be forced to compromise them, no matter how much time and money they might cost me.

'This case was a sham and a total abuse of the tribunal system, which is there to protect employees who have been mistreated. It is not there to aid those chancing their arm at landing a big payday. I hope that other companies will learn from this example and also fight off derisory claims.

'What has happened here is representative of a new wave of claim culture where some employees file spurious actions regardless of whose reputation it may smear in the process. I have spoken about this subject in the House of Lords and will continue to campaign to put an end to this practice, which has developed in recent years and is seemingly spiralling out of control. This has to be stopped.'

The one memory that stays with me on the day of the verdict is just how big a story it was – instantly. Frank PR emailed the press release to the likes of the BBC, Sky and the Press Association, then David Fraser made a quick call to the Press Association to check they had it. As he put the phone down and went to call Sky to do the same, he looked up at the TV on his desk. On the Sky broadcast, the big red 'Breaking News' bar displayed: 'Lord Sugar calls case "a sham and a total abuse of the tribunal system".' It must have been only three minutes after it left Frank PR's outbox.

I should have stopped there, but unfortunately one of my employees told me there was a possibility – because the claim was so derisory and because there was so much inconsistency in Stella English's evidence – that we could go back to the tribunal and ask to get some of our fees refunded. I initially said, 'No, don't bother – it's a waste of time,' but they kind of insisted, so we went ahead and tried that, but the tribunal would not agree to force her to pay us any money. I pointed out to my employee that this was now deemed a 'victory' by Stella English; that she had won a decision despite losing the case. Of course, the decision she had 'won' was that she didn't have to pay our fees. Not really a glorious victory whichever way you look at it.

She hired another PR consultant, Terry Mills, who was hawking around stories about her including one that was reported in the *Sunday Sport* on 6 October 2013 with the headline, I'LL SHOW YOU MY BOOBS FOR £25,000. The article alleged she was *skint* – obviously not so skint that she couldn't afford to pay a PR consultant!

The Stella English episode had a negative effect on me. Ann – and the rest of the family – saw all the aggravation I had got myself into with the tribunal issue, but then again, having been married to me for forty-seven years, she knows by now that I can't help getting myself into these situations where a matter of principle is at stake. My family, friends and colleagues can never understand why I make life difficult for myself, but I'm pretty tough-skinned even though these things don't go to your boots.

The whole episode was a nasty, horrible situation, I regret to say. Thankfully, it has been the only blemish on this great journey of being involved in *The Apprentice*. I suppose you come across these things in life and you have to endure them. Happily, as I've said a number of times, the vast majority of the ex-candidates are polite and grateful to have been given an opportunity to participate in this wonderful process.

16

MORGAN THE TYRANT

**Documentaries, Twitter wars with Piers Morgan
and new friendships**

Thanks to me giving Piers Morgan his big break on television (I like to keep rubbing that in) he had found himself a niche in the market and was presenting an ITV programme called *When Piers Met . . .* These were detailed documentaries chronicling a person's life and I'd seen the ones he'd done on Cliff Richard and Andrew Lloyd Webber. By the way, these documentaries are not to be confused with his *Life Stories* programme or the Saturday-night chat shows he does now.

Piers asked me whether I'd be interested in doing a full-length documentary called *When Piers Met Lord Sugar* covering my life story from childhood right up to the present. It sounded quite an interesting project so I agreed. A filming schedule was laid down, the first part of which was to be in Florida, where I had a house, so they could film my lifestyle there. The second part would be back in London in my old surroundings, including the council flat where I lived as a child and the primary school I went to. Having set the filming dates, we then had to abandon the timetable because, regrettably, Ann's father passed away and everything was put on hold; at one stage it even looked like the whole thing would have to be called off. However, eventually we were able to reschedule and I arranged an additional trip to Florida so that Piers could make his film. The programme was very successful; in fact, it was originally designed to be a one-hour documentary but it ended up an hour and a half long, including adverts. The ITV people must have loved it because it's highly unusual to let a programme run over the time it is originally allotted. The documentary is still available for anyone to view online at *bit.ly/amsbook_120*

Making the programme was interesting at some points, verging on hilarious at others. To start with, Piers was being as mischievous and rude as he possibly could, but he knew I could give it back with interest so there was some great banter in this film, some of which unfortunately didn't make the cut. One of Piers's trademarks, as anyone who's seen his interviews will know, is that he tries to get his guests to weep about the unfortunate things that have happened to them in life. While we were filming, the pathetic film crew and directors would take him to one side at times and say in effect, 'Go on, Piers, try to get him on to some sentimental story – we want to see the sad side of him. See if you can make him emotional because it would be a major coup to see this so-called tough guy from *The Apprentice* crumple. If we could just get a glimpse of a little tear in his eye, it would be fantastic.' I say this was pathetic because, although I didn't actually hear them say these words to him verbatim, you could tell that's what they were doing as in certain sections of the filming they would stop, make some excuse that the lighting was wrong or something like that, then pull him aside to have their little talk.

I said to him, 'Piers, these people are amateurs, son. Do they think I've just come off the bloody onion boat? I know what they're trying to get you to do, so forget it.'

Piers laughed and said, 'I know, I know, but you know what it's like in telly. They're asking me to do these things, but you're right, you're right. Anyway, let's move on.'

At one point Piers asked me, 'What's been the worst moment in your life?'

And here, if I say so myself, I went into my best acting mode. If BAFTA were looking in, they should have given me a bloody award for this alone. I changed my whole demeanour to appear uncomfortable; I put on a very serious face, took a deep breath and started to speak very slowly and very sincerely. 'Yeah well, it's a difficult one to talk about. I know you like doing these things and you've forced me into it, but if you really want me to say . . . well, my most traumatic time, I guess . . . [long pause] . . . was when you got fired from the *Mirror*.'

It was a hilarious moment. Even the camera crew couldn't keep their cameras steady and Piers himself burst out laughing. Unfortunately, because I'd tricked the producer, who thought he was about to strike TV gold, the actual sequence never got into the final cut. But if anybody wants to watch it, you can see it at *bit.ly/amsbook_122*.

While in Florida, Piers wanted to film me, Ann and him in the famous Matteo's restaurant in Boca Raton. Anyone who goes to Boca Raton will know that it's one of the best Italian restaurants around. The owners had agreed to allow filming in the restaurant and the camera crew had arrived a few hours earlier to set things up. The maître d' was a fellow by the name of Vinnie, and Vinnie – like many other Americans – did not understand that my first name is not Lord. 'It's Alan,' I've told him many times. It was hilarious the way he would come up to the table and flap around to get himself into the picture and say, 'Hi, Lord, is everything okay for you? Anything I can get for you, Lord?' I think we filmed a sequence of me trying to explain to him, 'Vinnie, Vinnie, look. I know that you Americans don't take much notice of anything outside your great country, but in Britain there are Houses of Parliament – it's a bit like your Congress. Now, one of our Houses of Parliament, where we formulate the laws of Britain, is called the House of Lords, and my title is *Lord* Alan Sugar. I was born Alan

Sugar but my title is Lord Sugar – in other words, Lord *isn't* my first name.'

He looked at me, still confused, and said, 'Okay, Lord, I got it.'

And still to this day, this fellow doesn't get it. And it just goes to show you that these Americans really don't 'get' anything outside of their own culture. I say that because if I were Senator Alan Sugar, Vinnie would not be calling me Senator; he'd be calling me Alan.

Piers wanted to film some of the things I get up to while I'm in Florida, one of which is cycling. I arranged for my local bike shop to loan Piers a Pinarello bike so we could be filmed riding up and down the Florida intercoastal roads. I was a little concerned that he was rather tubby at the time and that he might not be able to grasp riding a high-performance racing bike. So much so that I told the shop, 'Don't fit cleat pedals for his bike – fit the normal pedals you'd find on a regular bike,' as I didn't want the responsibility of this plumpish, pompous, arrogant, oversized chap falling off. As it happened, he turned out not to be too bad. He rode at a steady twenty miles per hour and actually managed to keep up, although the sequence we were filming only lasted about two or three miles.

There were a few other scenes filmed in Florida: a guided tour around my house, a glimpse of my Legacy 600 jet and all that kind of stuff. And then the Florida filming was over, and a few weeks later we did some filming in London where ITV had arranged for me to visit the council flat where I was brought up, in Clapton, which is part of Hackney. I had been back to the area on many occasions filming around the flats and talking about my East End roots, but the last time I was actually *inside* the flat would have been well over forty years ago, and they had managed to gain access for this documentary.

I'm sure it's very common that in people's childhood memories what they thought was a large place turns out to be much smaller when they see it as an adult. That was the immediate reaction I had when I walked into this flat. The council had done major renovations over the years but in general terms it was still the same physical layout. When I went in, I just could not believe how small the kitchen was, for example. My technical mind clicked into gear and I genuinely started to wonder whether something strange had happened over the years and they'd rebuilt the whole thing. But when I put things in perspective, the front door was where the front door always was, and at the back of the flat, the kitchen window was where the kitchen window always was, so nothing could have changed. It seemed absolutely tiny, as did the lounge, which had felt enormous when I was a kid. The current tenants had given the production company permission to film in the flat and had vacated the premises, but at the eleventh hour the agreement fell through. Unfortunately, therefore, extracts of my visit to the flat could not be included in the film.

The shrinking phenomenon occurred again when I was taken back to Northwold Road School. I'd thought the assembly hall was a massive place when I was a kid, but it looked quite small seeing it now. We strolled through the playground and I made the fatal error of telling Piers that my earliest recollection of being taken to that school was when I was five years old, and after my mother dropped me off, I started to cry and ran all the way home. When I said the word 'cry' his eyes lit up as if he'd just won the lottery.

'Cry?! Oh, so you're a crier then, are you, Lord Sugar?'

'Well, I *was* only five years old, Piers.'

'Oh, no, no, no, actually, I remember when I helped you out in the *Daily Mail* court case – there were reports of you crying there. And here you were crying at school. You're a bit of a serial crier, aren't you? Anywhere else you're going to cry?'

What a tyrant that Morgan is.

'There's one thing I will promise you, Piers. I will not be crying on your programme,' I said.

In one of the sequences, while he was talking to me and trying to stir up my emotions, I said to him, 'Do you remember when Gazza cried during an England match and then afterwards he was in a TV advert where they made fun of it by putting little tubes behind his ears to squirt loads of fake tears?' Then I took out a little bottle of eye drops and said, 'Look, Piers, I'll drip them into my eyes for you if it makes you happy; if it makes you feel better.'

He just would not give up with this crying thing. As we all know, he usually manages to achieve tears on his chat-show-type programmes, which incidentally he has asked me several times to appear on. I've turned these down flatly and told him, 'We've already done it once. We did a proper documentary and I'm not going to do another one of those things because you're going to be raking up the same old stuff, and I can't be bothered, to be quite honest with you.'

The reason he keeps pestering me to do it now is because, since those days, we are famously known for our Twitter wars. In around 2009 I joined Twitter and he joined at roughly the same time. From that moment onwards, we have been bantering and rubbing each other up the wrong way. This has become rather popular on the social media network, and it's reached such a crescendo after so many years that ITV see as TV gold the idea of two people who keep ripping into each other on Twitter finally meeting face to face on one of their programmes. And that's one of the reasons I decided I wouldn't do it. Perhaps I'll hold that moment in stock for another time, and another programme.

On balance I was very pleased to have participated in the documentary. It was an exciting project and definitely fun to make and I suppose that really says it all. The reason I turn down most things is because I can't be bothered to do them and I don't find them rewarding. Over the years I've been contacted by lots of production companies who have the seed of an idea for a programme format and want me to consider being the lead presenter. I didn't dismiss these requests out of hand. It was always worthwhile having a read to see what was actually on offer and what their ideas were. Having said that, none of their ideas were any good at all. Certainly I wasn't going to get involved in a programme that was attempting to rip off *The Apprentice*.

However, there were some documentaries that I did participate in. Aside from the programme with Piers, I've been involved in a few documentaries for the BBC who told me they would always give me some airtime if I came up with a topic I was interested in. I did a one-hour documentary on football which was also quite enjoyable to make because I met up with a lot of the old football cronies I was involved with in my Spurs days. I interviewed several agents; I interviewed the chief executive of the Premier League; I even interviewed Karren Brady in her position as director of West Ham, as well as a few other people in the industry. We were discussing the general rise in the fortunes of football.

As I say, I gave up my time to do this programme simply because it was an enjoyable thing to do. I've always told the BBC that if they wanted me to do more documentaries then I would do them gladly, as long as they are on subjects I understand or enjoy.

On another occasion, I was asked to comment in a documentary that the BBC production team was making about Bill Gates. When the production team came to film the interview, they were very interested in the content I gave them, particularly the history of the computer industry in the UK and some of the stories of me having run-ins with Microsoft in the early days. So impressed were they that they went back to the ranch and decided they wanted to make a documentary on me, which they did. The commentator was Fiona Bruce and we spent a couple of days in Spain with me on my bike again, this time riding down a winding road in Istán. Tracking me was Fiona, driving my Lincoln Navigator vehicle with the back open, allowing the cameraman to perch there and film me. Talk about saving money – we must have broken every health and safety rule going, but this was Spain. We couldn't have got away with it in England.

Whenever I'm asked to do a programme like the one with Fiona Bruce or the football documentary, the BBC production people seem to think I have all the time in the world. I always have to tell them upfront that I will do the documentary for them, no problem at all, but they have a maximum of two days of my time, which of course doesn't have to all be in one chunk – it can be half a day here, a quarter of a day there – but two days is all I will allocate to them, and respectfully, if they cannot accommodate that, then I fully understand that we can't go ahead.

In the case of the football documentary, after it was agreed that I was going to do it, a young lady from the BBC production team came up to me and said, in a matter-of-fact manner, 'Right, we'll need about eight days of your time to do this, Lord Sugar. We need you to go to Germany to watch Bayern Munich and we want you to go to Greece and see Panathinaikos, and there's a possibility we might need you to go to Spain to watch Real Madrid . . .'

I stopped her in full flow and said, 'Hold on a minute, hold on, hold on, love, hold it! Look, I'm not going anywhere. I am going to London, that's all I'm going to do. And if that's not good enough, we'll have to forget it.'

Someone else came back to me and we sorted out a two-day filming schedule. The content I gave them for that football programme, in my opinion, was fantastic. However, when they showed me the first cut, I could not believe my eyes. Here I was, called in as the guru to reflect on the way that football's finances had grown, and they hauled in some so-called experts from accountancy firms who write all these lengthy boring reports on football finance statistics. I would say without exaggeration that the one-hour film they produced had fifteen minutes of these boring people waffling. I got on to the BBC and said, 'Look, I've been wasting my time here

– and you were going on at me about going to Bayern Munich, Real Madrid and all that stuff. I hate to think I'd have done all that only to see these boring stuffed shirts waffling away. The whole point of this programme was to see me giving certain people a grilling about the way the football industry has gone; not to listen to some bloody accountant rattling off statistics, which is boring, boring, boring.'

Anyway, I made my point and as usual it was seen as encroaching upon the creative geniuses' territory, but I think it's fair to say I got about eighty per cent of what I wanted. As for the other twenty per cent, they couldn't help themselves; they just had to leave in some of the boring stuff.

Great Ormond Street Hospital has been the beneficiary of a lot of money raised between me and Piers Morgan on the various bets we have made publicly on Twitter. One of the first contributions he made was after a bet that he would have more followers than me by Christmas of 2010. He lost and had to pay up. On the other hand, I have to admit that I have contributed significantly because we normally have a bet every football season on whose team, Tottenham or Arsenal, will finish higher in the Premier League. From time to time we've also had bets on the Tottenham v Arsenal matches. The banter on Twitter with other celebrities is quite interesting because we all tend to follow each other, and if they're Arsenal supporters I like to wind them up. Dara Ó Briain, for example, the host of You're Fired, is an Arsenal fan, as is Dermot O'Leary from The X Factor, and I have fun winding them up. Having said that, I don't get many opportunities – it's normally the other way round because Arsenal have consistently been better performers than Tottenham as far as their Premier League position is concerned.

When I joined Twitter in 2009 I started to use it as a way of advertising the things I was up to, including – when *The Apprentice* was on – answering my Twitter followers' questions about the show. Shamelessly, I would also use Twitter to promote some of my businesses and my autobiography, which came out in 2010. It occurred to me, having seen what was going on in the US, that my Twitter name *@Lord_Sugar* could appear on screen in *The Apprentice* programme in exchange for me tweeting comments while the programme was being broadcast. This idea of mine was totally rejected by the BBC. Maybe they hadn't even thought about it, but certainly they said it was not possible. I guess their reasoning was that it would look like Lord Sugar was exploiting the licence-fee-payers' money by publicly advertising his Twitter handle, and because I was also promoting various non-*Apprentice* things on my Twitter feed, I reckon they might have thought this was unacceptable, so my idea was turned down. However, these days, as we all know, most popular BBC programmes have a Twitter reference. For example, on *Question Time* they actively invite people to participate on Twitter using the handle *@BBCQuestionTime*, an innovation which I felt *I* had brought to the BBC – of course, I'm not naive enough to believe they'd ever admit that.

Instead of agreeing to put my handle on screen, they decided, one series later, that they would display *their* handle and came up with some convoluted system whereby – and I still to this day don't understand it – they would show it on screen at the beginning of the programme and any comments tweeted to it would be forwarded to me, and then I would look at the comments and tweet the people back where necessary. A chap actually came to visit me from the BBC to explain how it was all going to work. In the end I respectfully declined and decided to take matters into my own hands. Just before the programme went on air, I would go live on Twitter and start priming my followers that I'd be coming online and talking them through the show. Obviously I was never going to spoil anything and I would always wait until a particular event had appeared on TV before I commented on it. This has become tremendously popular, to such an extent that the system occasionally crashes when too many people tweet at the same time, and I sometimes have to wait a few minutes till it all settles down. Then I get all sorts of messages from the Twitter service saying that my tweets are trending, worldwide! I seem to set the Twitter world alight when I tweet while the programme is on, and as I say, not just in the UK – I repeat, worldwide.

I was told by Fremantle Media that *The Apprentice* is one of the biggest trending topics. It's interesting because Fremantle, being an international company, have been contacted by some of their contemporaries in America saying, 'This is very strange. We've seen on the social network reports that *The Apprentice* is trending out of all proportion.' Of course, the *last* question they'd be asking themselves is: might this have anything to do with events *outside* America? They had to be told, 'It's not the US *Apprentice* with Donald Trump; it's the UK *Apprentice*,' to which they said, 'Ahh, we understand now. We thought it was odd because the US *Apprentice* is not currently being broadcast – we wondered how it could be trending at number one worldwide.'

I wish someone would have said to them, 'Yes, there are other things that exist outside America, you know.'

The power of Twitter is quite amazing. So much so that in my latest contract with Boundless, believe it or not, there is a clause that actually *obliges* me to do live tweeting when the programme goes out. So what started off as Lord Sugar's stupid idea has now become a cast-in-concrete contractual obligation!

As we've seen earlier, Boundless is the name of the division now responsible for producing *The Apprentice*. Fremantle Media, the owners of Talkback Thames, had secured the services of a consultant who came into the company to analyse the activities of Talkback Thames and – to make a long story short – they split Talkback up into various different divisions. The division that was going to deal with *The Apprentice*, going forward, was named Boundless. However, they were still owned by the head company Fremantle.

Prior to the reorganisation, Lorraine Heggessey, Talkback's chief executive, had hired other personnel including Sara Geater, a lawyer by profession and a very experienced lady who ran some of the production departments at the BBC. It was Sara who, from then on, I would be negotiating with on contracts. From a corporate structure level, Sara sat in between Lorraine and Jacqueline Moreton. I'm telling you all this because one day I was trying to contact Lorraine by email and I received a bounce-back message. I thought that was odd; maybe our server or their server had gone down. To my surprise I discovered that she'd turned up to work one morning and was told, without notice, 'You're fired.' They shut off her email, packed up all her stuff and sent her on her way.

It was a massive shock. I had no idea why they'd made that decision. Rumour has it they blamed her for losing one of the big programmes they used to make for ITV, *The Bill*. Personally, I thought if that was the *real* reason then it was a little unfair. Lorraine's remit was to bring in new business and new programmes and I guess Fremantle thought she wasn't doing such a good job. But it was a big shock to me, as well as to Michele Kurland and everybody at Talkback/Boundless at the time. Sara Geater was made temporary CEO of Boundless and from then on all of my dealings were with her. It just goes to show how ruthless the TV production business can be. When all is said and done, it *is* a business and it is run by some hard-nosed people. All the same, I think there could have been a nicer way of dealing with Lorraine if they didn't require her services any more. To dispense with her in such a harsh manner was quite shocking as far as I was concerned.

Lorraine's departure from Talkback happened little more than a week before a wedding anniversary party she and her husband were throwing. I'd been delighted to accept an invitation and the event illustrated the sheer number of people she knew in the television world, because the place was jam-packed full of TV celebrities, including Rob Brydon, Rolf Harris – say no more – and many others.

Lorraine's husband, Ron de Jong, saw me as I came in and said, 'Look, we're here to enjoy ourselves tonight. I'm sure you are sensible enough just to go with the flow and not talk about Lorraine's dismissal.' I imagined it must have been a bit of a downer for her, but as I remember, everybody there had a great night and certainly the Talkback affair was not discussed.

I have since met Lorraine on several occasions. Shortly after her sacking I had lunch with her. We never actually discussed the reason *why* she was fired; we just talked about the dramatic nature and the suddenness of it. She told me she was going to start her own business, which had something to do with a conglomerate of small production companies, and obviously I wished her well.

One side effect of being in the TV business and meeting all these new people was that you kind of grew a whole new bunch of friends, like Lorraine. And on special occasions such as my sixtieth birthday, when my wife wanted to put on a big bash somewhere, as well as my normal circle of friends and family I decided to invite my new-found friends from the media industry. So in 2007, some of the cast of *Comic Relief Does The Apprentice* including Cheryl Cole and Karren Brady came along, as well as production people such as Michele, Kelly and Lorraine. Also there were Daisy Goodwin, Patrick Uden, Roly Keating and Peter Fincham, who was then Controller of BBC1. And not forgetting of course Nick, Margaret and a lot of my business associates. Michele had secretly commissioned Andy Devonshire to film all my grandkids walking over the famous bridge that we see in the titles of *The Apprentice*, where the candidates seem to be bouncing across. This was a great surprise and a great film with excellent work again by Andy. It must have taken a hell of a lot of work to organise and coordinate all the kids.

Similarly, in 2008, Ann and I celebrated our fortieth wedding anniversary and again we had a rather lavish bash, with a lot of the same people invited. I've certainly picked up a lot of new acquaintances and friends as an unexpected by-product of my involvement in the television industry.

Of course, my very good friend Nick Hewer is someone I've known for decades. And as series after series of *The Apprentice* rolled out, I was not the only one being contacted by various media companies and asked to participate in TV programmes. Nick, who used to be my PR consultant years ago, who was almost accidentally thrown into the role of my advisor on *The Apprentice*, turned out to be a fantastic character in his own right. We're all aware of Nick's raised eyebrows, his cutting one-liners and his witty descriptions of events; all encased in his posh demeanour and rather dapper look. And so one would not be surprised to hear that he himself was starting to get demands for his services. Initially, this was for speaking events. He was travelling all over the country giving talks for various organisations and making himself, as he put it, quite a bit of money.

'Look, I struggled for years trying to make money in the PR industry – and *you* weren't the most generous, Alan, although you always looked after me,' he used to say to me. 'And now, here I am on television getting paid to do this *Apprentice* thing which is very nice of course, and people are also throwing a bit of money at me for speaking, so I'm making hay while the sun shines because I'm no spring chicken.'

'Absolutely,' I said. 'More power to your elbow, mate. Get on and do as much as you want. Yes, make hay while the sun shines.'

This escalated beyond just doing speaking engagements – he started to appear in other TV shows. BBC Northern Ireland commissioned him to do a programme about farming. Now, Nick is a bit of a country lad. He was brought up in Wiltshire and he loves his tractors, so he took the opportunity of being a John-Harvey-Jones-type troubleshooter for small Irish farming businesses. The programme was called *The Farm Fixer* and it was quite interesting. Obviously the Northern Ireland wing of the BBC had an allocation of funds that they had to spend and they took the opportunity of hiring Nick to do these shows because he loves the country life and, in fact, he does have Irish blood. As one would expect, he did an excellent job presenting the programme.

He also teamed up with Saira Khan, the runner-up from series one, and did a few little gigs with her, but of course the biggest thing that we know him for now is as host of *Countdown*. And if ever there was a programme made for Nick, *Countdown* is it. He was the perfect choice.

Nick has always been very conscious of the fact that, as he puts it, he owes all his media success to me. He would never do anything that would encroach upon *The Apprentice* or compromise its integrity. More to the point, he will go to great lengths to ensure, as a friend, he doesn't do anything to upset me. He will always come and see me and tell me about offers he's been made by television companies. I won't say it's to seek my approval because he knows he doesn't need that, of course, but he values my opinion on whether a project is worthwhile doing. That said, I think in the back of his mind he wants to be sure I'm okay with him doing his other ventures.

He came to see me while we were filming *The Apprentice* and told me that he'd been offered this opportunity to do *Countdown*. I said to him, 'Bite their hand off, Nick. Absolutely do it.'

His concern at the time was how it would mesh in with him filming *The Apprentice*. I said to him, 'Nick, you are perfect for *Countdown* so this is what you should do. Go and tell them the truth. Say to them, "I will do *Countdown* for you, but there's a window of time when I can't do it. We start filming *The Apprentice* around the middle of September so I'll be out from then until the middle of November. Now, if you can accommodate me to do your *Countdown* programme outside of that window then I will definitely be able to do it, but *The Apprentice* comes first."'

And sure enough, the people who produce *Countdown* accepted that proposal, and that is how it has been right up to series ten of *The Apprentice*. He managed to merge all that work on top of doing *The Apprentice* for me, so I say good luck to him.

I mentioned earlier that Daisy Goodwin moved on to pastures new and started her own production company. Well, Daisy's a shrewd lady and very well connected within the television fraternity. She's known for being able to get commissions – she will go and pitch a proposal for a programme to a television broadcaster and sell the idea to them. Daisy, who was by now running a company called Silver River, rang Nick and asked him to call in to their offices just off Tottenham Court Road for a chat about a project under development. She wanted to know if Nick would present a BBC documentary on working into old age, given that that was exactly what Nick was doing! Provisionally titled *The Town That Never Retires*, the programme would look into the issues surrounding the need to work until late in life if in the future the state pension were delayed until people were seventy-plus years of age.

Nick suggested to Daisy that if he teamed up with Margaret, the two of them, both of a certain age, would have great impact. Daisy thought that Margaret would never go for it because she had not enjoyed life in front of the cameras. Nick's response was, 'Leave it with me. I'll talk to her.' And Nick did indeed persuade Margaret to join him, so the dynamic duo of Nick and Margaret were back on our TV screens. Nick said he felt there was a Nick and Margaret brand to be exploited, and how right he was.

Margaret, as we know, left *The Apprentice* to pursue her academic studies, but aside from that she found the schedule too gruelling. However, she accepted the proposal put to her by Nick to join up with him and make a series of documentaries which were broadcast on BBC1. I've seen a couple of these already with the pair of them sitting in the back of a taxi bickering with each other. I think it was a brilliant move by Daisy and Nick. While the programme was probably made as a way of covering the BBC's remit to licence-fee payers that they will broadcast on issues of public interest, and wouldn't normally expect a large audience, people might well tune in just to see Nick and Margaret back together again. I should explain at this point that as part of the above remit, money has to be spent not just on entertainment programmes like *The Apprentice* or *Strictly*, but also on other issues of public interest, and it's in these areas that Nick and Margaret were filmed doing their documentaries.

So not only have I become a media star, but Nick too has become a media star, followed closely by Margaret. Nick loves every moment of it, as I do. And Margaret? Well, she still goes on a bit about not liking being recognised on the Underground, but I suspect that's waning a little now because it's what she used to say when she was in *The Apprentice* – so if she really hated it that much, she wouldn't put herself up for it again with the Nick and Margaret show. On the other hand, I do sympathise with Margaret if her main reason for quitting *The Apprentice* was the strain on her poor feet, because that *was* a killer.

Having said that, I am absolutely in awe of Nick's energy levels. Not only does he walk around following the teams on *The Apprentice* for weeks and weeks, he's up and down the motorway to Manchester recording *Countdown*, then he's off to give a speech somewhere, then he's down to his little château in France to liaise with his Polish builder about fixing something, then he's back in England and off to meet his partner, Catherine, an astute businesswoman in her own right, then up to Manchester again by train for another three days . . . Unbelievable energy and stamina for a fellow who, at the time of writing, has just turned seventy-one!

And he still finds time to organise an annual Christmas drinks party at his club, the Reform Club. He puts on a little bash there every December to which he invites me and some of the people involved with *The Apprentice*, as well as a lot of old friends and new people he's met in the media industry.

He reminded me that I once threw him a surprise party for his sixtieth birthday at the Dorchester hotel. We did actually manage to keep it a surprise and I got him there under the pretence that we were just going to have dinner. I remember pulling him out of the bar where we met, then dragging him off to see some fancy car that was being promoted for some corporate event – just to get him out of the way while the guests were assembling for the big surprise. And he *was* surprised. It was a very nice night, just before the days of *The Apprentice*. In fact, it was shortly after that party that I set him to work on Peter Moore and co. to get me the *Apprentice* gig. At the party, being the PR man he is, and even though he had no clue whatsoever that he was going to be the guest of honour, he'd written himself a speech within about fifteen minutes.

'Bloody hell,' I said to him, 'did someone spill the beans, Nick? Did someone let on about this party?'

'I swear to you, no. But, Alan, why are you so surprised? While you've been sitting there munching away at your food, I realised it was inevitable that I was going to have to make a speech, so I've written this out very quickly – because that's what I do! Remember, I *am* a PR man.'

I've jokingly said to him that now he has this new-found wealth and has turned into such a mega media star, he should bear in mind that on 24 March 2017 I will be seventy and so – hint hint, nudge nudge, wink wink – if he felt like having a surprise party for me, it will be his chance to reciprocate.

17

ALL FIRED UP FOR THE NEW FORMAT

**Looking for brains not bollocks in series seven with
Jedi Jim and the Nodding Dog**

When I was contemplating doing more series of *The Apprentice*, I had growing concerns – after all my experiences so far – about placing the winner in a job amongst my other employees. As I've previously stated, the new boy or girl sometimes doesn't blend in with the rest of the staff, and then there's always that jealousy issue over the £100,000-a-year salary. With this in mind, I decided there needed to be a change.

Another factor affecting my thinking was that the world had gone into financial crisis, and I decided that if I were going to do any more of these *Apprentice* programmes, we would need to theme them in such a way as to say, 'We recognise the current economic crisis, but we can combat the situation.' It was small-business owners and start-ups who were struggling – most of them to get finance – so I decided that instead of offering a job to the winner, I would change the prize to be a *partnership* with the winner on a fifty-fifty basis plus an injection of £250,000 into the new business. Obviously, once I'd thought up this idea, I had to run it past the production company, explaining my rationale to them. They in turn had to seek approval from the format owner Mark Burnett and also the BBC.

I was quite confident that all parties would sign on to my logic, and happily they agreed it was an excellent idea to change the format and give it a more exciting new element. They also recognised that in light of the then economic situation, it was very timely and appropriate.

And that's one of the reasons *The Apprentice* remains so popular. Even though it still has everything that people loved about it at the beginning – the strong characters, interesting business lessons and boardroom grillings – the programme hasn't been afraid to evolve. Many other programmes become naffer versions of themselves over the years because they refuse to change at all, but I think *The Apprentice* walks that line very well and I'm proud of the flexibility and cooperation shown by the production company and the BBC.

So in summary, my new offer to the candidates was, 'Instead of winning a job with me, why not win me as your investor? Instead of a £100,000 salary, why not a £250,000 investment into your business idea? I will bring not only my cash to the table, but also my forty-plus years of experience in business.'

Changing the format meant that the production company would have to change their methodology in the applications process in as much as when recruiting potential candidates for the show, they would now be looking for people who had the seed of an idea for a business, who were able to put together a business plan and who'd already attained some experience in their field. We publicised this change on the *You're Hired* programme at the end of series six, stating that Lord Sugar would be changing the rules so that the prize going forward would be a business investment.

When the production team started auditioning for series seven they were meeting people who up till then would never have applied for a job with me; people who weren't 'natural' employees but who had started a business or who were passionate about an idea they had. It was an exciting prospect for the production people too, but of course it was also risky. I was all too aware that at the end of the series, when I'd decided who'd won, I could be well and truly stuck with this person! They weren't just going to be an employee in one of my companies, whom I might see at the office occasionally; they were going to be my business partner.

Thus there were a lot of implications in this change, and it also demonstrated my total commitment to *The Apprentice* process. Many people would have taken on hosting *The Apprentice* and then been happy, after filming, to walk away and just wait for the next series. However, by changing the format and entering into business with the winner, I was making a long-term commitment.

That year's winner, Tom Pellereau, was a perfect example of the different sort of candidate we got with the change of format. Now, Tom is a very nice fellow, a slightly eccentric inventor-type boffin, and had it been the old prize of a job within my company, it would be fair to say that although he might have gone far in the process, it's unlikely he would have won. But as an investment, Tom had exactly what I was looking for. His zany sort of mad inventor-type mind is always coming up with ideas – he's got that sort of brain. And I am a product man, and always have been, so I could see I could help Tom with the actual nitty-gritty of running all facets of the business. The gamble paid off and we proved to ourselves that the idea worked. It also felt like we were capturing the mood of the country at the time. And I have to say, the way it turned out showed we'd got it spot on and we've stuck with the investment as the prize ever since.

Series seven wasn't all plain sailing, however. That year the house we found for the candidates was in Sheen, south-west London, and it caused us major issues. As you can imagine, finding a house large enough to accommodate sixteen people (including rooms for them to use as offices and rooms for the crew to use to store filming equipment as well as accommodation for the house team) and all within easy reach of central London, on a tight budget, is no mean feat. Ruby Evans was really hard-pushed to find something. I recall her saying that the house in Sheen was really the only option because everything she had tried had failed and it was getting far too close to when we had to start filming. The house was very nice and the candidates were very comfortable but it was a nightmare from a logistical point of view. During the rush hour it could take literally hours for the candidates' cars to get into town. Moreover, the house was directly under the flight path for Heathrow which caused the sound crew no end of problems. One of them timed it and found they had a gap of less than three minutes between each plane going over.

The new format obviously worked because the viewing figures broke the all-time record, and the series at its peak attracted over ten million viewers; a figure that only the biggest and most popular TV shows ever reach.

People often underestimate *The Apprentice*. It's all too easy to sit at home in the armchair and write off candidates as useless, when actually some of the things they pull off would be considered pretty bloody good by industry experts, especially bearing in mind these people have stepped straight into a new branch of business for the first time. I don't think anybody understands the pressure these people are put under in order to perform. And that, combined with the competitiveness of the process and the fact they want to be seen to be performing well in front of me, does from time to time make the whole thing look a bit chaotic.

So it does annoy me quite a lot when I see on social media people calling the candidates numpties and brain-deads, because what appears to be them messing up is in fact a result of this terrible tension. But people are quick to snipe. My old friends at the *Daily Mail* hauled out Luke Johnson to slag me off and rubbish the programme in general. Stuart Rose of Marks & Spencer, when asked about *The Apprentice*, once famously commented, 'If I spoke to *my* staff like that, I would have been fired ages ago.' I famously replied to those critics saying that if I got hold of them, or indeed my friends and business captains like Richard Branson or Philip Green, and stuck *them* in a house and rang them up at seven o'clock in the morning and said, 'Right, get your arses down to Heathrow airport – you're going to Germany and I want you to come up with a new range of crisps to sell to the German market – you have to formulate the flavour, design the branding and packaging, draw up a marketing campaign and get back here in two days' time,' I wonder how well these people would do? To be honest, even if I were asked to do it, I'd find it quite difficult considering I was under a time constraint as well as trying to win a competition for the best product. Ironically, Luke Johnson was once a participant in a kind of fly-on-the-wall-type programme where they came into his company to see how it operated. From what I heard, he threw a wobbly, had a tantrum and walked out.

I wrote to Stuart Rose after he made his comment and told him I didn't think it was appropriate for a leading businessman to criticise me or my programme in such a way when he didn't really understand what he was talking about. He responded by saying perhaps we should get together and have a cup of tea. I declined.

In series seven, there were some real surprises along the way. I kicked off in Boardroom Zero and said to the candidates, just to add a bit of spice, 'I'm not looking for a sleeping partner – I am not Saint Alan, the patron saint of bloody losers.'

Edward Hunter was the first person to be let go. He was an accountant from one of the biggest accountancy firms in the country. I mentioned to him that on his résumé he said, 'I am Lord Sugar's dream.' However, I respectfully pointed out that on this first task, never mind dream, he'd been a nightmare, and that was why I fired him. The excuse Edward gave for failing always sticks in my mind. He said it was hard for him to lead the team because he was the shortest!

When I asked the opposing team what they did, Melody Hossaini went into a long boring ramble. I decided it was time to hear from the rest of her teammates so I said, 'Right, we've heard the Melody, now let's hear from the chorus.' Bloody hell, could she talk! She was also responsible for coming out with the famous statement, 'Don't tell me the sky's the limit when there are footprints on the moon!'

The new prize on offer had attracted a different calibre of candidate, potentially capable of running a business, and the way the first few tasks panned out proved we'd been right to change the format. I was beginning to see that amongst these sixteen candidates there were definitely some bright sparks. On one task both teams made over £700 in a day just by collecting and disposing of rubbish from different businesses, but the most successful performance that year came in the ninth week, when I asked the teams to come up with a new brand of biscuit and pitch them to three major supermarkets. Helen Milligan (the runner-up in that series) was project manager, and her team came up with a biscuit called Special Stars, aimed at kids. When they pitched them to Asda, Jim Eastwood, who was a big character on that series, came out with some outrageous claims of what they'd be doing to support the product. However, the supermarket saw past all that nonsense and could see that in essence it was a very well put together product and brand. And, believe it or not, they ordered 800,000 units! So while the haters and snootier ends of the press are often looking to do *The Apprentice* down, they regularly overlook the huge business successes we've achieved, such as in this biscuit task.

One of the things that came out of series seven was that some of the candidates were already established in industries they would have wanted me to invest in if they won. One such candidate was Zoe Beresford, who was a drinks manufacturer. On this task, which Helen Milligan won by selling 800,000 pieces, Zoe, someone with experience in the food-and-drink industry, came up with zero orders for her product and consequently she was fired. This illustrates the point I was making earlier that, under pressure, so-called experts and experienced people can't hack it sometimes.

I had to give Jim a special award after his performance on this task. He had told the buyers from Asda that his team would spend millions on promoting these biscuits with a huge TV-advertising campaign, tie-ins with new kids' movies, etc., etc. Of course, he could never have delivered what he promised, so in the boardroom I awarded him the BBIW – the Biggest Bullshitter in the World award. I told him, 'You can talk the hind legs off a donkey, but what I've forgotten about bullshit you haven't learned yet.'

Now Jim Eastwood was a glowing example of the type of person we've had in the boardroom most years I've done *The Apprentice* – the sort of bloke who thinks of himself as a bit of a tactician.

You will recall that in the first series of *The Apprentice* I told candidates not to underestimate me. I said this because I knew that at least some of them must have come in thinking they'd be able to pull the wool over my eyes or outmanoeuvre me, so I wanted to get two things understood right from the start. Firstly, that they were dealing with someone who, during the course of my career, has seen it all, done it all and bought the T-shirt; and secondly, that I believe you can be shrewd in business but still be an honest trader.

Unfortunately, Jim was one of these people who tried to employ the tactic of being a little bit slippery in the boardroom. The most striking example of this was on a task when I told the teams to design a new mobile phone app. One of the reasons the boys' team lost was because the description Jim had written for the online marketplaces which sold the apps was totally useless, absolute gobbledygook. The project manager was a fellow by the name of Leon Doyle, a fast-food marketing entrepreneur who if I didn't know better looked as though he could be Piers Morgan's lovechild.

As this was a technical task to do with smartphones I recall asking his team when they got back into the boardroom, 'Good team leader? Steve Jobs or out-of-a-job?' When the result was announced, his team had lost. As it was a phone app task I couldn't resist borrowing a slogan from one of the network operators, Orange. I told the losing team, 'On the subject of phones, the future is not bright. In fact, the next application one of you might be making is a job application.'

When they got back from the losers' café, I asked Leon who he wanted to bring back into the boardroom and he nominated Jim and a chap called Alex. Jim looked as if butter wouldn't melt and launched into this impassioned speech about how Leon had made the wrong decision and how everyone else but him was at fault. Leon must have been impressed by the speech because, having said he was bringing Jim back, quite rightly, for messing things up, he changed his mind and let Jim off the hook! I couldn't believe my ears and neither could the production team listening in. It was one of the best examples of someone talking themselves out of trouble in the boardroom that any of us had ever seen. In fact, on the *You're Fired* programme after that episode, Dara Ó Briain christened Jim Eastwood 'Jedi Jim'.

I'll never forget the face of Glenn Ward, the candidate who was brought back into the boardroom to replace Jim. Poor Glenn's face was a picture. Here he was, thinking he was in the clear for another week and getting ready to go back to the house, only for Jedi Jim to change Leon's mind and make him choose Glenn instead. Not a happy bunny, as you can imagine. He was safe though, as Alex was fired. However, later on, in the task to do with designing a free magazine, when Glenn was trying to defend his position to me, I said to him, 'Glenn, you describe yourself as a barrow boy done good.'

'Yes, Lord Sugar, I promote live music and I'm a social secretary at a football club.'

'So you're a bit of a Del Boy then? I was wondering if you were one of those people who thought that *Only Fools and Horses* was a business documentary.'

Vincent Disneur was another interesting candidate who was half Belgian. He was banging on so much in one of his explanations as to why he wasn't responsible for something or other I had to cut him short.

'I know you are Belgian and that's where the waffles come from, but can you please cut the crap and tell me why you shouldn't be here in the final three?'

He used to come out with some classic stuff, leading with his chin in the boardroom. In week three I set a task for the teams to buy ten items for the Savoy Hotel, which was about to reopen after a major refurbishment. Vincent told me he'd left a lasting impression with all the suppliers he negotiated with. I recall saying to him, 'So you reckon you'll be remembered long after you're gone? Let's see if I remember you.'

In week four I set a task offering beauty treatments. The teams had completed the task and I opened the boardroom session with another of my classic lines. 'Right, you've done the *beauty* stuff – now you've got to deal with the *beast* side of things – me!'

Vincent was a bit of a handsome-attack character and every week his skin tone seemed to change. We all suspected he was using some kind of spray tan as he looked a bit orange. On that task, one of the things his team missed out on was securing the spray-tan product to sell. I told the team they might have lost the spray tan because Vincent had used it all before they started.

Vincent was in team Logic, which had lost the first four tasks. On task five, which was an advertising task for pet food, once again he took the brunt of my criticism over the name he'd decided on for their dog food. I said to him, 'With your team's track record, clearly Winalot wasn't on the agenda, was it?'

I continued, 'I have this dream that one day I will walk into this boardroom and you lot won't be here – never mind Logic, you should be called Tragic!' Jedi Jim made his usual slick, impassioned plea about how well he did and the excellence of the team's dog food. I shut him down by stating, 'In the old days there were rumours about what went into the contents of dog food, which prompts me to ask: I don't know what *you* are made of – is it brains or bollocks?'

Another thing I'll always remember from that series concerned Tom Pellereau. He had been in the losing team in the first five weeks and raised the issue in the task I had set about recycling rubbish to turn into cash.

'I've lost five in a row, Lord Sugar,' Tom said, 'and I'm not happy.'

'Yes, I'm aware of that. I know I like recycling, but it seems I have recycled you enough times in this boardroom; and as you know, my boardroom disposals get taken away in the back of a taxi.'

Right from the first occasion when I addressed the candidates in the boardroom, whenever I was explaining things or giving them advice, Tom had this habit of nodding towards me as if to say, 'Yes, I fully get it; I understand.' And this nodding carried on right the way through the whole series.

There was one task I really had my heart set on doing; a task I had carried out myself forty-three years earlier! I said, 'We're going to go back to basics and we're going to replicate how I started my business up.' I got them all to turn up at a big North London warehouse which had a massive array of products. I gave the teams £250 each and told them they should select and buy whatever products they required from the inventory. The teams had a van each and I told them to get out there and start selling. The key thing about this task was that they should replenish their stock when they'd sold out. In other words, if they'd decided to buy fifty umbrellas and they'd gone out into the street and sold them all, they were supposed to come back and buy some more.

As I say, the purpose of this task was to replicate how I started my business back in 1968 when I bought a minivan and a bit of stock, and went out in the morning and started to sell. In the afternoon I took some of the cash I received and went back and bought some more stuff and carried on doing that for a whole week, and at the end of the week I counted my assets. So this task was *not* to be a headless-chicken sell-everything free-for-all, and then come back with nothing but a wad of money; it was all about counting the assets – the assets being the cash you have in hand plus the value of your stock – and the team with the greatest assets would win. It was important they grasped the idea that the object wasn't to sell out of everything, because in theory, the next day you could be back in business again buying and selling more stuff.

The setting of the task took place in the warehouse itself. Instead of the candidates being lined up like a load of tailors' dummies as they usually are, I had them sit around on the boxes as I walked among them explaining the task. I recall going right up to Tom Pellereau and saying, 'And if you don't stop bloody nodding, I'm going to stick you inside the back window of my car.'

Now Mark Saben, the series editor, has a good sense of humour. And one of the products he asked the warehouse people to put forward was a nodding dog for cars. Our little in-joke. I remember at the end of that task, Mark gave me one of these dogs to take home to remind me of my outburst at Tom, the nodding candidate.

Because this was the first time I'd be going into business with someone, we decided that the interview stage, which used to be the penultimate episode, would now be the final. So the penultimate task for this series was one where the teams had to open up a new fast-food type of restaurant. It was an excellent task for which we invited a lot of industry experts along to appraise the results. At the end of the task, I had to fire Natasha Scribbins who, even though she had a degree in hospitality, contributed very little. This left four candidates, who would go head to head in the new-style final.

Because of the format change, it was very important that the business plans of the final four candidates were scrutinised very carefully in the final. Now this is an unusual sort of situation, and has often been commented on in recent years. When I requested we change the format the BBC pointed out that my decision for hiring or firing candidates *must* be based upon their performance in the process and *not* on what business I fancied going into; otherwise it would make a farce of the whole process – and I wholeheartedly agreed with that. Although the candidates are asked to enter the process by putting forward their business plans, when I meet them for the first time in Boardroom Zero I explain that I've only had a very quick look at the headlines of what their business ideas are about. One of the reasons they've been allowed into the process is because I have no objections in principle to any of the business ideas I've seen – that is, from a *headline* point of view. However, I make it very clear to them there is simply no point at this stage in doing what I call a deep-dive investigation into their plans, because what I need to do is see the candidates performing throughout the course of the process to ascertain whether they are good business people or not. At this stage, the fine details of their business plans are totally irrelevant. In fact, their business plans are locked away in a safe until I am ready to view the ones belonging to the final candidates.

For the final interviews I decided to get myself some new advisors. Claude Littner, of course, had been my advisor from the start and remained as one of the panel. Margaret Mountford was called back because of her experience in the process. Additionally, I decided to bring in a couple of younger people who were already in business so they'd be of a similar mindset, hopefully, to the potential winners. I chose a fellow by the name of Mike Soutar, a very successful businessman who has his own publishing company producing promotional magazines, and another enterprising young businessman called Matthew Riley, owner of Daisy Telecoms. Matthew is an entrepreneur who built himself up from scratch into a

multi-million-pound business. So there I had a panel of very serious people who would be able to give me their opinions on the
individuals.

The final four candidates were: Jedi Jim Eastwood, a sales and
marketing manager; Susan Ma, a skincare entrepreneur; Helen
Milligan, an executive assistant to the CEO of Greggs the bakers;
and Tom Pellereau, the zany inventor.

Now I've always made my own mind up about the candidates
in terms of who to fire, despite the fact that I do get a few hints and
tips from Nick and Karren (and in some cases Michele Kurland) as
to their personal opinion on certain individuals. Susan Ma, for
example, was in a task where we sent the candidates to Paris to sell
certain products to leading retailers there. Regrettably, and I'm not
sure whether it was nerves, she made a couple of daft comments.
Sometimes when candidates are in front of the cameras they think
they have to say something; they think they have to be seen to be
talking rather than standing around like lemons. And Susan came
out with her classic saying, which I continue to remind her of. It
was in relation to a children's product her team was proposing to
sell, and Susan's famous line was, 'Do the French like their children?' It haunts her to this day. There was another comment she
made when her team was evaluating a car product, 'Do the French
drive a lot?' Well, considering one can spend half one's life stuck in
a traffic jam on the Champs-Elysées, you can imagine that those
two statements did not engender much confidence among Nick,
Karren and Michele, and they planted a little bit of concern in my
mind that perhaps this very young girl, who after all was only
twenty-one, should not be considered a serious business partner
for me.

And so the final began. Jedi Jim was interrogated by the panel.
His business idea was to start some kind of pseudo-charitable
foundation to do with schools. Helen Milligan's idea was to move
on from working in Greggs to open up her own patisserie and tea

shop. She toyed with the idea initially of a concierge service, some-thing that was set up to arrange events for people such as getting them tickets for the theatre or football matches, bookings in hotels and all that kind of stuff. I had preached throughout the course of the process that people need to go into a business that they have some experience in so this came as a bit of a shock. When it was pointed out to her that the proposal seemed a little bit strange, she rethought it and came up with the obvious idea of opening her own tea shop and patisserie, which of course are very popular these days. Susan Ma's business plan was to manufacture and market a range of natural cosmetics that she'd formulated herself. I consid-ered Helen and Tom to be the strongest contenders, and so regretfully I had to let Jim and Susan go.

It was an interesting final boardroom and a very tough decision to make, but as I said before, my heart is in products, and Tom had once successfully designed a very innovative nail file and had sold it in moderate volume. There was an issue over some business deal he'd tried to do with the nail file in the US that went wrong, which frankly was as clear as mud to me. However, what supports my principle that I will not let the business plans put forward at the start influence my final decision, is the fact that Tom's proposal was for what he considered an innovative office chair. Having observed him through the process and recognised him as a product design man, I felt that the rekindling of his novel nail file would actually be a big hit in the UK if handled well. And so, after a lot of deliberation and deep thought, I decided that Tom was going to be my first business partner. It's worth mentioning that had it been the old system, Helen (who had done brilliantly throughout the process) might well have won, especially if one were looking to take on a cool and competent employee rather than someone who's always sparking with new ideas.

One of the tasks we had in this series was to represent Groupon, a company that arranges for special offers of discounts for various services or goods from an array of retailers, and I believe that after Jim left *The Apprentice*, he went on to represent them in Ireland. I am not sure how that worked out, but Nick, who tends to keep in touch with some of the Irish ex-candidates, says that in the end he went back to work for his old printing company as a sales manager. Nick also says that Jim married the prettiest girl in Cookstown, County Tyrone, and the two of them can be seen strolling around town – the Posh and Becks of Cookstown.

After deciding on Tom as the winner, I felt excited that the new scheme had worked well and I'd found a credible business partner. For the first time in years I looked forward with enthusiasm to meeting the winner knowing that I didn't have to dump him in the midst of my employees and go through the same old aggravation. Instead, we would be starting a small business from scratch. It was a kind of injection of adrenaline for me, and even though I was running multi-million-pound companies at the time, to start something up again was an exciting proposition.

I believe that people even to this day do not understand what a massive opportunity winning *The Apprentice* provides. In the real world, if you want to start your own business – even if you had £250,000 – you would first need some premises. Secondly, you would need to get the usual things set up: payments for rent, rates, electricity, telephone lines and internet connections. You'd need to buy desks, chairs and computers, arrange for your new company to be registered at Companies House, arrange for your company to be registered for VAT . . . I could go on – basically a hell of a lot of stuff for an inexperienced person to do. The beauty of my offer to the winning candidate is that they will come into my general organisation and occupy part of the premises. They will then be able to draw down upon the skills and expertise of all the people I have in what I call the boring side of business; in other words,

I have all the accountants and lawyers and IT experts they would need. All the winning candidate has to do is get on with producing their product or service and concentrate on selling. Of course, they will be charged for the cost of using these people, so if for example they require the services of our in-house IT manager to assist them in developing their website or setting up their computer system and email, they will pay the hourly going rate we pay our IT manager plus a thirty per cent surcharge. This is designed to replicate what their true cost would be if they had to do it themselves. This means they won't be burdened with the cost of a full-time IT manager, but will have the facility of being able to call upon him as and when they require, on a pay-as-you-go basis. And the same procedure exists with our lawyers and accountants.

And so in the case of Tom, he decided on his company name, Aventom Ltd, and all of my people set to work on his behalf to register the company, apply for VAT registration, deal with PAYE, secure web domains and that kind of thing; for which his company was charged accordingly. Now I'm not sure whether non-business people will grasp everything I've just explained, but I can tell you as a businessman that anybody wishing to start a business would bite your hand off to have all this offered to them, because what you *really* want is just to be able to concentrate on what you're in business for, and in Tom's case it was to develop and launch a new range of nail files and buffers.

Once Tom had clued himself up again on his nailcare range, we recognised that they needed to be produced in the Far East. Tom had no idea how to deal with the Far East, whereas of course my people had over forty years' experience in this: the mechanisms of importation, duty, freight and all that stuff. So once again he drew down on the expertise of some of my staff on the same pay-as-you-go basis.

There was a lot of scepticism from the outside world, especially from our friends in the media, that this £250,000 investment was merely a scam – that I wouldn't actually be putting £250,000 into the company but instead would make up some waffle about the added value and services I provide. They just didn't think I was going to put my hand in my pocket. So mean and suspicious were they that within days of Tom being announced as the winner of *The Apprentice*, someone from the media contacted David Fraser of Frank PR and told him they'd been to Companies House and seen that this new company Aventom had been formed but they couldn't see any sign of £250,000 being injected. These scoundrels really make me sick; they're always out there looking for the negative side; always looking to cause trouble. In fact, this journalist – who when all's said and done is just a bloody journalist – was clueless as far as balance sheets and share structure was concerned. It was immediately pointed out to him by one of our accountants that if he had half a bloody brain, he would see that the share capital was injected and £250,000 was indeed there in the assets on the balance sheet of the company – so basically go and get stuffed. That was the first and last time that year it was ever questioned, but because of that incident, the first thing I now do, just to reassure the *Apprentice* winner, is open the new bank account and immediately deposit the money.

Now any new company will of course make losses in the first few months. Consider that Tom had to start paying rent for the space he was occupying; he had to buy computers and pay for all of the other previously mentioned services. And, naturally, developing a new product and a brand, as well as developing a website, takes time. After a few months, Tom came up with the name Stylfile for his products; then came the decision to get them made with the assistance of one of my production people in the Far East; then he had to take the decision on how many he was going to buy for stock before he could get underway to start selling.

I was a little concerned at one stage. I figured that this type of stuff needs to be sold in leading retailers such as Boots and Sainsbury's. Having spent forty years dealing with these people, I know you can't simply knock on their door and expect to get an order. Even if you have the best thing since sliced bread, these companies tend to buy in phases. They usually have a ranging period which can be several months before they are prepared to take stuff in. Here I have to take my hat off to Tom and say he did an exceptional job when he got himself an audience with Sainsbury's and Boots and managed to convince them that his new, innovative S-shaped Stylfile nail file was a must. He convinced them that as winner of *The Apprentice*, with so much publicity behind him, it would be a no-brainer for them to stock his product. And in an unprecedented move, Sainsbury's and Boots decided to take them in, based on some support advertising that Tom managed to arrange in certain women's magazines.

Of course, winning *The Apprentice* attracts a lot of attention, and unlike anyone else starting up a new business, Tom obviously had a tremendous advantage because of his position, so when he picked up the phone to people like Sainsbury's and Boots and announced himself as Tom Pellereau, winner of *The Apprentice*, which they'd no doubt seen on telly, you can understand why they answered the phone. This advantage is part and parcel of the wonderful opportunity afforded the winner of this programme.

Today, Tom has a range of fifteen products and is represented in Sainsbury's, Boots, Tesco, Asda and Waitrose. More importantly, he has a viable business set-up, and what's encouraging is that he now has four of his own employees, plus those he subcontracts from my organisation. I'm also pleased to say – conscious of the eagle-eyed media – that bearing in mind there were losses in the first six months due to the burning costs of the company, he still managed to turn a significant profit in his first year of trading, and has remained profitable ever since.

*

As I've said on many occasions and in my previous books, if I hadn't entered the electronics industry, one of the industries I may well have entered into was cosmetics. I like it because cosmetics are low-cost, high-margin products surrounded by a lot of marketing and advertising. I remember when I was a kid at school enjoying an exercise where we had to come up with a cosmetic product and a marketing theme for it. It was my forte. And just a few years later, a few pals and I got together and made a range of cosmetics to sell on a market stall. My friends lost interest and I ended up having to flog them all. Perhaps I should have stuck at it, but then again I can't complain – I did go on to be the largest manufacturer of computers in Europe, after all.

With my interest in cosmetics, it's not surprising that finalist Susan Ma stuck in my mind. Her business plan concerned the special range of cosmetics she had made from a formula invented by herself using some exotic ingredients. The USP (unique selling point) of the product was that the ingredients were all natural. I recalled how hard-working and vivacious this young lady was during the series, and so, about nine months after the programme, I called her up and asked her to come and see me. She was very surprised to hear from me and asked me why I'd contacted her. 'I'm interested in finding out about your business and what you're doing – how you sell and how you manufacture,' I told her.

She came along to my offices and explained to me that basically she made this product in a kitchen at home with her mum's help, and then took the product out into the marketplace – quite literally, on market stalls – and sold it. She gave me some samples of the products, which I asked my wife to test out. Ann told me they were very good indeed, and the fact they were natural, with no harmful ingredients and not tested on animals, was also a very good point.

I was very impressed with Susan and having ascertained exactly how she produced the stuff, where she got the ingredients and the bottles, how she made the packaging, etc., it was clear to me she had tremendous knowledge of importing stuff from China and doing things which had taken some of my employees many years to learn. This tempted me to put a proposition to her and say that, although she was not the winner of *The Apprentice*, I was prepared to start up a business with her on a fifty-fifty basis by injecting not £250,000 but £200,000. Obviously she was delighted and I explained exactly how it would work – in the same fashion as it was working with Tom. I told her how the backroom support would allow her to freely run her business.

And so we started Tropic Skincare Ltd in 2011. Initially, Susan's business model was based upon some of the successes she'd had in the marketplaces, but also she had taken a stand at the Ideal Home Exhibition and been very successful selling her products there. Like Tom, she too had acquired a bit of fame by being on *The Apprentice* and I think it fair to say that she played upon that to get a little PR so people would visit her stand at the exhibition. So initially our business revolved around selling at the Ideal Home. This was relatively successful but rather expensive and the profits were moderate. However, because her product range was so excellent, it had been spotted by a group of women who worked for a social-selling network originally owned by Virgin. From what I understood, Virgin decided to drop Virgin Cosmetics and someone else had taken it over using a new name – and now they needed products. They asked if they could purchase some of Susan's stuff so they'd have other things to offer their clients at their cosmetic-selling parties. I didn't quite understand this concept myself, but what I *was* clear about was that I wasn't prepared to lose any money out of the £200,000 I'd injected. I remember explaining to Susan very carefully that she could do what she wanted and sell what she wanted, but she must not extend any credit to these people. By the way, just to make it quite clear, this company was by now nothing to do with

Richard Branson's Virgin Group; it was one of his old companies that had been taken over.

As sure as eggs are eggs, the person running this company said they would buy mega amounts of Susan's stock but needed sixty days to pay. I put the kybosh on that straight away, and I have to say that Susan was a little disappointed at the time because she saw big opportunities for sales. At that point I gave her her first business wake-up call: if they love your product so much, just play hardball; be a hard-nosed businesswoman and tell them, 'If you want it – it's cash upfront – otherwise forget it.' And, believe it or not, they accepted those terms, and the business started to expand rapidly as a result of profits made on the stuff being sold through this social-selling organisation.

Susan, being the brilliant young entrepreneur that she is, thought to herself, 'Why do it for someone else? Why not do it for ourselves?' And to cut a long story short, that's exactly what Tropic Skincare does at the moment, now having over three thousand 'ambassadors'. I attend Tropic's biannual event in Birmingham where I speak to them, encourage them and present awards to their best salespeople. And this business is going from strength to strength; not just for Susan and me, but also for the ambassadors themselves. Some of them are earning astronomical amounts of money monthly, and for most it's not even their main job.

Even though Susan is young, I still don't know where she gets her energy from. I really have no idea how she manages to organise the vast number of products in her range – designing them, formulating the ingredients and testing them, coming up with the packaging, and manufacturing them in the factory we now have in Croydon.

I fast-tracked this whole story because this book is about my experiences in television. I could write another whole chapter just about Tropic Skincare, a fantastic thing to be involved in. For me, as a man who runs multi-million-pound companies, it's like going back to the old days of starting from scratch, but the thing is, this is not scratch any more – this is mega bucks coming in.

So was Susan an example of letting the wrong person go? Was it an example of choosing the wrong winner? No. Tom was the deserved winner, and so would Susan have been perhaps, had I not been swayed by some of the people who formed an opinion of her based on a couple of silly remarks. In the end it turned out to be a win-win situation, and Tom's and Susan's paths cross frequently when we have our regular board meetings at my head office. It's fair to say there is mutual respect between the two of them because they are in somewhat similar businesses.

Now here's a strange piece of fate. Not only is Susan my business partner despite not winning *The Apprentice* that year, she nearly didn't get into the process at all! The production people reminded me how she pestered them so much and demonstrated such determination; she was the first candidate to fight her way into the process after the application deadline had closed, and when she managed to get that concession agreed, can you believe it, she turned up late at the auditions. They told me she kept calling, saying she was on her way. They were about to close the door and she arrived with a minute to spare for the start of the audition process.

I also recall Dara asking Nick, who was in the audience at the *You're Hired* show, to comment on Susan. Nick said, 'Well, *I* would invest in her,' which I thought was quite strange since he was one of the three people who kind of turned me off her. What was even funnier was that Michael McIntyre, who was on the panel in that week's show, said, 'You're in the wrong show, Nick,' referring to *Dragons' Den*.

The BBC of course raised an eyebrow a year or so later in suggesting to me that going into business with one of the fired candidates was not really in the true spirit of the programme. I fully understood and accepted what they were saying; however, I pointed out that this didn't happen instantaneously with Tom being declared the winner; it was later. At the end of the day, this was the first year of the revised format and it was uncharted waters for me, Talkback and the BBC. So while everyone concurred that I had done nothing wrong in investing in Susan, it was agreed that for future series there would be a set period before I could invest in anyone other than the winner.

Having said that, I have to say respectfully that there has not been the temptation for me to do so since series seven, but I do still have the option.

So, am I loving this opportunity to start up new businesses with the winners? Has it given me new incentive and a new enthusiasm for *The Apprentice*? Absolutely yes.

18

BAFTA SHMAFTA

**The award-winning second series of *Junior Apprentice*
and my BAFTA revenge**

In August 2010 the BBC confirmed that a second series of *Junior Apprentice* had been commissioned. Once again it featured sixteen-to seventeen-year-olds, but it was extended to an eight-episode format rather than six. One of the things that sticks in my mind for this series was the clothes the candidates wore. It wasn't just the outsized suits; it was that as the series rolled through, I noticed that every time the candidates came into the boardroom they were wearing the same clothes. I asked Michele Kurland at the time, 'What's going on here with these kids?' Then it dawned upon me that, unlike the senior *Apprentice* where the candidates were filmed getting into the taxi in their coats and scarves, *Junior Apprentice* was being filmed in summer so their day clothes could be seen. I guess you could say it was a little oversight by the production people and that they should have asked the candidates to bring a coat or a scarf with them, but then again it might have looked a bit stupid when there was blazing sunshine throughout the whole of the episode.

Actually, this reminds me of my little visit to the *Dragons' Den* studio when I was doing the *Children In Need* sketch. When I was talking to Theo, Peter and Duncan I asked them why they always seemed to wear the exact same clothes on the programme.

I wondered why it was because I don't do this on *The Apprentice*. As any viewer will notice, each time you see me in the boardroom or setting a task, I have a different shirt and tie and suit on. The reason, they explained to me, is that they tend to record *Dragons' Den* programmes in large blocks over a week, and what they show on any one programme can be mixed and matched from separate weeks' filmings. So, for example, if Theo were to wear a red tie one week and a blue tie the next, and the finished transmitted programme had sequences taken from both weeks to create a good balance of content, the viewers would be confused by the fact his tie was changing colour. In the dressing room at the *Dragons' Den* studio, there are duplicate sets of the same shirts and ties so they can remain clean. I'm not so sure about Peter Jones's striped socks though – I doubt whether they'd be able to find enough pairs of those in the whole country.

Moving on to the second series of *Junior Apprentice*, this time we had twelve candidates from all walks of life. Michele had employed the services of Colm Martin as series editor, and we had the usual debates over which candidates would be in the process. I particularly loved young Mahamed Awale. He was a short, dapperly dressed fellow, and one couldn't help but notice the massive watch he was wearing.

One issue we came across was that there were two viable candidates both called Harry – Harry Maxwell and Harry Hitchens. At one stage we debated whether two Harrys would confuse the viewers, but they were such brilliant kids, I kind of insisted to Colm and Michele that we keep them both in. I just decided I would call them Harry-M and Harry-H, and that's what I did from Boardroom Zero onwards.

In the first week, I separated the candidates into boys and girls as usual, and the first task was to sell frozen treats: ice creams, frozen yoghurts, that sort of stuff. When I heard in the boardroom about the chaos in the girls' team trying to produce the ice cream,

I tried to introduce a bit of light-heartedness and said, 'Forget Ben and Jerry, this was more like Tom and Jerry.' Nevertheless, despite their mix-ups in production, the girls had a better pricing strategy and swept to victory.

When the losing boys' team came back into the boardroom, my attention was drawn to James McCullagh, a young Irish lad from Londonderry. This boy could bunny off a scratch – he was non-stop talk, talk, talk, talk, talk. He reminded me a bit of Jedi Jim. Project manager Harry-H brought James and Mahamed back into the boardroom. Despite Mahamed's fantastic look and his sparkling banter, he performed poorly and regrettably had to go. Interestingly enough, this was the first time for a few years (both junior and senior) that the losing project manager was not fired in episode one.

In week two, Ben Fowler, a young lad from Birmingham, was fired as it was clear he was a bit out of his depth in the process. I started to get a little concerned that perhaps it was too much for him because he hadn't performed well in either the first or second tasks. Lewis Roman was the boys' project manager and I was really impressed at his honesty – he actually admitted to me that I would be justified in firing him. I admired his candour and the fact that he'd been willing to take risks and put himself at the forefront of the task, which showed he had a bit of spirit in him. This ultimately saved him from being fired.

For the third task, I mixed the teams up a bit. They had to set up their own floristry business and sell flower arrangements to hairdressing salons and theatres. Lizzie Magee's team won the task by a mere thirteen pounds! On the losing team, Harry-M was a major annoyance to his teammates; in fact, during the task, Hannah Richards and Gbemi Okunlola simply ignored his input. I asked Hannah who she was going to bring back into the boardroom with her and Harry-M was chosen, along with Zara Brownless.

It became obvious quite early in the process that Zara was a very sharp young lady who was already starting to shine through. She was a tiger and did not deserve to be brought into the board-room. As for Harry-M, annoying as he was, it turned out he was right in the advice he gave the team and so for that reason, regret-fully, I had to let young Hannah go.

In all series of *The Apprentice* I like to introduce an advertising task. This time the candidates had to create their own brand of deo-dorant, and market it by way of a television advert. Zara had announced that her ambition in life was to produce films and doc-umentaries, so this task was right up her alley. Harry-M was the other project manager.

It was the closest decision in any of the advertising tasks since *The Apprentice* had begun, but ultimately Zara's team won, which meant that once again Harry-M was in the losing boardroom. A pattern was starting to emerge here – it seemed that his teammates and housemates didn't like him very much; though to be fair, in many of the tasks he was actually the engine of the team. It just so happened that despite the work he put in, his teams never won.

Another popular task is when I send the candidates out to find ten items, but this time there was a rather novel twist on it. We got permission from Madame Tussauds to film in their building and I set the task there, explaining to the candidates that they had to go and find ten props for use with the waxworks.

One problem I always find on this task – and not only on *Junior Apprentice* – is that the candidates do not spend enough time sort-ing out who is responsible for getting what, and who is going where. On this occasion, Haya Al Dlame's team immediately left Madame Tussauds without organising themselves properly. It really was a case of the left hand not knowing what the right hand was doing. At one point, two of their team were chasing around separately to find the same item! However, young James came to the fore on this task. From what I heard from Nick and Karren, he was unbelievable in the way he negotiated with the vendors. The other team, led by Lizzie, suffered a heavy defeat at the end of the day, due in part to Harry-M leading them on a wild goose chase trying to buy stuff. Despite that, he escaped the boardroom that week and I let Hayley Forrester go.

In the penultimate task, I arrived at the candidates' house to inform them that I wanted them to produce a brand of popcorn in various flavours and to market them to companies such as Odeon Cinemas and Morrisons supermarkets.

The problem with having twelve candidates and the series only being eight episodes' long is that when we got near the end of it, we had to adapt the format. So I also had to break the bad news to the candidates that only *two* of them would be going forward from this task into the final. This meant that the *entire* losing team would be fired, along with one person from the winning team; someone who perhaps didn't contribute as much as the others. I know it sounded a bit cruel, but we'd brainstormed it so many times as to how we could sort it out, and we concluded that this was the only way we could deal with it.

I have to say that both teams came up with great products. James's team created a type of Mediterranean popcorn called La Popcorn, while Harry-H's team created an American-inspired pop-corn called Empire State Popcorn – Harry-M wanted to call it Smoochies, only to be ignored again. Both teams did very well. Empire State Popcorn got orders for 95,000 bags from all three retailers, but La Popcorn got the overall win with 120,000 bags.

Now remember – these are kids; kids making record-breaking sales of a brand-new product they had innovated themselves. So to fire some of them was a horrible duty because it was such a close-run contest. In fact, Harry Hitchens was a real contender in my eyes – a very sharp and astute young man. I felt very sad having to let him go as part of the whole team along with Harry-M and Lizzie. Unfortunately, Harry Maxwell was never in a winning team, which I believe is an all-time record.

I was then faced with the even worse task of picking someone from the *winning* team to go too. The winning team comprised James, Zara and Haya. It was very difficult firing Haya, a young lady who did so well throughout the process. However, the other two candidates, James and Zara, had risen to the top and shone through as the best of the bunch that year, along with Harry-H who, if he'd been in the other team, may well have ended up the ultimate winner.

For the final I gave the two remaining candidates the task of designing a new video game, with the help of the previously fired candidates. Being Irish themselves, both Michele and Nick had tremendous admiration for James McCullagh. I, too, admired him because he'd started off in the process like a bull in a china shop, but as the weeks progressed, and after a few little pointers from me, he settled down and showed us what an astute young man he is. Colm Martin is also Irish, so I had three Irish people subtly chipping away in my ear that perhaps James would make a great winner. I reminded everyone that it's not about who we like; it's the success of the task that's the issue – in other words, what was the best product and how was the final task managed?

I have to say that these subtle nudges were starting to niggle me a weenie bit. I had to go away and think things out logically and rationally; to try to be professional and not simply choose Zara as the winner out of sheer belligerence because the other three were batting for James. In the end I genuinely believed that Zara came up with the best proposition in the final and was also an outstanding performer throughout the series. And for that reason I chose her as the winner of *Junior Apprentice*.

Zara scooped the £25,000 prize and, just like Arjun the year before, she has very sensibly not drawn down on it too much. She contacted me after winning and asked me to fund some Apple equipment plus editing software so she could start pursuing a production-company business. Not only did I readily agree to it,

I managed to get my company Viglen to negotiate much better prices than she ever would have got buying it in a retail store. But to this day, the lion's share of Zara's funds is still sitting in the bank while she sensibly waits until she's ready to start her business. And I have to say, my nose tells me that this young lady, Zara Brownless, is going to make it – whether it's in the TV production world or in some other form of TV-related business. She is one shrewd cookie.

I referred earlier in the book to BAFTA and my terrible disappointment at not receiving an award for the first series of *The Apprentice*. As you may remember, Lorraine Heggessey sympathised with me at the time and said that she would put my name forward on any future programmes nominated for a BAFTA. (BAFTA allows you to either name the 'production team' or four individuals.) However, Lorraine had left the company, of course, and I have to say it was an oversight on my behalf not to check that I was one of the named individuals when I heard from Sara Geater and Michele Kurland that the second series of *Junior Apprentice* had been nominated for a BAFTA. What's more, I heard that Jane Lush, the lady who had introduced both me and *The Apprentice* to the BBC, was part of the BAFTA committee which helped to decide which programme would win. I remember her emailing me telling me she was so excited that *Junior Apprentice* had been nominated and hoped that it would win.

And so, on the night, I went to the awards ceremony with Nick, Karren and the whole production team including Colm Martin, Michele and Andy Devonshire. To my surprise, we won. I say 'surprise' because I thought the BAFTAs tended to be given to fresh new programmes, and as we'd won a BAFTA for the main *Apprentice* on series one, and had failed to win our nominations on series two, three and four, I assumed that because the show was no longer novel we wouldn't win on this occasion either. However, I guess it was the fact that this was a different twist – with juniors – that swayed the judges.

So up we jumped onto the stage, and muggins here grabbed hold of the award and started to make a speech, in which I said, 'I feel a bit of a fraud, standing here with the most prestigious award you can get in television, because in the audience we have people who have spent the whole of their lives in TV, either acting in it, producing it, directing it, commissioning it, and then there's me, a businessman that has come along and is standing here with this great award, so I can appreciate how some of you may be feeling, and to those people all I can say is . . . [I paused for a second] . . . bleedin' hard luck!'

That comment got a great deal of laughter. I then went on to talk about the very hard work of Michele Kurland, not only for this series, but also for how she has been the engine behind the whole of *The Apprentice* and how remarkable she's been in all the effort and devotion she's given the series. I also paid special tribute to Andy Devonshire to let the audience know that he's the man responsible for those fantastic sweeping aerial shots of London that we've all got used to seeing.

I then decided it was time for Michele to speak. And just as I turned to Michele, Colm Martin came running over, dragged the BAFTA out of my hand and plonked it into Michele's hand. She gave her speech and thanked all the people involved in production, then we were ferried off to the media room where I had to do a Q&A with the media about the programme and have photographs taken holding the award.

On this occasion, the actual awards were given to Michele Kurland, Colm Martin, Andy Devonshire and some woman called Darina Healy. This Darina was in the background at Boundless. She had some fancy title, but I rarely saw her on the set. I've since learned she was Head of Production; in other words, she was Ruby

Evans's boss. Michele Kurland might say she was her right-hand woman, but from my perspective she was someone up the pecking order in the company, possibly in charge on the finance side of the programme.

As we walked off the stage, I'd overheard Colm saying to the others, '. . . Well, he's not getting *my* one,' referring of course to me.

So once again I was disappointed, but more to the point I was furious with Colm Martin. Here is a programme that without me they wouldn't have even thought of! Putting aside all the artistic genius and the fact that these awards are for the producers – if you don't have a programme to produce, you can't get an award. And it was *me* who persuaded the BBC to make this junior version of the programme – it was my idea completely (how's that for being a 'creative') – and yet once again there was no award for me. My wife was shaking her head when I got back to my seat. She couldn't believe it, again! And Nick and Karren were furious too, not for themselves, but because they felt really humiliated for me. And believe me, I could tell it was *genuine* concern – they felt outraged and they complained bitterly to Sara Geater.

At the dinner event afterwards, Sara pleaded the Fifth Amendment. 'I knew nothing of this; I don't know anything about who got nominated, blah, blah, blah.' I told her that Lorraine had agreed in the past that whenever *The Apprentice* was nominated, my name would be put forward. She came up with some kind of feeble explanation afterwards: 'No, BAFTA won't allow it; the BBC won't allow it because you're not actually the producer; you're the talent.' Well, if that was correct, why agree to put my name forward?

I told her that was total bullshit, then I turned my back on her and walked away. She came after me, saying, 'Well, let me see what I can do with the BAFTA people.' I told her not to waste her time.

'We've been there and done it before, and there's nothing you can do. The damage has been done.'

Sitting at the table, I was boiling up inside. So much so, I stood up, pointed at Colm Martin and asked him to come away from his table and talk to me.

'What the bloody hell do you think you're playing at, pulling the BAFTA out of my hand in front of five hundred people?' I said to him. 'What's the idea? You've got your BAFTA for your so-called creative genius, so what the hell were you doing dragging the award out of my hand? I don't need you to tell me that Michele deserves the award. If anything, she's the *only* one who deserves it. You certainly don't – you just happened to be in the right place at the right time because Michele appointed you to my *Junior Apprentice* programme. I do get it, you idiot – I know I was not on the list, and I have no intention of taking Michele's well-deserved award.'

His reaction to that was, 'Oh, I don't want to talk to you tonight on this wonderful, wonderful occasion. I really don't want to talk to you tonight – you're spoiling it for me.'

'Never mind bloody spoiling it for you. You're lucky I don't bloody chin you here and now. You totally make me sick. This programme is nothing without me and you bloody know it.'

Michele Kurland got wind of my anger and came over and told me that Colm was a very nice man and I really shouldn't get angry with him.

'Michele,' I said, 'much as I admire and respect you, please just shut it, because this is a bloody disgrace, and you know it as well as I do. Michele, you deserve this award – there is absolutely no question about it, and if there were only one award to be given out and it was a choice between me and you, I would make sure *you* got it. But there were four separate awards given out and one went to bloody Darina, the bleedin' accountant. I am pissed off.'

At the end of the evening I told Michele that I needed to take one of the awards with me because, once again, the BBC wanted to interview me the next day. She said she would arrange for me to get it. I could see they were frightened I was going to pinch an award so I told her I would never do a thing like that; I just needed it for photographic purposes and I'd get it back to them in no time. This was a little porky.

These BAFTA awards are like hens' teeth. Other ceremonies might provide duplicate copies, but they only make a certain amount of BAFTAs each year (like the Oscars) so there was no chance of asking them for a replica.

I'd worked out in my mind that I was going to call upon the services of one of my genius engineers, Mr Vitus Luk, a man I'd employed for thirty-odd years. Originally I met him in China; he is one of the most resourceful mechanical engineers I've ever met in my life. I phoned Vitus the next morning and told him about last night's goings-on at the BAFTAs. I explained to him that the award was basically a brass statue mounted on a marble slab, and what I needed him to do was make some copies. Now Vitus is a very straight and honest chap, but he sympathised with me when he realised the injustice of the situation. To cut a long story short, I delivered the BAFTA to Vitus who, in just one day, managed to make a special mould which can be used for casting bronze or brass. The award was back with me by the next day, and I returned it to Boundless.

Vitus set about sending the mould off to his cronies in China. From what I understand, the pouring of brass is quite a specialised technique, and if this mould of his didn't work perfectly, the whole exercise would have been in vain. But Vitus being Vitus, his mould was perfect, and a few weeks later he sent me pictures of five shining BAFTA replicas.

The problem now was how to procure the marble base. Vitus had taken detailed measurements of it and sent me a drawing, but he said he was having difficulty locating a perfect colour match for the marble, which he had also photographed. So while he had made the main brass pieces, we were struggling to find the marble.

With my mind always working at 100mph, on a bike ride one

day I rode past a company which makes marble worktops for kitchens and bathrooms. I took the opportunity of popping in there and showed the guy the drawing Vitus had made of this little cube of marble. Funnily enough, the fellow knew who I was; not just off the telly, but also because his company was a supplier to my real-estate company where marble items are sometimes required to fit out the washrooms in the offices we build. He immediately agreed to help me procure the right material for the bases.

'Come back in a week and I'll make you some. How many do you want?'

'Six would be good,' I said. It's always good to have a spare in case one gets messed up.

Sure enough, I went back a week later and he had perfectly engineered these bases with exactly the right colour of marble. I couldn't thank him enough and asked him to send me the bill, but he refused. As I had previously told him about the little scam I was up to, he said it was a pleasure helping out.

Finally, with the combination of the marble bases and the brass replicas Vitus had made earlier, he assembled the finished awards, which looked brilliant. So excited was I that I showed one to Ann. She was not amused. 'What's the good of that? It's not the real one.'

'That isn't the point, that it's not the real one. The point is, morally, we deserve it.'

'Yes, I agree,' she said. 'It's still not the real one though.'

I said, 'Well, who will bloody know whether it's the real one or not? You see me in the papers standing there with the award in my hand – any normal member of the public would assume I would have one. Of course *you* know why I haven't got one, but I was plastered all over the newspapers with it when we won it the first time, and also when we won it the second time, so while it may be a bit cheeky, I feel it's a good coup.'

I took four of the awards to the studio while we were recording a new series and I showed them to Nick and Karren. I told them I was going to give them one each as they certainly deserved it for all the work and effort they'd put in. Then I cheekily decided that I was going to take the opportunity of a break in the boardroom to film Nick, Karren and me talking about our BAFTAs. As I was about to be very rude, I realised that getting the production people to film me would compromise them, so I didn't ask. Fortunately, my grandson Alex was at the studio that day, so I asked him to video me on my Samsung S4. I then made a speech, with Nick and Karren sitting beside me, in which I said, 'Now, Talkback Thames/ Boundless have enjoyed the commissioning of [*Junior Apprentice*], all brought about by me coming up with the idea, so it was delightful for us in the recent BAFTA awards to have actually had the programme win things, but it was dampened down by the fact that when it came to me standing up there, speaking on behalf of everybody, having photographs taken, doing all the PR, that the actual award . . . I didn't get one! They gave it to a bleedin' accountant! So all I can say to Talkback Thames and Boundless and Fremantle is this: having got you the job, I feel very bitterly disappointed in your selfishness, but there is one final thing I can say to you . . .' Then as Nick, Karren and I whipped out our replica BAFTAs, I added, 'F*** you!'

If you'd like to see that clip, you can watch it via the following link *bit.ly/amsbook_136*

After that, I'm sure I'll never ever win a BAFTA award now for anything I do. Certainly I've blown my chances of getting a lifetime achievement award. Actually, it wouldn't surprise me if BAFTA came after me for the infringement of the copyright of their award. If they do, I say: Bring it on, BAFTA, I'm here waiting for you!

The Apprentice was nominated again in 2015 and to be fair to Patrick Holland, he stuck me on the list as part of the production team. However, I told him that we should not hold our breath as I was a hundred per cent sure that *The Island with Bear Grylls* would win, as it was the only *new* programme from the category we were listed in. That's what BAFTA do, they always award the new programme – and as I predicted, *The Island with Bear Grylls* won.

Back to the awards themselves, always with an eye on a deal, I say: BAFTA, if you need any more of these things made, I can knock them out much cheaper than your current supplier. Say £59.99 for quantities of 100–2,000, or £39.99 for 2,000+. I can even do plastic ones for unlucky nominees at £5.99, all plus VAT of course, through my new company Amsaward.

Now I mentioned my grandson Alex. He is a regular character who often turns up at the filming of *The Apprentice* and has been doing so for quite a few years. He obviously loves the programme but more to the point he has aspirations of being in the theatre or working either on television or in TV production. Alex has a wonderful nature. People often comment that you don't think you're speaking to a fourteen-year-old; it seems more like a conversation with a forty-year-old. He's one of those kids who's really adult in his ways and is very sensible. Whenever he's allowed, he comes along to watch me filming *The Apprentice* at weekends or in school holidays. In particular, he loved watching *Junior Apprentice* being filmed, and he also likes to come to some of the events like *You're Fired* and *You're Hired*. On occasion, if time permits, he'll come to watch when we're actually filming a task being performed, such as the final. Everybody in the production company knows Alex. He doesn't get in anyone's way. He sits and chats with the production people on their level.

His devotion to *The Apprentice* is not exclusive, however. He was with me while we were filming one Saturday and he kept asking me, 'Papa Al,' which is what he calls me, 'when do you think we'll be finished tonight?'

I said, 'I don't know, Alex. We're still waiting for the candidates to come back from the losers' café, then we've got to do make-up and all that stuff, you know the drill. By the time they get in here, by the time we sit down, by the time we film . . . it could be another couple of hours.'

'Well, I want to get home because *Strictly*'s on tonight.'

'Oh I see. Well, it's going to take as long as it takes.'

That evening he was sitting in the gallery watching me being filmed in the boardroom. I was on my final bit of dialogue, just about to make my decision.

According to Michele, all of a sudden Alex shouted out, 'Come on already, fire one of them – I want to get home and see *Strictly*!' Apparently there were hysterics in the gallery.

As well as Alex, some of my other grandchildren occasionally come along to the boardroom to watch the filming. Ann has also been there many times to experience it herself. Andy Devonshire brings his kids along from time to time and we have a bit of fun and banter with them, letting them have some chocolates from what's virtually a confectionary stall laid on for everyone there. Ruby Evans had a little girl who would frequently be seen running around the set, again helping herself to the chocolates and crisps on offer. So all in all there was a bit of a family atmosphere there, and everyone knew everyone else. From time to time other production people would bring in their kids and, of course, they would ask for photographs with me or Nick or Margaret or Karren. Alex, for example, wanted to have his photo taken sitting in the boardroom chair pointing his finger in the famous 'you're fired' pose, and many of the other kids did the same.

I recall when Alex was a bit younger, I told Ruby and Michele that we'd have to have a very serious talk with him and make him sign what is known as a non-disclosure agreement.

'Alex,' I said to him, 'you must understand that this programme is a secret while it's being recorded, and you can't tell any of your mates at school what happened or who's been fired, or indeed who any of the candidates are. It's a policy of the BBC [ha ha, now it was my turn to use the BBC as an excuse] that anybody who comes in here has to sign this non-disclosure agreement.'

I think at the time he was around twelve years old and he took it very seriously, though quite honestly I don't know how Ruby, Michele and I kept a straight face. Joking aside, I had to do it because you know what kids are like. He might have blurted out who won or who got fired. To this day, he won't even tell his mum and dad, his brothers and sisters, or indeed Ann, who's been fired whenever he knows the result.

19

'IF I WANT A FRIEND, I'LL GET A DOG'

Awarding the Turnip Prize and looking for the Marks to my Spencer in series eight

My wife, Ann, having been married to me for over forty-seven years, has heard all my anecdotes, jokes, quips and put-downs. She tells me I am like my Uncle John who – as I described in my first book, *What You See Is What You Get* – was the first businessman in the family. He ran a hardware store in Victoria and was famous throughout the area for the display outside his shop which had lots of little plaques with silly jokes on. For example, he'd stuck one on an old-fashioned broom with a long handle, which read, 'This broom was made by a tall girl named Jean – as such it is very hygienic.' Pathetic, I know, but Ann has watched every series and likens some of my *Apprentice* quips to Uncle John's. The difference is, he had lots of time to think them up.

In Boardroom Zero of series eight, I was off and running with some of my gems. 'Don't try to hide,' I warned the candidates. 'We're not playing *Where's Wally?* here – I'm not looking for Lord Lucan.'

And, as usual, one or two of my comments backfired. There was one fellow by the name of Michael Copp who was sweating profusely, which prompted me to say, 'Michael, you look like you're sweating. You're not nervous, are you?' Little did I know the poor fellow had a really bad cold at the time.

The auditions yielded another bunch of sixteen very interesting candidates and, having proved in series seven that the new prize format worked, we decided to stick with it for series eight. First of all, though, I was about to encounter some more changes of personnel. Most importantly, Mark Saben, who'd been series editor for two years and had overseen the change in format – changing the prize from a job to an investment – decided he wanted to move on. Mark had worked his way up *The Apprentice* ladder since the second series. I spoke to him at length, asking him why he'd decided to give it up because we'd worked very well together. As with all types of production, if you have a team that has done things before, then the quality of the product will remain high. However, despite my talk with Mark, it was clear that he wanted to go. He felt that he had done so much on *The Apprentice* and had built himself a reputation within the industry. Now he wanted to capitalise on it and move to a new production company where, allegedly, they were going to offer him a shareholding. I did explain to him at the time that a shareholding in a private company isn't worth jack shit, but it probably came across as sour grapes; as me trying to come up with an excuse to make him stay.

I'm not quite sure whether the shareholding ever materialised, but clearly he was flattered having been head-hunted by this company who'd been given the job of producing a new and exciting programme for the BBC called *The Voice*. Obviously, as *The Voice* was very much a reality-TV show, whoever approached Mark felt they were going to draw down on his wealth of experience on *The Apprentice* over many years. I heard a bit later, as the months went by, that it didn't work out exactly as Mark thought it would with regard to *The Voice* and I understand he ended up doing something else for the company.

At least Mark Saben's role as series editor was going to be filled by someone I'd come across before, Cate Hall. She'd worked on *The Apprentice* in the past, directing both on series three and the *Sport Relief* episode. Since then she'd been working for other production companies on programmes such as *Turn Back Time: The High Street*. Michele Kurland, of course, was still in charge of the whole thing.

There was another new face on the scene, a gentleman by the name of Patrick Holland, who was appointed managing director of Boundless. The management structure had changed quite a bit since Sara Geater had taken over from Lorraine Heggessey, and with Patrick in place, I now found myself with yet another new person to discuss matters. Patrick was responsible for *The Apprentice* among other programmes produced by Boundless.

We also decided to shake up the tasks quite significantly in series eight and did a number of different things. Cate was very good at coming up with task ideas, so that year, as well as the classics such as design and advertising, we tried some different things too such as 'upcycling', where the candidates had to buy second-hand tut and flog it on for a profit in fashionable areas like Brick Lane. This upcycling involved getting hold of tatty old bits of furniture, adding some value to it and reselling it. Not just furniture either. For example, if they found an old tennis racquet they could upcycle it by fitting a clock in the centre and putting it on sale in one of these fashionable outlets. Quite an interesting task.

Another new task we introduced involved sending out the candidates to source deals for an online discount website, which at that point was a new business model that seemed to be gaining popularity. We also asked the candidates to come up with a fitness franchise that they could license, which again was new territory for us. Overall, some of these new tasks worked extremely well, others less so, but on a long-running series like *The Apprentice* it's always good to keep striving for fresh ideas.

People often ask me whether I can spot a winner right from the very beginning. The answer is: not really. On this series there was a lady by the name of Bilyana Apostolova who was a risk analyst by profession. I could tell from her general demeanour that this was a very clever and wise person. She had worked for banks and was obviously qualified in her field. However, when it came to the first task – to create a souvenir to sell to tourists – she led the girls on a wild goose chase all over London, which ultimately lost them the task.

I remember speaking to her in the boardroom after she tried to apply her professional experience to a very simple task and ended up overcomplicating it.

'Bilyana, you're sitting there talking like a City strategist – this is a two-bob outing: go and buy a bit of stuff, print your name on some T-shirts and go and flog them on the street. This is not a take-over of Goldman Sachs.'

What also sticks in my mind was the way she kept reassuring her teammates that she knew Primrose Hill very well and then went off in the wrong direction. When we got back into the board-room, the girls started ganging up on Bilyana – so I had that going on in one ear, while in the other ear the only information I had available to me was the advice of Nick.

I'm not sure whether the girls ganged up on Bilyana because they'd recognised she was a real contender; all I can tell you was that the girl was very, very shrewd. However, I was placed in an untenable situation because Bilyana didn't really defend herself very well against all the allegations being thrown at her by what looked like a bunch of sharks, smelling blood. So regrettably, this person whom I'd mistakenly thought was a real contender, possibly even the winner of the series, fell at the first hurdle. I'm not being bitchy here, but she was also a beautiful-looking young lady and some of the girls might have been a little bit jealous of her. Just an observation.

*

Of course, as with every series, we got the usual *Apprentice* cock-ups. I remember on the design task I asked them to come up with a new household gadget and to be honest both teams' offerings were pretty poor. The boys designed something for the kitchen called the EcoPress. You were supposed to put your food waste into it and mulch it down, but the thing was *tiny* – like a cafetière. I told them it looked like it had been made for vegetarian dwarfs. The girls made a splashguard which you stuck to the edge of the bath so you didn't get wet while bathing your kids.

For that task we had arranged some brilliant companies for the candidates to pitch their products to, including, would you believe, Amazon. It's understandable that the teams would be intimidated by a meeting of that scale, but the girls lost their heads completely and ended up asking Amazon to take a million units off their hands! When I found out, I couldn't believe what I was hearing. I saw the footage months later and I had to laugh – Karren's face was a real picture. I'm surprised she managed to control herself and not step in. It was a feisty boardroom and the team ended up turning on each other over a number of issues. In the end, Maria O'Connor was fired as I couldn't ever see her being able to get on with her teammates. It came out that she'd hardly contributed at all, even falling asleep in the car when the rest of them were trying to brainstorm ideas.

As ever, a few of the candidates tried to lay low and sneak through the process under the radar. I had warned them about this in my opening boardroom speech with my *Where's Wally?* and Lord Lucan schtick, though some of them did try. But after doing seven series of *The Apprentice* my radar was well tuned in and I got rid of them. Another tactic the candidates often employ is to try and be pally with me. Many's the time one of them has said, 'I'm an East End boy just like you, Lord Sugar.' This is another futile strategy I told them not to bother with.

'I'm not looking for a friend,' I said. 'If I want a friend, I'll get a dog.'

On another occasion I sent the teams off to produce different condiments, and had set up an appointment for them with a trendy grocer on the Kings Road. The trouble was, one of the teams had so many problems in their manufacturing process, they didn't have a sample ready for the meeting. They went along anyway and pitched the product without a bloody sample! I suppose you have to give them marks for bravery. Michael Copp, an East End lad who ran his own kitchen furniture company, failed miserably on that task and, as I mentioned, he wasn't helped by the fact he'd got this terrible cold. I got the feeling that when he was fired in that episode it came as more of a relief to him than anything else.

One of the big characters that year was a market trader called Adam Corbally. Adam ran a fruit and veg stall in his home town of Glossop in Derbyshire and had expanded successfully, allowing him, I believe, to invest in property. He was an absolute self-starter and you had to admire him, but he couldn't for the life of him shake off his market-trader instincts. He was so keen to sing his own praises to me in the boardroom every week that I asked him if he had taken on the role of Modesty Manager.

One week that springs to mind was when I'd sent the candidates off to make street food in Edinburgh. When I briefed them, I explained that this task was *not* about coming up with some cheap meat pies – street food these days can be very gourmet and chic. However, Adam couldn't stop himself and ended up producing meatballs out of the very cheapest meat he could find – they had a cost price of something absolutely ridiculous like 47p per portion. Actually, it was one of those occasions where there was a very good chance that the wrong team might win simply because they'd managed to get the cost price so low. However, not only was it a bad business move, he'd completely ignored what I'd asked him to do – the brief had been *gourmet* street food. This situation happens on

The Apprentice from time to time when candidates try to be clever by taking the *letter* of what I've asked them to do and ignoring the *spirit* of it. There's a good example of this in a later series which I'll tell you about. Sometimes people seem to forget that I'm not looking to go into business with someone who wants to get around what I've asked them to do rather than dealing with the problem properly. Of course I appreciate smart, innovative people in business, but I'd rather team up with a straight shooter. As I said in the opening boardroom, 'I'm looking for a partner – the Marks to my Spencer; the Lennon to my McCartney.'

During the task, Adam's team decided they would go and position their stall near the famous Hearts football stadium in Edinburgh and sell his meatballs to the fans milling around the ground at the Hearts v Rangers match. That might have worked, but his teammate Katie Wright, who was in charge of pricing, decided to charge a ludicrous £6 per portion. They didn't realise that football fans wouldn't dream of paying six quid a go, even for decent food, let alone that garbage. I interrogated the team. 'Where were you trying to sell them?'

'At the Hearts/Rangers game, Lord Sugar.'

'How much were they?'

'£5.99, Lord Sugar.'

'£5.99 at a Hearts football match? They don't pay that for a striker!'

Katie Wright piped up, 'Lord Sugar, I go to football matches where it's £6 for a burger.'

'Really? £6 for a burger? Where do you go? Chelsea?'

I went on to question Adam. 'I've got two problems here, Adam. One: you can't sell. And two: you went off in the wrong direction and made a load of cheap stuff.'

'Lord Sugar, I *do* believe it was gourmet.'

'Listen, I've had pictures shown to me of these meatballs and I've got to tell you – I've seen things like that at the zoo on the floor of the elephant enclosure! I don't know how you can tell me this is quality stuff. There's one thing you *can't* cook and that's the books – the figures don't lie.'

But despite his cock-ups on that task, I didn't fire him. Katie had to go because of her ridiculous pricing policy. In fact, Adam survived all the way up to the last task before the interviews, but in the end it was all a bit much for him. I decided that although he was a great self-starter, he was a bit out of his depth, as demonstrated in a task I set in week eight, to hold an exhibition of urban art. My dialogue with him in that boardroom session says it all.

'Adam, you're in the fruit and veg business – how did you feel in this art task? What you've come up with won't win the Turner Prize; more like the Turnip Prize!' A very nice hard-working chap, but sadly he had to go.

As I said earlier, we're always trying to think up new tasks and to be on trend. One of the things that has kept *The Apprentice* fresh is to have tasks that show new innovations and new trends in British business.

A particular trend at the time was the growing market in English sparkling wine. I decided that the promotion of a new brand of English sparkling wine would be at the centre of one of my favourite tasks – the advertising task. The candidates had to come up with an awareness campaign for it, including making an online video. One of the teams thought they'd try the humorous approach and produced the most horrendous lead-balloon advert you've ever seen, directed by a Northern girl by the name of Jenna Whittingham. I remember telling her in the boardroom after I saw the advert, 'Well, Spielberg can rest easy, that's for sure.' It featured some naff bride on her wedding day kicking off about the fact that she'd been served champagne rather than English sparkling wine, but that wasn't even the team's biggest blunder. The worst bit was that they'd called their wine 'Grandeur', which as Nick quite rightly pointed out is a *French* word, so probably not best suited to English wine.

In the end though, it was Jenna's awful attempt at producing a funny advert which let them down, going against everything they'd been told about marketing English sparkling wine as a quality product; not in a jokey context. The advert reminded me of one of those sixties comedy films. I remember saying to them in the boardroom, 'I know I may remind you of Sid James, but I didn't tell you to go out and make *Carry On Boozing*. I was half expecting Kenneth Williams to pop in and say, "Ooooh, maître d' – where's my Grandeur gone?"'

Later on during that post-mortem, we saw a classic example of a candidate trying to force my hand and ultimately coming a cropper. Stephen Brady was in my sights on that task because he, along with Jenna, had come up with that terrible advert. He knew he was close to being fired, so he tried to bargain with me, saying that if he could just project manage the next task, he'd guarantee me that he would win. In the end I decided to fire Jenna for the shocking advert, and took Stephen at his word and made him project manager the following week. He lost and he was out the door.

In the end, series eight was won by a fellow called Ricky Martin who came from the recruitment world. Now I think Ricky would admit that at the beginning of the process he was quite brash. He said he was 'the reflection of perfection' and that he was a shark at the top of the food chain. He came across as arrogant, though certainly he was a great talker. His brashness didn't help him too much in the beginning because he ended up being brought back into the final boardroom at least four times. The first occasion was on the condiment task when Ricky was in charge of the production side. There had been some sort of mess-up with the recipe and they'd had to chuck a load away. In the boardroom Ricky kept on about how he'd rescued a whole batch – he would not stop going on and

on about it. Anyway, in the end it turned out he'd produced something like twenty extra bottles; hardly the Dunkirk-style rescue he'd
made it out to be when he was claiming to be the Henry Ford of the
condiment world. But as I said, over the weeks Ricky learned to
shut up a bit and listen a bit more, and he really started to grow. He
is a classic example of someone who is highly intelligent and clearly
picked up the plot as we were going along. One could see how he
understood every facet of the process as the weeks went by.

It was a tough decision choosing Ricky against another very
credible finalist, Tom Gearing. Tom was a young man who worked
with his father in the fine wine investment trade, and I recall Nick
in the final boardroom of the series suggesting to me that this business would be something different for me and that I should give it
serious consideration.

Personally, I was a bit confused and maybe a little concerned as
to how Tom, who was already in business with his father, would be
able to break away and set up a new company with me, as he would
have had to give me his full attention if he were going to be my
business partner.

I chose Ricky in the end; not for that reason alone it must be
said. Ricky's business was all about starting an employment agency
that specialised in recruiting people for the medical industry, in
other words, scientists who worked in drugs companies. Ricky
himself is highly qualified and has a degree in biochemistry with
medical biochemistry from Cardiff University. So it was his wealth
of knowledge in the field combined with, most importantly, the
business acumen he showed throughout the course of the series
that led me to choose him as the winner.

An interesting side issue was that Ricky was an amateur
wrestler. In fact, there are pictures all over the internet of him
in his wrestling attire. These sorts of things didn't prejudice me,
however, as I'm very broad-minded. I just ignored all the rubbish
in the media saying that a wrestler was coming into *The Apprentice*.

Ricky turned out to be quite a character. I'm not sure whether he pursues the sport these days; I think most of the wrestling he does is with the numbers in our new business. But under normal circumstances, if someone would have said to me that one of your candidates is a wrestler and he is coming into *The Apprentice* process, I would have said to them, 'Really? Well, he's got no chance of winning.' So there you go – one thing had nothing to do with the other. One thing I would say though: you wouldn't want to mess with Ricky. He is a big lad, that's for sure.

We went on to set up our joint business HRS (Hyper Recruitment Solutions) which in its first year made a fantastic profit. He has really impressed all my support staff, and the business has continued to expand. So much so, he outgrew the area of my premises I'd allocated for him, and he now has separate premises of his own. This is exactly the sort of thing I would expect from my joint business with the winners; that they would end up standing on their own two feet, albeit with my support team assisting on accounts, IT and all the boring stuff. He now has around twenty employees and is constantly recruiting new staff for HRS itself.

Ricky has made a real name for himself in the specialist recruitment market, but it wasn't easy in the early stages. It was difficult for him to gain recognition from serious industrial chemical and pharmaceutical companies such that they would ask him to recruit employees for them. What's more, Ricky had to start from scratch finding new clients, even though he had very good connections from his previous company, because, as anyone in the recruitment business knows, one is not allowed to pinch one's old clients. There are very strict rules prohibiting it.

There's no question about it, Ricky's business was a great investment for me as HRS is going from strength to strength. It further endorses the change of format I introduced – from a job to a business investment – as a masterstroke.

*

Series eight was recorded around November 2011 and it was to be broadcast the following March. The big job of editing would take place during the intervening period, so in January or February I'd normally be expecting a call from Michele and the editing team inviting me to come in and have a quick look at some of the stuff they'd started to patch together. However, much earlier than that, while I was away in Florida, I was surprised to receive a voicemail message from Michele saying she would like to talk to me. Before I called her back, my mind started to wonder what it could be that Michele wanted to speak to me about. You know how sometimes you just get a feeling about something? Well, I knew that it wasn't going to be good news. It couldn't be anything to do with filming because that was all done; it couldn't be anything to do with editing because it wasn't time for that yet; and it couldn't be anything to do with broadcasting because that was miles away.

So when I finally got in touch with her it didn't surprise me one bit when she told me she was leaving Boundless. She had decided to take up a new challenge at Sky TV. Sky was starting to get very adventurous in its programming and wanted to produce special new shows like *The Apprentice* that had obviously been successful.

Even though I was expecting bad news, it still came as a very disappointing blow to me because Michele had been an exceptional and hard-working person on *The Apprentice*. In fact, one has to say that she really crafted it and owned it and made it what it is today. I don't wish to undermine anybody who has taken over from her, but I think the template and the general tone and thrust of the programme were set by Michele and me. Together we were the main architects, and as I often say to people: 'If it ain't broke, don't fix it.'

Of course, Michele knew this would come as a blow to me and she very cleverly pre-empted my disappointment. Knowing that we had a good understanding during the editing process with regard to what I wanted included as business messages in the boardroom scenes, she realised that handing the job over to some unknown person would not be the best thing as far as I was concerned. Most people wouldn't have bothered addressing that problem; they'd have just cut and run and said goodbye. But Michele went to the trouble of tracking down Peter Moore because she knew that I had, and still have, the utmost respect for him. Peter had turned down doing the second series of *The Apprentice* because, as he said to me after series one, 'No, I've done it. I want to move on. New challenges and all that.' However, on this occasion when Michele contacted him, he agreed to act as 'executive producer across the edits' out of friendship to me, and we'd work together on the edit. So when Michelle called me, she had already mapped out what she was going to say: telling me that the bad news was she was leaving and she was very sad and very thankful for the support I'd given her over the years; but the good news was she'd convinced Peter Moore to step in and help with series eight.

Peter did as good a job as he could, given he was taking over someone else's work; however, I'm not sure that he and Cate Hall hit it off. I have no reason to say that, but I can imagine it from Cate's point of view: this was the first time she'd been given the responsibility of fully editing a series and then in steps somebody for whom she knew I had great admiration. I have a lot of respect for Cate also, and she went on to do two more series with me, but I suspect there might have been, I don't know, a bit of jockeying for position. I say these things because Peter, by his own admission, is not the easiest fellow to get along with, albeit a brilliant talent, and a Spurs supporter! I still invite him from time to time into the boardroom at White Hart Lane when there's a special game on. And I still have to remind him to wear a jacket and tie when he comes along; something that continues to be alien to him and others in the arty-farty world of television.

*

Series eight started broadcasting on 21 March 2012 and the final was aired on 3 June. Shortly after the final, the snipers were out in force again, trying to intimate that the £250,000 had not really been injected into a company, despite these slurs being squashed the previous year with Tom. I really hadn't thought they were thick enough to try it again, but then this was a different so-called investigative journalist from another newspaper. We effectively told him to catch up and have a look at the rubbish written by somebody else last year, and we sent him a copy of our answer, saying in effect, 'Put that in your pipe and smoke it.'

Apart from the media sniping, what I'd started to notice was another problem emerging from this £250,000 deal. In the past where the £100,000 job caused friction amongst some of my employees, this £250,000 investment gave rise to abuse from spiteful people on social media trying to run Ricky down. Some people in the recruitment industry took to Twitter to insult him and say how he was never going to succeed in this very crowded market. Then there were the usual trolls, or keyboard warriors as they like to call themselves; the scum who sit around all day in their dressing gowns, tweeting comments like, 'Who the hell does Ricky Martin think he is?' and 'He's a bloody wrestler; he's not a businessman,' and many more insulting remarks that I won't publicise.

This type of sniping can be very demoralising for the winner, in this case Ricky. I had to spend quite a bit of time, as did my staff, telling him to completely ignore all of this rubbish because effectively it's just jealousy. I mean, who in their right mind wouldn't love to make their business dream come true by going into partnership with me with a £250,000 injection into a new company? The prize is fantastic; it's not a joke or a con – as Ricky realised when he saw the money go into the bank account. It's actually an entrepreneur's dream. Just think about it: you don't have to worry about the boring side of things like doing the accounts, VAT, rent and rates, electricity and telecoms. You get all that done for you and charged back at realistic rates to your new company – and all *you* have to do is concentrate on the business side of things. Some start-ups fail because the entrepreneur gets bogged down with all this boring stuff and is unable to concentrate or focus on the real deal. So I told Ricky to snap out of thinking about the social media rubbish. I didn't want him to waste time worrying about whether the adverse comments were going to affect me and my decision.

'You need to get yourself a thicker skin, Ricky,' I said. 'Don't worry about me – my skin is as thick as leather as far as snipers are concerned. You have to realise this is par for the course when you get into the real world of commerce.'

In the end, the sneering doubters and the trolls were put in their place. The proof of the pudding is always in the eating and Ricky's accounts are published for all to see. Anyone who bothers to look will see that the business has been a blinding success. So much so that both partners in the business, he and I, have been able to enjoy dividends, in his case to help him finance the purchase of his new house.

20

'SWEATING LIKE A PIG IN A BUTCHER'S SHOP'

Young Apprentice and why Karren Brady will never fly with me again

Picture the scenario. I – someone who has no patience whatsoever – am told to arrive at seven o'clock in the morning to film the setting of a task. Picture me sitting in the car, stuck in traffic, getting really wound up, and then turning up at the location, my temper frayed, and being asked to get in and out of the car two or three times so they could film the perfect arrival shot. I would be close to breaking point, then suddenly series director Andy Devonshire would appear on the scene, full of the joys of spring.

'Good morning, Lord Sugar. How are you this morning? Everything's set up for you. We're all ready to roll whenever you are. So, in your own time . . .'

He had this way of diffusing a fraught situation. Whereas I was about to tear off the head of the next person I met, Andy's disarming manner made me look at the production person and think, 'This lad's been up since five this morning. He's set up all this stuff and he's only doing his job; it's not his fault I got stuck in traffic. Okay, all right, let's go.'

Apart from being a very talented person, Andy's calming nature was a bonus for everyone so it was a sad day when, before the third series of *Junior Apprentice*, I received a very nice letter from Andy telling me he had decided it was time for him to move on and stop doing *The Apprentice*. His letter was really heartfelt and written in an apologetic tone. He told me how he'd enjoyed all of what he'd done, particularly working with me, but the amount of time he had to allocate to *The Apprentice*, which was evident in his attendance during filming, was impacting on the amount of time and attention he could give his expanding family, so regretfully he was moving on and thanked me for my understanding. He had been with the show since series one.

Andy's dedication to *The Apprentice* was unbelievable. I remember when we were in the middle of filming the final of series six, he received a message from his wife that one of his children had been rushed into hospital. Of course, the immediate reaction of everyone on the set was, 'Andy, get the hell out of here and get down to the hospital.' However, Andy didn't just drop tools and vanish – only after he had advised all his team about the day's filming did he shoot off. A few days later his child was recovering well, though Andy was not able to attend the final boardroom filming. He arranged instead for another experienced person from Boundless to take his position in the gallery. So all in all, Andy was very devoted to the programme, and while I fully understood his reasons for leaving, it was a hammer blow to us all. We wished him well, and to this day he remains an ardent follower of *The Apprentice*. He's always emailing me and telling me how he's enjoying the series.

I believe that after having a short period of rest, Andy got back in the saddle directing *The Great British Bake Off*, and was series director on the early editions of Channel 4's *Four Rooms*.

I talked earlier about the gentlemen's agreement I had regarding the inclusion of my boardroom comments. This agreement was honoured very well by Michele Kurland, but she had now left and other people weren't quite so keen to stick to it, despite having the agreement spelled out to them. On series two of *Junior Apprentice*, for example, Colm Martin decided to try and challenge my position. However, as Michele was his overall boss at the time, he reluctantly conceded after much debate. Now, however, we were about to enter a new era with a whole new bunch of people who had to be introduced to the process of making *Junior Apprentice*, which by now had been renamed *Young Apprentice*.

A gentleman by the name of Graham Sherrington was seconded to take over Andy Devonshire's role as series director. Graham had been involved in programmes such as *Top Gear* and *Grand Designs* in the past. He explained to me that he was going to step in and do this *Young Apprentice* as a one-off in between the other contracts he had. He was a nice enough fellow and very professional. He had obviously read the manual, as it were, left behind by Andy on how to make a series. Considering he'd never done it before, he did a very good job.

Patrick Holland, who had taken over from Michele, still had the problem of finding a new executive producer and series editor for *Young Apprentice*. He hired Claudia Lewis as executive producer and Laurence Turnbull as series editor. Claudia was looking after the *Four Rooms* series at Boundless, while Laurence had previously worked on programmes such as *Trawler Wars* and *Big Fat Gypsy Weddings*.

The senior version of *The Apprentice* was also being prepared and Cate Hall and Francesca Maudslay, whom I'll talk more about later, were going to run that, so it would have been an impossible task for these two people, who'd been working on *The Apprentice* for quite a few years, to have taken over and done *Young Apprentice* as well. Hence these other people had to be appointed.

So there I was starting all over again with a new bunch of people. Now as I've said before, 'If it ain't broke, don't fix it.' The trouble is, new people coming in to do a new job in a very popular and famous programme are naturally excited at the thought of taking on this rather prestigious task. They have their own feelings and ideas about how things should be run and they want to make their mark. One can't blame them for that at all. However, when I sat down and listened to Claudia Lewis and Laurence Turnbull blue-skying their ideas for *Young Apprentice*, it reminded me of one of my sayings: 'It's like watching your mother-in-law driving your Ferrari off a cliff.'

Having been through series after series of *The Apprentice* and having amassed a great deal of knowledge on how things should be done, I found myself having to burst the bubbles of their enthusiastic ideas and explain, one by one, why they wouldn't work. Of course, I had two choices. I could have let them make the mistakes and fall flat on their faces, which ultimately would have resulted in a poor-quality programme – something I would never do – or instead, interfere. I'm sure they thought I was interfering when I would say to them, for example, 'Sorry, that can't work because of this or that reason.' So I spent a lot of time getting the new people on track. Effectively this was wasted time, which was down to all these senior management changes. I should have known by then that this is telly. Most people would have said, 'You know what? Just let this new lot get on with it.' But I'm not that kind of person because the integrity of the programme is paramount to me. To be fair, Claudia and Laurence did listen in the end. I'm sure they appreciated what I was saying to them and they took it in the right way.

However, things didn't kick off too well because when it came to the audition process for the final candidates, Claudia had been called away to Spain as her sister wasn't well, so the final auditions and the selection of candidates who enter the process were all done in her absence, albeit she saw copies of their CVs and video clips of them – but not a good start. As previously, the series was to be eight episodes long and we started out with twelve candidates.

One of the big problems we anticipated in making the third

series of *Young Apprentice* was that the filming was going to coincide with the London 2012 Olympics. This presented us with a very serious problem. The tasks call for a huge amount of movement around London, with teams often having to visit four or five different locations each day when they do market research, visit design houses, pitch to customers, etc. As it is, the teams often end up running late because of traffic, so you can imagine how much worse it would be with the Olympics on and the candidates sitting in the Chryslers in total gridlock. Ruby Evans, who was still line production executive, looked into this issue for weeks. She did a lot of clever work with schedules and dates, and the final was moved up to Manchester, which worked around the issue entirely.

The series started off with a task I was extremely keen on. It was based on one of my earliest experiences in business. As a kid I used to go and collect leftover rags from the garment traders in the East End and sell them on to rag-and-bone men. I set the teams the task of sorting through a ton of old clothes and trying to make money from them; selling some of them on as 'vintage' at higher-end retailers; others on second-hand clothes stalls.

The boys' team must have thought all their Christmases had come at once because one of the series' great characters was a lad by the name of Patrick McDowell. He claimed he'd already set up his own fashion label and that he wanted to be a fashion designer later in life. At school he had won the Textile Designer of the Year award at the age of thirteen, and I have to say, having experienced Patrick throughout the course of the process, if Britain is going to have new fashion designers, he is certainly the right calibre of person to be one of them.

Having agreed to be project manager for the boys' team, Patrick immediately turned his attention to spending a load of time and money on customising and tailoring some completely bonkers stuff, including – I kid you not – a wetsuit kimono. Karren showed me a picture of this thing in the boardroom and I remember saying to the team that they'd made something even Lady Gaga wouldn't wear! I asked Patrick if it was intended to be worn to a cocktail party on the *Titanic*.

This bizarre item was nonetheless interesting and it drew people to his stall. Of course, he never managed to sell it. In fact, at the end of the day they sold all their customised stock to one retailer for forty quid – and lost over a hundred pounds in doing so. This contributed to their failure in the task and the girls' team, led by Ashleigh Porter-Exley, won. On the boys' team, a very nice young man by the name of Max Grodecki ended up being fired, basically because of his poor sales performance despite saying he had experience in vintage clothing. As a side story, at that time I was the executive chairman of a company called YouView who were producing a new television viewing system on behalf of seven shareholders: BBC, ITV, Channel 4, Channel 5, Arqiva, BT and TalkTalk. One of the shareholders' executives was a chap by the name of Max, and apparently, when Max was fired on *Young Apprentice*, it had a knock-on effect in the boardroom at YouView. I heard that emails were flying around saying 'Lord Sugar has fired Max', with a little clip attached of me saying, 'Max, you're fired.'

In week two I set another task in which one of the candidates, Sean Spooner, was also a so-called expert. The task was to come up with a cookery book and pitch it to three retailers. Sean was an aspiring publisher (in fact, I've heard that he has gone on to start a publishing business) so was chosen as project manager. Maria Doran in his team had the idea of a cookbook aimed at professional women. She thought it would be good to have a target market. They called it *The Professional Woman*, and didn't actually mention that it was a cookbook anywhere on the front cover; it just said something like 'Fresh, Quick and Healthy' which sounded more like a lonely-hearts advert!

The other team came up with something aimed at students leaving home for the first time called #WheresMummy. As a keen Twitter user I thought the idea of the hashtag and tying it in to social media was quite clever, but one thing I hadn't counted on was just how poor these kids' spelling was. It contained so many spelling errors it looked unprofessional and the retailers were not impressed. As I told them in the boardroom, spelling is not my forte, but even I wouldn't confuse eight rashers of bacon with eight rashes! Nevertheless, the girls' book got more orders than the boys', and I ended up letting Sean go. He'd failed to deliver in his supposed area of expertise.

There were some funny moments during the series due to things that the kids had simply never heard of. On the discount buying task I'd sent the teams off to buy ten items for the Coliseum Theatre to use as props in an opera. One of the items they'd been asked to get was a candelabrum. The teams had absolutely no idea what it was; one of them thought it was a spare part for a washing machine. I recall saying to them in the boardroom, 'Bearing in mind that the task was to find props for an opera, how could it have been part of a washing machine? Did you think they were doing a production of *The Repairman of Seville*?'

I also made a little play on words and asked them whether they tried to buy one of the items for a *tenor*. This resulted in a load of blank faces in the boardroom. Another one of my lead-balloon jokes that backfired.

This particular task gave rise to lots of fighting in the boardroom, and these youngsters were a really feisty bunch. Andrew Tindall's team won the task, but despite the win I wasn't happy with their performance because they'd received a lot of fines and this task was all about spending the minimum. In fact, their fines outweighed the amount they'd spent. In the boardroom, Amy Corrigan viciously attacked the losing project manager, Steven Cole, as well as David Odhiambo. This played a large part in my decision to fire her over the two boys, even though David was the first person in the history of *The Apprentice* to appear in the board-room three times in the first three weeks. My decision to fire Amy, however, was borne out by Karren who informed me that Amy had been the main protagonist in the previous weeks' arguments.

As I said, there was a bunch of really fiery characters in that year's *Young Apprentice*. One in particular – Maria Doran – stood out. Maria had a right temper on her and I remember one occasion in the boardroom when she got so worked up that she had to take lots of deep breaths in order to calm herself down. She got herself into a right tizzy; she was just so passionate she couldn't keep a handle on herself.

There were a number of interesting tasks that year – creating a new brand of hair product and making a TV advert, running an afternoon tea business in a stately home, picking items to sell at a music festival, and creating a children's club experience and selling the rights to holiday providers.

One of the stand-out moments in the series was on the TV advert for the hair product. Maria came up with the idea of a delib-erately tacky hairspray called *Strexy* and decided to play up the tackiness in the advert. Ashleigh thought this was a bad idea and attempted to take control of the task on the second day. This led to a lot of friction between her and Maria when they were filming the video. The advert was generally praised, although it was felt the 'girl power' message was a bit dated.

Andrew came up with a brand of hair gel called *Chameleon*, which was a fatal error. It was supposed to appeal to people want-ing to stand out from the crowd. However, as Nick pointed out – albeit too late for them to change anything – chameleons actually *blend* into their environment; they don't stand out. Andrew also decided to incorporate some humour in the advert whereby the actor had a bit of toilet paper stuck to his shoe; a joke which the trade executives viewing the advert felt misfired.

The other team's advert was clearly the better one. The trade executives thought so, and I completely agreed with them. Maria had led her team to a win. In the losing team, Navdeep Bual was fired. She did not really contribute to the task and, quite honestly, I didn't really see her as cut out for business. I felt she had more potential in other areas. She was a very clever girl and I suggested to her, before letting her go, that maybe she ought to concentrate on her ambition of becoming a lawyer.

There was some great boardroom banter from these young kids. Once, when he was talking about a teammate who was under stress during a task, Andrew Tindall came out with, 'He was sweating like a pig in a butcher's shop.' Brilliant.

The final ended up with four candidates – Maria and Patrick on one team; Ashleigh and Lucy Beauvallet on the other – and their task was to create a new sports brand and put together an advertising campaign.

I explained earlier that the final was to be held in Manchester to avoid the congestion in London due to the Olympics. Nick and Karren travelled up to Manchester ahead of me and observed the teams carrying out the final task. Because of other business commitments I had, I arrived just before the teams made their final presentations. To add a bit of glamour to this sportswear task, and due to the fact we were in Manchester, through my football contacts I got in touch with Rio Ferdinand and asked him whether he would be a judge on the panel to help me decide which team had come up with the best sportswear product. His presence really added something to the day and the kids were so excited to see this famous Manchester United and England player.

In the end I plumped for the proposal put forward by Ashleigh and Lucy's team. And so, regretfully, Patrick, who'd been a great candidate and a great character, was fired, together with feisty Maria.

After a final discussion in the boardroom, I picked my winner.

It was a difficult decision. Lucy was very gifted academically and performed very consistently throughout the process, but she was a little too quiet and lacked a bit of confidence. Put simply, she wasn't as strong as Ashleigh, who'd shown throughout the course of the series that even though she was only seventeen, she had a mature head on her young shoulders. She was always calm and collected in the boardroom and never seemed to get flustered. She got the plot much quicker than the other candidates and emerged as the well-deserved winner.

I'd hired a twin turboprop aircraft to fly me up to Manchester and now I gave Nick and Karren the good news that they could come back with me on the plane rather than sit in a train for hours, and we could go out to dinner later at my local restaurant, Sheesh in Chigwell. However, I didn't realise that Karren was a nervous flyer. Now over the years, Nick has flown with me all over the country. In fact, he'd been with me once in this very same aeroplane on a flight to Glasgow. On our way back, one of the engines had conked out and we'd had to make an emergency landing somewhere and wait for a new plane to come and pick us up.

For the flight back from Manchester I decided I was going to fly as number-two pilot. Shortly after we took off we encountered some turbulence. One bump resulted in a shriek from Karren in the rear cabin when the coffee she was drinking flew out of the cup and hit the ceiling. She wasn't convinced it was the turbulence and I imagine she and Nick may have concluded that my piloting abilities were not very good. I did explain to her that I had no influence over the weather and that I'd tried to warn them both by gesturing with my hands from the cockpit that we were about to enter some turbulence. To this day I still think Karren blames me.

*

Like the previous winners of *Young Apprentice*, Arjun and Zara, Ashleigh has only drawn down a moderate amount of money from her £25,000 prize. Unlike the previous winners, Ashleigh didn't go on to university. She has called on my advice more as she makes her way through the world of work, and I've had to keep her on track a couple of times. She was from an ordinary working-class family who never would have envisaged her having this £25,000 war chest knocking around, so there were some silly ideas she came up with from time to time. For example, she told me she was going to set up a business encouraging young people by inspirational speaking – she said she would need a vehicle to get around to her various engagements and asked whether I would forward some of the money for her to buy a car, as it would be part of the tools of her trade. On further investigation of her business idea, this didn't seem like a great thing to spend the money on, so I suggested she have a rethink.

Ashleigh has since left education and went to work at an estate agent where she gained experience in selling property. And at one stage she heard about the opportunities that existed in Dubai where people were allegedly making loads of money in commission for selling real estate there. She called and asked me whether I'd be pre-pared to fund her flight to Dubai plus accommodation costs. I asked her to explain what exactly she had in mind. She told me that she'd found a firm of estate agents in Dubai who had said in effect, 'If you want to come and work for us, you have to pay your own expenses and subsistence, and you will be working on a commission-only basis. What we will give you is a desk to operate from.' I explained to her that this was really not a good idea, and once again suggested she have a rethink. More recently she has come up with a far better idea, which did have some legs, and I asked her to produce a business plan before I agreed to forward the money.

The idea of the £25,000 prize, as I said in the very first series of *Junior Apprentice*, is not for the winner to go out and buy a second-hand Porsche to flash around to their mates; it's there as a fighting fund for when they've finished their education and/or have obtained some experience in the field in which they're going to operate. And for all three of the young apprentices, I have made sure, and will continue to make sure, that the money is not released to them unless it's for a good practical purpose.

With the *Young Apprentice* series recorded, it was now down to the editing process and, as usual, several weeks went by before I saw anything of interest. However, I started to encounter some resistance from Claudia Lewis when it came to my suggestions. Here was a classic example of someone not wanting to sign on to the gentlemen's agreement I'd reached with Michele and Lorraine previously. For the first few episodes it was reasonably okay in the sense that my business messages were being included, but later it got to the stage where I started to get a bit hot under the collar. This was exacerbated by some scheduling issues at the BBC which I considered a real problem. The programme was going out on *Thursdays* – that was a problem for a start as everybody knows that *Wednesday* is the traditional *Apprentice* day, not Thursday. It was also starting on 1 November and concluding on 20 December. This was smack bang in the middle of the peak-season programming, up against some major ITV programmes and Christmas specials. Despite my protestations to the BBC when I heard about the scheduling, there was simply nothing I could do as they wouldn't budge. Regrettably, the ratings went down because of the competition on Thursday nights, and a new series of a popular programme that was starting on ITV. I found it quite demoralising that all the work and effort we'd put into *Young Apprentice* was being undermined by this.

In the end, I got so disheartened that when it was time for me to comment on the editing of the later episodes, I kind of lost the will to live while I was arguing with this Claudia woman, and said, 'Listen, love, do what you bloody want; I'm not interested any more. The programme's being slaughtered in the ratings, and quite honestly it doesn't matter what we do now – it's going to continue to lose its ratings because of the competition we're up against. So knock yourself out and do what you want.'

'Oh, Lord Sugar, no, please. Look at the programme. Please give me your comments. Honestly, I really *do* value your feedback.'

'Nah, not really, love. I can't be bothered, to be honest with you. I've lost all heart with it, because when you work as hard as we did and see what's going on as far as the scheduling's concerned, I'm afraid to say it is demoralising. As I just said, it makes no difference what we do, so there you go.'

Funnily enough, *Young Apprentice* was nominated once again for a BAFTA, but didn't win. I didn't think it would. I remembered that the senior *Apprentice* won a BAFTA in its first year and was nominated the following year without success. So I told people not to get too excited as it would be highly unlikely that *Young Apprentice* would win a BAFTA two years running. My prediction was correct.

I got the feeling the BBC themselves were not that happy with the idea of making more series of *Young Apprentice*, and this feeling was borne out after I was contacted by the production company to tell me that the BBC were keen for me to continue with the senior *Apprentice* and would like me to sign up for at least another two years. I followed up those discussions with Mark Linsey who was Controller of Entertainment Commissioning, which meant he was responsible for the commissioning of *all* the BBC's entertainment shows such as *The Apprentice, Strictly Come Dancing* and *The Voice*. He's also Deputy Director of BBC Television these days which means that he stands in for Danny Cohen when he is away or unavailable. Mark politely said that the BBC didn't really want to do any more *Young Apprentice* series.

I was disappointed and have always felt that the bad scheduling of the programme, which initially stemmed from the complaint made to the BBC about my government role, doomed *Young Apprentice* from day one. But by now I think that mentally I also conceded that I wouldn't push to do any more as it took quite a big chunk of my time; particularly through the summer. Indeed, Ann, who was a great fan of *Young Apprentice*, had kind of complained to me that I was absent for a large chunk of the summer holidays. So in the end it was killed off.

I think it also coincided with the fact that under Danny Cohen's new leadership there was pressure being brought to bear from the outside world to make cost savings across the whole of the BBC. I believe directives came from the BBC Trust stating that savings had to be made as there was no more money to be taken from the licence-fee payers, and although I have absolutely no confirmation of this, I simply guess that the cost charged by Boundless to the BBC for making *Young Apprentice* was a considerable amount of money, and that ditching it may have gone some way towards the economic savings that Danny Cohen had to make. I also think that Danny considered twenty weeks of *The Apprentice* per year would make the public tired of the brand, and by keeping the main series only, it would retain its specialness. Personally, I believe that with good spacing, both series could have survived. What I do know is the public loved *Young Apprentice* and to this day I still get lots of people, especially on Twitter, asking me when it's coming back. In the end it was a victim of rescheduling brought about by some external issues and events. And being the truthful and honest fellow that I am, I normally respond by saying, 'The BBC decided not to do any more of them.'

I remember talking to Danny and suggesting that perhaps the real reason was: too much Sugar on TV. This is quite an interesting point because, as people will know, certain celebrities pop up all over the place on TV; not just in the programme they're famous for. They're often asked to do other programmes for the same broadcaster. With me, however, apart from a few documentaries I'd done for the BBC, there was always a reluctance to discuss any new format idea I might have. For example, I had an idea for a show where I would be an arbitrator or a mediator, which I put to Talkback at the time when Lorraine Heggessey was CEO. The conceptual idea was that I would deal with commercial or personal disputes between people and act as an arbitrator – a bit like Judge Judy on steroids. I had a vision of how this could work very well, but when it came to negotiating a format, I couldn't agree terms with them to do it. In fact, Talkback thought the idea was so good that despite me thinking it up and them not being able to agree format terms with me, they ended up taking up my idea and doing it themselves using Gerry Robinson, whom Michele Kurland had worked with before in another type of business show. When I finally saw the broadcast, it was quite frankly pathetic. There was one episode where somebody was talking about their cats and how they would leave their legacy to them – real scintillating stuff. Needless to say, the programme was a complete and utter flop, and completely different to what I had in mind.

I also think the production company and the BBC now see me in just one role, so each and every time I have some ideas for a different format, they politely tell me that it's of no interest to them. It's as if they wish to preserve me solely for *The Apprentice*.

21

'SOMEONE HERE THINKS
HE'S NAPOLEON!'

**Nick doing his own stunts and filming series nine
with the wishy-washy poxy boxy**

A simple lesson in life is that experience always allows you to learn what to do next time. Consequently, I became very proficient in what to do when faced with the baggy-jumpered, beanie-hat-wearing, brightly-coloured-scarf-around-the-neck brigade, all displaying their artistic genius. I'm talking about the directors of the BBC's trails.

As I mentioned earlier, the first *Apprentice* trail I saw was for series one, where they'd actually taken a compilation of clips from the show and patched them together to make an advert for the arrival of a programme never seen on UK television before. That kind of trail is not rocket science to produce; it simply requires a certain amount of cooperation from *The Apprentice* production team to provide the trail-makers with the rushes (I know I'm sounding like a TV luvvy now). Over the years, however, as the series became more popular, the marketing division of the BBC, who are responsible for promoting programmes, actually made custom trails from scratch.

At first I found it hard to grasp that the production team on *The Apprentice*, who knew every detail like the back of their hands, were barely consulted with regard to the content of the trails. This separate marketing division took control and operated in a world of its own. They kind of invented a whole story for the trails and made a mini-film which didn't use any of the actual footage from the series. These were very expensive productions and were an indication of how well the BBC got behind the series.

I was of course featured in most of these custom trails. They were all made in a studio where in some cases a mini-boardroom was created as a set. I was surprised to see the size of the crew. You had the director, naturally, but also one bloke with a rag cleaning the desk, another with a brush dusting the lens, the gaffer – a bloke who fixed things if they went wrong – another geezer with the famous clapper-board and five runners asking if you wanted coffee, tea, cold drink or a sandwich. And there was a buffet fit for a queen set up for the crew, who of course must be fed! It was an amazing sight.

Being a novice back then, I fell for it hook, line and sinker. 'Your call time at the studio [meaning when I should arrive] is 9 a.m.,' they'd say. I'd get a whole list of events that were going to happen: wardrobe, make-up, tea break, film scene one, etc. The bottom line was it resulted in me being needed for five hours to film a trail that lasted twenty-five seconds when broadcast.

What wasn't amazing but bloody boring was the amount of times I was told to say the same thing over and over again to get what the director, a mini-Spielberg, described as perfection.

'Okay, take twenty-five – just one more time, Sir Alan. I know you are frustrated but we just need to get it right.'

I mean, how many bleedin' times can you say, 'Will you send the candidates in now please.'

They drove me nuts to such an extent that I would start to lose it and tell them, 'That's it – I'm out of here in five minutes.' Near to a Jeremy Clarkson moment.

When I was asked to appear in more trails in later years I would say, 'No problem, but here is the deal. You have me for one hour, so you set everything up, do all your scenes with the other people, take all the shots that you need. Use one of your runners to stand in for me to get your eyeline, focus, lighting and all that bollocks; then I come in – bish bash bosh – I do my bit and then sod off.'

'Oh dear, dear, dear,' they laughed condescendingly. 'I'm afraid it doesn't work that way, Sir Alan. It *would* be nice if we could do that, but in reality you will be needed for at least three hours. We'll try and fast-track it of course, as we know you're a busy man.'

'Er, no, mate. Did you read my lips? You have one hour, otherwise I am not doing it, simple as that. So go tell Fellini he has to work around it.'

Honestly, I wasn't being unreasonable or having a diva moment. Of course I wanted to support the programme and drum up viewers. As everyone at the production company and the BBC knows, I always give my full support to the series. But having experienced the waste of my time, I knew it could be done. It was just a case of them recognising they had to change their methods, and to make a long story short, that's what happened. And that's what happens today if ever I'm asked to do trails.

There were some great trails. One showed a scene of complete carnage and disaster in the boardroom, which looked like a bomb had hit it. There were candidates lying on the floor, across the table and hanging on the wall. My bit was to walk in and look down at a candidate on the floor – while holding his business plan in my hand – and say something like, 'You will have to improve on this to be able to stand up in my boardroom.' It was very funny.

I recall Margaret disapproving of this trail. She said it was a disgrace to portray such a scene and it misrepresented what really goes on in the boardroom. I remember telling her to lighten up and stop being a bloody lawyer. It was just a bit of fun.

I think the best one was the *Goldfinger* trail where I was depicted as Mr Goldfinger, the character from the James Bond movie. There were scenes of me riding around in my car, and in a restaurant, where people's faces would turn to horror when they saw it was me pointing at them. There was an antique clock containing a person's face carved in gold – the face spoke and said, 'Thank you for the opportunity, Lord Sugar.' The funniest thing was when Nick had to perform his own stunt. He had to dive in front of Karren to protect her as I was about to point at her. On the set there was a large mattress on the floor so, all suited and booted, Nick dived across the front of the camera and soft-landed on the mattress, which of course was not in view. Tom Cruise, eat your heart out, is all I can say. They overlaid the *Goldfinger* theme tune on top of the trail, and I have to say: credit where credit's due, I know I take the mickey out of these creative people, but on this occasion what they produced was brilliant.

The BBC knows its audience and so, for example, they might show a trail for *The Apprentice* before the start of *EastEnders*, knowing that many viewers watch both programmes. As another example, BBC3 is known to have a very young audience, so despite the fact that *Junior Apprentice* was shown on BBC1, it made sense to promote its arrival on BBC3.

People often ask me, 'Since you've been involved in television doing *The Apprentice*, has it helped your business?' Back in the early days this was a worry for Jane Lush. Her big concern was that the programme should not be seen to help promote any of my business interests. Well, as I've explained, there was very limited branding to do with my company in the programme itself. Outside the programme, the honest answer is this: as far as any business is concerned, my participation in *The Apprentice* has not helped in any way, shape or form; except it's true to say I can pick up the phone to most people that my companies would be interested in doing business with and get an audience with the boss so that my people can go and talk to them. But that's where it ends because business is business, and there's no justifiable reason for anybody to do business with me simply because I'm the host of a popular television show. At the end of the day, any business proposition we're offering a potential client has to stack up on its own. So I'd say at best I can get an audience. Some may say, 'Well, that's an advantage in itself,' which I think one has to concede is true, but the point is, it goes nowhere as far as the bottom line is concerned.

Outside of business, restaurant reservations are much easier to get. In fact, some places rather enjoy having a semi-celebrity there, particularly those in the West End of London. On many occasions after being in a restaurant a short while I'd see a load of paparazzi suddenly appear outside, no doubt called there by the staff looking to promote the restaurant; to show that showbiz types go there. Once, Nick, Karren and I were leaving a restaurant in London after having dinner, and as we came out there must have been twenty photographers. Their cameras flashing away nearly blinded me and resulted in me walking towards the wrong car!

Very often in restaurants someone will come up to me and say, 'I know who's going to be fired next week. I can tell, because at the end of last week's episode – when they showed you pointing your finger and saying, "You're fired!" – I remember who was sitting where you were pointing, so I know [for example] it's going to be Charlie.'

'Really?' I say. 'Well, actually, maybe that sequence you saw of me pointing my finger was filmed five years ago. But to be fair, let's analyse what you've just said. First of all, if the programme hasn't broadcast yet in which you think I fired Charlie, how do you know that Charlie's sitting at that end of the table? He might have been sitting there in last week's episode, but how do you know he'll be sitting there next week?'

I'd see the person's face drop and they'd walk off with their tail between their legs, disappointed that their theory was wrong.

And then you get the other type of person in restaurants who just wants to talk to me about anything. Sometimes I even get followed to the loo by people who want to stand next to me and talk. I spoke about this once on *The Jonathan Ross Show*. Some men might understand where I'm coming from here – when you've got someone standing next to you at the urinals nattering away, your intention of going to the loo is thwarted and you're unable to get any pressure up, so you end up leaving and going back again a few minutes later. Maybe it's an age thing. I got so fed up with this that on one occasion, when I was out to dinner with my daughter and son-in-law Mark, I asked him to be my minder in the loo!

'Follow me, Mark,' I said, 'and kind of hang around and stand next to me so I can get a bit of pressure up.'

How ridiculous does this sound? Nevertheless, it's true.

The strangest thing about being involved with *The Apprentice* was the reaction from my staff in all my companies. Before the first series started there was a lot of publicity about Sir Alan Sugar being in a new TV show, as well as the BBC trails. You would have had to live in Siberia to miss it but, as far as my staff were concerned, it was as if nothing must be said. In fact, it was even stranger when the show started to transmit. I would walk into the office the day after an episode had been broadcast and go into a meeting expecting some chit-chat about last night's show. Instead we just got on with things. I don't really know how to explain it – I guess the staff and other executives know me so well that they might have thought I'd take exception to comments on the show. So there was a silence. I guess they were talking about it amongst themselves, of course, and one couldn't help notice the sweepstake charts on the office walls, as there are in many other offices up and down the country, on who the winner will be.

For *Apprentice* series nine we decided to shake things up a bit. Both Cate Hall and Francesca Maudslay had worked on the programme long enough to have a real awareness and respect for why we do certain things a certain way and yet be able to change things here and there, hopefully for the better, as we were always looking to freshen up the format slightly. When the candidates gathered for Boardroom Zero, I gave them my opening speech and set the first task, but before I sent them off I decided to ask them – for the first time at the beginning of a series – what their business ideas were.

I had told the production people that usually in Boardroom Zero the candidates just sit there and listen to me going on and on, explaining what the whole process is about, who Nick is, who Karren is, all that stuff. This time I wanted to have a little chat with some of the candidates to get a rough picture of who they were and what their business plans were about. It was kind of an icebreaker. So I went down the line talking to some of them, and they gave me a quick headline of the businesses they were pitching to me.

Of course, before all this I had seen the video clips of the candidates and heard the usual outrageous boasts. For example, Luisa Zissman said, 'I've got the energy of a Duracell bunny, the sex appeal of Jessica Rabbit and a brain like Einstein,' while Jaz Ampaw-Farr said, 'I am half machine!' Jason Leech claimed that his effortless superiority would see him through, and Zee Shah, who once worked at Phones 4u, said, 'I am like Napoleon; I am here to conquer.'

I got straight down to business and said, 'I've got a pile of CVs here. It's full of the usual BS – "I'll give 110 per cent", "I'm the greatest entrepreneur since sliced bread", "Failure is not an option; I think outside the box, inside the bleedin' box" – all the usual clichés. To be honest with you, I'm sick and tired of that bloody rubbish.'

After asking a few of the candidates to outline their business plans, I turned to Leah Totton. 'I see we've got a doctor in the house, is that right?'

'Yes,' said Leah.

'Well, you'd better be on standby. Someone here thinks he's Napoleon!'

I turned to Zee and said, 'You know what happened to Napoleon, right?' He nodded. I continued, 'Well, consider me as the Duke of Wellington in this process.'

Another change we had decided to make to Boardroom Zero was to ask the candidates to decide who the project managers were going to be there and then, rather than go to the house and have the usual round-the-table discussion.

Before I'd even said what the task was, Jaz put her hand up to volunteer. I told her at the time it was very brave to jump in like that without even gauging how the rest of the team felt – she should have at least listened to what the task was all about. Anyone who's ever watched *The Apprentice* must have seen me bleating about not taking on a job unless you have some sort of experience in it.

The first task was excellent and gave us some great footage. I'd arranged two shipping containers full of imported products, which were waiting for them at the port of Tilbury in Essex. The candidates had to go and collect their products in the middle of the night and then find buyers for the whole of the next day. The idea was that London is a city that is always trading, day and night, and the art of the task was to match the right products to the right trades to be able to keep selling all day. It was no good picking products with a short shelf-life that would only sell in the morning; but then again it was also not right to select products that people only bought later in the day. So all in all there were quite a few nuances and twists in the rules for this task.

Filming a twenty-four-hour task like that was no mean feat. The camera and sound crew, as well as the drivers, worked it in shifts, but the production team and candidates of course had to be awake the whole time. We had not told the candidates beforehand that the task would be taking place overnight, though they had been warned to sleep right up until the moment they were collected and brought to the boardroom for the first time. I think Cate and Francesca were up for something like forty hours in total. It was all worth it though as it was a spectacular way to start the series.

One major coup was filming at the port of Tilbury. Tilbury had been featured in one of those Channel 4 idents where the structure of the port had been made to look like it was forming the Channel 4 logo. It looked amazing, but was a huge job for our team to take on. Imagine trying to light an area within a massive port in the dead of night, then film a load of candidates running around like loonies all over the place. Add to that the fact that it's a working port – with customs and import rules and massive health and safety considerations – and you have one very tricky filming location.

The boys' team won that task. However, when I questioned them before we knew the result, I had cause to criticise Tim Stillwell because it was reported that he didn't do much. He'd just hung around, kind of hiding.

'What are you doing there, Tim? Standing there quietly? I hear you didn't do much on the task. You know that sometimes you can step back so far you fall off the bloody cliff?'

'Lord Sugar, I thought the way to prove myself was in sales.'

'So what did you sell then?'

'Hi-viz jackets, Lord Sugar.'

'Blimey, they must have seen you coming!'

However, once it had been announced that the boys' team had won and I was about to send them off for a treat, Tim piped up with an apology, stating that he'd taken my feedback on board. I told him, 'Tim, your team won! Shut up – don't dig yourself a hole. Just shut up and go.'

On the girls' team, Jaz had spent far too much time on the motivational side of leadership, doing lots of whooping, high fives and cheering and stuff like that. When I questioned her on this, she didn't like my criticism and sighed, 'Oh man!'

'I'm not "man"; I am Lord Sugar.'

'Sorry, Lord Sugar.'

Not only did her team find her motivational approach patronising, it was totally ineffective. My initial instinct about Jaz turned out to be right. She made some very poor decisions and so became the first candidate to be fired. At one point her team was trying to sell golden lucky cats in Chinatown – the one place in London where the shops could source the exact same thing for a few pence.

Knowing the headlines of the candidates' business plans allowed me to assess their so-called areas of expertise when it came to synergistic tasks. This happened on week two when the task was to come up with a new brand of flavoured beer. I made two of the candidates – who both wanted to start a drinks business – opposing project managers. The boys came out on top despite one of their team, a Liverpudlian fellow called Kurt Wilson, making some idiotic managerial mistakes. He sent a bunch of people to produce the beer, not one of whom was a beer drinker! In fact, one of the people he sent to the factory was Zee, who didn't drink for religious reasons. I asked Kurt, 'Why on earth did you send people to a brewery who don't drink? I mean, why did you send Zee? He's as dry as a cream cracker in the Sahara Desert.'

By week three I was keen to see if the girls could pull together and win for the first time, so rather than mix the teams I thought I'd give the girls one last chance to prove themselves. The task was to design a piece of flat-pack furniture. The girls came up with the Tidy Sidey, which they said was a multifunctional side table, but I said was simply a box on wheels. They spent the best part of two days coming up with this thing and it really was just a bloody box. I recall my conversation with them in the boardroom. Since they had tried to think of a fancy name for what was just a box on wheels, I picked up a glass of water and described it as a portable hand-held beverage interface. I called their product, 'Tidy Sidey, wishy-washy, poxy boxy,' and added, 'This was a design task where

– to use all the business clichés you lot tend to come up with – you're supposed to think outside the box, and all you thought of *was* a bloody box!'

Somehow they managed to get a few orders for it from smaller retailers, but neither of the two massive retailers I'd set up for them bought any. The Tidy Sidey suffered from 'committee syndrome'. Every single member of that team had a different idea for the product, so what they ended up with was a horrible mish-mash. By trying to please everyone, they ended up with nothing in design terms. They tried to explain that the product was easy to assemble in that it was glueless, which resulted in another of my Uncle John quips: 'I think you mean clueless.'

Sophie Lau, one of the team, tried to argue that it *was* very functional. I agreed it was – in the sense that I could wheel it out to the bloody skip and throw it away.

On the other hand, there have been times when the candidates have produced seriously impressive products. The same week the girls came up with the Tidy Sidey, the boys designed a chair with a very clever sliding system that turned into a table. It was one of the best products I'd seen in all my years in the boardroom. Obviously it still had some way to go in terms of finessing the design, but the concept was clever, and the architect of that concept was Welshman Alex Mills, who in this particular case was allowed to express his idea to his teammates, and they let him get on with it. In the short period of time they had to come up with this thing, Alex had designed something that would have taken some companies weeks to do.

One of the stand-out candidates from series nine was a gentleman by the name of Jason Leech. Now Jason was a lovely fellow and had a different background from most of the other candidates. He was an academic who wanted to start a business, and although he lacked a lot of the industry experience some of the others had, he had real strengths in other areas. Most of the other candidates liked

Jason but thought he was a bit *too* nice and a little weak. However, over the course of the series he really started to blossom. I was very impressed the week he came out of his shell and sold a caravan for around £10,000. In fact, after the winning team left the boardroom it occurred to me that I hadn't complimented Jason. I got the production people to run after him and tell him to come back. You can imagine what was going through his mind. His face when he walked back into the boardroom was a picture I won't forget; he looked like a rabbit in the headlights. He had no idea why he was called back and must have known this was an unprecedented move in *The Apprentice* – indeed, I had never done this before. He must have thought he had done something wrong and that maybe I was going to fire him.

'Hi, Jason, sorry to call you back. Don't worry, young man – you have a worried look on your face – I just wanted to personally say how impressed I was with your caravan sale and the way you've at last shown some great business acumen. That's all. I forgot to say it when I first heard the result, so I thought I'd call you back to say well done.'

After that, I saw the colour come back into his face. He was obviously very relieved. 'Oh, thank you so much, Lord Sugar. I really appreciate that.' As he left the boardroom he was kind of walking backwards out of the door and bowing and thanking me for my kind words. He was a nice, charming fellow, I have to say.

Some of the other candidates didn't do so well selling caravans. When I took Alex to task on the subject, he started rambling on in his defence and boasting about his current business, saying that he made products for the Royal Family.'

Surprised to hear this claim, I asked, 'You've sold stuff to the Royal Family?

'Yes, Lord Sugar. My company made plaques for the Royal Family.'

'Really? Are you sure? Did you pitch to the Queen then? Or to the corgis?'

That year's advertising task was to come up with a campaign for a new dating website. Jason, maybe fired up from his previous win and compliments from me, put himself forward as project manager. I think it's fair to say that as well as he did on the caravan task, this task was the complete opposite – he did a pretty poor job. He dithered and hesitated, and struggled with the amount of work they needed to do in such a short time. Meanwhile his teammate Luisa got more and more frustrated with him. Nick's opinion was that Luisa's constant questioning of Jason, rather than being helpful, caused him to lose confidence and dither even more. In the end Jason told the team that he wanted to abdicate as project manager and let Luisa take over.

I'd never heard anything like it! There had been times when teams had had major fall-outs, but replacing a leader mid-task was unheard of. Nick and Jason both felt Luisa had contributed to the problem rather than fix it, but Luisa was adamant that she was trying to save the day – something I always tell the candidates they should try to do if they see things going wrong. That said, I didn't like what I was hearing about how Luisa had behaved, and told her so in no uncertain terms.

That advertising task was one of the most extraordinary we'd had for years, not only because of Jason's abdication, but also because of the campaigns the teams came up with. Jason's team devised a dating site for the over-fifties called Friendship and Flowers, which was so bland that it looked like something from God's Waiting Room.

Even though Jason did not perform well, the fact of the matter was that the implementation of the task in general was poor, and Neil Clough had a lot to answer for. I questioned him about the aspects of the task he'd been involved in. 'Neil, where did you get the name Friendship and Flowers?'

'From market research, Lord Sugar.'

'Where did you go? A funeral parlour? Your advert makes *Last of the Summer Wine* look like an action movie.'

However, Jason had reached the limit of his business abilities and he knew it. As nice a chap as he was, I just couldn't accept him giving up and abandoning ship like that. I said to him, 'Picture the scenario here. You're in charge on the sinking *Titanic* ship – you don't just *give up*, do you?'

Jason replied, 'Look, if I were in charge of a sinking ship, my first concern would be all the women and children.'

I just shook my head. The other candidates quietly giggled that he had taken me literally. At that point I knew he'd come to the end of the line, and it was with a heavy heart that I let Jason go. However, Luisa also left the boardroom that day with a very clear message that I was not going to tolerate any more reports of her browbeating behaviour.

The other team came up with a site for young professionals, called Cufflinks. Alex decided to be the face of the advertising campaign. He cast himself as a nightmare date called Herbert. He was wearing an extraordinary outfit and a face full of make-up. If memory serves, he looked like some sort of transvestite witch. To understand how bad that was, you'd have to recall what Alex looked like in real life. For some reason better known to him, he had manicured eyebrows! I recall on one occasion when they were being driven around in the Chryslers, one of the other candidates said he looked a bit like Dracula. He really did look a bit weird, though he seemed like a nice, hard-working chap.

There was something charming about Alex, but his teammates never seemed to take him very seriously. Week after week he came into the boardroom saying that he'd put himself forward to lead the team, but they never took him up on the offer. He didn't project manage until week nine when I set them the task of coming up with a new ready meal. His team decided to produce one for kids called 'Deadly Dinners'. I could see what they were trying to do – they were hoping to draw on the fact that kids like gruesome things and slugs and snails and all that sort of stuff. But perhaps the word 'deadly' wasn't quite right for a product aimed at kids, and the skull they had on the packet definitely didn't help.

'Deadly Dinners?' I remember commenting. 'What's next? Lethal Lasagne? Homicidal Hummus?'

The teammates were squabbling in the boardroom after they'd lost, all trying to place the blame on each other, which prompted me to say, 'It's like a bloody microwave meal in this boardroom – things are getting heated and we're going round in circles.'

The product clearly was not accepted by the retailers they pitched it to. Having said that, we noticed in the episode that the kids did actually like the stuff. The point was, however, that the retailers felt the mothers would not buy the product because of the nasty branding. I also guess it didn't help that when Myles Mordaunt was in full flow doing the pitch to the retailers, Alex was completely throwing him off by loudly popping the film lid on the microwave ready meal.

That year we sent the candidates to Dubai for the discount buying task. Zee stepped up to be project manager on the basis that he had lived and worked in Dubai. He said he knew it like the back of his hand, but when they got out there he quickly fell apart, and it all went to pot. He led his team to all the wrong places and they made a lot of bad decisions. One of the things they had been asked to buy was a flag of the UAE for the flagpole at a new hotel complex. As you can imagine, it was a massive flagpole requiring a large flag for which they'd been given the measurements. However, when phoning the instructions through, Kurt managed to mix up centimetres and inches, and when they went to collect the flag, it was about the size of a napkin! Later in the boardroom I could not resist a little dig at Kurt. When I was talking to the other team, led by Myles, I said, 'Myles, or as Kurt might call you, Kilometres, tell me what your team got up to.'

When I heard how badly Zee had messed up, I told him, 'You said you knew Dubai like the back of your hand – well, you must have been wearing gloves! If I'd sent you out to buy twenty camels you'd have come back with a packet of fags.' He had failed big time on this task so I said to him, 'I don't think Napoleon was ever fired from Phones 4u, but today, Zee, you're fired from this process.'

Some of the female candidates didn't like Zee very much – they thought he was not very polite. I recall on one occasion when the candidates entered the boardroom, Zee opened the door, walked in and let the door swing back in the face of Natalie Panayi, who made a point of saying, 'Thanks very much, Zee. Very gentlemanly of you.'

As usual, by the time we got to the interviews episode I had narrowed the field down to the candidates who seemed to have the most about them in business terms. We'd decided that year to make the final task one where the finalists would actually launch the business plans they were proposing, not only to me, but also to a number of industry experts. This meant that the interview programme was moved to the penultimate episode.

One person I really had my eye on during the final run-in was a young man by the name of Neil Clough. Like a lot of candidates he came into the process making all sorts of claims about how brilliant he was, but over the weeks he learned to control himself and started to exhibit the sort of qualities I was looking for in a business partner. The problem came when we got to the interviews. In Boardroom Zero ten weeks earlier, Neil had mentioned his idea was an online estate agency. I thought no more about it until we got to the interviews episode and my advisors pushed him for more information. It turned out that Neil had completely neglected to think his idea through. His plan just didn't stack up – not even nearly. Worse still, when all my advisors explained this to him and asked him what his Plan B was, he stuck stubbornly to his idea and refused to budge an inch.

I have to say I bent over backwards telling him that one side of his plan seemed okay – a website for consumers to bypass estate agents and sell their houses themselves. However, it was the second part of his plan – where he said he was going to get the agents to use his website as well – that was flawed. Claude and I explained this massive error to him several times, saying to him, 'Your idea would screw the agents out of their fees, so how on earth could you then expect them to pay to be on your website?' Nevertheless, he still bluntly refused to change his idea, which left me no choice but to let him go.

It was a total shock as I had assumed Neil was a cert for the final. I told him that he was the right man with the wrong plan. I don't mind admitting I was sad about it because he was a very hard-working person and I had genuinely felt he was a contender. However, his total stubbornness in not listening to the advisors or me – even after we'd suggested many times that he change his business plan – ultimately cost him. I'm sure he regrets his refusal to change to this day.

I know this all must sound like a bit of a farce. When a candidate has done so well throughout the process and then fails at this stage, people often say to me that it's not fair. But a bad business plan is like a bad task – it shows the candidate has failed to think things through. I'm always looking for a *credible* business partner, and how they've put together their business plan is really important. It *was* very disappointing that someone as promising as Neil, who'd done so well for eleven weeks, had failed to think his plan through and, worse still, would not listen to advice.

As it happens, Neil has done very well since the series and tells anyone who will listen how positive he found the experience. He even told Cate and Francesca he'd do it again if he could. One of the things he's been doing a lot of is motivational speaking, which he first discovered he had a talent for on the corporate entertaining task, when he gave a brilliant motivational speech to a room full of paying clients.

The most surprising thing to come out of the interviews episode were the details of Jordan Poulton's business plan. He described it as an immersive mobile experience. I asked him to clarify what that meant. As far as I could tell, it sounded like what happens when you drop your phone down the loo!

Jordan was another bright fellow, but it turned out that having got through almost the entire process, he had neglected to mention to me that the idea he was pitching for my investment was actually someone else's company – all he had was a gentlemen's agreement to prove his own involvement. What Jordan was asking me to do was to not only go into business with him but also with some unknown partner of his! Needless to say, these are not the sort of terms I can go into business with someone on, especially as Claude discovered that in Jordan's proposal he was only offering me fifteen per cent of the business for my £250,000. I don't know what he was thinking – it's like he'd got me confused with one of the bloody Dragons.

The whole concept of the programme is that the candidates come forward with their business ideas, and the winner and I start a business on a fifty-fifty basis where I inject £250,000. Jordan was being too clever by half and consequently he left the process at that stage.

As I've said before, I never go into the nitty-gritty of business plans until the very end of the process. I just take a quick look at the headline and category in general to make sure I have no problem with it, because whoever wins is going to be the expert and do all the work. There is no point wasting time diving deep into sixteen business plans if they are not going to be at least in the final five of the process. On top of this, of course, the BBC wanted an assurance that I would not favour a particular candidate on the basis that I liked their plan more than the others'. The winner has to win on his or her performance in the process. Naturally I agreed as this is fair.

As a result I rely on the candidates to have well-thought-out ideas that they own themselves. However, incidents like Jordan's and Neil's business plans kind of throw a spanner into the works. One might argue if these matters were thrashed out at the beginning, the candidates would either have to come up with new plans or decline entering the process. I don't see how to avoid these surprises as I am stuck between a rock and a hard place. Either we dive deep into the candidates' plans upfront to see if there are any anomalies or we just hope these were rare incidents.

One of the candidates, Leah Totton, was a young Irish lady who'd just qualified as a medical doctor. She had played it very cool for many weeks, not getting too involved in arguments in the boardroom. This resulted in her slipping under the radar a little, as no one seemed to point the finger at her for the failure or indeed the winning of the tasks. It got to the stage where I turned to her and said, 'Leah, it's about time I started to hear from you as to what you've actually been doing here throughout the course of this process.' In response, she exploded with words and I got some very fast-talking explanation. She spoke at a hundred miles an hour, a trait she still has today.

Her business idea was to open a beauty clinic where she would perform various treatments on her clients. She reeled off a load of treatments she was thinking of, including one that was called facial fillers. She explained that she could conduct these treatments on young ladies during their lunch break, and called the service 'lunchtime facial fillers', to which I responded, 'Sounds like a big sandwich to me,' and added, 'If that's the business you want me to go into, it will raise a few eyebrows.'

In week six I had set a corporate entertaining task. Leah, who was project manager, had dithered and changed themes three times by trying to consult with her teammates. I decided it was time to rattle her cage a bit in the boardroom over her indecision.

'Leah, you're a doctor – you're trained to diagnose things and then make a decision. So if I came into your surgery with a stomach pain, you wouldn't put it to the vote whether I should have an enema or my appendix out, would you?'

Luisa Zissman was another credible candidate, who was already running a business – a website supplying people with baking accessories that one uses to make things like cupcakes. After the interviews episode, it ended up with Luisa and Leah as the finalists. While Luisa had been a rather disruptive and aggressive candidate throughout the course of the process, one had to admire the fact that she was correct in a lot of what she said, and she certainly had her head focused on business, as indeed did Leah. And in the final they had to present their businesses to industry experts.

Luisa's idea was a company that would supply baking accessories, while Leah's business plan was a skincare clinic that would offer various types of treatments such as Botox and other non-surgical, non-invasive procedures. It was an excellent final. Both girls had worked tremendously well on presenting their propositions. Uncharacteristically, this tough girl Luisa broke down a bit behind the scenes, thinking that she'd messed up her presentation, only to be comforted by her team of ex-candidates who told her not to worry and that she'd done very well. But, overall, my thoughts were that Leah had demonstrated to me throughout the course of the process her true professionalism, and my mind was made up that Leah would be the justly deserved winner.

Before I move on to talk about the business that Leah set up, an interesting point I would like to pick up on is that Cate Hall and

Francesca Maudslay had both worked in the background on *The Apprentice* for quite a few years, but for series nine Cate was promoted to executive producer and Francesca took over as series editor. It's a classic example of working one's way up the ladder as you would in industry, like Sir Terry Leahy, for example, who started on the shop floor in Tesco and eventually became the Chief Executive Officer.

Francesca has an amazing photographic memory about *The Apprentice* and we often joke with each other about it. I suggested she go on *Mastermind* with her specialist subject being the details of *The Apprentice*. Occasionally, when we have a few minutes spare during filming, I'll test her by saying something like, 'Series four, episode seven, who got fired?' And, believe it or not, she comes up with the correct answer just like that. She's an expert on everything to do with *The Apprentice*, so who better to be in charge of a series than her? And who better to help remind me of some of the facts and figures during the writing of this book? She has been a great help in refreshing my memory.

One of the things the whole team at Boundless has in common is how hard they work. Compared to other industries I've been involved in, I've never seen people work as hard to get so much achieved in such a short period of time. Francesca and Cate, together with the rest of the team, certainly burn the candle at both ends and make an amazing contribution to the success of the programme. And, most importantly, they are passionate about getting it perfect.

As with Ricky, winner of series eight, Leah's win generated a lot of adverse publicity, primarily from competitors in the industry we were about to enter. This fell into two categories. The first was a sort of general negativity, saying that this business plan was doomed to fail because the market was very crowded. The other type was very spiteful and came from so-called experts in the field who started to cast doubts on Leah, a qualified doctor, saying that she wasn't qualified enough to be able to run a clinic of this type, or indeed conduct the particular procedures which were being offered.

This upset Leah and she had to spend a lot of time with Frank PR trying to fend off all this negative stuff. Of course, the media loved it when somebody who put themselves forward as an expert effectively slagged off this 'fortunate' winner and her £250,000 windfall. It was quite a nasty situation and another eye-opener for me on the reaction to the winner of *The Apprentice*. But, despite all this, we stuck to our guns and set about getting the clinic started, which I would say was one of the most complex things I've been involved with since we changed the format. The other winners, Tom and Ricky, simply needed an office to work from; not premises in a prime location specially customised as a clinic. And that was just the first of the issues.

I've always made it clear to the winners that I'm going to start the business with them on a fifty-fifty basis and that the £250,000 investment is going to be injected on day one. But after that, forget it – you're on your own and you have to provide your own funds and work within that budget. And so, when looking for premises where the clinic could be located, Leah had a bit of a reality check. Her original idea was to be somewhere like Knightsbridge or Kensington. However, the rents being demanded by landlords in those areas would eat straight into the £250,000 investment. So the first thing Leah had to do was rethink the location. It was decided we would focus on the very busy City of London area where people could come in after work, or even in their lunch breaks, to have the treatments.

Whenever people spoke to me about Leah's new business back then, there was always the same inevitable question both from the media and others: 'Lord Sugar, will you be going to Leah's clinic for treatment?' I told them that businesspeople like me *would* be able to pop in at lunchtime. They could go in looking like me and come out looking like Justin Bieber.

As Leah was to learn, you can't just find some empty premises and say, 'Right, I'm going to make this place a clinic.' Not wishing to get too complicated, but there are certain restrictions on what you can use premises for, such as retail or offices. There is a special usage category for things like dentists, therapists or the type of clinic Leah wanted to set up, so that restricted her options. Eventually, with the assistance of my employees in Amsprop, my property company, Leah managed to home in on premises in Moorgate which needed a complete refurbishment. Once again, with the assistance of our construction people at Amsprop, that work was undertaken, but all in all, the rent plus refurbishment costs considerably dented her fighting fund. And bear in mind that all this takes time. From the day she was crowned winner of *The Apprentice* and officially started her new company, Dr Leah Ltd, it took several months before she was up and running, ready for business.

Interestingly enough, the choice of the name, Dr Leah Ltd, was something Leah herself was originally against. If one recalls the final in which I discussed it with her, she actually said she didn't want it at all, and came up with the name Niks – which is 'skin' backwards; her logic being that her treatments would turn back time on one's skin. I recall saying to her it sounded like a good name for a wine bar for Mr Hewer to open.

I explained to her that Dr Leah would be the best name for this business, simply because if she won, she would be known as the person who won *The Apprentice*; her name is Leah and she's a doctor – so what better publicity can you have than calling your company Dr Leah? Eventually, Leah realised this was the best name for the company – I think after consulting with her friends and family. I told Leah that a famous doctor, Dr Sebagh, was very successful in London and Paris, and that she should try to model herself on this person; and that's partly why I came up with the name Dr Leah.

Putting aside the adverse publicity, there was some positive stuff that came out of being the *Apprentice* winner. Various manufacturers started to contact Leah to see whether she would be prepared to use their equipment in her clinic and, to Leah's credit, some very good commercial deals were done with these people based upon, of course, some reciprocal publicity from us to promote their machines. And they would help promote Leah's clinic too.

The clinic opened on 22 January 2014 and initially there was a flurry of business due to the general interest in her being the winner of the *Apprentice*. This was the first time I'd been involved in a business that carried out some kind of medical procedure on people, so I discussed with Leah the fact that we had to ensure everything was done in the correct and proper manner. Not only was her reputation as a doctor on the line, but my reputation was on the line too. With that in mind, we could not afford any mishaps.

There were two main issues that concerned us, the obvious being the danger that something might go wrong when carrying out a procedure. To overcome this, Leah found some doctors who had years of experience with Botox, and initially employed them on a consultancy basis to do the work until she became a fully fledged practitioner in that area. The other important issue was the ethical side of things as regards what age group we would be prepared to treat. For this, our rules were: unless you were over eighteen (or twenty-five for Botox) we were not going to treat you in our clinic. As we know, there have been lots of reports in the media of young girls in particular who want to have these types of procedures done, sometimes without the permission of their parents, and this is something that neither Leah nor I subscribe to.

Some of the negative publicity came, predictably, from certain newspapers asking us questions like, 'What age group will you be treating?' This kind of alerted me to make doubly sure we had a fail-safe system whereby no underage people would be able to slip through the net. I mention all this because one day a woman came into Dr Leah's clinic with her daughter. The woman said she wanted to book in her daughter, who was fourteen years old, for a cosmetic procedure. Both Leah and I are convinced this was a blatant plant from a newspaper, itching to publish headlines saying that we would carry out procedures on a child. Nasty as it sounds, there are some very horrible people out there, particularly from the media, who try to set traps. It was good in the sense that we picked it up immediately due to my warnings to Leah that she should have a very careful vetting system, from the receptionist to the online booking service, and this system is in place. All this goes to show the ridiculous amount of pressure this particular winner was under; all brought about by snipers from the media and snipers from within the industry. I mean, can you imagine the newspaper headlines if a treatment were performed on a fourteen-year-old child?

I think it fair to say that the start of the business was slow, and Leah was becoming a little nervous about the lack of clients coming in. To her credit, she went out on the road, visiting some of the local offices in the City, giving out flyers trying to popularise her clinic. I kept telling her, 'Your business will grow based upon recommendations and repeat business. You have to build a clientele and you have to be patient.' I also kept reminding her of Dr Sebagh, whose business is flourishing – you cannot get an appointment simply because his existing clients keep coming back.

As expected in the first year of trading, the company made a loss. This was no problem at all considering the costs that were incurred in setting up the place, and the void period when no trade could take place. However, I'm pleased to say that everything I'd told Leah about building up her clientele has all come true, and she is now trading very successfully and profitably. That said, when I get together with Leah in business meetings, I have to spend half the time giving her a wake-up call and suppressing some of her very adventurous ideas for expansion and opening multiple branches.

22

AN AMAZING MILESTONE REACHED

**Filming series ten with twenty candidates
and a trip to New York**

As we started to plan for the next series we realised it would be the tenth anniversary of *The Apprentice*. It's unbelievable how time flies. I certainly had no idea all those years ago in those early meetings with Peter Moore that the series would still be going strong a decade later. Some of the crew, like camera supervisor James Clarke, have worked on every single series, and getting to the tenth year felt like a big anniversary for them too. One of the former members of the production team came back to join us for series ten: Stephen Day, who'd worked on a number of earlier series alongside Mark Saben, came back to take over the role of series editor because Francesca – the *Apprentice* mastermind – had stepped up and was now executive producer alongside Cate Hall.

One of the big changes for series ten was the timing. The 2014 World Cup meant that our usual summer slot would be a total nightmare – any matches that clashed with *The Apprentice* would obviously take priority, meaning that we would have been shunted around the schedule. And even if the game were being shown on ITV we couldn't expect to compete with a World Cup match. So the BBC quite rightly decided we would transmit in the run-up to Christmas instead, with the final taking place the weekend before Christmas – incidentally, the day after the *Strictly* final – so the BBC did a big marketing push for what they called 'Winners' Weekend'.

It's not often that a show of this type lasts ten years and it felt like a huge milestone. The BBC was happy to produce an extra programme called *Ten Years of The Apprentice* and all of us at Boundless thought it was important to mark the fact it was the anniversary. We decided there should be a few little references to past series, though we knew we shouldn't push it too far. It was important that the tenth series stood on its own two feet just like any other series and not feel like a giant look back.

We wanted to start the new series off with a bang and I had an idea after I was told during the auditions that the production people were finding it very hard to whittle down the best candidates to sixteen. Hearing of their dilemma, it dawned upon me that, this being the tenth series, maybe we should give some other people the opportunity rather than send them away saying, 'Sorry, try your luck next time.'

So we discussed whether, instead of having sixteen candidates, we could consider twenty. My only negative thoughts on this were, 'Hold on a minute, this may sound like a bit of a gimmick.' I've always maintained that I don't want to do things that will make *The Apprentice* gimmicky just for the sake of it, albeit it was the tenth-anniversary series and it was right to do something special.

With respect to the format owners, I had noted that in America the producers of *The Apprentice* went off the rails a little bit by introducing what can only be described as gimmicks. The viewing audience saw straight through them and this may have contributed to the demise of the ordinary 'civilian' version of *The Apprentice* in the US. And so a lot of discussion took place between me and the production people as to how we could hand-on-heart justify the additional four candidates, as well as consider how it would work in filming. The justification in my mind was that, yes, this was the tenth anniversary and, yes, the production people *were* struggling with so many credible candidates. It occurred to me: why not pick the best twenty, rather than just sixteen, and send four good contenders away, as I might be sorry later that those four had slipped through the net. And so it was decided we would take the opportunity and have twenty candidates.

But there were some downsides to the idea. Having twenty people meant we'd have to find an even larger house and we'd also have to up the number of microphones and crew members in order to get decent coverage of that many people. Extra cars would be needed to run them around, and then there was the extra food and pampering for twenty candidates. All of this had to be taken into consideration and discussed with the BBC. In the end the BBC must have felt the idea was good and they agreed to the twenty candidates.

Of course, the upside to this was having the freedom to be able to fire people as and when I saw fit. Over the years there had been several occasions on which I'd felt like my hands were tied slightly; occasions on which several people really deserved to go, but I'd had to fire just one person, or sometimes two, in order not to completely mess up the number of people remaining later in the series. To be fair to all the candidates, we basically need to keep a balance of people when we set up the teams for ongoing tasks. Again, I was a bit concerned that if a multi-firing was going to happen, it should not come across as a gimmick. It had to be very clear to the audience that it was fully justified as it would be unfair on candidates to be fired just for the sake of sensationalism.

I made it very clear to the production people that the risk was that if we had a bunch of excellent candidates, when we got towards the end of the series, say episode ten or eleven, we might have far too many people around to deal with.

'If that happens,' I told them, 'I'm sorry to say that's what we're going to have to put up with. But if that's not the case, then it will be completely at my discretion if I decide to dispose of more than one person on a task. And if I do, I will make sure that it's backed up by the information given to me by Karren and Nick.'

Karren and Nick were brought in on this discussion and I pointed out to them that it would be more important than ever that they gave me their full and frank opinions on the twenty candidates when they were out with them in the field.

This new arrangement meant the candidates couldn't do something we'd seen them do every year at some point, which was to figure that as long as there was someone else on the team whose performance was weaker, they could always point the finger at that person. For the first time it wouldn't be enough just to avoid being the weakest person on the losing team – they would have to contribute positively in order to be allowed to stay.

Karren, Nick and I were really excited about starting the tenth series. Since *The Apprentice* became hugely popular, every year when the process starts and we're filming the opening boardroom, I can see this knowing look in the candidates' eyes that says, 'We've got this programme sussed – we know what's coming.' So for series ten when it came to Boardroom Zero I wanted to prove to them that, actually, they knew absolutely nothing.

We started by letting sixteen candidates come into the boardroom where I gave them the usual eyeballing and explained that things were going to start off slightly differently. Then I called the receptionist and said, 'Would you send the rest of the candidates in please.' It was a big shock to the candidates already in the room, and it made very good television. The production people had kept four people hidden so the initial sixteen had no clue.

As soon as we had introduced the other four candidates, I explained to them that the reason there were additional candidates was because we'd had difficulty narrowing it down to sixteen as there were so many good contenders this year, and I'd decided I was going to give some other people a chance. Then I said, 'As you all know, the process usually lasts twelve weeks. Well, the bad news is – the process is *still* going to last twelve weeks, which means there will be occasions when more than one person will be leaving the process. So I feel it only fair to tell you now – don't expect, in any of the tasks I'm going to set you, that just one person will go. At my discretion, there may be more than one of you that goes, so put that in your pipe and smoke it.'

I was happy when I got that off my chest because not only did I want them to know it, but I wanted that part of my introduction speech to be shown in episode one so the public understood my position.

As it had worked well on series nine, I decided again to get to know some of the candidates in Boardroom Zero. I spoke to a few of them just to get a rough idea of what their business plans were about, and who they were and what they'd done. Steven Ugoalah, for example, was a social worker from Canada who'd been working in the Arctic and Antarctic. To try and lighten the mood I said to him, 'What were you doing? Counselling penguins?'

I also had a few words with Columbian Felipe Alviar-Baquero. Felipe was a likeable fellow. On his CV and video clips he always spoke about himself using his name, summing up with, 'Felipe's strategy in this process is just to be Felipe.' When I read on his CV that he was a lawyer, I said to him, again to keep things light-hearted, 'I see you've had some terrible jobs over here – one of them was advising Arsenal Football Club?'

I mentioned how the candidates looked like they thought they knew it all – well, one person who didn't fall into that category was Mark Wright. He had come over from Australia a year earlier and had never watched a single episode of *The Apprentice*; indeed, the first time he ever saw my face was in the opening boardroom!

After having a brief word with the candidates, I asked the boys and girls to choose their project managers for the first task there and then. This time the teams had a discussion amongst them-selves, perhaps having learned from series nine when Jaz jumped in so quickly and shot herself in the foot.

For the girls' team a lady called Sarah Dales took charge, mostly because during my little chat with her I brought up that she'd said on her application she could sell ice to the Eskimos. (I told her she'd be all right with Steven, who'd been up in the Arctic.) So when it came round to the girls' team deciding on a leader, given that they'd be selling products used in the first tasks over the last nine series, she was the obvious choice. During my initial chat with Sarah, I could not help noticing the long list of things she'd done in the past. She claimed to be a hypnotherapist, with one of her speci-alities being to cure erectile dysfunction. I remember turning to Nick and warning him not to look into her eyes.

I knew right from Boardroom Zero we had a right bunch on our hands that year and I was proved right. No sooner had they left the boardroom than Sarah started driving her team round the bend. She laid out her strategy. 'Tomorrow, we're going to put on loads of make-up, high heels and short skirts.' That went down like a lead balloon with some of her teammates, who refused to lower their standards. Sarah interrupted: 'Remember, I'm project man-ager. Okay then, let's half of us go dressed up; the other half are going to look semi-average.'

In fact, the girls' team won the first task, but that was more an indication of how awful the boys' performance was rather than any sort of positive indication of how well the girls did. Sarah's leader-ship was dire. I remember one of the most cringeworthy moments of that first task was watching her trying to flog a bucket of clean-ing products to London Zoo for something like three hundred quid. It was really mortifying.

When they got to the boardroom at the end of the task, the teams told me the names they had chosen. The boys had gone with Summit, suggested by Essex boy Daniel Lassman. I asked him if he'd just shouted out, 'Hold on, I thought of summit!' The girls had chosen to call their team Decadence. I think they believed they were being clever as it was a play on the word decade (for the tenth-anniversary series), but it just sounded bad. Nick had to explain, in his inimitable way, the negative connotations of the word decadence.

'It *is* an odd name to choose,' he said to them, 'bearing in mind it combines decay, decline, even moral turpitude, with loads of self-indulgence.'

The girls' faces dropped. It was an excellent moment in the boardroom.

I told the girls they should rethink their team name. I didn't need to know it right now, but they should go off and come up with another name for the rest of the series. That aside, the girls did win the task and the treat we gave them was to send them off to a private pod on the London Eye – this echoed the very first treat we'd given the winning team ten years earlier.

Once the boys' team found out they'd lost, they all ganged up and tried to blame everything on Steven Ugoalah. Steven stuck out as a strong personality right from the start. I remember when I saw the video clip of his audition I knew straight away we had a big character on our hands. Sometimes people get intimidated by the process and end up shutting down a bit or being calmer than they were in the auditions, but not him! He was exactly the same in the process as he was before it.

Now if there's one thing I hate, it's people trying to make someone a scapegoat, and it was quite obvious to all of us that the boys had gone off to the café and given each other a little nod and decided that what they were going to do was pile all the blame on Steven when they got back to the boardroom. Now although Steven did have a bit of a hand-grenade personality, there was no way the loss of the task was his fault, and having consulted with Nick and

Karren, I told the boys' team in no uncertain terms that I wouldn't stand for any of those sorts of calculated tactics.

One candidate who tried to lay low and not get noticed was Scott McCulloch, who had claimed in Boardroom Zero to be a combination of Gandhi and *The Wolf of Wall Street*. After a dire performance in the first task I pulled him up on it and told him, 'Never mind the bloody *Wolf of Wall Street*; you're more like the bleedin' Poodle of Petticoat Lane.'

Only one person was fired in week one, a chap by the name of Chiles Cartwright, but I did reiterate that I would take advantage of being able to clear out the dead wood early on, and there were a number of multiple firings at the beginning of the series, mainly because they'd left me no choice.

In week two, for example, I did something unusual and suggested very strongly that Robert Goodwin, a tall fellow who wore very eccentric clothes, should seriously consider being the project manager for the task as it was about wearable technology. He'd told me in Boardroom Zero that his business plan was all about fashion and that kind of stuff, and so, as I'd preached over the years, it's a no-brainer that somebody who has some interest or knowledge in that subject should be the project manager. So while I never appointed him as such, I strongly hinted at it when I set the task. When the boys' team got together to brainstorm the task, I was told by Nick that Robert ducked the project manager position. He'd shied away and passed the buck, saying that although he *did* want to go into fashion, this task wasn't high-end enough for him so he wouldn't be leading it.

When the boys' team lost, it was one of the easiest firings ever to get rid of Robert. He thought he'd played a clever game in avoiding being project manager; however, before the boys' team left for the losers' café I said, 'Now, I get the feeling there's going to be a lot of finger-pointing at one particular individual, Robert, for not taking up the project manager's position. So I'm going to make it a lot easier for everyone . . .' I turned to Robert: 'I don't like people who bottle out – so, Robert, you're fired.'

In his audition video, Robert had said, 'My absolute worst nightmare is getting to age forty with a fifty-grand salary and a four-year-old Toyota.' I recall speaking to Nick and Karren after he was fired, telling them that Robert's worst nightmare had turned into a pipe dream.

There was a look of relief on the faces of the remaining boys, thinking they were now in the clear. I quickly wiped away the smirks by saying, 'Right, Robert's been fired – as you no doubt would have all suggested – so *that* excuse has gone. Okay, you chaps, go off to the losers' café and we'll carry on from there because as I told you when we first met, I have the flexibility of removing more than one person on a task.'

It was Scott who had stepped forward to project manage that task. He had done so because I'd criticised him for not doing much the week before. However, he'd stupidly jumped in and volunteered despite not knowing anything about the subject. His only claim to fame was that he once went to a seminar in which wearable technology was the topic. It was a complete and utter shambles and so Scott was also fired on this task.

The product the boys had produced was a joke. It was a T-shirt that included a built-in camera. I remember saying to them in the boardroom, 'When the retailers saw your T-shirt with a camera in it, they must have thought whoever talked you into that brought out the real meaning of the term "They saw you coming". I've seen some bad products in my time but not many as bad as that. I can see why the retailers didn't buy any – even shoplifters would bring them back!'

The girls' team didn't do much better with their solar-powered jackets with LEDs. The solar panels were on the shoulders, which made the jackets look ridiculous; I told them I was no fashion guru, but to have solar panels on the epaulettes took me back to the days of the American TV soap *Dallas* and Sue Ellen with her power dressing. I enquired whether the LED lights were for someone to land a plane on.

Nurun Ahmed had been coerced into being project manager on the basis that she sold scarves in an Asian boutique, which was a very weak connection – it didn't make her an expert in wearable technology. I was annoyed with her and her team, and reminded them that a project manager needs to have experience in the field the task is about. It prompted me to say, 'I once did a paper round but that doesn't make me Rupert Murdoch.' I told her teammates they had well and truly lumbered her by making her the leader, and said to Nurun, 'It's not just the jacket that's been stitched up here.'

My hand was slightly forced in the third week by a young lady called Lindsay Booth. I'd sent the teams off to make and sell scented candles and that sort of stuff, and Lindsay's team lost. I told the team it was an easy task and that anyone could have done it – I didn't care whether they were a butcher, a baker or indeed a candlestick maker. When Lindsay walked back into the boardroom after they'd been at the café, you could see in her face that she was totally and utterly resigned to being fired. She'd done nothing of merit on the task – I think she sold something like £12 worth of candles; pretty dismal in a team that made over £1,500 profit.

When I started to push her a bit on her performance, she just fell apart and admitted she hadn't been any good. She said she wasn't the person she expected to be in the process. It was very sad but my hands were tied – she'd pretty much admitted she was out of her depth, which was a rather appropriate pun since she owned a swimming academy.

'As a swimming instructor, you're drowning here!' I said to her. 'This is a tough environment and these people are like sharks.'

There was no fight left in her and, before we moved on, I said, 'With regret, I think it's best you leave now.' She was another example of someone who had mistakenly believed they had what it took to get through this gruelling process. However, after three weeks she'd realised it wasn't for her. I have to say, it's not very often that people pull out themselves.

On that task there were massive rows within the girls' team over who should decide what went into the candles. Sarah was getting it in the neck from her teammates who had wanted to use aloe vera in the make-up of the candle. Having listened to the team arguing about ingredients and banging on about Sarah being to blame, I recall saying, 'Never mind bloody aloe vera, it sounds like goodbye Sarah.'

There were plenty of stand-out characters on series ten, one of whom was a cheeky Northern chappy by the name of James Hill. On this task he tried to misrepresent the price of the candles, and Karren pulled him up on it. When he came into the boardroom I gave him what-for.

'James, I heard you were telling a few porkies about the candles. Do you know what ethics are?'

'Yes, Lord Sugar. Sorry, Lord Sugar.'

'Just so there's no confusion, ethics is not where Southend and Colchester are.'

In week four, the flexibility of having twenty candidates really paid off. I'd tasked them with coming up with their own YouTube channel with a view to it going viral. One team's offering was utterly pathetic – it was called 'Fat Daddy's Fitness Hell' and involved filming Felipe being put through his paces doing sit-ups and all that. I remember commenting in the boardroom, 'One good thing came out of it – it's always nice to see a lawyer tortured!' But as for the video, it really was bad, and I told them, 'The only way this will be going viral is if you kiss someone with the bloody flu.' Unsurprisingly, the team lost. When it came to the final boardroom of that task, I looked at Sarah, Steven and Ella Jade Bitton sitting opposite me and realised that I didn't believe any of them deserved saving. I remember thinking, 'None of this lot is going to make it as my business partner, so what's the point?' I fired the lot of them, then rang the house to let the remaining candidates know that no one would be coming back tonight. That put the wind up them.

One of the tasks that year was to run a coach tour, and while Nick got a lovely day trip full of historical information and a tour of Blenheim Palace, Karren had to spend the day on a coach with James Hill and his team, who'd decided that the best way to pass the time was to have a singalong of nursery rhymes. Karren called it 'the coach journey from hell' and I'm not sure she's forgiven me yet. When we got into the boardroom Karren explained what had gone on and how the whole trip was a fiasco. They'd been visiting Hever Castle that day and had to describe what had happened to Anne Boleyn. I recall telling James that if Anne Boleyn's neck had been as thick as him she might still be alive.

In the end James came a cropper as project manager in week eight. I'd sent them off to select and sell products at the Royal Bath and West Show. James described himself as a bit of a Del Boy. I pointed out to him on a couple of occasions that bragging about being Del Boy wasn't really the wisest thing to do since Del Boy was *not* a successful entrepreneur.

James relied on his instincts a lot and wasn't much of a strategist. On this particular task he'd sent his sub-team off to assess all the products and talk to the vendors. Later, when they called to give him their feedback from these meetings, James just decided to pick the products himself, despite never having seen them! If that wasn't bad enough, James carried on making mistake after mistake. He and Roisin Hogan, an accountant from Ireland, had gone down to the show to meet a stall holder there to try and secure a product to sell the next day. One of the products was a range of hot tubs; the sort of thing you might put in your garden. Anyway, both teams really liked this product so James thought he'd put on a charm offensive – however, he kept calling the stall owner Derek when actually his name was Anthony!

I remember saying to James when he got back to the board-room, 'You keep saying you're like Del Boy but I reckon you're more like Trigger – he's the one who was always calling Rodney "Dave".'

Even worse than that, having lost out to the other team on the hot tubs, James then lied to the rest of his team and pretended he'd deliberately chosen another product – I'm not sure how he thought he was going to get away with that one. Poor James, when I saw the cut of the episode that Francesca had sent me through, I really did feel sorry for him. He made a plea from the heart not to fire him, but regretfully I had to let him go.

Felipe's team won that task, but there was real aggravation in the team. Daniel Lassman had won the right to sell the hot tubs, but Mark Wright persuaded project manager Felipe to let him sell the products the next day. Daniel was furious with Felipe, saying, 'You've let Mark get inside your head.'

Daniel was another big character in the series and not popular amongst the candidates. He was always claiming he was expert at everything and I had to burst his bubble on many occasions. In his audition he said, 'There's no "I" in team but there are five "I"s in individual brilliance.' Modesty was not one of his greatest attrib-utes.

I've never before met a person who, despite evidence to the contrary, would keep saying, 'Lord Sugar, I am the best salesman . . . I have sold the most here . . .' whereas, in reality, on many of the selling tasks he sold nothing!

'Young man, you are deluded!' I said to him. 'In fact, you're one of those people who thinks that if they say something often enough they'll convince themselves it's true. The facts show that you didn't sell anything!'

But this was water off a duck's back. He would simply say,

'Yeah, but I'm a great salesman.' Unbelievable. I also said to him, 'Daniel, you claim to have learned from every mistake you've ever made – you must be a bleedin' genius by now.'

To his credit, however, I have to say that although he rubbed everyone up the wrong way in the early stages of the process, he did change his ways week by week. I'm sure he will be one of those people who looks back and reflects that *The Apprentice* process was good for him because by the end of it he'd become a different person. I remember him remarking in the boardroom about how he was now a reformed character. In fact, he even got compliments from his arch-rival Mark Wright and those two were always at each other's throats. If ever there was a testosterone fight in *The Apprentice*, it was the one between Mark and Daniel, and to a certain extent James Hill. The three of them didn't really get on. I recall saying to Daniel that if I put him in a team of one he'd still have an argument. I suspect that on his CV he missed out the bit where he got kicked out of charm school.

Series ten had some extremely ambitious tasks, none more so than when we sent the teams off to do the advertising task in New York. We had wanted to film in the US for years and I'm glad we made it for series ten, as it gave the task a great sense of scale. We managed to negotiate some terrific access too, such as getting the candidates' adverts displayed on the digital billboards in Times Square. They also displayed a picture of Karren, Nick and me for promotional purposes, which is quite a nice little keepsake.

The only downside of the New York task was that it was totally and utterly exhausting. The production team over there knew they had a limited amount of time to get all the footage they needed. There was no way they could go back later if, for example, they accidentally forgot to get a shot of a particular building or whatever. So the few days they were there were absolutely jam-packed. Then there was the issue that only half the candidates went out to New York – the rest of them stayed in the UK. This meant that

Cate, Francesca and Stephen Day had to start work when the UK candidates woke up and didn't finish until the New York candidates went to bed. This left them very little time for sleep themselves, and they all looked completely demented by the end of it.

As usual, the advertising task was great and I had a team of New York advisors whom I spoke to by phone. The task was all about creating a new drink for the American market, which as you can imagine is very crowded and competitive. One of the teams (which included James) came up with the brand 'Big Dawg', which I thought was quite good. Karren told me in the boardroom that James had fought hard to be part of the team that went to New York – he was absolutely desperate to go. I told her this didn't surprise me because, with no offence to our cousins in the States, *some* Americans are stereotypically loud and obnoxious, so I could actually see how James would fit in perfectly there.

Felipe was project manager of the other team. They came up with a health drink called 'Aqua Fusion' which was a dubious shade of orangey yellow. I remember commenting in the boardroom that the colour looked like something Big Dawg had done up against a tree. The Aqua Fusion campaign was quite dull and boring. I told the team, 'They say New York is the city that never sleeps, but I tell you – this advert would send anyone to sleep.'

Around that time, my Twitter enemy Piers Morgan had been fired from his job at CNN so I couldn't resist another Uncle John quip. 'Felipe, you showed your product to America and America didn't want it. You made the Piers Morgan of drinks – it was as bad as that.'

One episode that turned out to be very controversial was the discount buying task. To celebrate the tenth anniversary of the show, the list of things to buy consisted of various products which I'd asked the teams to get over the last ten years. One of the products was a full-sized anatomical skeleton. I'd picked this item because we knew there were only a couple of places they'd be able to find one and, as it was fairly expensive, I thought it would be a good opportunity to see their negotiating skills. While one team found just the right thing, the other team thought they'd try to be clever. It was Felipe who managed to find a paper skeleton kit at a bookshop which could be cut out and assembled – it was a nifty thing but it was by no means what I'd asked them for. It had cost them less than fifteen quid, and when Felipe was questioned by his teammates about it, he kept saying, 'Well, I am a lawyer and Lord Sugar's wording never said that it had to be *built*.'

When we got into the boardroom, one team had their skeleton hanging there on its stand, while Felipe's skeleton was laid flat on the table like a pad of paper. I was utterly shocked. I said, 'What the hell is this?' Felipe went off on an explanation based on the legal interpretation of my rules, saying that it *was* an anatomical skeleton.

I pointed to the other team's skeleton and told Felipe, '*That* was exactly what *I* wanted. Your thing looks like a skeleton that's been run over by a steamroller.' I continued, 'If I were invited to your birthday party and you told me to bring a cake, how would you feel if I turned up with flour, butter and eggs?'

Incidentally, despite the fine imposed upon Felipe's team for the skeleton, they could have still *won* that task had it not been for another stupid mistake by Mark Wright and Katie Bulmer-Cooke. One of the items I'd asked them to go out and get was a specific length of rope. They got the rope but it was too long. I remember telling them in the boardroom that all they needed to do was pop into a shop somewhere and borrow a knife or a pair of scissors, because if they'd come into the boardroom with the correct length, then believe it or not, even with the skeleton cock-up, they would have won.

Felipe was a very nice chap, and obviously a very good lawyer, but on this particular occasion, I had no alternative but to let him go. Now I got a lot of stick on Twitter for that decision, saying I'd got it wrong and by the letter of the law Felipe had got it right; that I'd got rid of him because he'd pulled the wool over my eyes; that I didn't want him to make a fool of me, blah, blah, blah. Well, people are entitled to their opinions, but I felt at the time that he was trying to be smart.

Felipe knew he'd taken a big gamble; he was trying to be clever and it backfired on him. As I've said before, I don't want to go into business with someone who tries to find a clever way around doing what I've asked. What's more, if I'd have allowed the skeleton, then the other team would have lost and ultimately one of them would have been fired and lost out on the chance to win the prize – despite doing the right thing. Basically, I'm an honest trader and I'm not about to start making trick decisions like that, which I personally thought would have been unfair. I remember talking to Cate and Francesca about it afterwards and they agreed with me one hundred per cent.

Another massive coup for that series was securing the Leadenhall Building for the interviews episode. We had held the interviews at the Institute of Directors for the past three years but thanks to series director Robin Trump, we were able to use the Leadenhall Building. Robin, who had done an excellent job behind the scenes on previous series, had taken over from Andy Devonshire for series ten. When I met him I recognised him as someone who'd worked on *The Apprentice* before. I understand he was Andy Devonshire's apprentice and, from what I saw, he must have learned a lot of Andy's tricks. I must admit when I heard that Andy would no longer be working on the show, I was wary of what his replacement would be like. However, while not wishing to undermine the excellence of Andy, I have to say that Robin really did pull it off and did a very impressive job on the first series he was in charge of.

One of his tasks was to find a space in the heart of the City of London where they could film the interviews. This was no mean feat. After all, which big corporation would be willing to put up with the massive inconvenience of having us host our interviews in their office building? On top of that, there was the issue of confidentiality. The interviews programme is one of the hardest to keep under wraps – all it takes is one of the staff in the office building to take a sneaky photo of the candidates waiting in reception and put it on Twitter or Facebook, and the whole thing's blown.

When they went to have a look round the Leadenhall Building, known as 'The Cheesegrater' because of its distinctive shape, it was still in the later stages of development. The outside of the building was constructed but there were no fixtures or fittings inside. In fact, when Robin and Cate first visited the place, they had to wear full safety gear with hard hats. But in the end we pulled off this great coup in getting the developers to allow us to use one of the floors, about forty storeys up. It looked absolutely amazing with wonderful views over London. It towered above the famous Gherkin building, and when I first visited the location I stood at a window having some pictures taken with my hand stretched out as if it were resting on top of the Gherkin. We played around a bit and I took some photos of Nick and Karren as well. During the interviews episode, this great location enabled me to say to the candidates, 'Now this place, like each of you, is not yet open for business,' which worked very well.

Bearing in mind that series-eight winner Ricky Martin's business was all about recruitment, and that his business had really started to flourish, I decided to use Ricky as one of the interviewers in the programme. Who better than him to sit and talk to the candidates as someone who not only knows about recruitment, but also what it's like to be in *The Apprentice* process? This turned out to be a very clever move as there was no pulling the wool over his eyes.

One stand-out moment in the interviews was poor Solomon Akhtar, who got it right in the neck from Claude. Claude lost his rag with this guy because, having gone through eleven gruelling weeks of the process, he came up with a ridiculous business plan on two sheets of paper, one of which was covered in pictures of coloured boats. Claude went ballistic and threw him out of the interview. Solomon got so flustered he didn't know which way to turn – Claude had to point out to him that he was trying to exit through the wrong door.

To this day I cannot think what was in Solomon's mind because he was quite a clever chap. To be honest, I had my eye on him throughout the series, thinking he was a possible contender as he was very much into the technology business, an industry which I'd been involved in over the years. However, his business plan was a total joke. You can imagine the shock everyone had when Solomon presented this two-page piece of rubbish.

Daniel also struggled in the interviews. Mike Souter, one of my advisors, told me that contrary to claims in his CV, Daniel had not won any awards. I commented that perhaps his CV itself should have been awarded the Booker Prize for Fiction. When Daniel came into the boardroom I made it clear to him, 'Flannel is for the bathroom, not the boardroom. I understand you told Claude in your interview that all you need is cash, a good name and some contacts – you sound like a criminal on the run.' I had to let Daniel go at that stage.

It was an extremely strong final that year between Bianca Miller and Mark Wright. Mark had pretty much sailed through the process and was respected by the other candidates. I say respected – I won't say he was liked by all of them as he had shown a ruthless streak throughout the whole series. He was interested in winning and he didn't care who he trod on. Having said that, he also had a certain salesman's charm about him. It was his mixture of great salesmanship and smooth-talking that won so many tasks. Add to that his ruthlessness and you've got a prime candidate for winning this process. Bianca, on the other hand, was a very clever lady who worked for a major consultancy organisation and was already running a personal branding business.

It was a difficult decision to make. Bianca had made a few mistakes during the course of the series. One big clanger which lost her team a task was that she had granted exclusivity for the whole of the Borough of Westminster to one shop in exchange for them taking six units of the board game her team was selling. I pointed out to her in the boardroom that in the Borough of Westminster you have the most condensed area of retailers I would say in the world, and she had granted exclusivity on their product to some little backstreet shop on the strength of just six items, thereby shutting down the potential for other sales of the product. That incident stood out in my mind as an indication that perhaps she didn't quite understand the business side of things. On the other hand, the business proposal she came up with for the final was rather interesting – a line of ladies' tights to match different skin tones to be sold to various ethnic groups. Quite an interesting concept.

Fortunately, Karren, being a director of Sir Philip Green's Arcadia Group, which includes ladies' fashion retailers, was able to advise me on whether this concept had legs – an unfortunate pun. Karren told me there were some issues: the market was very competitive and Bianca was trying to focus too heavily on a special niche market at a very high price.

In Bianca's presentation to the industry experts I'd invited to the final event, she came up with a colour chart of various shades of tan. I told her this would be useful for me to show to my builder when he's choosing what shade of tea he requires. She had also hired some wonderful long-legged models to wear her tights, and they put on a great display to the audience. In the boardroom afterwards I commented, 'Ah yes, the models. Mr Hewer was smiling away to such an extent that I had to send him to a doctor to have the smile wiped off his face.'

Sharp as a needle, Nick responded, 'Yes, Mr Hewer had minor palpitations.'

Mark's proposition was all to do with getting people, as I put it, 'up the pecking order' on search engines, for example Google. This was also a market that is quite flooded with companies who provide this service to their clients. Mark claimed that he was already doing it for the company he worked for. He had come over from Australia to find his fortune and had become the top sales manager in the fastest-growing division of his firm.

As I've mentioned, at the final I had some industry experts there as advisors. Sitting next to me was the then managing director of Google UK. When Mark finished his presentation, this fellow turned to me and said, 'This guy is very good. He's done his homework and he knows everything inside out. If this were your old format of giving someone a job, Lord Sugar, then if you wouldn't have him, I would.'

Nevertheless, it was a tough decision to make because, as Nick pointed out to me in the boardroom, 'Alan, you are a product man. You've always been a product man, and Bianca's proposition is all about manufacturing and selling a product. I believe that she should be your business partner.'

In the end, though, I decided Mark would be the winner. It was disappointing for Bianca but I still remain in contact with her and gave her advice on starting this dream business of hers. I suggested that perhaps she should start in a small way, because the cost of goods means that it's not hard to spend hundreds of thousands of pounds. I told her – as I've told many of the candidates who have passed through my boardroom – that I'm always there to help and give advice.

So Mark came through as the worthy winner of the tenth series of *The Apprentice*. Mark's parents had flown over from Australia and had seen their boy win. At the *You're Hired* recording after the final, Dara Ó Briain asked Mark's father, 'Do you have *any* idea whatsoever what your son does for a living?' It was a very humorous moment when his father said, in his broad Aussie accent, 'I don't have a bloody clue! All I do know is, he's a hard-working, family-orientated lad and very clever.'

Mark, as winner of the £250,000 investment, once again experienced the same phenomenon that Ricky and Leah were subjected to when they won. In Leah's case it was her industry competitors, whose noses were about to be put out of joint, that created the problems. But as bad as that was for Leah, in Mark's case it was multiplied by a factor of a thousand. All hell broke loose on the social networks saying he had no chance whatsoever of succeeding; he was just running a me-too business and the ideas he presented on the programme were rubbish, etc., etc.

Then, while he was trying to establish the business and set up the website for his company Climb Online – which is a great name considering what the business is all about – the website was attacked by hackers in an attempt to shut it down and cause major trouble. The attack was so orchestrated and widespread that the host of the website got on to our IT manager and told him he'd never ever seen an attack of this magnitude in their history of running web hosting! He then said that as much as he enjoys our business and hosting all the other things his company does for us, with the greatest respect, could we move away because we were going to cause his servers to crash and disrupt everybody else they hosted. To compound the situation, Mark had already got some customers lined up for his new business and the danger was that these nasty, sabotaging idiots would attack those customers too, which would be the worst thing we could imagine.

So the start of Mark's business was not without aggravation. Eventually our IT people found the necessary hosting companies to protect his website; companies that are normally used to protect

organisations like banks and government institutions where pre-
venting infiltration is of paramount importance. Obviously these
hosting companies are far more expensive than we were used to,
but it was absolutely necessary in the end.

After overcoming those hurdles, Mark kicked off very well. In
fact, he has gone on record as stating, quite correctly, that he's been
the most successful *Apprentice* winner so far (in the fifty-fifty
joint-business format) because he turned in a profit within the first
couple of months' trading, which is quite an achievement. Since
then he's landed some very big accounts and has already started to
employ twelve or thirteen of his own staff.

So once again my concept of starting a small business is showing early signs of success. I do hope that one day the BBC will take
the time to look back on these start-ups. These success stories go to
show that *The Apprentice* is very authentic and that you *can* start a
business with a moderate amount of money and make it into
something big. To date, these five joint businesses (four with the
Apprentice winners and one with Susan Ma) employ more than
forty people directly, not to mention the additional backup staff
that I have in my main company.

I'm there to make sure the companies are run correctly and
properly, and the simple fact is I have now invested over £1,000,000
in these businesses. It takes me back to my early days of trading
and it keeps me fresh in this new world marketplace with all its
new ways of doing business, so different to what I experienced
during the meteoric growth of my own companies back in the early
eighties. The challenge of taking a small business into profit, creating employment for others, is what it's all about, and it's part and
parcel of what drives me to continue doing *The Apprentice*.

23

GOODBYE IS NOT THE END

**Nick and Dara leave, Karren is made a peer and
I look forward to series eleven**

There was another landmark event in the history of *The Apprentice*
during the *You're Hired* show, which was broadcast on 21 December 2014. It was then that, with deep regret and a heavy heart, I
announced to the audience that Nick Hewer would no longer be
doing *The Apprentice*.

During the summer Nick had spent a few days with me on the
boat that I charter in the South of France each year. One afternoon
we decided to have a little stroll in San Remo and chat about the
future of *The Apprentice*. The reason I suggested this chat was
because I was picking up signals from Nick that perhaps he'd had
enough. While I've already expressed my admiration for his stamina and the amount of work he's able to do, *The Apprentice* process
is a gruelling period of hard slog. You're on your feet all the time
and the hours are very unsociable. I think it was starting to take its
toll on Nick, and there were certain hints in his body language and
some of the things he said that made me feel that perhaps he
wanted to have this conversation.

And so, when I raised the possibility of him not doing any
more series, I won't say he jumped at it, but he graciously accepted
that perhaps the ten-year anniversary would be a very good point
at which to say it was time for him to move on. From his point of

view, I guess it would give him back those weeks spent filming *The Apprentice* every year so he could get down to his house in France and have a proper vacation in between recording *Countdown* and all the other bits and pieces he does in his busy schedule.

Having discussed the issue with Nick in August and agreed that he would no longer do *The Apprentice*, I had to inform the production company who in turn informed the BBC. We felt that rather than spoil the series, which was about to start broadcasting in October, we would keep the lid on Nick's departure until the final show. Apart from the production company, only Nick and his partner and me and Ann knew he was going, so it was relatively easy to keep it from the public.

The reality of Nick leaving took a while to sink in – for both of us. It wasn't until the *You're Hired* programme, which was recorded a couple of days before it was broadcast, that it actually dawned on me that in the next series Nick wouldn't be there, which would be very strange and very different for me. I mentioned on the show that I naturally turn to my left and see Nick sitting next to me in the boardroom, and the sudden thought that he wouldn't be there was quite a sad moment. I think that Nick, too, might have had slight reservations about giving it up, feeling that he would miss the whole thing, but at the end of the day he kind of accepted it would be the best thing for him.

Towards the end of the series ten broadcasts, Nick held a dinner party for about twenty people, all of whom had been key to the success of the show over the last ten years. Guests included Margaret Mountford, Karren Brady, Michele Kurland, Andy Devonshire, Ruby Evans, Lorraine Heggessey, Mark Saben, Patrick Holland, Francesca Maudslay and Cate Hall, and of course I was there with Ann. What a great night, and it showed the level of camaraderie that *The Apprentice* generates. The stories and anecdotes flowed thick and fast, and at the end Nick made a farewell speech and then presented me with a pair of gold cufflinks he'd had commissioned featuring my engraved initials and my family coat of arms, which he had designed for me when I was knighted in 2000. It was a wonderful way for him to stand down after ten years.

I made a point of wearing these special cufflinks on the night of the final *You're Hired* show and mentioned it to the audience. I also mentioned a horrible incident a few weeks earlier when Nick was mugged in the street in central London and his beloved IWC watch was stolen. He was very angry and ranting at me about it. He insisted that I, as a member of the House of Lords, should ask my fellow peers to do something about the safety of ordinary people in the street. I saw this as him setting me a task, so I set about making contact with the boss of IWC London and explained poor Nick's story to him, saying what a nice gesture it would be if they'd kind of help out in replacing his watch – nudge nudge. They were very good about it and I managed to pull off a deal which included me having to buy one also.

Another funny incident involving Nick was that he turned seventy during the filming of the last series and I wanted to find him a nice present that he'd really appreciate. He had been waffling on about some antique statue of a Japanese heron he had seen in an art gallery in St James's, London. He kept telling Karren and me how much he admired it but it was ridiculously expensive. I asked Nick what price he *would* pay for it and his response was quite far away from the asking price. I told Nick I would make an approach to the art dealer to see if I could get him a better deal.

To make a long story short, it took me three weeks to get the dealer down on price, during which time Nick kept pestering me.

'Alan, how are you doing in your negotiations on the bird?'

My reply would always be, 'Sorry, I'm not able to give you any positive news, mate.'

Finally I did a deal without Nick knowing, paid the bloke for the heron and told him to box it up. One day we were setting a task which happened to be in a gallery where there were loads of statues. I winked at Karren – who was in on the plan – and she took her cue and asked Nick how he was getting on with buying that heron sculpture.

'The bloody thing has gone,' he replied. 'It's not in the window any more. The fellow told me he would sell it, so I've lost it.'

The next time we went to the boardroom I told the production people about my little scam. I asked them to tell Nick, as soon as he arrived, that some idiot had left the window of his room open and a bird had flown in and messed all over his desk; and that he should wait until they'd cleaned it up. I then slipped in and mounted the heron on top of the box it came in, and placed it on the desk in his room.

I then got the production people to tell Nick that we were running late and that they'd done the best they could to clean up his room, but could not confirm the bird had flown away as they couldn't see it. They said they thought the bird might still be in his room, so he should watch out when he went in.

Nick was very confused and couldn't understand what was going on – delaying filming over a bloody bird? He went into the room and there was the heron on his desk. He could not believe his eyes. Obviously he saw the joke and we all had a good laugh, particularly about how Nick had been doing our heads in over this bloody sculpture. I told him that the only way to shut him up was for me to buy it for him for his birthday. The sculpture now stands in a prominent position in his home. He tells me he's forever grateful to me and really appreciates what I did for him.

Back to the last *You're Hired* show. It really *was* a time for departures on this tenth anniversary because Dara Ó Briain also announced he would no longer be doing this show. And Sally Dixon, who was responsible for producing and editing *You're Fired* and *You're Hired* for many years, also decided to move on. Some might argue there was a hidden message there somewhere in so far as three key people were leaving that night.

On the positive side that year, there was some great news for Karren Brady. Prime Minister David Cameron appointed her to the House of Lords as a life peer, and she is now known as Baroness Brady. I had the honour of being part of one of the most unprecedented scenes ever seen in the House of Lords when I brought her into the House at the introduction ceremony. To clarify, if a Conservative peer is being appointed to the House of Lords, then at their introduction ceremony, which is a rather formal affair, it is traditional that they are brought into the House by two Conservative peers. Karren, however, liked the idea of *me* bringing her in because of our association. We felt it was a little bit cheeky, not to say mischievous, which was quite exciting – that we would break the unwritten rules and that I, a Labour peer at the time, would be one of the people bringing her in.

Of course, I tried to sound this out with the officials at the House of Lords first, but they weren't very helpful in telling me whether it would be okay or not. Technically and legally it *is* perfectly okay, but I have to say there were a few concerns and frowns about it, certainly from the Labour side, and I believe it also raised a few eyebrows on the Tory side. Nevertheless, I brought Karren into the House (together with one of her associates from the Conservative Party) and, despite this unprecedented scenario, not one person batted an eyelid on the day. The ceremony went wonderfully well and we enjoyed a very nice lunch afterwards.

Karren's appointment raised an issue for the next series of *The Apprentice* – what did she want the candidates to call her in the boardroom? When I originally started doing *The Apprentice* I was known as Sir Alan, and interestingly enough people *still* use this name. I guess it's become ingrained in the minds of everyone who watched the early series of *The Apprentice* because one heard the candidates saying, 'Yes, Sir Alan,' 'No, Sir Alan,' so often. It was back in series six, more than five years ago, when I started to be called 'Lord Sugar' on the programme, yet half the people I meet on the streets today call me 'Sir Alan' – funny.

I asked Karren whether she wanted people to use her title and she said, 'No, no, I still want to be called Karren, but we'll see how it turns out.' There were a few jokes floating around at Nick's expense when Karren was made a peer in the House of Lords. There was Lord Sugar, Baroness Brady and Nick with no title. Typical of him, when questioned about it he told people that he didn't feel out of place and that he was retiring from the process anyway.

Once Nick's departure was announced, there was a flood of people asking me who was going to replace him, to which my standard joke-reply was, 'I'm putting a phone call out to Simon Cowell and a phone call out to Piers Morgan, just to see if either of them would be prepared to do it.' I was surprised at the high level of interest in this topic, and even more surprised at the number of people who approached me independently asking whether I'd consider them for Nick's position. Most of them were just interested in getting on telly and obviously hadn't realised that the criteria for being my advisor is to be somebody a) that I trust, and b) that I have known for many years; someone who knows me as well as I know them – so this was not an easy position to fill.

In the US, Donald Trump in his version of the programme used to rotate his advisors regularly – including having his own children in the show, something I *wouldn't* consider and neither would my children. I needed to replace Nick with somebody I'd had a similar relationship with – and that person was Claude Littner. I had known Claude for over twenty years, and of course he is very familiar to *Apprentice* viewers having been in every single series as one of my advisors on the interviews episode.

So I spoke to Claude about the role. He would, of course, be well accepted by the viewing public as he's familiar to them. He is very popular on *The Apprentice* because of his Rottweiler treatment when interviewing the candidates but naturally this new role would be different. He would now be walking around and following the candidates week in and week out while the process was evolving. Apart from the physical side of things, the main change would be that he would not be dishing out stick to the candidates but instead would be advising me in detail on what they'd been up to when out on the task, just as Nick, Karren and Margaret have done over the years.

Claude and I gave the matter a lot of consideration, and of course one mustn't forget that the BBC needed to have their input into it and be comfortable with him as the replacement for Nick. Once Claude confirmed he would be up for it, the proposition was put forward to the production company and the BBC, who spent very little time in confirming they had no issue and no problem at all with Claude, and recognised how popular he already was as an *Apprentice* character.

The question that many people asked me when Nick said he was not doing *The Apprentice* any more was, 'Lord Sugar, are *you* still going to do *The Apprentice*?' I usually answer that I will continue to do the programme for as long as I find it interesting, exciting and enjoyable with a great end result. I sometimes wondered whether they were asking, 'Are you *really* going to do more of those?' implying that it was getting a bit stale now; a bit samey. That was the kind of question I got from some of my close friends and family. However, if that's what they think then they simply don't get it because, as far as I'm concerned, every year is a new challenge, a new group of people for my ongoing message of enterprise in starting a business from scratch. Having said that, if I start to feel that what's being broadcast is not of the highest quality or is getting a bit old and tired, then I won't need anybody to tell me that the time is right to give it up.

I can assure you I *will* know when the time is right, just as Nick knew when the time was right for him. I certainly don't believe his departure from *The Apprentice* reflected that he felt it was clapped out, because clearly it's not.

That said, the most important issue which people seem to over-look is that the decision on whether or not I do *The Apprentice* is not my own – the BBC are the ones who decide whether they wish to recommission the programme. This is normally gauged by a lot of clever statistical analysis and market research to see whether the programme is value for money for the licence-fee payers, and that's all irrespective of what I have to say about it.

It is interesting to note that the format of a TV programme tends never to switch channels. If the BBC decided they no longer wanted to broadcast it, the format, which of course is owned by Mark Burnett Productions and licensed to Fremantle, could be sold to another channel but there would normally be a period of a year or more before it flipped. The only time I've ever seen it happen quickly is with *Big Brother*, which was traditionally on Channel 4 but was given up by them and sold to Channel 5. Apart from that, I don't recall any others.

Anyhow, that's all academic at the moment because the pro-gramme manages to attract such a great audience that the BBC is still up for it. Also, bear in mind that when we first started doing *The Apprentice*, things like iPlayer and Catch-up TV provided by the likes of YouView, Sky and Freesat (and on people's computers) were not available, so the audience was measured on the day of broadcast. These days the audience is measured not only on the day of broadcast, but also by the additional views it has on iPlayer, Sky+ and the various YouView-type devices. When you add all these together, the numbers are actually very impressive, nearing the ten-million mark. And I guess that's one of the reasons why the BBC still wishes to continue with the programme.

*

When I look back and reflect on my ten years in telly, one of the big things that comes out of it is my admiration for the BBC. In the beginning I was a little confused by some of the complex issues around what we could do and couldn't do on the show – all related to BBC compliance – the sort of stuff I've already talked about in this book. *Now* when I look back, I really do have to admire the BBC.

I suppose the best way to describe it is that the BBC and its management is like a giant fishbowl where you can look in and see every move. The world and its brother are there ready to criticise them – whether it's viewers moaning about some stuff that's been broadcast, the media criticising them for paying too much to their stars or the government pressurising them over their policies and criticising them over issues of scandals, such as the Jimmy Savile affair or, in more recent times, the firing of Jeremy Clarkson, etc. All these things are spotlighted because the BBC is effectively a publicly owned service funded by the licence-fee payers.

If you compare the BBC to, say, Tesco or Sainsbury's, where the bosses are driven by massive salaries and share options to make profits and cut costs, the BBC bosses by contrast are there to fulfil the charter laid down by the BBC Trust, which says in effect, 'You are spending public money so you have to ensure you give the public good value across the whole of the country. You have to make sure that all regions are catered for and all kinds of programming is made – not just comedy, not just drama, not just soap operas, and certainly no cheap American imports – and there have to be programmes which are of cultural interest as well as entertainment.' All of this makes the BBC a very complex organisation, and I certainly wouldn't like to take on the challenge of running that place. It's a terribly difficult job as they are always under the microscope.

And so, as a person who came into television thinking they were a bunch of plonkers, just being awkward, I've ended up as one of their biggest fans. I would say that effectively working for the BBC has been a great honour and privilege, and it goes down as one of the great milestones in my life. All the experiences I have been through in those ten years have made for an interesting and wonderful journey.

As I finish writing this book, filming for series eleven has not yet started, but the audition process has. And I'm able to say that the CVs and video clips of the candidates I have seen are quite impressive, so I'm sure we will have another bumper series.

Do I know how long I will be continuing in *The Apprentice*? The honest answer is no, not at the present. But of course there *will* come a time when I have to stop. And regardless of whether that is my decision or the BBC's, my years in television will always remain a great achievement and a source of pride in my life.

ACKNOWLEDGEMENTS

I'd like to thank the following: Ivor Spital for his research; Francesca Maudslay for using her amazing photographic memory to help with research on this book; and everyone in the various TV production teams that I have worked with over the years – it's been a wonderful journey.

PICTURE ACKNOWLEDGEMENTS

All photographs are from the author's collection with the exception of the following:

Page 1 top, page 2 bottom left, page 4 middle and bottom, page 5 bottom right, page 6 top, page 9 bottom right and left, page 12 bottom, page 14 top © FremantleMedia.

Page 1 bottom, page 2 bottom right © Andy Devonshire.

Page 2 top, page 5 top, page 11 bottom, page 15 top, page 16 top © PA Images.

Page 3 top © Tomos Brangwyn / Getty Images.

Page 3 bottom © Nicky Johnston/Camera Press.

Page 4 top left © Eamonn McCormack / via Getty images.

Page 6 bottom © James Clarke.

Page 7 top © BBC.

Page 7 bottom and page 11 top © BBC Motion Gallery.

Page 8 bottom, page 13 bottom © Frank PR.

Page 9 top © Danny Martindale / Getty Images.

Page 10 top ©Louise Devonshire.

Page 12 top, page 16 bottom © Francesca Maudslay.

Page 13 top ©Radio Times + Immediate Media.

Page 15 bottom © Rex Shutterstock.

INDEX